NURTURING HIDDEN RES

Michael Ungar's *Nurturing Hidden Resilience in Troubled Youth* is the first text in its field to examine resilience as a social construct. It offers a comprehensive theory of resilience and a model for the application of this theory to direct practice with high-risk youth in clinical, residential, and community settings.

Ungar's analysis of resilience and his approach to intervention focus on youth who are labelled dangerous, deviant, delinquent, and disordered. He explores how these youth discover and maintain well-being through discursive empowerment. Using detailed case studies, Ungar shows how high-risk youth explain their problematic behaviours, such as gang affiliations and drug and alcohol use, as strategic ways to compose stories about themselves that bring them experiences of control, strength, and acceptance.

Nurturing Hidden Resilience in Troubled Youth challenges media stereotypes and offers an alternative approach to social work practice. Timely and original, the work gives voice to troubled youth themselves, and suggests that we build upon, rather than resist, their constructions of resilience as a method of effective intervention.

MICHAEL UNGAR is an associate professor at the Maritime School of Social Work at Dalhousie University.

Nurturing Hidden Resilience in Troubled Youth

MICHAEL UNGAR

UNIVERSITY OF TORONTO PRESS
Toronto Buffalo London

© University of Toronto Press Incorporated 2004
Toronto Buffalo London
Printed in Canada
Reprinted 2008
ISBN 0-8020-8770-1 (cloth)
ISBN 0-8020-8565-2 (paper)

Printed on acid-free paper

National Library of Canada Cataloguing in Publication

Ungar, Michael, 1963–
    Nuturing hidden resilience in troubled youth/Michael Ungar.

    Includes bibliographical references and index.
    ISBN 0-8020-8770-1 (bound).   ISBN 0-8020-8565-2 (pbk.)

    1. Problem youth – Psychology.   2. Problem youth –
    Behaviour modification.   3. Resilience (Personality trait).
    I. Title.

    BF724.U54 2004   155.5'18   C2003-904477-7

This book has been published with the help of a grant from the Canadian
Federation for the Humanities and Social Sciences, through the Aid to
Scholarly Publications Programme, using funds provided by the Social
Sciences and Humanities Research Council of Canada.

University of Toronto Press acknowledges the financial assistance to its
publishing program of the Canada Council for the Arts and the Ontario Arts
Council.

University of Toronto Press acknowledges the financial support for its
publishing activities of the Government of Canada through the Book
Publishing Industry Development Program (BPIDP).

Contents

Preface

Our enthusiasm for narrative accounts of resilience in popular literature is unwavering. Anne Frank's (1952) *Diary of a Young Girl*, and
more recently works such as Frank McCourt's (1996) Pulitzer prize-
winning novel *Angela's Ashes*, Eric Weihenmayer's (2001) *Touch the
Top of the World*, the story of a visually impaired mountain climber,
and Denise Chong's (2000) *The Girl in the Picture*, a biography of Kim
Phuc, the badly burned child victim of a napalm attack during the
Vietnam war, have all provided evidence of resilience in lives lived.
As inspiring as these accounts are, they have not helped us to understand what makes an individual child survive and even thrive, while
another succumbs to life's challenges. The children who appear not to
succeed have come to be known as deviant, dangerous, delinquent, or
disordered. Typically we have called these children vulnerable, while
those who rise above their adversity, are labelled resilient.

Through years of clinical practice, research, and reflection on my
own life, and the lives of those whom I have been fortunate to know
in both professional and non-professional settings, I have become curious about the differences between resilient and vulnerable children.
Who exactly are the *invulnerables*, to use James Anthony's (1987) term,
and who the vulnerables? Frankly, I admit to my confusion in this
regard. The more I have listened to people recount tales of lives lived,
the less sure I have become of who are failing, who are surviving, and
who are thriving. This book is a search for a better way to understand
the pathways individuals, specifically children and youth who encounter a large number of risks while growing up, travel in search of
health.

When I began to rigorously examine these pathways I was fairly certain that success had something to do with experiences of power. My professional development took place in the 1980s and 1990s, a time in which we saw a proliferation of work on empowerment, feminism, and other critical perspectives in social work and psychology. I reasoned that healthy development must result from certain experiences of power, while less than optimal growth and functioning would coexist with what Michael Lerner (1986) described as surplus powerlessness and others have termed *learned helplessness* (Abramson et al., 1978; Peterson et al., 1993).

The Paradox of Context

It was a reasonable place to start but, strangely, one which soon presented me with a paradox. The youth with whom I worked who demonstrated dangerous, deviant, delinquent, and disordered lives resisted these labels and despite numerous interventions frequently refused to change their behaviours. They argued that through their high rates of recidivism, readmission to hospitals, and non-compliance with courses of treatment and medication, as well as their attachment to risk-taking lifestyles, that they were happier than if they complied with adult expectations for socially normative behaviour. While I had thought that if these youth became empowered they would change their self-destructive patterns, I had neglected to consider that they may already feel quite powerful as a result of their troubling behaviours. 'Odd,' I thought, that they resisted my interventions but continued to nurture power through activities that were conventionally unacceptable.

This pattern stymied interpretation until I began to encounter the growing literature on postmodernism and more specifically the writings of Michel Foucault (1965/1961, 1976/1954, 1980/1972, 1982, 1994/1973, 1994/1978; Fraser, 1989; Gordon, 1994), the prolific French philosopher who helped developed a method of inquiry that has allowed a plethora of explorations into social interactions. In Foucault I found a less deterministic notion of power, one that spoke more about power as evidenced in the way relationships are socially constructed. What I was observing with the youth with whom I worked could best be understood, so I reasoned, as a discursive battle between the language my colleagues and I used to describe children's lives, and the children's preferred, although underprivileged and localized self-descriptions. To these young people, it seemed, dangerous, deviant, delinquent, and disordered behaviours had a meaning far different from what I suspected. When I showed the humility to listen and gave them a space to speak and be heard, I began to understand that high-risk youth choose their pathways to resilience from within the economically, racially, socially, geographically, and even physically constrained choices available.

I have since then never met a youth who I can say wakes up and intends that day to make a mess out of his or her life. I have never met an individual who resists an offer of help that respects his or her efforts to survive. Nor can I any longer discern differences in the generic quality of the behaviours demonstrated by vulnerable and resilient children. Both strive to construct an identity as healthy.

This is not to say I have put aside the considerable literature on risk and resilience. Much fine work has been accomplished in the years since Emily Werner and Ruth Smith (1982, 1992) and Lois Murphy and Alice Moriarty (1976) were conducting their longitudinal studies of children. However, to demonstrate the relevance of a postmodern interpretation of resilience to this field of study I have purposely chosen to address only those parts of the resilience literature that either support what youth have told me or, as is more often the case, raise issues of discontinuities, incongruities, and anomalous or null findings that might be accounted for by a postmodern account of resilience grounded in the experiences of high-risk youth themselves. This approach is likely to alienate both modernists and postmodernists, as evidently both paradigms (or in the case of postmodernism, anti-paradigm) have tended to be thought of heuristically. Proponents of both approaches seldom like to see how developments in one paradigm may inform the other when the two are juxtaposed. This is what I have done throughout this book, combining the conventional literature, the voices of youth, and postmodern theory to show that resilience can be understood as a social construct. Just as postmodern thought has grown from a liberal critique of modernism, so too must a similar course be charted for a postmodern inquiry into resilience.

Privileged but Hidden Voices

Adolescents involved in the studies upon which this book is based came from a number of different institutional and community settings in several parts of Canada. While all agreed to share their stories, the strict rules governing the use of confidential material, especially that relating to young offenders, means that many of the stories that appear in these pages must necessarily be a collage of details, much of the material real, but some imagined in the spirit of the lives it hopes to mimic. The result is a series of anecdotes from my clinical practice and formal research cobbled together into the kind of conversations I have with many young people and their families. Sometimes, I have recounted verbatim conversations with research participants where I felt I could do so without giving their identity away. At other points I have chosen to present composite sketches of participants as substitutes for individuals whose identities must, of course, remain strictly hidden. None of the people portrayed actually exist as I describe them. Although some readers familiar with my work might think they recognize in these pages a particular individual, I would suggest the resemblance is more coincidence than fact.

Looking back at my own life, and that of many who are close to me, I see the same patterns emerge as found in the stories I am about to share. I continue to be exhilarated by the indomitability of children who exploit whatever environmental niche is offered them. I am reminded of Arne Naess (1989), the Norwegian deep ecologist, who spoke passionately of the intrinsic worth of all individual plants and animals and the arbitrariness of our assigned valuation of them. Similarly, I have found that leaving aside dichotomous thinking, I have been better able to value individuals for their constructions of resilience. Interestingly, these same antisocial and self-destructive people tell me that they would willingly choose more socially acceptable self-constructions if their talents were valued and access to health resources were made available. My work has never been so interesting, nor so engaging, since I began privileging what is a seldom heard voice in the field of interventions with high-risk youth: the voice of the youth themselves.

Acknowledgments

This book and the theory it presents has been simmering for years, like a pot of good Maritime tea, becoming thick and flavourful with time. I am especially indebted to the young people who shared their lives with me so that I could 'brew up' this account. It is their courage to chart their own courses through life that has been an inspiration in mine. Without their help refining the ideas I write about here, and setting me straight when my adult bias obscured the Truth, there would be no book.

Bringing this work to completion has also been greatly assisted by my many friends, colleagues, and most especially my family, who have always been the final 'member check' for anything I write. Not only have Cathy, my partner, and two children, Scott and Meg, reflected back to me the importance of this work, they have also supported me through the endless hours of writing.

Lastly, this book reflects the support of very special people like Eli Teram, who helped direct me towards the completion of the first phase of research, as well as Particia Kelley, Isaac Prilleltensky, and Geoffrey Nelson, who offered invaluable guidance along the way. There have been many others, including professional colleagues from around the world who contributed their thoughts and, of course, students like Anna Lee and Rhonda Brophy who assisted with the preparation of the manuscript. Finally, as I mention often throughout the coming pages, I am especially thankful to the many staff with whom I have worked in numerous settings over the years for helping me better understand high-risk youth and their pathways to resilience.

The following previously published articles (in revised form) are reproduced here with the permission of the journals in which they originally appeared:

Ungar, M. (2001). The social construction of resilience among problem youth in out-of-home placement: A study of health-enhancing deviance. *Child and Youth Care Forum, 30*(3), 137–154.

Ungar, M. (2001). Constructing narratives of resilience with high-risk youth. *Journal of Systemic Therapies, 20*(2), 58–73.

Ungar, M. (2000). The myth of peer pressure: Adolescents and their search for health-enhancing identities. *Adolescence, 35*(137), 167–180.

Ungar, M. & Teram, E. (2000). Drifting towards mental health: High-risk adolescents and the process of empowerment. *Youth and Society, 32*(2), 225–252.

As well, the verse on page 125 is reproduced with permission of Nancy White. 'Daughters of Feminists' is from her album *Momnipotent: Songs for Weary Parents*, available from coolname.com/nancy_white.

Truth isn't outside power or lacking in power: contrary to a myth whose history and functions would repay further study, truth isn't the reward of free spirits, the child of protracted solitude, nor the privilege of those who have succeeded in liberating themselves. Truth is a thing of this world: it is produced only by virtue of multiple forms of constraint. And it induces regular effects of power. Each society has its regime of truth, its 'general politics' of truth – that is, the types of discourse it accepts and makes function as true; the mechanisms and instances that enable one to distinguish true and false statements; the means by which each is sanctioned; the techniques and procedures accorded value in the acquisition of truth; the status of those who are charged with saying what counts as true.

Michel Foucault (1994/1977, p. 131)

Chapter One

The Social Construction of Resilience

The news this morning was not good. Last night, another male jogger in the city where I live was 'swarmed' by a group of youth. It happened while he was running through the Commons, a large open park bordered by intersecting roadways that creates a natural barrier between the wealthier white community of the south end and the working-class, ethnically diverse communities of the north end. Robbed and then beaten, the man was finally left alone when he collapsed on the pavement and stopped fighting back.

Such incidents leave us dumbfounded. Although statistically there is less violent crime among youth today than a decade ago (Blumstein, 2002; Carrington, 2001/1999; Cayley, 1998; Federal Interagency Forum on Child and Family Statistics, 2002; Tyyskä, 2001), it is easy to see why we perceive our streets to be less safe and youth more at risk of becoming dangerous, deviant, delinquent, and disordered. This incongruity does not, however, confuse high-risk youth when asked to provide accounts of their lived experience growing up amidst adversity (Caputo, 1999, 2000; Hoskins et al., 2000; Oglesby-Pitts, 2000; Ungar, 1995; Weis & Fine, 1993). In studies that document the rich narratives of high-risk youth and their depictions of their capacity to survive and thrive, even violent teens argue that they should be seen as healthy both in spite of, and as a consequence of, the risks they face. Strangely, these youth talk about their problems as pathways to resilience embedded in unconventional, marginal, and, too frequently, destructive behaviour. These constructions of health amid adversity can also inform postmodern clinical and non-clinical interventions that open up possibilities to effectively engage these young people in ways that avoid the resistance typically attributed to them. Such interventions are unlikely to make all our parks safe at night, but they are, as I will show, demonstrably effective in helping youth find acceptable and less harmful ways to construct powerful identities that bolster their experience of health without needing to hurt others.

Mad, Bad, or Sad?

Looking at children and youth as either bad or good, ill or healthy, vulnerable or resilient has over the past century changed from speculative musings by agents of social control to a codified system of assessment and categorization in which professionals have become powerful advocates for particular visions of social order (Blundo, 2001; Margolin, 1997). The continuing growth in size and scope of works like the *Diagnostic and Statistical Manual of Mental Disorders (4th edition)* of the American Psychiatric Association (1994) is just one example of the mental health industry's search for discursive tools that substantiate categorically what are thought to be problem behaviours among children and youth. As more and more young people are slipped neatly into these well-defined boxes, the meaning they construct for their behaviour and the context in which it takes place is overlooked. Accounts by high-risk children and youth of their experiences nurturing and maintaining mental health are very different from the explanations provided by their informal and formal caregivers. These accounts fit with an emerging view of mental health that challenges the authority of professional and lay health care providers to decide what are, and are not, behaviours associated with well-being. This alternative, although still a marginal point of view, can help professional and lay helpers, family members, and the informal community networks of concerned individuals that surround high-risk youth, more effectively support problem youth by showing us how to better exploit opportunities in impoverished environments to nurture and maintain children's mental health.

This book explores both the theory of resilience as a social construction and its practice implications in community and clinical settings. At root is an understanding of mental health as dependent upon one's discursive empowerment, the power one has to define one's own self as healthy. This work relies first upon a critical reading of the growing literature on resilience in at-risk children and youth. To this review are added the voices of marginalized youth who have participated in a number of qualitative studies that my colleagues and I have conducted over the past ten years (Ungar, 1995, 2000, 2001a, 2001b, 2002; Ungar & Teram, 2000; Ungar et al., 2001). This understanding of resilience as a social construction is the basis upon which were developed the postmodern interventions in formal and informal corrections and mental health and child welfare settings that are discussed in Chapters 7 and 8. As both a researcher and clinician, I found that it was not enough to ask 'What is happening among high-risk youth?' I also needed to answer the more difficult question, 'What can we do to help as a community of concerned professionals, paraprofessionals, and lay caregivers?' Significantly, the interventions that are discussed explore the complementary roles that professionals and non-professionals have in this work.

Resilience Defined

Resilience as a concept has been the property of well-intentioned researchers who have sought to define a particular set of outcomes, behaviours, and processes as indicative of well-being. Ann Masten, as one of the pioneers in the field, defines resilience as a 'class of phenomena characterized by *good outcomes in spite of serious threats to adaptation or development*' (2001: 228). Resilience may refer to either the state of well-being achieved by an at-risk individual (as in he or she *is resilient*) or to the characteristics and mechanisms by which that well-being is achieved (as in he or she *shows resilience to* a particular risk). But what are good outcomes? What does it mean to adapt or develop? Implicitly, such definitional ambiguity, which Masten herself recognizes, opens for discussion our definition of resilience. What are we to understand as resilience if socially accepted understandings of the term are not set in stone? What if youth have other ways of explaining personal 'pathologies' that may blur the lines between maladaptive and adaptive development? Given the opportunity, could these youth demonstrate that what are frequently understood as signs of disorder are, in fact, healthy coping or expedient adaptation to chaotic environments and stressors? As Sean Massey and his colleagues discovered through their work with gay men growing up in heterosexist environments, and women living with AIDS, 'We find no easy correlation between "objective" well-being and narratives of thriving' (Massey et al., 1998: 352).

One of the surprising things that youth tell me is that collaboration between professionals, paraprofessionals, lay service providers, families, and communities impedes the healthy development of children when caregivers participate in the construction of problem-saturated identities. High-risk youth challenge these identities by arguing, ironically, for recognition of the health-enhancing aspects of deviant behaviours such as drug and alcohol use, early sexual activity, time spent living on the street, self-inflicted injuries, negative peer associations, truancy, and custodial dispositions (Brown, 1998; Nylund & Ceske, 1997; O'Reilly & Flemming, 2001; Pipher, 1994; Robinson, 1994; Simon et al., 1997; Smith & Nylund, 1997; Tyler et al., 1992; Ungar et al., 2001; Weis & Fine, 1993; Ziervogel et al., 1997). These potentially self-destructive pathways to tenuous but healthy identities bring with them, youth tell us, a sense of meaning, purpose, opportunities for participation in social action, a sense of belonging and attachment, recreation, financial stability, personal and social power, social support, and even basic necessities like food and shelter (see Chapters 5 and 6). Mental health outcomes are closely linked to the control high-risk youth exert over the labels that define their health status, a control largely denied them in the mental health discourse of institutional and outpatient settings, their communities, and their families. There is much evidence that youth are doing better than we might expect (Federal Interagency Forum on Child and Family Statistics, 2002; Rutter et al., 1998; Statistics Canada, 1999, 2002; Tyyskä, 2001). For many children, patterns of deviance are healthy adaptations that permit them to survive unhealthy circumstances. The implications of this understanding of resilience among dangerous, deviant, delinquent, and disordered youth has the potential to dramatically change how caregivers and service providers respond to them.

This book approaches resilience from a perspective different from that found in the bulk of the resilience literature. While most of the risk and resilience literature anchors itself within the large and varied discourse on developmental psychopathology, the voices and interventions I write about are principally concerned with the construct of health, and a non-pathologizing discourse that is emerging in what are loosely categorized as postmodern, constructionist, and narrative understandings of health and health-oriented interventions (Gergen, 2001; Gergen et al., 1996; Smith, 1997; White, 1995). Results from two qualitative studies and material from my clinical practice will help to create a tapestry that better describes resilience. The warp of this cloth is the rich research tradition that starts in earnest with Norman

Garmezy and Michael Rutter's work in the 1970s that has produced a wealth of knowledge. The weave is the thickly described lives of the 43 high-risk youth and their families who helped co-construct the postmodern understanding of resilience presented here. Details of this research, including the participants, their families, and the procedures for the study are included in the Appendix.

I have presented this research and the literature within a theoretical frame of postmodernism, an approach to experiencing the world that has shaped my thinking and the way I engage with people in my clinical and research roles. Throughout this book an innovative understanding of resilience and its application to direct practice in formal and informal settings is presented. The interventions that are discussed based on this understanding can provide practitioners with the practicalities of one way (as a postmodernist, I would argue there are many possible applications) to apply this material in community, clinical, and institutional settings with high-risk youth and their families.

Clinical and Non-clinical Populations of Youth

Discovering resilience in vulnerable populations is not as strange as it may seem. Adolescents who exhibit an array of challenging behaviours have much in common with youth thought to be functioning normally. Research by Roger Hutchison and his colleagues (1992) studying the mental health of 187 institutionalized adolescents in a psychiatric facility demonstrated that despite the number of accumulated troubling life events each participant reported, these youth did not differ as much as might be expected from the general population of adolescents on measures of mental health. Hutchison et al.'s conclusion is a small part of a growing trend towards shifting our focus from categorizing high-risk youth based on how society views their adaptation (i.e., are teens institutionalized or rewarded for their behaviour) to an appreciation that teenagers cope as best they can given the resources they have available. Results such as these suggest clinicians can focus too much on individual psychopathology, neglecting the context of a child's behaviour and latent signs of health (Cowen, 1991; Magnus et al., 1999; Swadener, 1995; Van Hoorn et al., 2000; Velleman & Orford, 1999; Wolin & Wolin, 1995).

The high-risk youth whose stories follow understand terms such as *mental health, empowerment,* and *resilience* in ways different from those of their caregivers. Collectively, these adolescents articulate an alternative discourse on resilience that links mental health to experiences of power. They explain that the social discourse that defines them as high-risk youth is biased by generalizations about the state of their mental health. That discourse, they argue, is the greatest barrier to their experience of well-being, as it denies them access to health-enhancing self-definitions. Social institutions such as their families, communities, schools, and the helping professions have tended to punish high-risk youth for the ways in which they bolster their sense of personal and social empowerment (Brown, 1998; Lesko, 2001). As a society, we have rejected these youth's pathways to resilience.

Mark was 14 years old and 6'2" tall when I first met him. He had just been released from a psychiatric ward where he had been placed for six months following multiple suicide attempts. Mark talked about his mental health as very much dependent on experiences of control. His description of this control is typical of conventional understandings of healthy youth as documented in the mental health literature that emphasizes attributions of self-efficacy (Asendorpf & van Aken, 1999; Bandura, 1998; Cochran, 1988; Farrington, 1995; Webster-Stratton, 2001). The manner in which Mark expressed this control, however, which included his suicidality and subsequent identity construction as a patient, are anything but typical of what are accepted as benchmarks of successful adaptation.

When asked simply, 'What does mental health mean to you?' Mark and other youth like him talked about their need for personal power and social acceptance as preconditions for a positive self-regard. Mark explained: 'Mental health means being able to cope with life and my problems and able to control my emotions. And not being so severe in cases when I get angry, not going into a rage. When I get depressed not sinking so low, you know? Just able to control how I feel.' This 'being in control of your mind,' as 15-year-old Allison put it, was fundamental to how all the youth in the present study thought about their mental health. Peter, age 14, emphasized that his mental health hinged on 'thinking I'm an okay person, that I'm not lower than anybody else.' Beth, age 16, talked about being 'mentally strong,' and 15-year-old Lorraine said mental health was 'being able to make decisions for yourself ... feeling good about yourself and stuff.' Both the power and control necessary for feelings of mental health and definitions of one's self as healthy were, however, described by these youth as resources denied them by social institutions which view them and their behaviours as maladaptive.

Youth I meet tell me that one's state of mental health is sustained amidst adversity when there is sufficient power to attain both the resources needed to maintain health and the power to influence the way others define that health. Thirteen-year-old Margie's parents had recently separated, and she was having to decide where to live. Margie was candid about the stress and powerlessness that she experienced when with her family. She landed herself in therapy after she had slashed her wrists and threatened to overdose on over-the-counter medications. When asked specifically about the things that made her feel *healthy* and the things that threatened that health, Margie answered by describing her life with her parents since their separation: 'It's hard to decide who to live with. That's the worst ... It's like if I move in with one parent, the other will feel really bad ... I don't have a lot of freedom to do what I want. It makes me feel horrible. It just feels like I have to do things no matter what.' Margie patiently explained to me that the suicidal gesturing had helped her to cope by bringing attention to her heightened level of stress and causing her parents to work together to keep their daughter alive. Where professionals saw manipulation, or a triangulated child, Margie explained her actions as a way of asserting some control over a situation where she otherwise had none. It was a complex strategy that, paradoxically, achieved health through the expression of illness. Furthermore, Margie's self-injurious behaviour had drawn a close group of friends around her who could empathize with her. So much so that when she felt overwhelmed by the discord between her parents, the change of homes she experienced, conflict with step-parents, or her mother's ensuing poverty and depression, Margie said she knew how to signal her distress to others like her boyfriend Lance. 'I tried to slit my wrists last night,' she told me during one of our therapy sessions, 'I was really flipping out. I called Lance, and he stopped me.'

These expressions of control and power bring youth like Margie and Mark acceptance for how each wants to be seen. As they and other youth have shown me, if this acceptance upon which mental health depends is scarce in one sphere of their lives, they will seek it in another:

INTERVIEWER: What word would you use to describe what teens are looking for to keep themselves mentally healthy?

MARK: Acceptance. Yeah, I mean I've got lots of friends but the ones I hang around with most are *the ones who make me feel good about myself. And I know I can be myself with them.* They know me best. Like people who have stuck with me through everything. They know I have problems, and maybe they don't like it, but they accept it.

Mark described his life after being discharged from the institution as better, not so much because he was now healthy and normal, but that through contact with other disturbed youth he had experienced acceptance for who he felt he really was. His explanation of his health helps to construct a link between mental health and the empowering experiences that lead to feelings of acceptance. Mark said to me, post-discharge, 'I can really be myself now. Because I don't really care so much what people think of me. If they like me great, if they don't then f-'em.' Mark left the hospital having authored a powerful identity as a troubled youth who was healing and who was accepted by his equally troubled peers. 'In the hospital everyone knows what your problems are. And you don't get that feeling of rejection because they're in the hospital too,' he explained. Acceptance as a patient, like Margie's experience of suicidal gesturing, became a catalyst for finding a place among peers and in the community that, oddly, was more powerful and health-enhancing than the powerless position inhabited before being labelled clinically disordered.

Understandably, there is danger in providing a re-presentation of the voices of a marginalized population such as high-risk youth. There can be a tendency to overly determine the findings, placing what are fluid and evolving understandings of reality into neat boxes that overly structure participants' accounts of their lives. This problem is further compounded when one tries to make orderly sense of these lives as they are lived. Such efforts can undermine the sense of chaos, or as the Russian philosopher Mikhail Bakhtin (1986; Irving & Moffatt, 2002) calls it, carnival, the exuberant kaleidoscope of activity that emerges when disordered lives are described thickly.

With these caveats in mind, an understanding of resilience as a social construct and the growth in discursive power that youth experience as their pathway to health are only one unique account of the lives of the youth with whom I have worked. These results cannot be generalized, but they can be transferred from one cohort of troubled youth to the next. Yvonna Lincoln and Egon Guba (1985) talk of transferability as the qualitative equivalent of external validity, with the difference being that the onus is on the consumer of research to judge the applicability of findings to their own particular context. The local-ized truth, as revealed through the rigour of the methods used in this work, ensures only that what is presented is a reflection of what these youth and I together understood as our best co-construction of our experience. I say our, because as in any qualitative work, in my role as the principle researcher I am the research tool, biasing the way data are selected, coded, and finally understood. Of course, the youth and their families, and my many colleagues, have authenticated these find-ings as well, providing me with forums through which to validate this particular construction of resilience.

Growth and Resilience

There is a growing emphasis on developmental theories that explain the behaviour of problem youth as evolving along pathways that are complex, multidetermined, and contextually relevant (Dishion et al., 1999; Farrington, 1995; Loeber et al., 1998; Moffitt et al., 2001; Moffitt, 1993, 1997; Nagin & Tremblay, 1999; Sampson & Laub, 1997; Thornberry, 1998). Significantly, this categorical progression towards persistent deviance and disorder, and subsequent desistance, lends sup-port to a narrative account of the same phenomena. We have well-docu-mented proof based on conventional studies that the number of crimes committed is related to the degree of seriousness and frequency of delin-quency among an offender population, although different dimensions of these behaviours vary widely and can occur independently. It is diffi-cult, therefore, to make any broad generalizations about which troubled youth will commit which crimes (if any at all), how frequently they will commit them, nor of what particular ilk the crimes might be. When talking, then, of a criminal career, a great many factors and variables must be accounted for. Furthermore, low base rates in the actual number of children and youth who act out seriously, the sporadic nature of their behaviour, and the numerous confounding factors found to influence that behaviour make the specification of pathways to de-linquency (and by extension other forms of disordered behaviour) impractical and uncertain (Tolan & Gorman-Smith, 1998). What we do know for certain, however, is that a small portion of the population commits the majority of the crimes, with studies finding that 6 to 8% of the total population commit up to 70% of all reported criminal acts (see Farrington, 1995; Fleming et al., 2001; Loeber, Green, Lahey, Frick, & McBurnett, 2000; Moffitt et al., 2001; Rutter et al., 1998).

We have come to accept that children become troubled youth and that, ecologically speaking, developmental choices match the contingencies of environments and the risks children encounter therein (Conger & Simons, 1997). Such theories, I believe, are sound, and the patterns of growth they document are relevant to the lives of the youth with whom I work. However, the explanations for these pathways are problematic. Developmental psychopathologists and criminologists imply in their work that children all grow towards something which, as Nancy Lesko (2001) discusses in her review of adolescents in sociohistorical contexts, explicitly defines positive outcomes in terms of a particular model of functioning. Typically, the model fits best with the way white men create orderly homogeneous communities that reify definitions of what normal is supposed to be.

A constructed understanding of resilience shakes at the order implicit in the schematics of developmentalists like Rolf Loeber and his colleagues (2000; Farrington, 1995; Loeber, Drinkwater, Yin, Anderson, Schmidt & Crawford, 2000; Loeber et al., 1998), adding an inconvenient and messy bunch of competing discourses to what it means to grow up successfully. A plurality of narratives suggest multiple pathways to health that may or may not include deviant and disordered roots. A constructed understanding of health and resilience challenges us to reconsider how we know when we have developed successfully, an epistemological paradox in response to an overly ordered and biased ontology. Might it be better, instead, to think in terms of the performance of young lives as distinct from that of older lives? The ways youth perform their life stories (and even then, I am only speaking for the youth whose stories are privileged here) are adaptive and progressive no matter what the outcomes. To my knowledge, delinquent youth do not think of their performance of criminal acts as conduct disordered behaviour or as the result of poor parenting practices. Instead, they describe their lives as functional and, when detailed study is undertaken, in pro-social terms (see Gilgun, 1999; Hagan & McCarthy, 1997; O'Reilly & Fleming, 2001; Robinson, 1994; Totten, 2000; Tyler et al., 1992; Ungar, 1995). Objective assessment of their development one way or another imposes upon them a teleological account of their growth. We predetermine what we will accept as that which is acceptable. Starting from these premises, our interventions are doomed to failure (as evidenced by the high recidivism and readmission rates), as we have failed to inquire what youth themselves consider to be success.

When, then, is healthy not synonymous with normal? Normal functioning and health, for the social constructionist, are the labels typically given behaviours of people who appear to have internalized society's expectations of them (Foucault, 1976/1954; Sedgwick, 1982; Weedon, 1997). Foucault's (1982, 1994/1977) work shows that our subjectivity is constituted through power relations. In other words, how we experience ourselves depends upon how much power we have in our dealings with others and the identities co-created through these interactions. This power is exercised through a panoptic scheme of society that makes us feel sufficiently monitored to the point that we keep ourselves in check, ever leery of doing something wrong. The discourses in which we participate and to which we contribute become the same discourses that enslave us. Far from a dystopian vision of society, however, Foucault believed that by understanding this dynamic of power we come closer to regaining control of our subjectivity and to being able to oppose oppression. In the case of marginalized populations like high-risk teens, there are few opportunities afforded them to collectively voice their understanding of how their health is maintained, much less to be heard when they speak of their experiences. It is exactly this collective expression of differentness that is important to nurture. Foucault was optimistic that marginalized voices could participate more equitably in social discourse. To him, power is capillary, coming from below and embedded in social exchanges among both rich and poor, powerful and dispossessed. Those who hold power (even small amounts of power) are frequently convinced by the majority to ignore what influence they have.

In his understanding of power, Foucault is remarkably similar to Paulo Freire (1970, 1994) whose decades of work with peasants in Latin America has shown that through a praxis of knowledge coupled with action, even marginalized groups of people can achieve a degree of personal and social power by articulating their truth in opposition to the Truth of elites. Like Freire's, Foucault's writings are not abstract exercises, but attempts to discern from the past principles that inform the present.

Foucault's work is useful in trying to understand the alternate discourses of health found among resource poor youth who find resilience in odd and socially unacceptable ways. These youth are typically the ones whose lives we psychopathologize, seeking to explain their troubling behaviours relative to benchmarks of predetermined normalcy and pro-social behaviour. Foucault has shown that it is only in recent history that we as individuals have become these objects of psychology, knowable beyond ourselves. As Colin Gordon, writing about Foucault's work, says, 'the knowable individual has been the individual caught in relations of power, as that creature who is to be trained, corrected, supervised, controlled' (1994: xvi). When troubled youth do not fit with the social expectations placed upon them, their behaviour results in stigmatization, placement, incarceration, treatment and most often, exclusion. Such youth may or may not need help, but too frequently we prefer to train, correct, supervise, and control rather than understand.

So obsessed are we with our need to explain misbehaviour psychologically that, according to Foucault (1994/1973), we insist that those who contravene our laws must have reasons for doing so. Finding these essential causes allow us to fit individuals neatly within the discourses that define them. When they do not fit, as is the case for many of the youth in this study, Foucault believes we become upset, unable to fathom that an individual would act deviantly for any other reason than those we prescribe. Although the individual may insist he or she has no sufficiently dark motive for his or her actions beyond seeking pleasure, assuaging boredom, social experimentation or making himself or herself feel more mature (all explanations privileged in this book by the youth themselves), we dismiss these alternate constructions as unworthy of study and lacking in insight.

All this raises the issue of what is normal or healthy and the need to understand the symbolic interactions that give meaning to these terms (Mead, 1934). Sophie Freud (1999) points out that normality is constructed when a sufficiently large number of people influence social discourse by changing their behaviour in ways that make that which was deviant normal. She gives the example of female college students who were a generation ago embarrassed to tell all but their closest friends they had lost their virginity. According to Freud, heterosexual young women who have not had sexual intercourse are now more likely to feel that something is wrong with them, a view supported by others socially.

More conventional understandings of normal, as found in Daniel Offer and Melvin Sabshin's work (1974, 1991), show that normal can be defined in at least five different ways. These are: a lack of pathology, the utopia of self-actualization, the statistical average, the ability to negotiate life's developmental crises, and pragmatically, as those behaviours that do not require clinical intervention. Building on Offer and Sabshin's (1974) work, Walsh (1982) looked at family organization and found a wide array of methods to assess normalcy. Both these works assume that normal can be discovered.

The Power of Self-Definition

High-risk teens engage in a process of self-definition that, when successful, avoids the stigmatizing effect of the labels forced upon them when they appear to be other than normal. Acceptance of these socially constructed identities by those influential in the child's life is the fulcrum upon which the resilience of high-risk youth pivots. As Mark said, 'It's nice to just be accepted.' His self-definition as an ex-psychiatric patient has made him feel unique among his peers. He now sees himself as a resource to them when they need help in talking about difficult issues in their lives, in the process creating their own benchmark for what are normal and what are abnormal feelings and thoughts. Other teens in this study demonstrated the same effective solutions to coping with the marginalized identities given them as high-risk youth.

Pam, for example, is a 14-year-old known throughout her community for her violent antisocial behaviours and her role as leader of a small gang of teens who spend most of their days skipping school and on the streets. Pam explained that she does what she can to protect her fragile self-esteem. Growing up, she faced the multiple risks of having an alcoholic sole parent mother, dire poverty, sexual and physical abuse by her mother's partners, and then a number of foster and group home placements intended to protect her, but which only further exacerbated her already diminished mental health status. Each risk she confronted, and each episode during these confrontations, left her feeling increasingly disempowered and disenfranchised. Given all this, Pam's behaviour and resulting social identity are intelligible and empowering choices. She is a master at exploiting the few resources she has.

These resources were principally found through Pam's peers and the 'wannabe gang' (Gordon, 2001/2000; Monti, 1994) into which they made themselves. For Pam, mental health means 'having lots of friends, going out, being loved, knowing that you're accepted, just knowing that you're loved by at least one person can keep you mentally stable.' With her peers, Pam has found an identity that brings with it the power of acceptance. She works hard at being a leader among her friends to sustain her chosen self-definition. She says she would have preferred an identity that brought her wider social acceptance, but, like many of the youth with whom I work, in the absence of other choices, gangs of dispossessed delinquents offer an easily adopted and powerful forum in which to construct resilience. This does not mean that these teens are not aware of, and do not participate in, the dominant discourse that privileges conventional behaviour as health-enhancing. As Pam said, 'I read my predisposition report, and it said how I assaulted a person and all that. And I look at somebody else who's in jail and think that person's cool but deep inside I know that person's a retard because they're just messing up their life. Like I look down on myself for all this.' Although Pam's identity protects her by giving her some degree of power within her community, she knows how far she is from achieving a more widely accepted and healthier self-definition. Her experience with accessing conventional sources or power and a positive self-definition has, however, not been very successful. In her underprivileged and vulnerable state, a more likely expression of individual and group power for her is through destructive and delinquent acts. Her search for resilience is every bit as motivated as that of her more 'likeable' and 'socially acceptable' peers, but has taken her along a different trajectory through life.

Andrew is a 17-year-old whom I met while he was in custody for armed robbery. He had been diagnosed as 'suicidal' and 'depressed,' and he was on medication to deal with attention deficit disorder. Prior to his one and only criminal act, he had excelled academically and had experienced at school some measure of self-esteem, positive self-regard, and internality, all traits associated with a state of mental health (Bandura, 1998, 1999; Ziff et al., 1995; Zimmerman, 1990). While he exploited opportunities at school to demonstrate personal competencies and, arguably, was successful nurturing a healthy identity there, at home Andrew was thought of as 'stupid' and a 'problem.' Andrew explains the armed robbery as a desperate attempt to escape from a home where he felt threatened and powerless. Incredibly, he said, 'I didn't care what happened to me. I didn't care if I got caught. No matter. What's it matter if I'm here in jail or at home?' The fact that Andrew's scholastic achievements did not keep him out of trouble with the law raises questions about academic success as a buffer against delinquency (Battin-Pearson et al., 2000; Newcomb et al., 2002) and highlights the dearth of resources experienced by youth who must cope with emotionally abusive parents. Andrew reasoned that he could use his parents' words to his advantage and embarrass them by excelling as a problem child.

My purpose here is not to argue that only youth viewed as troubled nurture resilience, although such young people form the bulk of the case examples throughout this book, as these are the youth most likely to challenge us clinically and institutionally. My clinical work and research has also included conversations with youth who construct resilience in ways more typically understood as conventional expressions of health. Significantly, their resilience was explained in ways similar to that of their deviant and disordered peers. Beth, for example, is an intelligent and caring 16-year-old environmental activist and vegetarian who attends a fundamentalist church. Her history of early abuse, poverty, and being a witness to years of family violence is compensated for by her mother's strength and Beth's many talents. Beth asserts her identity forcefully and is accepted for her uniqueness by those whom she values. Even within the ultra-conservative church that she chose to join, Beth is confidently herself, making the church elders reconsider what is appropriate dress for a young woman. With a laugh, she told me, 'All the girls wear dresses. I wear pants and a tie.' In one form or another, high-risk youth seek the acceptance and mental health Beth enjoys. They achieve this by acquiring, maintaining, and most importantly, challenging socially constructed identities upon which their self-definition as resilient depends.

'Who you gonna believe?'

Who is going to listen to children tell it 'like it is' when their voices are largely silenced? We pay inadequate attention to the context in which research and clinical practice takes place, failing to recognize that what we know is skewed by how we go about the business of knowing. For example, while narrative accounts of resilience in our popular literature (Chong, 2000; Frank, 1952; McCourt, 1996; Weihenmayer, 2001) have provided evidence of resilience in lives lived, they have done so without the rigour of structured qualitative analysis to understand the mechanisms that promote healthy outcomes. Authors such as Robert Coles (1967) and William Beardslee (1989) have provided more complete accounts of resilience through the narratives of children who struggle within specific contexts of prejudice, war, and abuse. With few exceptions, however, case studies of resilience such as theirs have not led to a fuller exploration of the systematic and rigorous study of narratives of resilience grounded phenomenologically in the experience of youth themselves.

Two specific methodological shortcomings plague much of the conventional inquiry into resilience. First, our determination of what is a risk factor and what is not, as well as which risks are relevant to a particular study of resilience in a specific population, is an arbitrary decision given the plethora of possibilities from which to choose. Second, social and cultural factors that play a deciding role in determining what are good and bad outcomes make the notion of resilience a contextually specific and culturally biased construct. While the rigorous use of qualitative methods may help in this regard (Rodwell, 1998; Seale, 1999), it is imperative that whichever methodological paradigm one starts from, researchers elicit and add power to minority 'voices' that provide unique localized definitions of positive outcomes while accounting for the researcher's own bias inherent in his or her social location.

Although definitions of risk and resilience abound, there is a troubling amount of uncertainty reflected in the way both are conceptualized. As Jack Richman and Mark Fraser note: 'Resilience requires exposure to significant risk, overcoming risk or adversity, and success that is beyond predicted expectations. Of course, problems arise when researchers and practitioners attempt to agree on what constitutes *significant* risk and *successful* outcomes that are *beyond predicted* expectations. For adaptations to be classified as resilient, should the outcomes be *highly* successful adaptations or can they be adaptations and outcomes that are at the level of *social competence* and *functionality?*' (2001: 6; emphasis in original). This issue of the arbitrariness of the resilience construct has been dealt with by quantitative researchers through their refinement of measures, the expansion of their data collection to include more contextually relevant variables, and the adoption of powerful tools of analysis such as structural equation modelling. Michael Rutter's (1987; 2001) work demonstrates just such a growing tolerance for the heterogeneity of outcomes. Rutter notes that 'research findings consistently show a very large range of outcomes after the most severe forms of psychosocial adversities' (2001: 15).

Ann Masten (2001) notes there is a tentative consensus among developmental psychologists and others as to a shared set of common risk and protective factors that predispose children to specific outcomes across many different contexts. However, thirty years of study has left us with knowledge of risk and resilience related factors that is still rudimentary according to Masten. Masten views the analysis of both sets of factors as highly problematic. Risk factors, for example, can accumulate over time, co-occur and are typically bipolar, with elusive processes that determine their effects. She argues that there is an 'arbitrary naming' of these predictors, with different outcomes, negative or positive, seldom developed fully, and seldom understood for their etiology. We make these arbitrary judgments in regard only to 'the criteria by which the quality of adaptation or developmental outcome is assessed or evaluated as "good" or "OK"' (2001: 228). That criterion itself, we must remember, is culturally determined (McCubbin, Fleming, Thompson, Neitman, Elver & Savas, 1998; Ogbu, 1981).

Howard Kaplan (1999), in his comprehensive review of the resilience literature, highlights many of the contradictions in the evidence supporting a resilience construct as distinct from other health-related phenomena. What we decide are indications of resilientlike outcomes depends entirely on the causal model we use to explain those outcomes. Fortunately, and unfortunately, resilience is so broad and contextually heterogeneous a construct that it is not possible to argue beyond the simplicity of a particular causal model which children are resilient and which are not. Thus, explanations of resilience have been based on models that are both heuristic and teleological, predetermining findings as a result of their constrained and biased constructions.

To argue this differently, if one does not test for the variables that may potentially demonstrate a child's resilience, but instead examines other dimensions of the child that are biased towards identifying or labelling less successful child behaviours, one could come to the erroneous conclusion (a crime of omission, if one will) that the child was vulnerable instead of resilient. For example, Kerry Bolger and Charlotte Patterson (2001) show a causal relationship between the risk factor of abuse and the outcome of peer rejection. They demonstrate that the outcome of peer rejection is associated with problem behaviours and being at risk of abuse, noting in their school-based research that 'chronic maltreatment was associated with both increased aggressive behavior and a greater likelihood of being rejected by peers' (2001: 563). While this finding is heuristically sound, it reflects the assumption that the child's aggressive behaviour is a problem, rather than a solution that is improperly transferred from one life domain (home) to another (school). Despite consequences with peers, there are, in fact, many good reasons for a child's constructive use of aggression (Cirillo, 2000).

Reified as a list of factors and behaviours, we can neglect to encompass the multiple dimensions of risk and resilience phenomena, such as the variable impact a particular risk factor has over time (Windle, 1999). A history of parental alcoholism, for example, poses one type of risk to the young child, but a very different type of risk when that same child is a young adult being enculturated into a family pattern of substance abuse. The infant may experience the drinking as a disruption in his or her attachment to parents, while the older individual may experience parental alcoholism as negative modelling.

Mark Fraser has approached this same terrain slightly differently. He argues that the large number of factors that create risk are best understood ecologically. Fraser and his colleague Maeda Galinsky (1997) liken this approach to identifying the keystone in an archway. Keystone risk factors provide an intriguing view of risk, as one is forced to never lose sight of their embeddedness in a complex and interdependent structure. Fraser and Galinsky speculate that there may also be 'keystone protective factors,' although they say that so little is known about protective factors at this time that it is difficult to determine if these exist in more than theory. The emerging trend in resilience research is to investigate chains of events or factors and processes that protect individuals over time (Anthony, 1987; Carver, 1998; Garmezy, 1983, 1985; 1993; Rutter 1987, 2001; Seifer & Sameroff, 1987).

Among the frontrunners in the field of resilience research, there is a growing call to further contextualize the study of resilience (Glantz & Sloboda, 1999; Silbereisen & von Eye, 1999; Van Hoorn et al., 2000). Of particular note is Hamilton McCubbin and his collaborators (1998) who have brought together both stories and studies of the contextually specific aspects of resilience found among African American, immigrant, and Aboriginal families. In studies of African-American youth and their families, McCubbin, Thompson, Thompson & Futrell write: 'The resiliency framework is built upon the premise that even in the most chaotic situations where youth and family dysfunction appear to be the predictable outcome, the family unit and its members have competencies and abilities. This strength, particularly in the context of the community, albeit limited, allows the family to transcend the obvious deficiencies, seize opportunities to improve upon themselves, and fulfill their shared responsibilities to promote the development of its members' (1998: 295). McCubbin and his colleagues go on to note that 'applying standard measures to families of color has numerous limitations, just as there are limitations in taking African-American family and youth measures and applying them to other racial or ethnic groups. This ... suggests the need for a planful effort to develop measures which include ethnic considerations, but which are directed at common features of youth and family coping common across groups' (1998: 322). We are a way from such considered research, with development and use of these measures still at the 'embryonic stage.'

Resilience and Social Context

Both constructionist and ecological understandings of resilience are attentive to the social forces that exert an influence upon our understanding of at-risk populations. However, understanding how risk and resilience are the products of discursive debate requires a point of view that deconstructs our bias and positions us as informal and formal caregivers in a self-critical and reflexive relationship with what we think we know. I have found support for this critical stance not only from within academic discourse, but also occasionally among portrayals of resilience in the popular media. Sociologists who have taken on this task of documenting social portrayals of youth have shown that there exists a collage of perceptions and misperceptions among community members as to the health status of our children (Lesko, 2001; Miles, 2000; Stebbins, 1996; Van Hoorn et al., 2000; Weis & Fine, 1993; Williamson, 1997). For the most part, we have worried that youth today are more at risk and more vulnerable than ever before. Journalists have tried, but with only a few exceptions, failed to attend to the marginal discourses of adolescents growing up in disadvantaged environments. The media have preferred to paint a monochromatic picture of the risk-taking behaviours of socially deviant youngsters (Cayley, 1998; Gray, 2000; Miles, 2000; Williamson, 1997). Loud and boisterous calls for action to repress youth reflect our popular media's, and society's, neo-conservative view of children (Lesko, 2001). We are frequently told that more jails, boot camps, stricter rules, and a return to old-fashioned values are the preferred policy direction to take, even though youth themselves, when consulted, disagree vehemently (Brown, 1998; Caputo, 1999, 2000; Gregson, 1994; Hoskins et al., 2000).

In one example of a refreshingly different contribution to the discourse on youth, John Gray (2000), a senior columnist for the Toronto *Globe and Mail*, detailed an alternative view of young people. He took a close look at youth in metropolitan Toronto and found that a one-size-fits-all account of teen culture misses the mark. Yes, we can easily find in every inner-city high school the stereotypical 'class from hell.' But that is not the entire story about difficult-to-teach children who we tend to think of as being the most vulnerable. Gray writes of one class at Jarvis Collegiate:

> Right from the start in Mr Clark's class there is a fundamental conflict between the students and the day's lesson, which is the relationship between the sun, the Earth and the other planets. This particular class is in its own little world ...
>
> 'Vladimir, are you with me here?'
>
> Vladimir, sitting sideways, his baseball cap on backward, nods without looking up. He has been trying to get the attention of the four neighbouring boys, who are more important than Jupiter.
>
> It is an odd symphony. Mr Clark, the planets and discipline against the relentless counterpoint of conversations about everything except the universe.
>
> A girl in the back row who has arrived late spends most of the time trying to convince two girls three seats away that she has had a baby and that's why she is 16 in Grade 9. One of the doubters says, 'You're lying, give me DNA proof.'

To hear politicians and concerned parents talk, one would think this is a scene commonplace among today's students. It might exist, but a closer look shows that students today are much healthier than we like to think. In many parts of North America a third to a half fewer children are dropping out of school, with a concurrent and steady increase in participation in colleges and universities (Federal Interagency Forum on Child and Family Statistics, 2002; Statistics Canada, 2002). Even among the more at-risk youth Gray meets there is far less dysfunction than would be expected. Gray surprises himself with the discovery that for most youth seen to be at risk, our understanding of their world is shallow at best:

> Five students, a gang known as the Spadina Girls, were charged in a reign of terror that included assault, harassment, extortion and death threats against other Jarvis students.
>
> That is the kind of story that strikes terror into the hearts of parents and students. But at Jarvis, the students insist that there is no violence and no indication of gang activities.

James Bradshaw, 16, who is in Grade 11, laughs at the suggestion that students might be scared of going to school: 'Violence is never something that seems present or threatening.

'Even when that Spadina Girls thing was going on, I honestly couldn't tell you who any of them were. I never noticed. I woke up one morning and looked at the paper and found out there was a girl gang with machetes and stuff at my school, and I had no idea.'

Gray paints a picture, with lots of detail to back it up, that children today are more sophisticated, more mature, even harder working, than were their parents thirty years ago. So far we just have not wanted to believe it. Instead we persist in talking about a 'youth violence problem' (see Coordinating Council on Juvenile Justice and Delinquency Prevention, 1996), where there is nothing more than a few high-profile cases and an epidemic of media attention (Cayley, 1998). Crime has not increased and may, in fact, have decreased more than statistics show when increases in charge rates are accounted for (Carrington, 2001/1999).

If problems among youth are not getting worse, then how are we to understand the behaviours of the few youth who still appear to be acting in dangerous and destructive ways? There is good reason to believe they behave as they do to survive. Seriously troubled children exploit opportunities to enhance the power of their self-chosen identities in ways that, unfortunately, hide their resilience under the guise of dysfunction.

When Surviving Is Thriving

Despite a growing body of literature that speculates that youth have their own health discourse (Brown, 1998; D'Augelli & Hersherger, 1993; Nylund & Ceske, 1997; O'Reilly & Flemming, 2001; Pipher, 1994; Robinson, 1994; Smith & Nylund, 1997; Tyler et al., 1992; Weis & Fine, 1993), there have been few investigations of how children and youth construct a discourse of resilience despite interventions that label them dangerous, deviant, delinquent, and disordered. Enhancing the discursive power of adolescent research participants (and subjects of journalistic inquiries, as well) can lead to greater clarity in conceptualizations of mental health related phenomenon. Pat Noller (2002) in her observational work with youth and families notes the discrepant findings between insider, or subject, accounts of personal and family

history, feelings and thoughts, and the accounts of these same phenomena when documented by objective raters of people's dialogue,
individuals she calls outsiders. Such conflict in perception is not just
researcher bias or methodological error, but to Noller, important in
informing her findings. Noller has found that there are significant
differences in adolescent and parental assessments of communication
patterns in families, with adolescents viewing their experiences more
negatively. Noller concludes that adolescents see family interaction
differently than their adult caregivers.

When given the opportunity, youth in a number of studies have
shown that standardized measures of resilience and vulnerability ignore aspects of health indigenous to them as a marginalized social
group (Brown, 1998; Dryden et al., 1998; Nylund & Ceske, 1997). What
are taken as indicators of vulnerability can be the basis for child and
family resilience when the experiences of the research participants are
understood from the perspective of those affected. A similar connection between power and the social construction of mental health has
already been demonstrated in both clinical and non-clinical settings
with adults (see Abrums, 2000; Kavanagh & Broom, 1998; Lord &
Farlow, 1990; Massey et al., 1998; Stoppard, 2000).

The discovery of a substantive theory of resilience that can explain
the experiences of high-risk youth who appear troubled necessitates
that researchers question themselves and their methods. The diversity
of experiences that are reflected in the lived experience of high-risk
teens reflects a postmodern tolerance for chaos that is counter to the
rigidity found in some research in this field. Hearing the alternative
discourses of high-risk youth requires a commitment to humility on
the part of the researcher and practitioner in order to bracket his or
her knowledge as simply one of many ways of knowing. A not-knowing position in relation to the concepts under study frees the researcher
to reach a deeper understanding of the localized experience of the
'other' (Fine, 1994; Fine et al., 2000; McNamee & Gergen, 1992). It is
this type of knowledge generation that is needed if we are to perceive resilience in children whose lifestyles make us think of them as
vulnerable.

Like other aspects of our social order, what we accept as factual
descriptions of the experiences of youth, including their experiences
as resilient, are created through a process of externalization. As Peter
Berger and Thomas Luckmann first explained, 'social order exists *only*
as a product of human activity' (1996: 52). Our commonsense world,

which equates resilience with healthy lifestyles, represents the internalization of the order we participate in, projected onto everyday events. Social constructionism deconstructs through language our taken-for-granted world (Gergen, 1991, 1994, 2001; Stoppard, 2000; Weedon, 1997). Bakhtin, one of the early postmodernists, wrote, 'words belong to nobody, and in themselves they evaluate nothing' (1986: 85). Naively, we rely on the social discourse in which we participate for the meaning of the words we use. Bakhtin's work shows us that 'knowledge and the multiple truths of life are relational rather than representational' (Dialogue and Knowledge Construction for Practice, para. 3, as cited in Irving & Young, 2002). Postmodern theory has been criticized on this very point because it appears to disembody material concerns of individuals and groups, making them nothing more than the products of competing discourses. While in a strict sense this is true, in practice, we accept our everyday language as reality for the sake of our need to communicate. This does not mean that what we think we know is any more an accurate representation of our world than any other representation that someone else might choose to have. All we can say for certain is that our thoughts manifest themselves at a particular time and place in a way that reflects the language we have available to describe our world, and that the meaning that attaches to that language always develops through a complex weave of relationships.

Take, for example, Ricardo Stanton-Salazar and Stephanie Spina's work that highlights how minority youth seek resilience in contexts different from the mainstream. They write, 'We must seek to better articulate how the forces of exclusion and social oppression have become normalized within every institutional structure which minority families and youth must routinely negotiate (e.g., public schools, housing, job market, judicial system). We must better understand and articulate agency in light of the impact of oppressive ideological and structural forces and the different ways they are mediated within families, schools, and communities' (2000: 228). In their critique of the literature on resilience Stanton-Salazar and Spina conclude that 'existing models of resiliency reflect biases grounded in American values of free enterprise and individualism, and [are] historically linked to the Protestant Ethic' (2000: 230). This bias dismisses as irrelevant the folkways of people with stronger family connections, who may chart pathways to resilience that are not based on dominant value systems and in particular hold a network orientation to survival that dismisses individualism. These networks of supportive agents, which may include peers, families, and social and institutional supports, can break cycles of disadvantage by creating an 'advantageous structural configuration' (2000: 244). Stanton-Salazar and Spina suggest we change from understanding resilience as an outcome to seeing resilience as an optimal response to stress in a particular cultural context. While their critique is an important one, in arguing that resilience among some minority groups (Latinos, for example) is based on these networks they avoid the thorny issue of who enjoys access to these networks (do all people in the cultural group share access equally?) and individual or sub-group difference. Furthermore, just because we contextualize resilience does not mean that we do not still reify success as social mobility, implying one must move (normally up) to succeed.

The difficulty this poses for helping professionals is that it puts up for grabs much of what we want to believe is true in our professions. If language limits thought, then are there phenomena that we are observing but unable to name? Feminist theorists have presented convincing arguments that this is exactly what has happened in regard to women's experiences (Gilligan, 1982; Miller, 1991; Nylund & Ceske, 1997; Scheman, 1980; Stoppard, 2000; Surrey, 1991b; Van Den Bergh, 1995; Weedon, 1997). Women's anger, ways of knowing, dependency on relationships, are all phenomena that have been either misunderstood or, more often, pathologized. The problem has been that experts who hold knowledge regarding healthy functioning are self-referential, arguing, 'be like me' or 'be as I want to be,' all according to the social standards represented by the knower (McNamee & Gergen, 1992).

Kenneth Gergen (1991, 1994, 1996, 2001) has been the flag-bearer for postmodern influences in psychology, and indirectly, other psychologically oriented disciplines such as social work, psychiatry, and nursing. He challenges the three modernist themes of traditional psychological science, namely, 'emphasis on the individual mind, an objectively knowable world, and language as carrier of truth' (2001: 805). Instead, Gergen explains, 'whatever exists simply exists, irrespective of linguistic practices. However, once one begins to describe or explain what exists, one inevitably proceeds from a forestructure of shared intelligibility' (2001: 805). For example, while we may all talk about anger in our Western culture and have a high degree of certainty that we are using language in a similar way (as when we describe a child's outburst as a temper tantrum), Gergen points out that we are ill equipped to research constructs from another's culture different from our own. This is not just a case of not having language: it is a matter of not participating in discourse. For example, when Aboriginal communities in Northern Canada speak of 'land' I am convinced that what they mean by land as a resource is vastly different from the commodified and de-spirited notion of land that is embedded in my non-Aboriginal culture.

Of course, such deconstruction opens this present work to the same criticism. In the present use of conventional research I have made claims to truth, for example, crime is decreasing or resilience derives from experiences of power. I do all this unabashedly, except that I ask readers to place each statement in parentheses. There is nothing here meant to imbue these particular ideas with the stamp of an overriding Truth, only to position them a little more prominently inside an emerging discourse on what constitutes health and resilience among marginalized populations. As Gergen observes, 'all that is solid need not melt into air. Rather, theoretical perspectives constitute discursive resources' (2001: 809). Individuals in the scientific community, then, whose participation in the social discourse on mental health is most influential, decide what is and is not normal. Clearly, it has not been the case that adolescents are listened to much in this regard: 'Far too often ... the adolescent point of view regarding their health-related needs and rights is absent from public agenda' (King et al., 1999: xi).

A Postmodern Constructionist Therapy

My goal in the following chapters is to link the theory of resilience to an emerging discourse among high-risk youth that demonstrates a multiplicity of pathways to health, some conventional and accepted, many others marginal. By including the voices of youth themselves in this work, my hope is to provide readers with a more theoretically grounded portrayal of resilience among these youth. Further, over the years, my research has contributed to the development of a therapeutic approach that I have found useful in both formal and informal community and clinical settings. The therapeutic techniques that will be discussed are a practical application of postmodern constructionist therapies (Augusta-Scot, 2001; Freedman & Combs, 1996; Hoyt, 1996a; Madsen, 1999; McNamee & Gergen, 1992; Smith & Nylund, 1997; White, 1995, 1997; White & Epston, 1990) to the mental health problems high-risk youth and their families experience as a result of biological, psychological, social, and environmental risk factors. Postmodern therapeutic approaches, often grouped together under the phrase 'narrative therapy' (see Smith, 1997), are premised on the understanding that all knowledge is socially constructed and truth claims highly sensitive to the dynamics of power expressed through social discourse. As with other postmodern interventions, the approach outlined here views therapy as a process of meaning construction that takes place dialogically through the formal and culture-bound context of the clinician's relationship with those with whom he or she works. Their usefulness and effectiveness with adolescent populations is well documented (Nylund & Corsiglia, 1996; Sheehan, 1997; Smith & Nylund, 1997; Sparks, 2002). For example, Marni Sheehan's (1997) work in New Zealand with violent youth in families has demonstrated success in preventing further abuse of the adults by the children. Sheehan shows that the violence of youth is frequently embedded in the narratives of violence in which the family as a whole participate and that when youth deconstruct their part in this story, their violent behaviours stop.

While systems-based therapies have reified interactions between family members and allowed therapists to view them mechanistically, narrative therapy, and the social constructionism upon which it is based, has provided a different approach to people, their interactions, and their problems. Michael White (1988; 1995; 1997; White & Epston, 1990) is credited with being the first to clearly articulate what has become the mantra for this field: the person is not the problem, the problem is the problem. This has provided a profound shift in discourse among professionals who saw problems as either the result of imbalanced systems or the result of individual failings. A narrative therapy encourages a view of problems as social constructions created through language. As Harlene Anderson and Harold Goolishian (1992) explain, the implication of this view is that clients are the experts on the challenges confronting them as they participate directly in defining their own problems. Therefore, it makes sense that people who come to counselling are the ones best equipped to locate solutions.

Problems exist inside language. Narrative therapists emphasize that since problems do not exist inside people, they can be constructed outside as the products of language. In other words, individuals are de-centred from the challenges they face, with problems being understood as the products of interaction with others and the language we have available to describe our experiences. As will be shown, the techniques of narrative therapy are useful for both individuals and families, although they work especially well when there is an audience to help to deconstruct the discourses that sustain the meaning of the problems that people experience. Problems, after all, seldom affect just one person, and we therefore all play a role in their maintenance and resolution.

Another useful way to think about the stories that people tell about their lives is to think about them in terms of their landscapes of action and consciousness (Freedman & Combs, 1996). Landscapes of action refer to what we do to sustain the stories we hold to be true: how we parent, what we eat, where we live, who we play with, when and where we recreate, all add detail to the narratives that reflexively constrain our lives. Landscapes of consciousness refer to the way values, beliefs, attitudes, and our thoughts in general influence the construction of our stories.

Like narrative therapies popularized by Michael White and his colleagues, the clinical and community approach to intervention explored in the second half of this book is based on the stories we tell about our lives and how we construct our identity through our co-authorship of these stories with others. Unlike behaviourism, psychoanalysis, cognitive, or even systems-based theories, constructionist approaches such as this explicitly address how some behaviours become defined as mental illness while others are thought to indicate health.

Those familiar with feminist and other forms of critical intervention (Mullaly, 1997; Pease, 2002; Pease & Fook, 1999; Van Den Bergh, 1995) will likely find a comfortable fit between their current practice and a social constructionist approach. For example, feminist therapists like Stephanie Weiland Bowling and her colleagues argue that 'negative assumptions that therapists and adults make about youth can ultimately have a devastating effect on the lives of adolescents, especially if they are unfounded or unjust as stereotypes and assumptions often are' (2002: 214). Accordingly, even youth who are thought 'bad' by their communities deserve a fair chance to participate equitably in treatment. Following from their research with practitioners, Bowling et al. identify three values needed to underpin interventions with adolescents to create a socially just therapy that challenges ageist assumptions of ineptitude. Practitioners should first carefully listen to adolescent clients define experience of oppression: 'We [encourage] family therapists to actively assess for family and/or societal injustices that might be causing adolescents to either externalize or internalize anger about the injustice. To follow this guideline, it is important to recognize that the family therapist working with both the adolescent and parent(s) will need to be able to recognize and reduce inappropriate and oppressive power and control by parents over their teenager' (2002: 219). Second, therapists are advised to deconstruct gender issues with both the youth and their families, highlighting changes taking place socially in how gender roles are interpreted. Third, those working with youth are encouraged to flatten the hierarchy between themselves and their adolescent clients. As will be shown, all three of these aspects of an effective intervention are relevant to a constructionist therapy.

Such an approach privileges the marginal voices of youth, making it easier to intervene in ways that fit with the young person's search for health. When treatment is effective, it can nurture for high-risk youth what Michael White has called an 'emancipatory narrative' (1997: 221). White's work is overtly political, in that it seeks to add power to the silenced voices of those who are marginalized by allowing them to interpret their experiences in ways that give their stories power. The need for such an approach can be illustrated easily if one recalls how for many years stories told by children of their sexual abuse in institutions were dismissed as a sign of the *child's* deviance. Within a discourse of paternalism the child's voice was silenced in favour of that of the perpetrator's. With time, and the weight of evidence in support of victims' accounts, these children's stories have gained credibility. We now believe children and call them 'survivors,' attaching to them powerful labels that recognize the courage of their disclosures. Postmodern therapies are explicitly intended to attend to power imbalances such as those so evident in the lives of abused children. The context of the child's behaviour, and the child's lack of discursive power to explain herself or himself and be heard, is important to treatment. Unlike in traditional therapies, the postmodern therapist understands that his or her way of seeing the world is just one truth and that those who are being helped are likely to explain their world in other ways. As will be shown in subsequent chapters, in the case of high-risk teens this means that peer groups are places where teens sustain their health and that families are not always safe places – and incarceration or other forms of institutionalization may be desirable choices when one's life is in chaos. Furthermore, there is evidence that surviving and thriving, in the discourse of youth, can paradoxically mean anything from taking drugs and attempting suicide to attending school and being involved in one's community. It all depends how the child, choosing from the resources at hand, finds a sense of coherence in his or her life.

Overview

In the following chapters, a case is made for an understanding of resilience as a social construct present in the lives of youth who are known more for their problem-saturated identities than their personal well-being. However, unlike many other books that present theories of resilience, I have also included here a lengthy discussion of what professionals, paraprofessionals, and volunteers can do through formal and informal treatment to nurture and sustain narratives of resilience in high-risk youth. My intent is to demonstrate the applicability of a social contructionist interpretation of resilience to the actual day-to-day work of concerned caregivers and therapists.

Building a Theory

Chapter 2 presents background to this argument through a review of the conventional risk and resilience literature. Finding resilience in a high-risk child has always held much appeal for researchers who appreciate the novelty of the child's situation. A careful review of the literature shows many different ways that resilience has been understood, although most of research in the field shares a common bias towards preconceived notions of healthy outcomes. The definitional debates that occur in this field of research will be examined, with the hope of setting the stage for a constructionist interpretation. Next, the nature and variety of the biological, psychological, and sociopolitical risk factors that threaten health and the protective mechanisms, those processes that protect a child against risk and promote resilience, will be discussed. Much of the literature reviewed in the chapter, while not explicitly supportive of a constructionist understanding of resilience, provides the threads necessary to weave together the constructionist theory of resilience presented throughout this book.

Chapter 3 moves from the general to the specific, building a solid foundation for the theory that is presented. The chapter details a search for empirical proof to support a constructionist understanding of resilience embedded in the risk and resilience literature as demonstrated in the lives of high-risk youth themselves. An exhaustive review of the literature has identified a large number of discordant findings that have troubled researchers and practitioners. In searching for health amidst chaos, Chapter 3 examines evidence that high-risk youth nurture and maintain well-being through dangerous, deviant, delinquent, and disordered behaviour. A number of international studies are identified that directly support an understanding of resilience as both a social construct and present in the lives of high-risk youth who *appear* to be functioning poorly. It is argued that the subjectivity of those who intervene with these youth has led them to erroneously diagnose problems and overlook strengths. These diagnoses will be explored for their contribution to problem-saturated identities among troubled youth. Numerous other studies, meanwhile, have shown that high-risk youth construct health-enhancing identities through their problem behaviours. The chapter concludes by deconstructing what are tolerable differences in children and examines the intelligibility of their behaviours, their search for status, the way they maintain health in institutional settings, and delinquency as a pathway to well-being.

With the preceding chapters establishing that resilience is a social construction dependent on the power that high-risk youth enjoy in the social discourse that defines them, Chapter 4 moves forward to an examination of the link between experiences of power and mental health in the lives of the study's participants. Specifically, it will explore aspects of discursive power related to resilience. Chapter 4 completes a redefinition of resilience as a social construct through a discussion of the process of discursive empowerment and its contribution to health. This approach relies on an understanding of power as capillary (Foucault, 1982; 1994/1977), or shared among high-risk youth and their communities, which is a precondition for the equitable participation of problem youth in social discourse. Like other mental health resources, it is shown that when discursive power is shared, the health of individuals is enhanced. The remainder of Chapter 4 provides a detailed discussion of three aspects of power relevant to an understanding of discursive empowerment as a protective mechanism that sustains mental health. These three aspects include experiences of power through relationships, the power to control mental health resources, and the power to exploit opportunities afforded by these resources to experience one's self as competent. These aspects of relational power, control, and competence are shown to be pivotal to a child's experience of himself or herself as healthy.

Voices of Youth

Chapter 5 documents in further detail the grounded experiences of the 43 high-risk youth who participated in the two original studies discussed throughout this book. In this chapter, I examine how these youth acquire, maintain, and challenge identity stories. Teens report that they seek control experiences through relationships as a strategy to acquire self-defining stories as resilient. Identities are constructed by either exploiting resources in one discourse or 'drifting' between discourses. Maintaining health-enhancing identities involves strategies that sustain discursive power in different spheres of interaction such that a coherent story of self is constructed. Challenging self-constructions as vulnerable requires control experiences and a say over the mental health labels assigned to youth. Loss of control over health resources and issues of gender affect these identity constructions. The chapter concludes with a discussion of three approaches to discursive empowerment discussed by the youth: staying stuck, playing the chameleon, and assuming acceptance.

Chapter 6 furthers the analysis of the study's findings by examining institutional and community-based out-of-home placements to better understand how this process of discursive empowerment works in a specific context. As all 43 participants had experienced placement at some point in their lives, pathways to resilience were either interrupted or furthered through these experiences. Participants showed that identity constructions as resilient require continuity across spheres of social interaction. Behaviours in residential settings that may be problematic for caregivers are efforts by high-risk teens to establish continuities and discontinuities in their identity stories, depending on which is discursively more power-enhancing. Chapter 6 examines how the behaviour of these teens as they 'get put inside,' 'survive inside,' and then 'go home' reflects strategies employed by them to nurture and sustain health.

Practice Implications: Professionals, Paraprofessionals, and Volunteers

Chapters 7 and 8 move this discussion from the level of theory to practice. Chapter 7 presents a model of a non-stigmatizing constructionist therapy that reflects what was learned from high-risk youth themselves. Treatment focuses on health, proceeding in three phases: reflecting, challenging, and defining. Reflecting on a child's identity involves an examination of the child's self-constructions.

Genograms and sociograms 'with attitude' are used along with other artefacts of treatment to help engage youth in this first phase of a praxis of reflection leading to action. The social construction of memory and the process of externalization of problems (White, 1988) is also discussed. In the second phase of treatment, challenging identities, the way in which therapy can help youth construct new identity stories is examined through work with individuals and their natural supports and through work with groups. The third phase of treatment, defining, explores ways that new narratives of resilience, which are enhanced during the first two phases of treatment, can be shared with a child's family, peers, and community. The chapter ends with a lengthy case illustration. The material is presented in such a way as to emphasize the fluid nature of the work, as therapist, youth, family, and community move back and forth between reflection and action.

Chapter 8 examines the role that informal community supports and paraprofessionals play in supporting high-risk youth's constructions of resilience. As will be shown, continuity in discursive empowerment demands that all of a child's helpers and caregivers interact in the social discourses that define the youth and his or her health status. Chapter 8 begins with an examination of how volunteers, mentors, community guides, and paraprofessionals expand a community's helping capacity. These individuals participate actively in the intersubjective spaces occupied by high-risk youth much more than is possible for professional helpers. The chapter then explores the role of volunteers and, more specifically, a unique set of volunteers, called community guides. Building on John McKnight's (1995) work, these guides build bridges to inclusion for marginalized populations of high-risk youth. They add both instrumentally and discursively to children's mental health resources by opening spaces in their community for these youths' fuller participation. Chapter 8 then reviews at length the role of paraprofessionals, demonstrating through case illustrations the important and complementary roles they play in sustaining children's identities as resilient.

Chapter 9 summarizes the arguments made throughout the book, emphasizing the links between mental health, the process of discursive empowerment, and resilience. The development of the theory of resilience as a social construct is discussed as an exercise in hermeneutics, with its emphasis on language and power. It is this conceptual frame that leads us to understand discursive empowerment as a protective mechanism. The chapter concludes with a look forward to the future of work with high-risk youth.

Chapter Two

Resilience under Study

There is always an element of the unexpected when one meets a resilient child. It is like finding oneself at a surprise birthday party, the lights suddenly flicked on, and from out of the darkness something wonderful is placed before you. This enthusiasm is not misplaced in work with resilient children and youth. Such an upbeat tone is captured by James Anthony (1987) in his report on a study of children at high genetic risk for psychosis. In that study, 24% of the total sample were free of significant psychiatric disorder; another 15% were well adjusted and asymptomatic. Intrigued, Anthony and his colleagues looked closer at their data and identified a third subsample which, they found, showed an astonishing invulnerability: 'It was the third subsample ... that came as a surprise when the normal end of the spectrum of adjustment was explored with the new methodology. These children of psychotic parents were not simply escaping whatever genetic transmission destiny had in store for them, and not merely surviving the milieu of irrationality generated by psychotic parenting; they were apparently thriving under conditions that sophisticated observers judged to be highly detrimental to a child's psychosocial development and well-being. Unfavourable hereditary developmental potentials and environmental conditions were working together against these children, and still they thrived' (1987: 148). While the term *invulnerability* has been put aside in favour of *resilience*, a term more contextually relevant, there is still something in this literature that makes us think of superhumans.

Melissa is an example of such exceptional development. She had no desire, and according to her, no need to see a family therapist. When her parents finally forced her into my office at a community clinic, I had the pleasure of meeting a clever and resourceful 15-year-old who surprised me with her capacity to assert who she was and what she wanted to become. Her agreement to join her family for that first meeting had been a ploy on her part to make sure that they got the help they needed, not a recognition of any vulnerability in herself. With Melissa flanked on either side by her parents Libby and Bob, and with her older sister Kirsten following behind with a newborn in her arms, the family marched into my office and settled on the neatly arranged circle of chairs I had set out for them. Libby had told me earlier on the phone that they wanted to find someone who could help Melissa cope better with the onset of her father's mental illness. Bob had recently been diagnosed with bipolar disorder – after spending thousands of dollars cross-border shopping and then becoming violent and being placed in jail after provoking a confrontation with border guards upon his return home. Libby has had to work long hours to get the family out of debt, while Bob has been lying about the house and fighting endlessly with the children, forcing them to do the household chores that used to be done by Libby.

Although Bob is on medication, and his behaviour is more stable, Libby is still very anxious and worried, both about her husband and her children. She confided that neither parent has had much time for Melissa in the past two years. Melissa has been expected to replace her mother around the home and keep it running well, especially since the birth of her older sister's first child. Both the sister and her baby have moved in with Melissa's family. Melissa says she only gets attention when she does not do what she is told.

According to her parents, Melissa used to be a 'good girl,' always helpful, never upset, and pleasant to be around. By the time I met her, Melissa was reported to be suicidal, frequently truant, sexually active, smoking, spending money 'frivolously,' and refusing to go to church. Melissa did not deny these accusations straight out, but sat quietly listening. Then she calmly explained that she felt like she was being expected to replace her mother at home and that she did not feel ready or able to do the job. She just wanted her family to be back to how it was before her dad's illness.

When out with her peers Melissa described herself as being quite different from who she is at home. Among her friends she is an outgoing and assertive individual whom others rely on in times of crisis. She has a boyfriend, as her parents suspected, but insists that she maintains a great deal of say over how she expresses her sexuality in that relationship. In getting to know Melissa over the next few weeks, I was struck by the way she has coped with the challenges she has been confronted with at home and by how she has successfully nego- tiated with her peers a positive self-definition other than that of sub- stitute mother. The stress in Melissa's life is, in part, the result of her attempts to carry this positive self-definition back into her home. Mel- issa described herself like this: 'I usually see myself as somebody who gets along with practically anyone. I don't put down people for how they look or what they wear, especially 'cause most people have con- trol over what happens to them. I have that control. I make all my own choices. Like being with a guy or not, and who my friends are, and if I smoke or if I don't smoke and stuff like that.'

It was hard to doubt Melissa despite everything Libby and Bob had told me about their daughter's erratic behaviour. Instead I felt I was meeting a young woman who exuded self-confidence, to the point of being willing to break with conventional gender norms and excel in an automotive class at school. She said, 'I've been put down a lot lately this year for taking a lot of automotive classes. But it's just a bunch of guys high on themselves who think no girl can do as good as them. Everyone before pictured me as this person doing this very girl- like thing and never getting into stuff like that. And now all my friends are like "Ooo! How can you do something like that?" But I like it. Like now my friends think it's really neat that I'm into that kind of stuff even though they're not that kind of people ... I don't really try to be like my friends 'cause I think that's really stupid, but it's neat being different. Makes me feel good.'

Risk, vulnerability, and resilience have now become well studied phenomena in the social science literature. A young person like Mel- issa is typical of youth living with a number of perceived risks. The difficulty comes in determining whether she is vulnerable as a conse- quence, as her parents believe, or resilient, as Melissa prefers to de- scribe herself. The purpose of this chapter is to examine the research relevant to risk and resilience to present an argument that Melissa's health status is best viewed as a set of competing discourses on well- being and normalcy.

Definitional Challenges: Risk and Resilience

The personal and environmental factors that have been studied as barriers to health and well-being have come to be known as risk factors. As resilience is only present when there is risk, like two sides of the same coin, it is necessary to clarify what is meant by risk before proceeding to a discussion of resilience. Risk factors have been shown to occur as chains of events that can be interrupted by protective mechanisms. Personal risk factors may include constitutional traits like temperament, sensory–motor deficits, and unusual sensitivities, as well as indicators of unhealthy psychological development such as an inability to bear frustration or maintain relationships, lack of self-esteem, and feelings of incompetence. Environmental risk factors such as a family member suffering from a psychiatric problem, chronic and profound stressors, low socioeconomic status (SES) of the parents, low academic achievements of the parents, and poor family functioning may also pose a risk to an adolescent's mental and physical well-being. This partial list of the hundreds of factors identified in the literature is illustrative of the complexity of this field of research.

Furthermore, the field has concentrated on two separate questions, one dealing with outcomes, the other with the processes that produce them. This dichotomy reflects the theoretical diversity found in the research on high-risk youth. Broadly speaking, most researchers to date have conducted their work influenced by a diathesis–stress model that explains vulnerability as the result of exposure to risk: 'These vulnerabilities constitute an individual's diathesis, and are conceptualized broadly as characteristics of functioning that lower one's threshold of susceptibility to environmental stressors that may subsequently trigger the onset of maladjustment or psychopathology' (Richters & Weintraub, 1990: 69). When vulnerabilities are studied, they are examined as both outcomes and sequential processes that produce the outcomes. In either approach, as is the case for most of the work in this field, the emphasis is on the problems caused by risk, with fewer resources devoted to the discovery of health-related phenomena among high-risk children and youth.

Earlier, researchers like Michael Rutter and his colleagues (1983, 1985, 1987, 2001; Quinton et al., 1990; Rutter et al., 1979, 1990, 1998) who provided leadership in the field of risk research, discovered through their work with at-risk children whose parents suffer a mental illness that continuities in psychiatric disorders across generations could not be attributed to a set of simple causal factors. Rather, it was the *process* by which these factors interacted that predicted specific outcomes. Consequently, risk factors have come to be thought of as chains of events, rather than singular negative episodes. These chains, like the risk factors already listed, include a great many biological, psychological, and sociopolitical factors that threaten an individual's healthy development (Anthony, 1987; Carver, 1998; Fraser, 1997; McCubbin, Fleming, Thompson, Neitman, Elver & Savas, 1998; Rutter, 2001). This possible 'barrage of hazards' (Anthony, 1987) to which an individual can be subjected may or may not affect a particular individual. It depends on how the risks are perceived. Furthermore, normative life crises such as moving, the birth of a sibling, and school adjustments may be potential risk factors for the child who has insufficient coping resources (Dunn, 1988; Sampson & Laub, 1997; Walsh, 1998). Thus, we may speak of all children as potentially 'at risk' at some time in their lives.

Complexity

There is some debate concerning these pathways through life and whether these chains of events lead to predictable outcomes (Cohen et al., 1990; Huisinga & Jakob-Chen, 1998; Loeber et al., 1998; Moffitt et al., 2001). The resilience construct, however, as complex as it appears in the lives of high-risk children, makes it very difficult to identify a narrow set of risk factors that can account for the variance between healthy and unhealthy children. Thus, for ease of analysis, most researchers have concerned themselves with only one or two dozen of the possible risk and vulnerability factors.

We know much about the etiology of problem behaviours in what are commonly referred to as high-risk populations. For example, the greatest risks to the health of youth in Western industrialized nations originate from delinquent behaviours such as drug and alcohol abuse, dangerous driving, self-injurious behaviours (e.g., suicide, high-risk sexual activity), violence, and social factors, including the following: intra- and extra-familial violence, school failure, poor parenting, divorce or separation, and threats to the family's economic stability (Dahlberg & Potter, 2001; Emery & Forehand, 1994; Jaffe & Baker, 1999; Johnson, 1993; King et al., 1999; Prilleltensky & Nelson, 2000; Robinson, 1994; Vanier Institute, 2000; Webster-Stratton 1998). Although this list is lengthy, leaders in the field of resilience research acknowledge their inability to narrow down the causal, or keystone factors (Fraser & Galinsky, 1997) that either predict healthy outcomes among at-risk individuals or protect and divert children and youth from these problem behaviours (Kaplan, 1999; Loeber & Farrington, 2000; Masten, 2001).

Risk factors, according to Laura Kirby and Mark Fraser, 'may include genetic, biological, behavioural, sociocultural, and demographic conditions, characteristics, or attributes. Risk or vulnerability represents a heightened probability of negative outcome based on the presence of one or more such factors' (1997: 10). In our emerging lexicon, risk factors are distinguished from risk traits, which are those individual characteristics and conditions that predispose a child to problems during his or her development. Risk factors and risk traits, along with contextual variations and normative stressors, or critical life events, combine to create risk mechanisms that contribute to the vulnerability of individual children. While risk is generally thought of as conditions affecting entire populations, *vulnerability* is the term reserved to describe the individual child who is judged to be either 'at risk' or, in situations where risk factors are compounded, 'high-risk.' The multiplicity of terms and definitional to-ing and fro-ing is indicative of a field of study still in its youth.

Admittedly, the now all too common use of the phrase 'youth at risk' has resulted in a loss of the predictive quality that 'at risk' once implied. This present work will likely not add to definitional purity, but intentionally muddy the waters by providing risk with a plurality of signifiers from different stakeholders in children's mental health. Such ambiguity will not sit well with some, like Romeria Tidwell and Susan Garrett (1994), who observe that many youth who are already manifesting problems are still being referred to as at risk. The problem, as Tidwell and Garrett note, is when exposure to risk stops predicting further problem development? The child raised by an alcoholic parent may grow up to be an alcoholic, which in turn may place him or her at greater risk of poverty, violence, and disease. No part of this pathway, however, is guaranteed (Velleman & Orford, 1999). Similarly, Barbara Lowenthal (1999) argues that a young child's neurodevelopment can be disrupted by either a lack of sensory experiences that diminish brain activity or from negative experiences of maltreatment and neglect that result in abnormally active neurons. In both cases, future functioning is likely to be disrupted. In defending a singular conception of risk, we run into the snarl caused by a congestion of possible futures. In this present work I purposely use the phrases 'at risk' and 'high risk' in a less predictive fashion, preferring to avoid a moratorium on when or how risk affects a population.

Where definitional agreement has occurred, researchers have found the effect of risk factors to be multiplicative. The child with one risk factor to contend with is unlikely, we are told, to be affected negatively for his or her entire life. The child with three factors present is likely to feel their effect more than what would be expected if one simply added together the potential impact of each factor individually (Crick & Bigbee, 1998; Ellickson & McGuigan, 2000; Herrenkohl et al., 2000; Rutter, 1987). Such were the results of a five-year study of youth by Phyllis Ellickson and Kimberly McGuigan (2000) in which they found among children tested in Grade 7 and five years later that violent behaviours could be predicted based on the compounding influence of early deviance, poor grades, weak elementary school bonds, pro-drug middle school environments, and bullying or stealing behaviours. Just as a slight deviation in an aircraft's flight plan may result in it veering many miles off course, so too can a few critical incidents early in a child's life skew development for years to come. Robert Sampson and John Laub (1997; Laub & Sampson, 1993) hypothesize a similar set of deviations they call 'turning points' that are moments of a child's adaptation to risk that profoundly affect the child's future course of development.

More qualified but still empirically supportive findings that substantiate this theory of cumulative risk are to be found in a number of works, including that of Jean Gerard and Cheryl Buehler (1999), who offer a considered view of the complexity of this relationship. They found in a study of family risk factors and youth problem behaviours that 'contrary to the steep increases in problem behavior expected for potentiated risk, the findings are more consistent with a threshold effect of multiple risk exposure. The data indicated that the most dramatic increase in these measures of problem behaviour is between zero and one risk factor, with a slight leveling off at greater levels of risk exposure' (1999: 355). In 47% of cases of children with a risk factor of one, poor parenting quality was the single predictive factor, much more so than interparental conflict or family economic hardship. On the surface these findings would appear to negate the hypothesis of exponential growth in the impact of risk. However, a finer analysis led Gerard and Buehler to suspect that, where cumulative stress operates, it is the multiple stressors that mount on *the parents* that are significant and multiplicative (as when economic upheavals make fathers less effective as parents in two-parent homes), and this results in a threshold effect whereby the stressed parent fulfils his or her role inadequately. In some cases, Gerard and Buehler found, two-parent families showed this pattern more than did single-parent, female-headed families, as fathers were more likely than mothers to become stressed by external factors that only indirectly affected the children.

Such complexity in the interaction among risk, protective factors (a two-parent household), and children's well-being is typical. Thomas Dishion, Deborah Capaldi, and Karen Yoerger (1999) report that, even though better family management and monitoring of a child would be expected to reduce substance use, closer monitoring and positive affiliation with parents who themselves use substances can exacerbate the risk of experimentation with marijuana by youth. Unexpectedly, in the same study, involvement with deviant peer groups, an anticipated negative influence on teenagers, did not predict the onset of tobacco use. Such complexity has led some to conclude that these constructs are too all-encompassing to be successfully studied using traditional methods (Glantz & Sloboda, 1999; Guerra, 1998; Thoits, 1995).

Further complicating this problem is how a particular behaviour is viewed, as a sign of either weakness or strength. Let us consider the Pittsburgh Youth Study (Farrington, 1995; Loeber, Farrington, Stouthamer-Loeber & Van Kammen, 1998; Loeber, Green, Lahey & Kalb, 2000; Loeber & Hay, 1994; Loeber & Stouthamer-Loeber, 1998; Loeber, Drinkwater, Yin, Anderson, Schmidt & Crawford, 2000; Loeber, Green, Lahey, Frick & McBurnett, 2000). For seven years, 503 Grade 1 and 506 Grade 7 boys were followed, with data collection taking place annually. Among the most telling risk factors predicting persistent serious delinquency were, at the individual level for the younger boys, motivation, bad friends, low interest in school, and disadvantaged neighbourhoods. For both older and younger boys, the factors were being cruel to people, being manipulative, and possessing a low ability to feel guilt. The most protective factors, for older youth, were high accountability and good relationships with parents. For the youngest boys in the sample, accountability, trustworthiness, the ability to feel guilt, school motivation, and a non-disadvantaged neighbourhood protected best. These two sets of risk and protective factors were found to have summary domain scores ranging from .66 for the oldest boys to .56 for the youngest; both findings are significant. Boys with higher risk scores had a much greater likelihood of becoming persistent serious delinquents. The findings ring true for many of the youth in the present study, but with a difference: While others may see in such a constellation of attributes indications of risk or resilience, many of the youth who would be negatively classified under such a protocol argued that in their particular context, certain expressions of self may have added to their health and protection, while other more pro-social expressions, had they been pursued, would have threatened that same well-being.

If we revisit the Pittsburgh results, anomalies that support this perspective are evident. Loeber and his colleagues found that, of the boys with a combined risk and promotive score in the promotive end, some 17% were still at high risk for becoming persistent serious delinquents, given their behaviours. The researchers speculate that this may be because what they measured may have been more appropriate to mitigating risk in younger children. While this might well be the case, one may also question whether we need to revisit the dichotomous thinking about attributes of risk and protection that sort characteristics somewhat arbitrarily based on the biased and privileged positions of researchers. After all, studies of street youth have found that characteristics similar to being manipulative, in Loeber's study taken as a sign of ill health, may, in fact, be both functional and health promoting (Ensign & Gittelsohn, 1998; Hagan & McCarthy, 1997; Tyler et al., 1992). This issue will be explored further in Chapter 3.

Resilience Studied

In the conventional literature such as that just discussed, children, youth, and adults who manage to overcome the adversity to which they are exposed are referred to as resilient. As Werner and Smith explained two decades ago, resilience is a child's *'capacity to cope effectively with the internal stresses of their vulnerabilities* (such as labile patterns of autonomic reactivity, developmental imbalances, unusual sensitivities) *and external stresses* (such as illness, major losses, and dissolution of the family). Even through the most stressful experiences in the most terrible homes, some individuals appear to emerge unscathed and to develop a stable, healthy personality' (1982: 4; emphasis in original).

Since 1982 there has been little change in the construct of resilience. Resilience is thought to be found only in those who emerge from adversity with their health intact as evidenced by specific patterns of behaviour. Fluidity in definitions of health, coping, competence, and other related constructs, including resilience, is seldom part of the discourse on resilience. Most frequently, the approach to assessing resilience has been formulaic. Depending on the severity of the risk to which a child has been exposed, the context in which it occurred, the duration of time the child coped, and the level of support available at the time to help the child, researchers have been either optimistic or pessimistic about a child's future growth and development.

The literature on resilience varies greatly in its estimate of how many children survive and thrive. The myriad of factors that must be considered when measuring outcomes and the contextual specificity required in these measurements makes it difficult to compare studies. Even intelligence quotient (IQ) and academic performance – bulwarks of psychological research – have been called into question as benchmarks of success by those who see a child's emotional quotient or EQ (Goleman, 1994) as being every bit as important to his or her survival as IQ, and academic success as culturally less relevant or even problematic among some populations (Gooden, 1997; Simmons, 2002; Taylor et al., 1995). All we can say for certain is that resilience indicates successful adaptation such that a child thrives where failure would be expected. Estimates vary. Some say that only about 10% of at-risk children will grow up resilient (e.g., Higgins, 1994). Others believe that as many as two-thirds or even all at-risk youth may be expected to beat the odds (e.g., Wolin & Wolin, 1995). The differences in the estimates depend on the definitions of success, the risk factors considered, and the design of each study.

This ambiguity in the resilience construct has been addressed in a number of works over the past decade (see for example, Glantz & Sloboda, 1999; Kaplan, 1999; Masten, 2001), including that of Edmund Gordon and Lauren Song (1994) who challenged reified notions of success inherent in such studies. Characterizing the history of resilience research as imposing conceptual limitations, they found that 'the conditions we label as *resiliency, resistance, invincibility,* and so forth, are relative, situational, and attributional. Thus, the assumed meaning of the construct may have greater significance for the researchers who define or investigate it, than for the person or persons who experience it. If you think that I am a "loser," and I think I am a "winner," whose classification is to apply? If you define my status as poverty stricken, and my own experience is that of sufficiency, is my resource availability a high-risk factor? If it is my behavior that we are trying to explain, whose perceived reality is valid as an independent variable?' (1994: 31). Gordon and Song focused their research instead on acts of 'defiance of negative predictions' among a group of 26 African American men and women who grew up successfully, according to their own self-constructions of positive outcomes.

Resilience has always meant positive adaptation in the face of adversity. There is, however, some debate over whether to be resilient a child must not merely survive, but thrive, and thereby demonstrate exceptional outcomes or invulnerability. This more extreme definition is problematic because the judgment as to which child is resilient is complicated by subjective appraisals of what is exceptional behaviour given the risks present in a child's life (Carver, 1998; Freeman & Dyer, 1993; Massey et al., 1998). Measurement is further complicated by the competing visions that stakeholders have of what constitutes health in children. Researchers who collect data from more than one source in conventional research programs have found that measures of resilience are far from objective. As Michael Rutter and his colleagues explain, the relatively modest agreement between multiple informants on children's behaviour (teachers, parents, and children) 'is a consequence of the fact that people often behave differently in different situations; in part it reflects differences in the opportunities to notice particular forms of behavior; in part it may be a result of perceptual biases of various kinds; and in part it may arise because informants vary in the reference groups that they use' (1998: 12). Arguably, such problems of measurement may require mixed methods if one is to contextualize findings that originate from respondents' different social locations.

Despite this and other related shortcomings, a greater focus on resilience enhancing variables and processes in developmental studies has resulted in attention being paid to children and youth who resemble their problem peers on measures of risk, but demonstrate qualities associated with normative definitions of health. Such individuals are typically described as resilient (Garmezy, 1976, 1983, 1987,1991, 1993; Masten, 2001; Rutter, 1987, 2001). As Jane Gilgun (1999) has observed, the resilience construct has come to mean a set of both behaviours and internalized capacities. The combined effect of this focus on resilience has been to engage us increasingly in a salutogenic discourse focused on healthy aspects of people's lives in contrast to the more predominant pathologizing discourse in which professionals participate (Antonovsky, 1987; Cowley & Billings, 1999).

Within the resilience literature, studies cluster into three types. As Stuart Hauser (1999) explains, the first is *epidemiological* and found in case-specific narratives or large longitudinal studies that examine the

way individuals within an at-risk population achieve better than expected health outcomes. Analysis of the constellation of variables at
play in subjects' lives identifies protective and vulnerability factors. A
second type of study considers *life course development* and changes in
level of functioning through the study of patterns of adaptation and
coping following sequences of stressful events such as the divorce of
parents, onset of mental illness in a family member, chronic illness,
dislocations, or a change in economic status. In these studies, the focus
is not solely on risk factors, but equally on the way negative (or positive) life events combine with biopsychosocial risks to produce desirable or undesirable outcomes. Over the past 20 years, these studies
have changed their approach from an examination of antecedents and
pathways to illness to investigations of the protective factors at play in
lives lived successfully under adversity. A third type of resilience research is concerned only with *recovery after instances of trauma*, either
natural or human in design. In these studies, which share much in
common with the work on life events, the emphasis is on developmental pathways after the trauma occurs and predisposing behaviours
and attitudes that buffer the effects of the trauma.

These three types of studies have operationalized the resilience construct in at least four distinct ways. When juxtaposed, each may be
understood as a singular reification of what resilience is, although
none is sufficiently broad to capture the constructions of all research
participants. When designing studies, researchers have had to decide
whether resilience is to mean simply normative levels of 'good coping' after a child in a low-risk environment experiences an exceptional
but acute trauma (such as a single episode of sexual abuse) or resilience is to refer to the same child who sees within the crisis an 'opportunity for growth' and excels beyond normative levels of functioning?
Both understandings of resilience among children in low-risk environments are frequently in the literature (Benard, 2002; Dunn, 1988; Emery & Forehand, 1994; Luthar et al., 2000). Alternately, resilience may
refer to conditions of successful, but normative functioning being
achieved by a child who 'beats the odds' in life by mounting a successful challenge to the combined effects of chronic and acute stressors in a high-risk environment. Such a child may be one growing up
with an alcoholic parent who lacks supervision but nonetheless maintains sobriety and an attachment to school. Finally, resilience has been
conceptualized as the characteristics and processes typical of children
who grow up in high-risk environments but who learn from their life

experience and are 'inoculated' against further exposure to stress. In the past, these children have been thought of as 'invulnerable' and 'invincible' (Anthony, 1987). Figures 2.1 and 2.2 illustrate each of these four uses of the term *resilience*.

Specifically, resilience-related factors that have been identified among youth fitting all four descriptions are easily categorized as either compensatory, challenging, or protective (Garmezy et al., 1984; O'Leary, 1998). Compensatory factors are those aspects of an individual or environment that neutralize exposure to risk in the first place (Cairns & Cairns, 1994; Garmezy et al., 1984; Luthar & Ziglar, 1991; Magnus et al., 1999). Such things as faith, a positive disposition towards life, and as demonstrated by a youth like Melissa, an engaging personality and an internal locus of control, have all been shown to contribute to positive outcomes when a child grows up under adverse circumstances (Bandura, 1998; Kumpfer & Hopkins, 1993; Murphy & Moriarty, 1976; Werner & Smith, 1982; Zimmerman et al., 1999). For example, S.T. Hauser (1999) spent more than 20 years working with the same group of youth who had spent between 2 and 12 months during their middle adolescence hospitalized for a childhood mental illness. Through a narrative analysis of yearly interviews, Hauser demonstrated six characteristics associated with competent coping in early adulthood. These compensatory traits include the following: a capacity for self-reflection, self-efficacy or agency, recognition by individuals of their self-complexity, persistence and ambition, self-esteem, and a coherence to the narratives that these resilient individuals construct over their life course.

In contrast, challenge factors are risk factors that serve the function of enhancing resilience when the risk is manageable for the individual and enhancing his or her adaptive capacity over time. Such challenges, in the form of an illness, significant loss, or family disruption, are often thought of as acting as an inoculation against future stress during crises (Cairns & Cairns, 1994; Chong, 2000; Rutter, 1987).

Finally, protective factors are becoming more and more of interest to those who work with high-risk children and youth as it these factors that are thought to reduce the potential for negative outcomes. While compensatory factors are characteristics of individuals and environments, protective factors actively target specific risks and are thus better thought of as processes or mechanisms for growth. Families or peer relationships that provide stable networks of support, individual coping strategies that marshal much needed resources, better

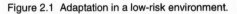
Figure 2.1 Adaptation in a low-risk environment.

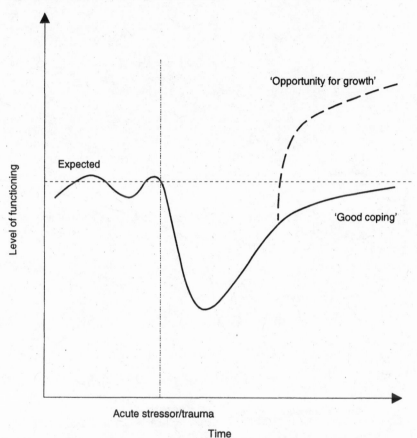

parenting practices that provide appropriate levels of supervision and guidance, and relocation to a safer community when one's own is found to be dangerous, are examples of protective processes that mitigate risk (Bender & Loesel, 1997; Gilgun, 1999; McCubbin et al., 1998; Recklitis & Noam, 1999).

Garmezy (1976, 1983, 1985, 1987, 1991, 1993) was among the first to think along the line of protective factors. He has been principally concerned with research on children in families where one or both parents have a mental illness or where children demonstrate resilience growing up in chaotic environments, for example, the children in war-

Figure 2.2 Adaptation in a high-risk environment.

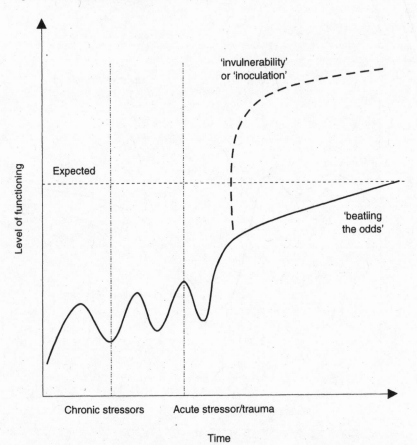

torn Northern Ireland and, retrospectively, the children in London during the Second World War. Garmezy characterizes his work as a third stage in studies of this kind. The first stage was the identification of children who show good coping despite risk. The second was the search for correlates of personal and environmental factors of relevance to these children. The third is the identification of the factors that contribute to these children's positive outcomes. Garmezy does not explicitly talk about protective mechanisms. He does, however, identify three broad categories of factors that he believes protect against risk. These three protective factors are the personality disposition of the child, a supportive family milieu, and an external support system that encourages and reinforces a child's coping efforts and strengthens them by inculcating positive values (1985: 219).

Rutter's (1983, 1985, 1987) early work took an interesting, and for the 1980s, novel approach to the same question of protective factors. Rutter found it important to think of protective mechanisms, rather than constellations of factors, that could predict healthy outcomes for at-risk children. A protective mechanism is a process over time that changes a child's trajectory in life by protecting him or her against risk. According to Rutter, reducing the amount of risk to which the child is exposed occurs in two ways. The first way is by changing the child's appraisal and cognitive processing of events. In this way, situations become less threatening when the child feels competent in his or her abilities to cope. As Rutter notes, 'protection may lie in the "steeling" qualities that derive from successful coping with the hazards when the exposure is of a type and degree that is manageable in the context of the child's capacities and social situation' (1987: 326). The second way the impact of risk is reduced is by altering the level of the child's exposure to risk factors. Thus, children in high-risk environments who have more structured home lives that protect them from extra-familial and intra-familial stress – home lives that include good communication, togetherness, sharing of activities, displays of affection, offers of support, mutual acceptance, and commitment to one another – are more likely to grow up healthy and weather both normative and non-normative life crises (Baldwin et al., 1990; Felner et al., 1985; Fick & Thomas, 1995; Hawley, 2000; Silberberg, 2001; Walsh, 1998).

Ana Fick and Sarah Thomas studied 110 disadvantaged children and youth attending a summer camp. They demonstrated that children's attitudes towards substance use and abuse (smoking cigarettes and drinking alcohol) were related to the level of exposure to violence in their homes and communities: 'Students who reported greater exposure to nonviolent conflict resolution within their families ... reported lower intention to smoke. The greater use of nonviolent resolution methods within the family may be indicative of more positive family relationships and processes, which may serve a protective function' (1995: xx). Findings such as these reflect what Rutter has shown to be patterns in the way protective mechanisms function when they reduce exposure to risk.

Rutter argues that protective mechanisms operate as critical turning points in a child's life that can redirect his or her development. For example, an interest in a particular sport or other extra-curricular activity that leads to an opportunity at school to participate and excel can be a critical factor in supporting a child's health (Doll & Lyon, 1998; Linney & Seidman, 1989; Rutter et al., 1979). From this experience of competence and self-efficacy in the gymnasium or after school club may come an expanded peer group, a heightened interest in school, and a greater likelihood of future success in non-sports-related aspects of life.

Sampson and Laub (1997; Laub & Sampson,1993) have thought in much the same terms as Rutter and his colleagues. However, they focused specifically on the principle of 'cumulative disadvantage' which results in critical 'turning points' in children's development and orientations either towards or away from delinquent lifestyles. Re-analysing the data gathered by Sheldon and Eleanor Glueck in 1940, Sampson and Laub developed a theory to explain the continuity children experience in informal social controls that incrementally influences the paths they travel through life. Thinking of delinquency developmentally, they examined the role that labelling plays in this dynamic process. In their discussion of a child with an aggressive temperament, they write, 'Aggression is a social behavior that, by definition, involves interpersonal interaction. Moreover, aggression and conduct disorder often generate immediate and harsh responses by varying segments of society compared to most personality traits ... aggression tends to foster physical counterattacks, teacher and peer rejection, punitive discipline, parental hostility, and harsh criminal justice sanctions ... Logically, then, the fact that much delinquency starts early in the life course implies that retaliatory efforts to suppress it also begin early. These repressive efforts accrete incrementally over time to produce developmental effects' (1997: 144). The result is a pattern of cumulative disadvantage that, through interaction with others and the labelling that occurs, predisposes a child towards persistent criminal behaviour.

Each successive episode of negative labelling acts like Rutter's protective mechanisms, only it produces change in the direction opposite to that desired. Denise Newman and her colleagues from the Dunedin, New Zealand, longitudinal study found there to be a great deal of continuity between the characteristics in temperament of three-year-olds and young adults' interpersonal functioning. The under-controlled children had the least favourable outcomes: 62% of them were boys, described during a 90-minute observation period as 'irritable, impulsive, and impersistent on tasks; they had difficulty sitting still, were inattentive, physically overactive, and emotionally labile' (1997: 208). It would not be difficult to conclude that many of the participants in the present study fared no better on measures of performance at age three. Children in the Dunedin study who grew up in more pro-social ways performed as well-adjusted, reserved, confident, and inhibited children. Both negative and positive characteristics have shown persistence into young adulthood and affect how development tasks are achieved. Given this, what are we to offer such children who seem predisposed to anti-social behaviour? It strikes me that most of our interventions are targeted at changing these young people, when the Dunedin results should encourage us to work better with their traits as shown. Youth themselves seem more comfortable making the most of a bad situation and exploiting resources that sustain their mental health. As will be shown, and counter-intuitively, high-risk youth frequently surprise us with their latent health (see Chapter 5).

The bias in most of this research has been to distinguish arbitrarily, and from within the bounds of culture, signs of vulnerability and health. Vulnerability mechanisms are shown by Sampson and Laub to cause negative changes in children's pathways to health. However, while Sampson and Laub identify delinquency as a negative outcome, high-risk youth argue that their responses to these critical turning points and subsequent choice of delinquent behaviours are functionally adaptive responses to risk factors. Persistence of these negatively perceived behaviours is the result of a dynamic process: 'the stability of behavior may reflect more the stability of social *response* than the time-invariance of an individual ... aggression is a social behavior embedded in ongoing social interactions with salient others' (1997: 154; emphasis in original). To the extent that labels accrue over time and become reified, high-risk youth will either become more adept at the negative roles assigned to them, or they will seek out alternative, more socially acceptable identities, which are generally assumed to better support feelings of well-being.

Fitting the Pieces Together

The relationship among risk, protective factors, and the positive outcomes thought synonymous with resilience is complicated by a mutual dependency of one upon the other, each an equal part to the puzzle of health. For example, John Pollard, David Hawkins, and Michael Arthur worked with a sample of Grade 6 to 12 students in five U.S. states to examine whether one needs both a risk and protection focus to address behavioural problems in children. They found that 'significant effects of protection in reducing the prevalence of problem behaviors are present only at the higher levels of risk exposure ... It should be noted that at these high levels of risk exposure, high levels of protection did not eliminate problem behaviors. Even among those with high protection, prevalence rates of all problem behaviors increased with more risk exposure' (1999: 151). In their conclusion, Pollard et al. support the idea that there is an interactive relationship between risk and protective factors, but that problem behaviours will still persist even when protective factors are present in the highest risk populations. In other words, protective factors do not extinguish the effects of risk, but they do buffer their effects, preventing further exponential growth in problem behaviours following risk exposure. Interventions that address both risk and protective factors simultaneously are the ones most likely to succeed.

Rutter's (1987) effort at conceptualizing protective mechanisms led to the identification of four specific types of protective experiences that were especially salient in the lives of high-risk children over time. The four were reduction of risk impact, reduction of negative chain reactions, establishment and maintenance of self-esteem and self-efficacy, and opening of opportunities. Rutter and his colleagues (Rutter et al., 1998) later expanded this list to include eight broad mechanisms that exert a positive influence on a child's growth. These mechanisms are the following: (1) those that reduce sensitivity to risk (previous successful coping); (2) reduction of risk impact (parental monitoring, child's distancing from a deviant parent); (3) reduction of negative chain reactions (successful handling of family conflict and effective problem solving); (4) increasing positive chain reactions (eliciting social support); (5) promotion of self-esteem and self-efficacy (successful coping with manageable stress); (6) neutralizing or compensatory positive experiences that directly counter the risk effect (a positive attachment to a healthy spouse); (7) opening up of positive opportunities (change of home, or access to career and educational experiences); and (8) positive cognitive processing of negative experiences (a positive orientation towards life and acceptance rather than denial of challenges).

Our understanding of protective factors and mechanisms has broadened over the years. Increasingly it is ecological, providing better predictions of health the more contextualized that research has become. For example, a study by Marc Zimmerman, Jesus Ramirez-Valles, and Kenneth Maton employed a longitudinal design to examine the link between helplessness, a risk factor, and mental health. Analysis of findings from two interviews spaced six months apart with 172 African-American male adolescents, found that 'sociopolitical control moderated the negative effects of personal helplessness on mental health outcomes ... Psychological symptoms did not vary as levels of personal helplessness increased for youths who reported the highest levels of sociopolitical control' (1999: xx). Zimmerman et al. note that we know much more about what causes pathology in this population about why or how some of these youth become well-functioning citizens. This is a common refrain among resilience investigators, especially those concerned with marginalized populations whose psychopathology has been overestimated because of a lack of cultural and racial sensitivity (Batey, 1999; Cross, 1998; Klevens & Roca, 1999; Tyler et al., 1992; Sharma & Sharma, 1999).

From Research to Narrative

The three categories of factors, compensatory, challenge and protective, which contribute to each of the four conceptualizations of resilience found in Figures 2.1 and 2.2, are characteristics ubiquitous among studies using a variety of methods including retrospective, cross-sectional, and prospective designs. Many of these same elements are also present in the narratives of the young people whose lives are recounted in the following chapters. Thus, while many of the youth interviewed for this study demonstrated patterns of resilience atypical of youth normally thought of as healthy, some participants did manifest resilience in ways more generally accepted. Unfortunately, unearthing these positive patterns proved at times difficult, for as I discovered, high-risk children live within a stigmatizing context that overlooks the positive characteristics that are more frequently identified retrospectively in populations of adults or older youth who have already distanced themselves from chaotic and stressful environments.

It was in this context that I met Peter, whose mother Joanne had requested help from Family and Children Services to prevent her from further abusing her children. Peter, age 14 at the time, and his younger brother, Luke, age 11, had on multiple occasions been severely beaten. Yet, Peter refused to see his abuse as a problem. He loved his mother and saw little need for counselling or other mandated interventions.

Peter never knew his father, with whom his mother had spent only a few months, living common-law. Joanne has had a long history of mental illness and continues to struggle with schizophrenia and depression. Nevertheless, she managed to parent both her children well, except for these occasional physical outbursts. Peter protected his mother from harsh criticism by denying the extent of the abuse. Despite his poverty and lack of consistent parental support Peter had succeeded well at school. In his community, though, he was viewed as just another problem youth who was on the streets too much and suspected of everything from abusing drugs to local property crimes.

In getting to know Peter, one meets a bright and studious individual who stands up for himself and his beliefs. He loves to debate issues and is proud of his straight 'A' performance at school. He also attends regularly a youth group run out of a community centre in another part of the city in which he lives and is involved in extracurricular theatrical productions. All these activities take him away from his home and community, but also inadvertently hide healthier aspects of his life from his neighbours – and even his mother. Peter's ability to negotiate the outside world has made him far less vulnerable to the negative effects of his abuse. Instead, he admires his mother for what she has managed to do. Her illness, he feels, does not interfere with his life, except when she keeps him up at night roaming the house talking to herself.

Broader Dimensions to Resilience

As demonstrated through such narrative accounts of lives lived, there are a number of aspects of life that are important to understanding resilience beyond those already mentioned. Most notably among these are the role of growth over time, the resilience of the family unit as a whole, and the cultural specificity of the resilience construct. The first of these, time, or more specifically, pathways to resilience, is frequently an aspect of resilience research. Resilience is not a static quality but instead an evolving set of characteristics and processes. I have already mentioned concepts like turning points and trajectories which have attached themselves to the resilience literature. Other work by developmental psychopathologists and criminologists has targeted specifically the pathways that individuals travel towards health and deviance. While many of these studies have been concerned with the life course of problem behaviours and mental illness, embedded within their findings is the detailing of lives lived in ways that achieve standards congruent with the researcher's own construction of health.

Robert and Beverley Cairns (1994), for example, used semi-structured interviews in multiple waves with a sample of almost 700 youth over 10 years. Combining these interviews with file reviews, they found that changes in expected life course from negative to positive could be accounted for by novelty in development (as when a child shows unexpected talents), measurement errors caused by aggregating data (making people's lives appear to be more stable, and therefore more at risk, than they really are), and real changes in development resulting from a significant change in circumstances and access to health resources (as when a child's school, neighbourhood, or family structure changes for the better). Such aspects of healthy growth are equally present in the lives of children like Peter whose unexpected talents, and access to a caring school environment allowed him an escape from a chaotic home.

Although correlational data have provided us with clues not unlike those found in the work of Cairns and Cairns or that of other notable researchers such as Werner and Smith (1982, 1992) and Terri Moffitt and her colleagues (1993, 1997; Moffitt et al., 2001), we are still largely at a loss to understand the motivations and nuances in these pathways to illness and health. Arguably, we need to know more about why children stop their troubling behaviours. But equally, for those engaged in troubling patterns, and for those who persist, we have failed yet to understand well their accounts of their experiences, nor fully considered the positive aspects of the behaviour that may diminish the need to desist.

A model of three pathways to different forms of serious or violent offending offered by Loeber and his colleagues (Loeber et al., 1998; Loeber, Green, Lahey & Kalb, 2000) has shown that there are predictable and orderly progressions to children's problem behaviours. Their three related pathways are distinguishable by the outcomes of either avoidance of authority, moderate to serious delinquent acts that include most property crimes, or violence against others (Loeber, Green, Lahey, Frick & McBurnett, 2000; Loeber & Hay, 1994). Although the work of Loeber and his colleagues has been well validated by others (Tolan & Gorman-Smith, 1998), they have themselves recognized that the tangle of reasons for these pathways is complicated by the health-enhancing aspects of some negative behaviours. Loeber and co-author Farrington write that 'some children engage in minor delinquent acts for excitement, adventure, or other emotions common among children. For these children, offending may be considered as part of the context of child development in which youngsters learn prosocial behaviors by trial and error' (2000: 742). Unfortunately, like most developmentalists, this qualified acceptance for the lifestyle choices of youth, when they are highly destructive and socially undesirable, as I will show later, does not extend so far as to understand aspects of these behaviour as *resilience-seeking*. Loeber and Farrington explain that such benign acting out is not really possible, as some of these same children are likely to be involved in more serious acts than those of which we are aware and that, for many, 'early status offences are stepping stones in pathways to serious, violent, and chronic offending' (2000: 743). Although we are getting closer, there remains the problem of distinguishing from among high-risk cohorts those children who will follow one of these three paths, and those who will desist altogether (Loeber, Green, Lahey, Frick & McBurnett, 2000; Nagin & Tremblay, 1999; Roberts et al., 2001).

A second aspect of resilience research that is emerging as important is the reconceptualization of resilience as a characteristic and set of processes found among families. Because risk factors occur in constellations and the processes that address them are necessarily complex, researchers like Froma Walsh have pressed us to think of the problem children face and their solutions contextually, rather than reducing each to its constituent parts. Understanding family processes as of a different order from individual experiences allows us a conceptual frame with which to examine the context-specific experiences of youth that predict negative outcomes and inform better interventions (Baron & Hartnagel, 1998; Freitas & Downey, 1998; Schissel & Fedec, 2001/ 1999; Silberberg, 2001; Silva-Wayne, 1995). There is mounting evidence that a constellation of factors at the level of the family, rather than solely those pertaining to individuals, are predictive of outcomes in at-risk children. Terri Moffitt and her colleagues found that, in relation to family factors, 'boys and girls whose mothers were negative and critical, who faced harsh discipline, inconsistent discipline, and family conflict, whose families moved frequently, who experienced multiple different caregivers and spent longer periods of time with a single parent, and who grew up in social economically disadvantaged families were at increased risk of developing antisocial behaviour' (2001: 101).

Walsh, in her work on resilient families, notes the diversity of family forms and the functionality of each: 'Families that don't conform to

the "one-norm-fits-all" standard have been stigmatized and pathologized by assumptions that alternative forms inherently damage children. Families of varied configurations can be successful. It is not
family *form*, but rather family *processes*, that matter most for healthy
functioning and resilience' (1998: 16; emphasis in original). Walsh explores many different families' responses to risk, demonstrating that
health exists concurrent with risk factors such as family breakdown.
Conceptualizing resilience as family-based, or system-based, is an important bridge between modernist and postmodernist paradigms and
how resilience is understood in each. In both instances individual characteristics are secondary to interpersonal processes. Dale Hawley and
Laura DeHaan (1996) lend further support to the idea that families as
a unit create resilience based on a shared view of reality and a common cognitive process that underpins a sense of coherence that protects the family as a unit. This same quality of coherence in the family
or relational system is pivotal to a salutogenic discourse and has appeared in a number of studies. One such is the examination by Myron
Oglesby-Pitts (2000) of male African-American children and their pathways to health that demonstrated the importance of family cohesion
(how well the family works and plays together, communicates, and
supports one another), a sense of religious faith, and a high level of
parental expectation.

Not all pathways, however, are so easily discerned. Richard Velleman
and Jim Orford (1999) conducted a series of long interviews with 164
adult children of problem drinkers who self-identified and with another 80 adults in a control group who did not have the same history
but were matched on key demographic and social variables. Their
findings indicate logical but inconsistent patterns in growth. Teens
from homes of problem drinkers may be more prone to delinquency,
but they are also much more likely to score higher in sociability and
peer group affiliation. In fact, Velleman and Orford comment, 'The
present findings that the offspring of problem drinking parents, as a
group, do not have much poorer adulthood outcomes than compari-
sons ... is contrary to the expectations engendered by the strong ACOA
(Adult Children of Alcoholics) movement in the USA and elsewhere'
(1999: 230–1). Reductionist arguments of causality and risk do not
hold up well when studies are designed that put aside conventional
constructions of the health of at-risk individuals and their families.
Other authors, like Beth Swadener (1995), propose that we move from
a discourse that supports a view of children and families as being at

risk to one that challenges our 'othering' of those who are less privileged. Swadener's work in educational settings starts from the premise
that all families are 'at promise.'

Beyond pathway and family considerations, the study of resilience
also requires a cultural caveat when deciding which outcomes are to
be chosen as benchmarks of health. Some studies have gone to great
lengths, in fact, to account for the obvious bias that culture creates in
their sample. Murphy and Moriarty, in their classic study on vulnerability, coping, and growth in children and adolescents in Topeka,
Kansas, took great pains to describe the context in which their study
took place and to situate the participants in time and place, arguing
that research on children 'has to be seen as relative to the culture, or
rather subculture, in which the children were observed' (1976: 18). To
their credit, Murphy and Moriarty acknowledge the limits of their
own work in this regard, although subsequent references to their findings seldom limit the generalizability of the Kansas findings beyond
the culture of the American plains states. Contextual difference between and within samples, if noted at all, is usually left unresolved.
Frequently, studies on resilience have controlled for the effects of culture, race, ethnicity, gender, and class rather than reflecting on the
bias inherent in their designs. My own research sees in the potential
hegemony of norms an important keystone concept necessary to understand resilience as it is actually experienced by high-risk children
and youth.

Summary

In this chapter I have brought together a variety of different understandings of resilience as currently reflected in the literature. It remains an ambiguous field, with content spread across a number of
different disciplines including psychology, education, social work,
medicine, and criminology. While there is agreement that for resilience to be present there must be exposure to risk, the nature of resilience has been conceptualized in at least four distinct ways, including
good coping, opportunities for growth, beating the odds, and inoculation against future stress. Supporting each conceptualization are studies that have investigated compensatory, challenge, and protective
factors. More recently the field has become most concerned with mechanisms or processes that protect children against negative outcomes
over time.

Throughout this discussion, a long list of possible factors associated with resilience has been discussed. There is an unwieldy matrix of hundreds of factors that appear in the literature that have been used as indicators of healthy outcomes and an equally daunting number of risk factors that interact one with the other as both dependent and independent variables. My intention has been to provide one cognitive map through this maze, raising the question as to why some factors and processes are chosen as a proxy for specific outcomes while others are not. Case illustrations show that in the lives of high-risk youth, there is a complex association between risk and resilience, with access to health resources playing an important role in how children construct health amidst adversity. In the next chapter anomalies in the research will be further explored to show that resilience is contextually specific and contextually constructed.

Chapter Three

Progressive Dilemmas in Resilience Research

Concepts such as risk, vulnerability, and resilience have been studied tautologically, with an emphasis on outsider constructions of subjects' realities. For example, take Joseph Burger's perspective on resilience published in a special edition of *The Journal of Emotional and Behaviour Problems* (1994). In his article, 'Risk, Resilience, and Protection,' Burger reviews the findings of a number of major studies that have most influenced our understanding of resilience. His conclusion is that there are two types of resilience, unhealthy and healthy.

> 'Healthy' resilience is expressed through pro-social, compassionate, har-
> monious, adaptive behaviors. In contrast, 'unhealthy' resilience is seen in
> the use of aggressive, controlling, withdrawing, or self-destructive be-
> haviors.
> Negative resilience is counterproductive. Such behaviour may have
> some short-term use as a coping mechanism, but it does not heal. These
> strategies poison human relationships and preclude the development of
> healthy resilience. (1994: 8)

There is no empirical evidence for this notion that some resilience is bad and some good. Burger, like many others, states what seems intuitively obvious, but cannot be authenticated in the narrative accounts that high-risk individuals themselves share.

Tommy was invited to participate in the study discussed in Chapter 1 and joined the research project while still in a secure juvenile detention centre but receiving mental health counselling in his community. Tommy says he copes with his violent past by finding one powerful self-definition and tenaciously holding on to it. In the presence of adults, Tommy is a quiet, withdrawn 16-year-old. He is a strong, good-looking young man who has been in and out of jail and foster homes for years. Tommy's mother, Debbie, has moved the family many times throughout her son's life. She talked of five different men who were fathers of her eight children; in some cases, she was not quite certain who was really the father of which child. Alcoholism, spousal abuse, and child abuse characterize the history of this family. Of his siblings, Tommy most idealizes his 17-year-old-brother Joe, who has spent time in jail for theft and assault. 'No one messes with him,' Tommy explained.

Tommy describes his friends as being like brothers to him. He had hoped that his mother would remain where she was, although her most recent partner was violent and an alcoholic, and it appeared unlikely that she would be with him for long. The family had only welfare coming in, which meant there was no money for Tommy to join a hockey or football team. He attended school sporadically, but hoped one day to become a mechanic.

Despite this bleak picture, Tommy did very well while in detention, maintaining his level of privileges and, through the discipline of natural consequences, learning to control his anger. He felt good about the advances he had made in his school work and enjoyed the many sporting activities provided for the boys while inside. Once out of custody, Tommy spent most of his time hanging around with friends, intimidating other people, but he did not continue to break the law.

Tommy's life story is a dramatic example of how a youth can choose to behave in a way that manipulates authorities into meeting an adolescent's needs. Given the problems confronting him in his home environment, Tommy's solution has been to construct the one powerful identity which is readily available to him, that of delinquent. On the street he will do just about anything to sustain this personae as a tough guy among his peers: 'I want people to think I'm tough. Like every time I'm walking down the street if people stare at me I'll go up and ask them what they're looking at. And ask them if they've got a problem or something. It gets me angry when people are staring at me when I'm just walking down the street. Makes you wonder why they're looking. But they always say they ain't got a problem and walk away.'

Understanding a youth like Tommy is complicated until one appreciates the contextual relevance of his behaviour, the nature of the judgments made by outsiders of the intelligibility and necessity of the boy's behaviour, and one places value upon his ability to negotiate for mental health resources with care providers and community services.

Mental health resources are diverse, ranging from the emotional (self-esteem, coping skills) to the physical (housing, employment, health care) and sociopolitical (a say over our community's institutions). Threats to our sense of *wellness*, a term now in vogue, can come from a lack of any number of resources including 'physical health, food, job status, and life opportunity' (Cowen, 1991: 404). Problems attaining these resources result from structural inequalities, not individual in-adequacies. As William Ryan's ground-breaking work on 'blaming the victim' showed years ago, social problems 'are not unique to the individual, and the fact that they encompass individual persons does not imply that those persons are themselves defective or abnormal' (1976: 18). The power to access wellness resources is not equally shared by all.

Nevertheless, we continue to blame the victims of oppression for their lack of access to the resources necessary to sustain mental health. In turn, the victims blame themselves, adopting the language of their oppressors and contributing to the definition of their own deviance and unhappiness (Lerner, 1986). The alienated youth we see rioting on the 6 o'clock news seldom have any critical consciousness of the his-torical and sociopolitical factors that led to their anger and frustration. Most likely they accept their labels of 'deviant' or 'criminal.' These youth are both subject and object in this game of self-definition. They group themselves into categories like 'punks,' 'rockers,' 'hippies,' or 'alternatives' in opposition to the labels adults assign to them. How different would our view of these youth – and the view they hold of themselves – be if, instead, those in power labelled them 'powerless,' 'discarded,' and 'survivors.' These definitions are explicit as to the role society plays in the conditions that breed the anger, apathy, and unhappiness so commonplace among deviant youth.

Research has shown that children like Tommy, who are aggressive with others, experience peer and family rejection more often than their non-aggressive peers do (Asher, 2002). However, we are not entirely certain of the mechanisms by which this takes place. Why would Tommy choose this set of behaviours over others? How does this behaviour address his lack of health resources? In terms of peer rela-tionships, we know from the work done by Moffitt and her colleagues during their longitudinal study of almost 1,000 youth in Dunedin, New Zealand, that 'boys and girls who were rejected by other chil-dren during the primary school years, who reported affiliating with delinquent peers, and who felt marginalised from school and conventional peers were significantly more likely to be involved in antisocial behaviour' (2001: 105). Tommy's pattern of behaviour fits with Moffitt et al.'s findings, although his explanation for the pattern is non-pathologizing. Complexity in explanations is to be expected, given the recent findings by others such as Nicki Crick and Maureen Bigbee (1998), who have demonstrated how victimizers and victims in school-yard settings may form distinct groups and that each learns about their role and is further reinforced in that role through the pattern of aggression and submission experienced during contact with each other. Relational aspects to both manifestations of maladaptive behaviour depend on networks of relationships (Crick et al., 1999). Similarly, constructions of resilience to be explored in this book occur within these relational networks and may for convenience's sake be thought of as one other dimension, albeit paradigmatically different, of what is already a well-studied interaction.

Unlike other reviews that have discussed the complexity inherent to studies of resilience (Gilgun, 1996a; Glantz & Sloboda, 1999; Kaplan, 1999; Kirby & Fraser, 1997; Luthar et al., 2000; Masten, 2001; Rutter, 2001), my purpose is to demonstrate two competing discourses, one conventional or ecological, the other unconventional or construction-ist. The articulation of this alternate constructionist discourse is in-tended to draw attention to the problems of studying resilience in different contexts, the problem of discerning valid definitions of posi-tive outcomes, and the challenge of developing effective interventions that are congruent with the experiences of marginalized populations of youth. This unconventional discourse is hidden among the null findings and confounding variables of quantitative research and among the extended narratives of qualitative studies.

As shown in the previous chapter, the literature on resilience has successfully documented a wide range of ecological factors that corre-late with healthy functioning in high-risk children and families (An-thony, 1987; Combrinck-Graham, 1995; Gilgun, 1996a; Glantz & Johnson, 1999; Hauser, 1999; Luthar et al., 2000; McCubbin, Thomp-son, Thompson & Futrell, 1998; Richman & Fraser, 2001; Sharma & Sharma, 1999). That body of knowledge, impressive as it is, however, cannot help us predict which specific high-risk child will survive and/ or thrive and which will experience developmental and behavioural problems. In the absence of caring adults who can be trusted, the health-seeking child like Tommy explains his reliance on troubled peers as the best strategy for coping. Is this thriving, resilience, or merely surviving? If we avoid making judgments of Tommy's behaviour we may see these aspects of his health. I would prefer that youth find other ways to achieve well-being. Nevertheless, pathologizing what may indicate well-being is not helpful to Tommy nor in informing a treatment plan. As will be shown in Chapters 7 and 8, a construction-ist perspective on resilience can inform a more engaging process of social intervention and clinical treatment. All we know is that resilient children and youth are characterized by individual, social, and envi-ronmental qualities that we have come to associate with resilience – leaving the construct open to criticisms that it is nothing more than a tautology (see Tarter & Vanyukov, 1999).

When one adopts a not-knowing stance in relation to one's practice, it is difficult to discern among high-risk youth which factors pose a risk and which open opportunities for growth. As the saying goes, 'That which doesn't kill you makes you stronger.' Defining a particu-lar characteristic of an individual or environment as a risk factor de-pends on the context of both the observer and the observed. It is seldom easy to see, in isolation, what the effect of a specific event or condition will be. There is an old Chinese tale of a wise peasant and his son. The young man falls from a horse and breaks his leg. Al-though the son is upset at himself, his father counsels, 'This could be bad, or this could be good.' Shortly thereafter, army recruiters come to draft the son into service. But the young man is unable to go because of his injury and is instead left on the farm with his father. Like many of the troubled youth discussed in the chapters that follow, one is never quite certain how the challenges that confront these children are going to affect their trajectories through life.

A constructionist approach to resilience, reflecting critical, socially just, or postmodern interpretations of the construct, in both research and practice contexts, builds upon the conventional literature to pro-vide complementary accounts of resilience-related phenomenon (see, for example, Braverman, 1999; Cross, 1998; Dryden et al., 1998; Felsman, 1989; Gilgun, 1996b; Ladner, 1971; Lightfoot, 1992; Martineau, 1999; Michell & West, 1996; Ungar, 2001a; Yellin et al., 1998). This inquiry is timely, even for mainstream investigators. As Albert Bandura has com-mented, 'We are more heavily invested in intricate theories for failure than in theories for success' (1999: 215). Bandura was referring to the role individual and group self-efficacy play in resilience, noting, for example, that many people overcome addictions without treatment. Although his argument is about cognition and the power of the mind to create psychic environments, Bandura's point would seem to open the possibility that these cognitive spaces are also constructed spaces dependent on discourse in which one may or may not participates as an equal (self-efficaciously).

Similarly, as Kenneth Dodge and his colleagues show in a variety of work (2001; Colwell et al., 2001; Dodge et al., 2002) on social information processing, social knowledge, and their effect on children's development, 'some children reliably have problems in processing peer provocations, whereas other children reliably have problems in processing peer group entry stimuli' (Dodge et al., 2002: 72). Such findings speak to the complexity in children's interactions with their peers and with other aspects of their environment. I do not doubt that the differences Dodge and his team of investigators measure exist as a demonstrable pattern. However, while I remain intrigued by such findings, I prefer to ask how then do such children negotiate for peer acceptance (and therefore sustain health), given these attributes? In other words, whose problem is these children's complexity and differentness? Children with these processing deficits still participate in a discourse on health through which they construct an identity as powerful or marginal. Indeed, as Thomas Dishion (2000) has shown, there is a great deal of consistency in a child's peer ecology from one setting to another. Youth who are most distressed and externalizing that distress in both their home and school environments are also the ones most likely to seek the attentions of a deviant peer group. Dishion finds it surprising, however, that there are positive affect dynamics that result from deviancy training and early sexual activity. Despite these findings, Dishion speculates 'that emotional distress and negative mood could be an amplifying mechanism with respect to vulnerability to positive reinforcement' (2000: 1122) that comes from association with deviant peers. It is just as likely, however, that youth seek out these positive experiences with their troubled peers to compensate for negative feelings across other domains of their lives (school, home, and community).

From a postmodernist perspective, a child's system of meaning, as evidenced through his or her attributions and cognitive processing, depends on the language available to that child to describe lived experience. A child who has the experience of cautious acceptance at home or even lack of attention and care would be expected to misperceive – or more accurately, construct differently (from a child with different experience) – the motives and behaviour of a group of friends. In such a situation, the pattern that children who are less supervised show of more externalizing behaviours is reasonable (Colwell et al., 2001). But the mechanism through which contextual factors, especially peer associations, skew a child's development is one that can be understood discursively as well as ecologically. To consider these outcomes as a processing problem overlooks the child's performance as adaptive from the child's point of view, even if the behaviour is constructed by others as antisocial.

Knowing What We Know and Don't Know

Definitions of health and well-being are context specific. Howard Kaplan has written: 'A major limitation of the concept of resilience is that it is tied to the normative judgements relating to particular outcomes. If the outcomes were not desirable, then the ability to reach the outcomes in the face of putative risk factors would not be considered resilience. Yet it is possible that the socially defined desirable outcome may be subjectively defined as undesirable, while the socially defined undesirable outcome may be subjectively defined as desirable. From the subjective point of view, the individual may be manifesting resilience, while from the social point of view the individual may be manifesting vulnerability' (1999: 31–2). Given such limitations it seems to me that many studies of resilience suffer from problems of construct validity that result from a lack of authenticity to their findings. This problem could be addressed by checking in with subjects (or participants) as to their constructions of the concepts under investigation (Lincoln & Guba 1995; Ristock & Pennell 1996; Rodwell, 1998).

As an example of this problem, let us re-examine the findings from a study of a relatively homogeneous sample of students in Grades 7 through 12 at 11 secondary schools in northeastern Colorado. Investigators asked 1,588 students to complete questionnaires on their health-related behaviours. Then they measured variations in terms of the conventionality–unconventionality of responses. 'Conventionality–unconventionality has been conceptualized here as a dimension underlying and summarizing an orientation toward, commitment to, and involvement in the prevailing values, standards of behavior, and established institutions of the larger American society' (Donovan et al., 1991: 52). The researchers state that their expectation of the results was that 'greater psychosocial and behavioural conventionality (or less unconventionality), as measured in the theory, would be associated with greater involvement in health-maintaining behaviour (less involvement in health-compromising behavior)' (1991: 52). With such a biased beginning, it is not surprising that the study, indeed, documented patterns of behaviour in youth who obligingly behaved as expected by their parents (and researchers). The researchers predetermined that there was only one way to demonstrate health: through conventional behaviours. These kinds of normative postulates are dismissive of the lives of high-risk youth who live beyond such conventions – and who argue that their unconventional behaviour maintains their health. Donovan, Jessor, and Costa's work says nothing about health, but everything about health constructions among researchers who argue for mythical and homogenized values.

Thus, we might more aptly think of resilience and health as context specific. A child chooses to adapt in ways that are most effective, given the available resources. Adaptive patterns that might seem unhealthy are not ends in themselves, but part of a process of growth that teens define as empowering. As is to be shown later, in some instances, the behaviours of dangerous, deviant, delinquent, and disordered youth can actually be more effective in nurturing and maintaining their mental health than can conforming to widely accepted, but constraining, social norms. Deconstructing the competing discourses on health that result is a Foucauldian exercise, although it also shares much in common with the work of symbolic interactionists such as Ross Matsueda and Karen Heimer (1997). We are already familiar with instances of discursive resistance to psychological hegemony. We need only to think of the 'aggressive' and 'oppositional' behaviours of Western women who rejected the passivity of their stereotyped roles over the past hundred years or so (Stoppard, 2000; Van Den Bergh, 1995). Their behaviour awoke in one generation after another (of both women and men) a consciousness of women's oppression and the misogyny of a society that compels such conformity. The real question, which has not being adequately addressed, is *who* defines what is healthy and what is unhealthy? As Mastueda and Heimer discuss, pluralist societies contain a diversity of perspectives that organize communication: 'These perspectives at times crystalize into distinct social worlds, in which groups organize around a common set of concerns and viewpoints. These subcultures can give rise to new ways of solving problems or adapting to the environment. At the same time, they can give rise to a parochialism that generates deviant behavior from the standpoint of other groups' (1997: 167).

A Constructionist Discourse on Resilience

Results from qualitative and quantitative studies, combined with anecdotal evidence provided through extended narrative accounts of lives lived, suggest that we might better understand resilience phenomenologically. Leo Rigsby points out that in much of the resilience literature judgments regarding desirable and undesirable outcomes are made from some normative frame of reference: 'Inevitably, such expectations are contextually bound in time and place and culture. Such benchmarks frequently reflect values of, and assume access to resources characteristic of, White, middle-class families' (1994: 88). Preferring instead a more contextualized understanding, Rigsby defines resilience as 'the response to a complex set of interactions involving person, social context, and opportunities' (1994: 89). Furthermore, it is important that we question the need for normative outcomes and expectations that have been formulated to support predeterminations of health. Rigsby sees our talk of resilience as a façade for political correctness: we hide behind studies of health our true intent, which is to invoke its opposite – 'non-resilience' and pathology.

This is precisely the problem when we read of resilience studies conducted using samples of convenience: Frequently these samples are found in schools and universities. These are contexts where the participants are already pre-selected and, on the whole, less at risk than their peers who are either not in school, or if they were, would be far less amenable to lengthy paper-and-pencil tests. In their study of the role played by social support, self-esteem, and social activities on stress and depression in children, Michelle Dumont and Marc Provost (1999) insist that they distinguished between three distinct categories of children: vulnerable, resilient, and well-adjusted. How valid are their findings when the sample of 297 Grade 8 and Grade 11 adolescents came mostly from, in their own words, 'middle-class intact Caucasian French-speaking families' (1999: 348)? (French was the dominant language in the host community.) Using a matrix of nine predictor variables (self-esteem, three coping strategies, social support, and four areas of social activities, including delinquent and antisocial acts), there was significant separation among the three groups. However, it is most telling that 'on the basis of all 9 variables, 70% of adolescents were correctly classified into the 3 original groups ... More specifically, both the well-adjusted group (72.4%) and the vulnerable group (82.4%) were correctly classified; the resilient group showed a somewhat lower percentage of correct classification (58.3%)' (1999: 353). Although 58% is a reasonable proportion, as a predictor of a group classification, it means that more than four out of 10 participants may have been improperly classified as non-resilient under the criteria used. Furthermore, it would seem that the researchers' ability to discern vulnerability was much higher. This leads one to wonder whether the real purpose of Dumont and Provost's study was not simply to identify instances of disorder in a group of middle-class, low-risk children – and not to understand the phenomena of risk and resilience at all.

Review of the conventional resilience research shows a number of studies that raise questions about the validity of the resilience construct used. In a simple, well-designed study, Richard Morgan (1998) examined the relationship between behavioural outcomes, as indicated by the level of privileges children attain while institutionalized, and factors associated with resilience. Based on the literature, Morgan hypothesized that children in residential treatment who demonstrate a more internal locus of control would achieve significantly higher average scores than children in the same setting who demonstrate more externality. It is interesting that Morgan himself predicted the possibility of a negative relationship between these variables:

> It seems logical to suggest that, since internal locus of control is related to more successful outcomes in resiliency studies, that [sic] it may also be related to more successful, i.e. better level scores. It must be stressed that this remains only a conjecture however, since it seems possible to also imagine the opposite direction of this relationship, that an internal locus of control, since it may suggest more of a sense of empowerment, may cause these children to, in fact, question and rebel against a well-defined set of rules and expectations precisely because they see themselves as having more options, as being more capable of effecting change compared to those children who are more externally oriented vis-à-vis locus of control who may just simply go along with the structure of the program because they feel rather powerless to change or manipulate the system. (1998: 44)

Given that both hypothesized causal relationships are inductively valid, it is not surprising that Morgan arrived at a null finding: 'It would seem that locus of control is independent of the behavioral level score and that some other dynamic must be involved which would account for the variation of behavioral level scores' (1998: 120). If Morgan had introduced greater complexity in his design, or sought to understand the meaning that the children themselves constructed phenomenologically, he may have found patterns to the compliant or rebellious behaviour among participants that predict positive outcomes.

A study by Irene Cirillo (2000) did just this. Using both qualitative and quantitative methods, Cirillo examined the constructive use of aggression among a sample of 32 adults abused as children. She demonstrated that an 'oppositional stance rather than passive victimage' is associated with better mental health outcomes. Contrary to popular belief, an oppositional or defiant stance in people who have previously been victimized can become a useful personal resource to sustain well-being. In Cirillo's study, which was empirical even in its qualitative aspects, an appreciation for an alternate and highly localized construction of aggression (that of adult survivors of abuse) was built into the design.

That children will act in ways contrary to what their caregivers expect is a truism of parenting. Rather than dismissing these misguided or problematic adaptations by children, these behaviours, when understood within an alternate discourse of resilience, tell us much about the child's construction of his or her world. In an exploration of children's constructions, Jerome Bruner (1987) notes that the young child may appear to be egocentric, when in fact, he or she simply lacks experience of another's perspective. In other words, we cannot expect young children, nor even adolescents, to adopt pro-social behaviours simply because those are what their caregivers see as most likely to enhance resilience. Morgan recognizes but does not address methodologically the perspective of the children he studied. Work by investigators who have tried to approach research participants differently has helped to demonstrate this alternate perspective of an at-risk and under-resourced child.

Thirty years ago Joyce Ladner (1971) studied black girls coming of age in a high-risk urban environment. She found among those youth much more health than she had been told was there. 'Placing Black people in the context of the deviant perspective has been possible because Blacks have not had the necessary power to resist the labels. This power could have come only from the ability to provide the *definitions* of one's past, present and future. Since Blacks have always, until recently, been defined by the majority group, that group's characterization was the one that was predominant' (1971: 2). A preoccupation with deviance among certain marginalized groups, including vulnerable or at-risk youth, has made researchers blind to the normalcy that is present (Nettles & Pleck, 1994).

This pattern is apparent in Neerja and Bhanumathi Sharma's (1999) review of 21 studies of at-risk youth in India, in which they found that Western notions of family and family functioning failed to account for the Indian experience. Even at-risk youth, who were expected to report trauma or conflict with family (mirroring Western models of concurrent risk), did not demonstrate a detachment from, antagonism towards, or history of abuse by their family – this, despite the vulnerability they displayed. The authors explain it like this: 'What the child at risk experiences as "family" may not conform to the dominant culture's norm of a family. The physically distant family of the street child, the single-parent family of a fatherless adolescent and a large extended family with several village-based relatives of a migrant slum girl – all provide succour to the vulnerable child. The important lesson that emerged from the research data is that the risk factors could well be moderated by resilience factors within the child's family' (1999: 413).

Arguably, when we construct studies with greater attention to the relativistic nature of resilience, we discover a less teleological and less arbitrary understanding of resilience phenomena. Jane Gilgun's (1999) study of young men in prison for violent offences showed that expressions of agency can be anti-social. Gilgun found that even when their performance led to criminal behaviour, these offenders accounted for what they had done as a way that they had achieved pro-social goals: 'Many of the persons whom I interviewed and who were in prison for various acts of violence also displayed a strong sense of agency, but they sought to succeed in often extreme antisocial ways, such as being the most vicious, intimidating person they could be or in being the best drug addict' (1999: 61). Thus, association of agency with resilience is a valid approach to measurement, but the expression of that agency must be understood within the context in which it occurs.

Gilgun's results, although perhaps unsettling, are supported by another study, predominantly of males. Katherine Kelly and Mark Totten (2002) examined 19 adults who had committed homicide when they were teens. They documented the participants' minimizations, cognitive distortions, histories of abuse, and early experiences of being bullied, living in poverty, and other trauma. All of these factors, the participants said, account for their violence. Nevertheless, there remained a great deal of variation among participants as to the circumstances that led to their murderous acts. For some it was simply that events spiralled out of control. For others the murder may have been an act of mercy, once their victim had been hurt accidentally or intentionally wounded. For most the murder was predictable but not inevitable. As Kelly and Totten explain:

> Trauma left them with a terrible emotional legacy. Feelings of shame, anger, fear, frustration, hatred, and powerlessness were shared by our offenders. These feelings are not uncommon in the general population. Many young people are harmed as children – some severely – and they do not turn these emotions into homicidal behaviour. Our participants turned their negative feelings into a variety of behavioural responses. They sought to protect themselves, to increase their social status, to improve self-esteem, to feel powerful, to escape their horrible situations, or to make sense of their worlds – all through the use of violence to one degree or another. They *chose* antisocial behaviour, but their choices were constrained. Some modelled the behaviours of people around them – family members, community members, peers – and others emulated masculine ideals or the social value placed on violence. Others had limited ability to make pro-social or positive decisions because of mental illness, brain injury, and low intellectual capacity. (2002: 248)

Understanding lives lived under such constraints, and the harmful decisions that individuals make in such circumstances, does not excuse the choices made, but it does make them more intelligible as attempts to survive and thrive.

On a less dramatic note, Marc Braverman found in his look at tobacco-smoking patterns among adolescents that 'if adolescents initiate smoking in an attempt to signal a maturity transition, gain entry into a peer group, seek physical sensation, or cope with stress, it is reasonable to ask whether the smoking fulfilled the goals in question (as well as, perhaps, to examine the adolescents' powers to articulate those goals). Although we recognize that these instrumental functions are at the core of the tobacco uptake process, we do not typically investigate whether tobacco use constitutes an *effective strategy from the adolescent's point of view*. In other words, our studies need to accommodate questions about how tobacco use may be related to successful or unsuccessful adjustment to the developmental tasks of adolescence' (1999: S71; emphasis added). Of course, this is not an argument for supporting smoking among young people. But Braverman's emphasis on conducting investigations of substance use and abuse that include the perspective of adolescents themselves is likely to produce better results regarding the pathways children travel towards adopting unhealthy and healthy behaviours. As previously demonstrated, most inquiries into such phenomena arrive at predetermined conclusions: they assume that one set of behaviours is maladaptive, while another more conventional set is adaptive, thereby missing the important generic functioning of protective mechanisms in face of limited resources for power.

A wide and varied cohort of authors have challenged notions of homogeneity in healthy behaviours. They argue from behind the critical lens of culture, gender, and race that in specific contexts negative and troubling behaviours are, in fact, signs of health. The concept of resistance, as when a youth resists either interventions, dominant cultural norms, or pressures by caregivers to change antisocial behaviour, has been frequently confused with vulnerability, especially in girls. Jill Taylor, Carol Gilligan, and Amy Sullivan, in their discussion of adolescent females, note, 'Girls' active attempts to maintain connection with others, and with their own thoughts and feelings, are acts of resistance and courage. That these actions often result in psychological distress or land girls in trouble with authorities – or both – points not to deficiencies in girls but to the need for social and cultural changes that would support healthy development in girls and women' (1995: 27).

Nicki Crick (1997; Crick & Bigbee, 1998; Crick et al., 1999) has made a career out of looking at patterns of aggression in girls. She also argues for a need to better understand behaviour from a gendered perspective. According to Crick, there are two types of aggression: girls more commonly demonstrate relational aggression, as opposed to male forms of overt aggression. When relational aggression is understood, girls may be every bit as violent as their male counterparts and resist stereotypes as victims or passive members of what have been perceived as male-dominated street families (Hagan & McCarthy, 1997; Totten, 2000; Whyte, 1955). Relationally aggressive children tend to be more internalizing, while overtly aggressive ones tend to be more externalizing. Most interestingly, though, children who follow the stereotypes of how they express their aggression are actually found to be healthier than their peers who express aggression in gender non-normative ways. Should this surprise us, when expressing aggression is one way that marginalized youth say they gain respect from peers and power within their communities? Expressing aggression in non-normative ways would further alienate a teen of either gender from his or her peers, threatening the health of a constructed status because of the likelihood for rejection. The lesson is clearly that youth are wise who express aggression in gender-specific ways. Furthermore, there are benefits to be derived from these negative behaviours.

What about the boys? Totten (2000) conducted a qualitative study of 90 marginalized male street youth in a mid-sized Canadian city. He found stereotypical interpretations of masculinity which brought these young men access to power that was otherwise denied them. Although Totten points out that he recognizes these behaviours as socially unacceptable, he also notes that the youth themselves argued that their misogynist, racist, and homophobic behaviours were efforts by them to sustain a powerful identity when other paths to health were unattainable.

Although not remotely condoning these behaviours, Totten uses his findings to propose a set of interventions to address the needs of these youth in ways that can provide them with alternative and safe lifestyles while crediting their experiences and deviant constructions of health.

A constructionist discourse need not be an excuse for rampant relativism. But, with its implied anarchy between competing definitions of health, a constructionist discourse fosters a critical appreciation of the differences in the power available to those who are marginal in the discourses on health, or who have only limited access to health resources. An alternate discourse on risk and resilience does not define all deviant behaviours as functionally adaptive. Nor should we accept all constructions of resilience as equal. Discursively, we privilege the contributions of individuals more or less. I personally struggle to accept the work of some researchers who have applied the constructs of risk and resilience to populations that are neither oppressed nor disadvantaged, making victims out of oppressors and mistakenly labelling so-called problems as so-called vulnerabilities (see, e.g., Dugan, 1989; Dumont & Provost, 1999). This conceptual error is made by Christina Sommers (2000) in her examination of what she calls 'the war against boys.' Sommers attempts to challenge the assumptions made by Gilligan and her colleagues about the oppression of girls. Although she pokes some holes, Sommers fails to address the broader contextual issues of risk, which connote different meanings for phenomena, for example, the decreasing representation of young men in higher education. Although this 'exclusion' may resemble what occurred previously for young women, males are now underrepresented in post-secondary education because of a confluence of social factors, not because of systematic discrimination synonymous with the risk previously experienced by young women. To say both populations are at risk avoids other, more significant, issues of power – which young men and women themselves can speak to.

The Usefulness of Two Discourses

Constructing an alternate discourse on health to explain children who resist conformity is useful not only to understand youth but to also provide treatment. In her examination of adolescent girls' resistance to medication, Jaqueline Sparks (2002) documents this type of resistance that, when properly negotiated, is a path to healthy functioning. But Sparks goes even further. In a truly postmodernist turn, she recognizes the need for a child's performance to have both an audience and supporting actors. In this regard, Sparks notes the collusion between service providers and parents who are both pressured from within a discourse on health that obliges them to administer medications:

> Those trying to help adolescents share a similar space of restricted vision and voice. Amid the din of powerful discourses, the 'gut feeling' that there has to be a better way disappears, and with it, the choice to stand up to and reject medication. Therapists who wish to help adolescents in ways other than encouraging medication risk finding their voices designated as non-scientific or 'paraprofessional,' their clinical expertise devalued and disconnected from their peers in a professional community ... Effective resistance offers clients and therapists a chance to affirm their own local knowledge. When therapy doors open and therapists shift their roles from expert diagnosticians to expert 'clienticians' – skilled encouragers of client connection, agency, and voice – the door opens to build a network of client voices of experience and expertise. (2002: 35)

My goal of offering an alternative discourse, one that recognizes the function of deviant, unconventional pathways to resilience in poorly resourced environments, is not an attempt to dismiss the bulk of the risk and resilience research, but to create a dialectic with it. Table 3.1 summarizes the contrasting elements of an ecological model of resilience as detailed in the previous chapter and the complementary constructionist model discussed here.

Table 3.1 Two discourses on resilience

	Ecological model	Constructionist interpretation
Definition	Resilience is defined as health despite adversity.	Resilience is successful negotiation with environment for resources to define one's self as healthy amidst adversity.
Theory	Informed by systems theory; predictable relationships between risk and protective factors; circular causality; transactional processes.	Non-systemic, non-hierarchical relationship between risk and protective factors; relationships among factors are chaotic, complex, relative, contextual.
Research methods	Investigations can be qualitative or quantitative, but knowledge is empirical, generalizable.	Investigations can be quantitative, but tend to be qualitative or employ mixed designs; interpretation is dialogical, relativistic, constructed.
Definition of health	Health outcomes are predetermined.	Health is constructed, with a plurality of behaviours and signifiers.
Risk factors	Risk factors are contextually sensitive • Risk impact is cumulative, factors combine exponentially • Attributions and belief systems are preconditions of risk • Effect of risk factors may also be neutral or protective	Risk factors are contextually specific, constructed, and indefinite, across populations.
Resilience factors	Resilience factors are • Compensatory: individual or environmental characteristics that neutralize risk • Challenging: stressors that inoculate individuals against future stress • Protective: multidimensional factors and processes that reduce potential for negative outcomes and predispose child towards normative developmental paths	Resilience factors are multidimensional, unique to each context, and predict health outcomes as defined by individuals and their social reference group: • Characteristics identified by individuals compensate for self-defined risks. • Challenges build capacity for survival relative to the lived experience of individuals. • Protection against threats to well-being comes from the exploitation of available health resources.

This discussion is intended to move us one step closer to a comprehensive, contextually relevant understanding of these constructs to avoid their becoming lost amid other explanations of health. An ongoing interest in both risk and resilience provides us with the hope that a strengths-based perspective finds empirical and phenomenological support. Just as Alice Miller (1991) has spent her career arguing for a better understanding of children in context as their psychological drama unfolds, so too, do resilience researchers seek to understand the propensity for health among at-risk populations. Adding new information to this discourse may help us to perceive unrecognized patterns, authenticated by at-risk individuals themselves, that account for the exigencies of health-seeking behaviours.

Discursive Empowerment Leading to Resilience

Exactly where a child will find his or her path to resilience is difficult to say. Many studies have tried to predict with certainty the exact constellation of factors that foster resilience. The extraordinary diversity of events in the lives of high-risk youth, as captured in the present study of 43 young people, makes it more likely there are a variety of pathways to resilience. Such variability suggests that correlational hypotheses are a weak reflection of individual experience. It is not specific events that distinguish vulnerability from resilience: it is the process by which high-risk individuals gather the resources needed to sustain an image of themselves as healthy that creates resilience. The randomness of these resources and the process by which they are exploited, including the resource of discursive power, will determine whether a child is resilient or vulnerable. When it comes right down to it, resilience is all in a name.

Figure 3.1 presents a model of the substantive theory generated through the 43 case studies explored throughout this book and explains the way high-risk youth co-author self-constructions as resilient. The figure identifies the process of discursive empowerment as a protective mechanism mediating the impact of risk factors, leading to self-definitions by high-risk youth as resilient. Although presented schematically, readers are cautioned to not overly reify the model nor mistake its orderly portrayal of events for the way it is for all youth. All that can be asserted is that for the youth in this study, a dialogically hermeneutic process (Rodwell, 1998) helped to discover this particular model that explains the commonalities shared in these young people's search for resilience. From this model we learn that *resilience*

Figure 3.1 The relationship between discursive empowerment, mental health, and resilience in high-risk problem youth.

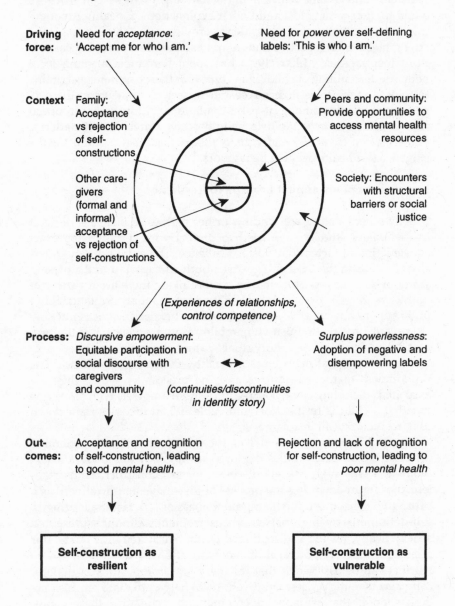

is the outcome of negotiations between individuals and their environments to maintain a self-definition as healthy. The model illustrates how experiences of discursive empowerment allow youth to better contend with the negative effects of the risk factors that contribute to poor mental health. Discursive empowerment promotes positive mental health outcomes found embedded in the unique self-constructions of dangerous, deviant, delinquent, and disordered youth.

High-risk youth argue that both acceptance of, and power over, self-defining labels is the driving force behind their behaviour. The context in which they live presents them with an array of biological, psychological, and social risk factors with which to contend. This context filters and limits the experiences available to them to exploit mental health resources that sustain healthy identity constructions. Experiences within a healthy matrix of relationships, control over mental health resources, and opportunities to discover and demonstrate personal competencies are three pivotal experiences that influence how a teen expresses his or her health construction. The result (whether in placement, on the street, or at home) is discursive empowerment or surplus powerlessness. Michael Lerner defines surplus powerlessness as 'conscious, though misguided, assessments of how much one can accomplish in any particular moment. The set of beliefs and feelings about ourselves leads us to feel that we will lose, that we will be isolated, that other people won't listen, and that in turn leads us to act in ways in which these very fears turn out to be true' (1986: 13). Teens describe their adoption of the stigmatizing labels thrust on them by others as part of a self-perpetuating cycle of powerlessness that leads to threatened mental health and self-definitions as vulnerable. In contrast, discursive empowerment satisfies the needs of high-risk youth for control over self-constructions as both healthy and resilient. When high-risk youth are able to employ strategies that promote either continuity or discontinuity in their identity development across different relational spheres, they are better able to influence which of these two processes they engage in. Denied access to this power, the high-risk youth in this study say their mental health status becomes threatened, and their experience of the risk factors that confront them more debilitating.

Research has shown for decades that social forces affect mental health outcomes (Bronfenbrenner, 1979; Lewin, 1947, 1951; Reynolds, 1934). But it has been difficult to identify the component parts of those forces and how each specifically functions to inhibit or enhance well-being.

Within the mental health literature, there has been an identified need for a meta-level construct that can explain a wide range of complex associations between factors that affect health (Fraser & Galinsky, 1997; Kaslow, 1996; Masten, Morison, Pellegrini & Tellegen, 1990).

Although paradigmatically distinct from an ecologically all-encompassing construct, discursive empowerment resolves many of the issues challenging positivist researchers. Such a construct proposes a process that enables individuals and their families, peers, and communities to have sufficient power to influence the discourse that defines them as healthy or, pejoratively, mad, bad, or sad. For example, Sybil and Steven Wolin (1995), in examining the resilience of teenaged children of alcoholics, note the paucity of descriptions in the language we have available to describe these children's resilience. Embedded in a discourse of pathology, we neglect to see the latent and active elements of resilience in these children, mis-diagnosing behaviours that appear to sustain negative transgenerational stories. Wolin and Wolin tell the story of a young man who drops out of school and to outsiders appears to be following his parents' lead, until in conversation with him one discovers that he deals drugs as a way of gaining employment and providing money to his younger brothers who would otherwise go without food or clothing. Intertwined with the damaging influence families (as well as peers, schools, and community services) can cause, we require an equally robust assertion of the positive challenge these risks pose. As observed in the lives of youth like Peter, Tommy, and Melissa, the chaos of their lives may potentiate growth and resilience.

Of course, the danger for lives that are lived in opposition to dominant norms is that the patterns established in adolescence calcify and become rigid reactions that others expect of such young people. Murphy and Moriarty (1976) in their classic study refer specifically to the negative labelling to which children are subjected when their behaviour is non-conforming. They were concerned with 'adultocentric labels such as "withdrawn," "resistant," "aggressive," and dichotomous categories such as "pathological" versus "normal."' In expressing this concern, they say, 'It seemed to us that children were seen through special glasses, constantly judged in relation to their conformity to adult demands, expectations, and pressures' (1976: 334). From a constructionist point of view, labels are more difficult to resist when the dominant story that supports them is invested with power by those in positions of control. Commonly, these power brokers, which include mental health professionals, have believed that there is much stability in personality development from adolescence to adulthood and that dysfunctional behaviour early in life predicts later maladjustment (Bardone et al., 1998; Jaffe et al., 2002; Roberts et al., 2001). Such narratives serve only to stigmatize at-risk youth, with the resulting reluctance, generally, to notice hidden narratives of resilience. Enculturation into the discourse of the helping professions brings with it a reliance on teleological theories. We predetermine outcomes, and frequently, the means by which they are achieved. Nancy Lesko correctly observes, 'Adolescent development has been driven by an imperative for individual improvement and "higher" achievements in cognitive, emotional, and psychological understandings. Because this developmental demand seems to come from nowhere, we are barely aware of its pull toward a certain set of characteristics that define maturity, rationality, and responsibility, and the simultaneous demotion of other possible definitions of adulthood. The hierarchy and selectivity are muted' (2001: 191).

In regard to high-risk youth (and other marginalized populations), we have tended to lack sufficient knowledge of the 'other' to ask if what we hope to accomplish through our interventions and research actually meets the needs of those whose lives we encounter. This, of course, strikes at the heart of a debate within the helping professions, as they struggle with postmodernism in its many forms (Gergen, 2001; Gergen et al., 1996). How do we help if there are no predetermined goals, no meta-theories to guide our work, and all truth is relative (see Brotman & Pollack, 1997; Howe, 1994; Leonard, 1997; Ristock & Pennell, 1996; Sands & Nuccio, 1992)?

This is problematic. However, one can take a positive orientation towards the challenges posed by postmodernist thought. Jane Gorman has noted, in reference to social workers, that helping professionals can position themselves as 'affirmative postmodernists [who] acknowledge the value of the consensual reading of a text or the shared understanding of a human experience and thus avoid the extreme nihilistic relativism characteristic of skeptical postmodernists' (1993: 250). Once we accept that our understanding of resilience (and our performing what we understand to be health-enhancing acts) is dependent on our participation in a collective social discourse that says that what we are doing is a sign of resilience, we come face to face with the thorny problem of relativism (Chambon & Irving, 1994; Gergen, 2001; Gorman, 1993; Leonard, 1997). If resilience can be anything that any group says it is, what then, in truth, is it? How do we determine if a child is resilient if not by objective measures? Peter Leonard (1997), addressing this postmodern dilemma for human service workers, has proposed a useful compromise to balance the demands of theory with the expediency of practice. Leonard explains that each society, bound by its social and historical context, holds to truths that are 'universal by consent.' These consensual positions allow groups with unique knowledges to unify, issue by issue, for a common purpose without falling prey to essentialism. The idea is a powerful one. What we accept as truth is not 'the truth,' but a widely trusted social construction reflecting the time and place in which it occurs. These truths are not immutable. Each constituent in social discourse decides if it is in his or her best interest to participate in a particular construction of reality. Although we might find it difficult to believe, our allegiance to our beliefs changes over time.

The practicality of the counsellor's material day-to-day occupation confronts the potentially disembodied theory of postmodernism and the unsettling feelings it brings with it. In practice, there is no need to accept a radical relativism that argues each person's reality is uniquely her or his own. Humans are by nature social creatures and, as such, construct meaning through shared language structures. Intersubjectivity in our discourse means individual understandings of the world must necessarily share social meanings between people. The problem of relativism, however, remains ever present. Nevertheless, as Ronald Labonte notes, 'Many persons with disease, disability or unhealthy lifestyles experience themselves as being very healthy' (1993: 17).

This problem is further compounded because the practices that we employ to control problem individuals are enacted from within sociohistorical contexts (Foucault, 1976/1954, 1994/1978; Margolin, 1997). Take, for example, research that has investigated the needs of women street workers and exotic dancers, many of whom would have grown up as high-risk youth (Egan, 2000; Hancock, 1999; Schissel & Fedec, 2001/1999). Addressing in policy what the women themselves identify as needs (e.g., safer working conditions, health care, and political power) pits their interests against the values of groups that seek to solve the problem of street workers and exotic dancers in other ways. Helping is made more difficult when the 'clients' or 'patients' oppose the well-intentioned efforts of service providers to solve what they perceive as problems (e.g., getting women off the streets). Accounting for these different social agendas is part of the process of inclusion that contributes to the empowerment of those whose voices are silenced in our political discourse.

Even the most dangerous, deviant, delinquent, and disordered youth understand that personal characteristics such as powerlessness, causing harm to others, depression, and uncontrollable anger are problems both personally and socially. However, when the voices of high-risk youth are privileged in the social discourse, these characteristics and the way they manifest behaviourally are explained as solutions to problems rather than as problems themselves. Through their performance as actors in an alternative peer culture discourse, youth empower themselves and challenge the commonly held beliefs of others. The entire process is reflexive. As these newly generated understandings gain credibility socially, youth internalize them, coming to believe their truth is the Truth. The first step in this cyclical process is creating a space for marginalized voices to be heard. As participant-observers within an alternative discourse, such as that heard here, we are not simply a passive audience to these expressed truth claims. Our responsivity, whether articulated or not, acknowledges the authenticity of what youth themselves have to say. What is enunciated has a way of being effected by its enunciation. Each individual who responds to what high-risk youth have to say become part of a struggle by these youth for discursive power.

Changing Interventions

What, then, are we to do to if we want to help? How do we express a postmodern sensibility and still perform some function for the good of others? Fred Newman and Lois Holzman (1997) posit a postmodernism – they might say a post-postmodernism – as a challenge to our tenacious need for an epistemology, even as we espouse our desire to do away with epistemology. After knowing, they say, there is only activity, which is the performance of knowing. The epistemological lens that confines us to thinking in ways that become fixed, even if disguised as narrative ways of knowing, frequently neglects a self-critical perspective. Instead of theorizing about youth at risk, an alternative is to see the accounts youth offer of their lives as a performance, an activity to which we too can respond at the level of activity, rather than knowing. In both therapy and research, it has been useful to talk with participants about 'our talk' and how our performance when we speak together plays out what each of us expects of the other and of ourselves. The substantive theory as presented here, the charts, and the discussion, are all necessary discursive tools for me to share with readers something about the lives of high-risk youth. Nothing here, however, *is* their lives. The distinction between the map and the territory remains. All I know for certain is that the youth have told me that the constructed reality I portray here re-presents their world to varying degrees. The youth with whom I work tell me they perform to survive. They literally play at being bad (Ungar, 2002). The danger in this re-presentation, however, is that the story will replace the individual veracity of lives as they are actually lived.

Newman and Holzman explain, 'A revolutionary shift beyond modernism entails moving beyond epistemology (frames of mind, points of view) altogether' (1997: 11). They contend that we get trapped by our need to find new ways to see things, perpetuating yet another epistemology, even if this new one is a more social epistemology, one that finds knowledge through social relations. This book falls prey to this same drive to the essentialist middle, an unfortunate reasonableness that discourse demands. The reader is cautioned that what is being conveyed is twice removed, first by it being told rather than shown by participants, and next by my recounting of it here. To suspend knowing and accept the uneasy feeling of being tossed about by competing constructions of resilience is to accept what young people actually do as expressions of an ontological movement towards survival. There need not be the assumption that there is some end point to all this, some pattern true for all participants. And yet, that is what I am left with, a collective will to express a singular truth as co-authored by the youth and me together. More accurately, there is no singular pathway to resilience.

Newman and Holzman seek to break down just such epistemic dualism, arguing against the notion that there is the knower and the known. Language is the divider. Lev Vygotsky said: 'Thought is not expressed but completed in the word' (in Newman & Holzman, 1997: 43). To the postmodernist, our thoughts are only there insofar as they can be expressed, not isolated events beyond their utterance in a social context. Theories of ourselves are finished thoughts that we use to create order about us. Young people like Tommy express their experience of their world, their drive for coherence and health, not by thinking but by doing. In this way they are exemplars of postmodernity. Often I find that they cannot express their experience of their world even if given the desire and opportunity to do so: they lack the words to account for what they do. How does one tell another that the performance of delinquent acts is fun, when the word fun is so heavily laden with the bias of acceptable and well-resourced outlets for its expression? In practical terms, our language is a tool to account for activity, but it has little or no bearing on the performance of the activity, only the way we co-construct meaning after the fact. One of the social therapists working with Newman and Holzman explains while working with a woman who is trapped by depression, 'It is far more likely that you're depressed because of what you're *doing*, rather than that you're doing what you're doing because you're depressed' (1997: 120).

Summary

To resolve inconsistencies in the risk and resilience literature attention needs to be placed upon people's own constructions of their health. In this chapter I have contrasted two discourses on resilience, one based on an ecological model, the other paradigmatically different and constructionist. Although distinct, findings from the first can be used to show the usefulness of the second. While a constructionist approach to resilience raises questions about findings from more mainstream research, that research is still useful in accounting for resilience-related phenomena when individuals authenticate the applicability of the theory in their lives.

Reinterpreting the results from a number of studies, and reviewing work more synonymous with constructionist perspectives on adolescent health, I have tried to demonstrate that our beliefs about what is happening among problem youth is less important than it is to hear and appreciate their accounts of their activity. Through teenagers' performance individually and collectively, with us adults playing the roles of both audience and supporting actors, high-risk youth construct for themselves powerful identities negotiated with others based on the health resources to which they share access.

The approach taken here is a positive one, seeing in postmodernism the potential to apply in practice a not-knowing stance that privileges multiple points of view. This has not been an argument for relativism: a postmodern appreciation for multiplicity contributes to our tolerance and celebration of different behaviours depending on an individual's level of discursive empowerment. This theoretical approach to constructed resilience can be enacted in practice. The interventions it informs are to be discussed later.

Chapter Four

Discursive Resistance and Postmodern Youth

The argument made in the previous chapters for understanding constructions of health among youth makes us appreciate a whole host of ways that youth define themselves. The plurality of signifiers that youth seek, and achieve, is not unique to our time. What is different is that this plurality in experience and background is being understood as the expression of competing discourses. In our deepening understanding of privilege and how it is constructed, we are beginning to understand how marginalized groups negotiate collectively for power to define themselves and authenticate their world-view. The paternalism and homogeneity that typified earlier generations is still as strong as ever, although it is now the commodification of youth that is the greatest threat to their subjectivity in the West. In opposition to this, I see all about me an emerging 'postmodern youth' comfortable with expressing their marginal position and arguing for its acceptance. In hairstyles, music, clothing, relationships, recreation, and career choices, youth express a plurality of identities, many of which have not been seen before, or if they have, have never been so mainstream or so widely accepted. While each generation has thrust forward an alternate personae (e.g., the flappers in the 1920s or the hippies in the 1960s), what we see today is a postmodern expression of adolescence in which there are multiple and competing cultural motifs.

There is a constructed quality to the lives of youth that is both an expression of the flux and flow of their society and a more insular self-referential discourse that ignores that which they do not control. Judith Van Hoorn and her colleagues (Van Hoorn et al., 2000) documented the experiences of youth during the political turmoil in Eastern Europe at the end of the twentieth century. Surprisingly, youth showed a

remarkable insularity from the broader social and political forces transforming their countries. Youth in Pécs and Budapest in Hungary and
Gdańsk in Poland showed optimism that adults did not share, a phenomenon largely explained by the youths' focus on the private rather
than the public aspects of their lives. Although from the outside, the
adults could see the changes taking place in their children's lives, I
find it intriguing that the youth themselves in Van Hoorn et al.'s work
remained optimistic, even oblivious, to the economic and social up-
heaval taking place around them.

These results are not really that odd when we realize that youth in
more stable parts of the world show this same self-absorption, to the
point that for the vast majority of young people their lives are predictable, their values normative. The chaos and strife that we want to
believe exist among youth are sorely absent. Steven Miles (2000), in
his look at the lifestyles of youth, comments that there is 'a strong
argument for suggesting that by accentuating an image of young people
simply as a social group likely to feel the full force of society's more
negative aspects such as unemployment, drug misuse and teenage
pregnancy, the actual intricacies of young people's experiences have
been misunderstood. Not all young people are submerged in the melo-
drama of subcultural life or the terrors of drug addiction and alcohol
consumption. In many ways young people are an index of social *norms*'
(2000: 3; emphasis in original). Miles offers evidence that youth are a
'barometer of social change' (2000: 9) and that their lives articulate the
evolving relationship between the structural and the cultural. Young
people express their identities confined by the opportunities they have,
but with the capacity to choose from among the options that are accessible. Miles notes, 'Young people are not entirely free to control the
structural influences on their everyday lives as a means of constructing lifestyles in their own image, but neither do these structures completely control who it is young people are. In effect then, young people's
lives are an outward expression or negotiation of the relationship between structure and agency' (2000: 36). These themes of negotiation
with, and insulation from, broader social forces suggest that youth
create their own discourses of health and cope in ways that may not
be obvious to their caregivers who experience the world differently.

The power that teens derive from participation with others in their
alternative discourses is key to their motivation to seek out social
milieus where they are part of a powerful collective identity that they
experience as contributing to a sense of well-being. There is a dynamic

interplay between the power invested in one's group identity and the way that identity reflexively confers power on all group members. Take, for example, the contentious issue of teen sexuality. Teens argue that the way in which they express their sexuality is pivotal to their well-being and concurrent sense of self, although they often face enormous barriers to constructing a healthy sexuality because of a conservative discourse regarding teens and sex. That discourse constructs teenagers as either non-sexual beings (i.e., encouraging abstinence) or as beings with excessive sexual desires that make them potentially immoral or dangerous to themselves and others (Lesko, 2001). Frequently we find children lack the words to even describe their sexual feelings, leaving them vulnerable to others' constructions of their experience (O'sullivan & Hearn, 2002).

Case Study: Cathy

Like other participants, 15-year-old Cathy focused much of her personal energy on acquiring a positive sexual identity. She was referred to therapy after a series of violent outbursts at home that were thought to be unrelated to the issue of her sexual expression. It quickly became apparent, however, in working with Cathy and her family, that how she defined herself conflicted with how her mother and, in particular, her father viewed her and her behaviour. Cathy was very hesitant to tell her father that she was sexually active. She explained, 'It's just that for a lot of my friends when their parents found out, their dads were real mad and started calling them sluts and everything and I was really scared of that.' Cathy's challenge was to avoid being seen as a 'slut,' while gaining acceptance from those close to her for the way she expressed herself sexually. Cathy knew, however, that a disclosure of her sexual activity to her parents would be further complicated because of a family secret – Cathy's mother's early and prolonged sexual victimization. As Cathy explained, control of her sexuality was an important part of her experience of personal power, and her way of distinguishing herself from her mother.

Not surprisingly, Cathy practised the skills necessary to assert a more powerful identity construction out among her peers. Cathy's group of friends, the 'Alternatives,' use their collective identity to enhance each individual member's power:

I like the way they dress. They are kind of like the rebellious ones. The outcasts. And I just like being that way. You're not just a follower and you are your own person and everyone is just like you but that crowd is an individual crowd. It's like you are against everyone else. It's not just wearing black that's important either. It's that most of us wear outfits like that or long skirts. I think in the group you are still your own person and you follow your own trends but the trend is not against what everyone else is into. And that's what I kind of like ... but like, the Alternatives are a lot less popular than like the Hommies. Like, there's a lot more teenage functions for the Hommies than for the Alternatives. It seems like discrimination for who you are and what you want to be. I guess it's because the Alternatives are really violent the way we dance (she laughs).

Being an Alternative establishes Cathy and her peers as somehow different from others, a difference that pleases Cathy and makes her more willing to do the same at home. Working together as Cathy and her peers do, high-risk youth offer a much more powerful resistance to the social hegemony that has typically excluded them from the mainstream. When Cathy dances or dresses oddly, she at least knows she is in good company.

Like her peers, Cathy is less concerned with thinking about what she is doing than experiencing the power that comes with the activity of performing her identity construction. While upon reflection she understood the strategy to be effective as a way to both gain personal power and contribute to the power of her group, becoming an Alternative required an audience to successfully construct the identity. Cathy explains:

It's kind of fun to see the expressions the café kids have on their faces when we come to school in these long black dresses. And they are like when I was walking down the hall wearing this long black dress and this guy said, 'Oh my God, is that a witch?' I started laughing because it kind of feels good to be noticed but sometimes not in that way. I think if you're an Alternative it's a much smaller group basically than the Hommies. Then you're more noticed. If you're a Hommie then you're not noticed. You're just another person in baggy pants and a long jacket. But if you dress like we do then when you walk down the hall then people go, yup, there's Cathy.

When with her parents, Cathy uses what she has learned about control of labels from being an Alternative to carve out a new role for herself at home as an 'adult.' She believes she plays the role of the mature one in her family. She says she has had to take on the role of 'therapist' with her parents, in the process changing herself from the scapegoat for the family's problems to the one who is actively solving them. All this can be a bit bewildering, remembering that Cathy was the catalyst for the family entering therapy in the first place, not the family as a unit. Ironically, this role she assumes as therapist makes Cathy feel she is healthier than her parents, even though she is the one who has been the target for clinical interventions.

Unfortunately, becoming an equal participant in a family's social discourse is seldom a process that goes smoothly for youth like Cathy. Directives to teens to be good, to be quiet, and to not be themselves when their behaviour is troubling, ignore the deeply felt need by teens to establish equitable and fair relationships. Strangely, while Cathy admitted to flicking a cigarette into her father's face after being slapped for swearing at him (the incident that preceded her referral to counselling), she insisted this highly provocative act was her attempt to establish equality within an abusive relationship and not to dominate. Cathy explains, 'I kind of felt I had to do it, to kind of justify myself, to kind of say, "You were wrong and I was right. I wasn't right by doing this but you shouldn't have hurt me."'

Competing Constructions of Adolescence

Too often, constructions of health by marginalized individuals are silenced, just like the voices of the researchers who document the experiences of these others (Fine, 1994). The children whose lives are discussed throughout this book come mostly from homes atypical of the idealized post–Second World War family with two parents, a single income earned by the father, and adherence to a system of patriarchy that hides the injustices of privilege. Instead, many, although not all, of the youth who contributed their voices to this understanding of resilience come from 'postmodern' families. In a postmodern family the family's identity as a unit is negotiated. With sufficient power in the social discourse, a group of individuals may convince others that they are a family in the functional sense of the word (Vanier Institute, 2000). An emergence of new family forms, which has been met with a neo-conservative backlash that mythologizes the 1950s patriarchy (see Gairdner, 1992), has meant credibility for gay and lesbian couples (either alone or with children), sole parents (either by choice or circumstance), grandparents raising their children's children, non-sexual unions for the purposes of maintaining a household, and blended

families with permeable boundaries that allow for children from previous relationships to enter and leave periodically. These are all examples of alternative family forms enjoying differing degrees of acceptance. Whatever is normal today is normal because a group of
people decide it is.

Vappu Tyyskä's (2001) overview of the status of Canadian youth
paints a picture of a misunderstood generation that is as marginalized
today as were their parents, grandparents, and great-grandparents in
their own times. According to Tyyskä, most of the problems confronting youth today arise from social inequities, with youth particularly
vulnerable because of their ever-increasing length of dependency and
prolonged engagement in a process of becoming capably functioning
adults in a post-industrial age. Jeffrey Arnett (2000) has gone so far as
to propose a new developmental stage called 'emerging adulthood' to
capture the unique qualities of this period. Ignoring the structural
conditions that constrain youth, we are as a society preoccupied with
the notion that youth today have something wrong with them. The
differentness of their family forms only adds to our confusion and
pessimism. And yet, as Lesko submits in her study of constructions of
adolescence over time, we are frustrated by youth not achieving everything we expect of them but blind to our own failure to meet the
expectations of our parents a generation earlier: 'Socialization implies
a profound passivity of young people' (2001: 194). Lesko attributes
our understanding of adolescence to a broad set of oppressive social
forces that constrain us to thinking about youth in terms of phyloge-
netic order, a step-wise progression towards higher forms of behaviour
of which Lesko says the archetype is held out as the White Western
Male. Women, gays and lesbians, and people of any non-white racial
group are all a foil from which a discourse of evolution towards a
singular ideal of completion is constructed. The problem is more insidious, however, than just hegemonic pro-social expectations. By equat-
ing one set of behaviours and characteristics as the target for adolescent development, Lesko shows how we out of necessity create the
other, the unevolved and uncivilized, the juxtaposition and ensuing
construction of pathology ensuring the status of one child over the
other.

Although Lesko does not specifically address the issue of high-risk
youth, her argument is useful to understanding the function these
youth's dysfunction serves for the mainstream. Our construction of
them as other and their health status as tenuous allows us to conspire

towards conformity. This has been David Nylund's (Nylund & Corsiglia, 1996) argument in his work with the staggering numbers of children now labelled with attention deficit hyperactivity disorder. While these children's brain functions may be different from their peers, we have not asked ourselves often enough if our public institutions such as schools should be obliged to make space for more hyperactive youth. The argument is one centred on access to needed resources, rather than an overemphasis on individual characteristics that may pose problems of differentness, but do not necessarily indicate pathology.

A solution to this dilemma may be to focus on patterns over time that appear to mitigate the impact of negative risk chains rather than a more exclusive focus on outcomes that are always biased by their immersion in discourse. These protective mechanisms, as they have come to be known, are understood as processes that occur in the lives of at-risk children that can account for positive growth regardless of an individual child's strengths or the barriers he or she faces. John Richters and Sheldon Weintraub (1990) point out that, while 10 to 15% of children of adults with schizophrenia develop the disease, that fact does not say very much about what makes an individual child grow up to be schizophrenic. We have made too much of the prediction of risk, avoiding an analysis of the complex environmental stressors that affect the development of an individual child. A child who is at risk is no closer to schizophrenia than any other child. That child is not 10% schizophrenic. All we know for certain is that child has a parent with schizophrenia.

In the Stony Brook High-Risk Project, a longitudinal study of offspring of parents with schizophrenia and parents with bipolar and unipolar depressions, Richters and Weintraub tried to understand three possible mechanisms of vulnerability: genetic transmission, exposure to parental symptoms, and the indirect effect of parental psychopathology on family functioning. They found evidence for all three explanations of transmission of the disease, but they were cautious not to isolate singular causes. Instead, they note the way that patterns of parental behaviour, from the frequency of psychotic episodes to the way parents behave in their marriage, all affect the quality of the parenting they provide. There is an emphasis on the unique pathways through which children grow that demands an appreciation for the environments in which they live. Although they do not explicitly mention the threats to healthy functioning posed by an ill parent's lack of social power and the family's greater exposure to poverty or social stigma, Richters and Weintraub's approach would seem to point in this direction. The fact of the parents' poverty, for example, would not in itself predict illness in their offspring. Their social class would, however, affect the resources available to them to parent effectively. A parent from a higher social class might not experience stressors related to poverty, mitigating the risk to his or her children. The key variable is not the distal factor of poverty, but the proximal risk posed by an overstressed under-resourced parent who is trying to cope the best he or she can. We know from other studies of experiences of power in the lives of those with a mental illness that personal empowerment is threatened by the presence of a mental illness (Lord & Farlow, 1990). We also know from studies of families coping with the stresses of disruption, conflict, the criminality of the parents, and parents' lack of time and skill to supervise their children that these are qualities associated with the families of children who demonstrate problem behaviours (Brame et al., 2001; Farrington et al., 2001; Gorman-Smith et al., 1998; Nagin & Tremblay, 1999; Stern & Smith, 1999; Webster-Stratton & Hammond, 1999).

The questions asked by researchers like Richter and Weintraub are good ones. Understanding the vulnerability and resilience constructs requires an appreciation for the role played by wider social forces. A taxonomy of protective mechanisms is needed that can account for both individual and community factors that have an impact on a child's development. Reconceptualizing resilience, and by extension, vulnerability, as a social construct makes explicit this connection between individual experience and the social forces that affect mental health.

Tyyskä's sociological examination of youth shows that on almost all indicators, youth today are healthier than youth a generation before. This story of success is all the more puzzling when we hear the rhetoric against the postmodern family, which if we are to believe the talk show hosts is failing miserably at raising its children. When examined closely, even the most socially undesirable activities of youth (e.g., pregnancy, violence, dropping out of school, and the use of drugs) are showing distinct trends towards health as conventionally understood (Federal Interagency Forum on Child and Family Statistics, 2002; Rutter et al., 1998; Statistics Canada, 1999, 2002; Tyyskä, 2001). That our bias against youth persists says more about adult fears and vulnerabilities than about the experiences of youth themselves. If we were to add subjective accounts of well-being to Tyyskä's objective presentation of the numbers, we might find that in the plurality of discourses open to youth that even more young people would portray themselves as healthy, which is the result of resilient children and youth making the most of the resources that they have.

Resilient but Dangerous, Deviant, Delinquent, and Disordered

Many studies acknowledge the different ways children express their resilience. However, few extend their analysis far enough to imagine the resilience of dangerous, deviant, delinquent, and disordered youth like Cathy, Tommy, Mark, and others whom I have already mentioned. This perspective of high-risk youth remains marginal within the discourse on resilience, although it does exist. Take, for example, Werner and Smith's description of the resilient youth in their now classic study: 'The resilient adolescents in our study were not unusually gifted, nor did they possess outstanding scholastic aptitudes. What attributes they had, however, they put to good use. They were responsible, had internalized a set of values and made them useful in their lives, and had attained a greater degree of social maturity than many of their age mates who grew up under more favorable circumstances. They displayed a strong need for achievement as well, with an internalized appreciation for the need for some structure in their lives' (1982: 103). This description of resilience could equally apply to troubled teens as there is nothing in this or many other descriptions of resilient youth that indicates that responsibility, an internalized set of values, and social maturity must be expressed in one way and not another. The characteristics Werner and Smith describe are generic to any number of possible contexts in which children live, although the tendency has been to arbitrarily separate children who find success in ways their caregivers approve of from those who succeed on their own terms.

Even extreme behaviour like gang affiliation can be experienced by youth as an indicator of social maturity, a need for achievement, an appreciation for structure, and a system of beliefs relating to honour and duty. How are we to understand gangs: as fact or fiction?

Carol Archbold and Michael Meyer (1999) note that a problem that gains public attention is further perpetuated through a cycle of media and public and service provider attention. Detailing the construction of a gang problem in a small city that they call Cedar Springs in the late 1990s, Archbold and Meyer demonstrate the vested interests in creating a youth problem. While incidents of gang activity remained minor in Cedar Springs, or for periods of time were non-existent, the police officers who formed the gang suppression unit (GSU) began to feel threatened that they would be returned to regular duty. Justification for the decrease in gang activity was attributed to the work of the unit, with no one wondering whether or not gang activity had really existed in the first place. As a consequence, youth and young adults came to be viewed in a certain way in Cedar Springs as much because of the response to them and their activities, which were at times criminal, although rarely organized. The creation of the GSU to address a problem constructed beyond the experiences of those who perform the questionable activities is remarkably similar to the strategies Foucault finds elites using throughout history. Foucault (1994/1973) notes that the medieval monarchy did much the same as the Cedar Springs police force and gave itself the power to define what was and what was not criminal. According to Foucault, over the past millennium we have given elites this power to define normal, discounting the veracity of our own more narrowly constructed experience.

The operation of a gang suppression unit can be a salve on a community's collective uneasiness with unruly adolescents. Unfortunately, official hyperbole misdirects limited financial and human resources and misunderstands the patterns of group association among youth. One cannot help but wonder, with so much hype about gangs in Cedar Springs, how many youth went out in search of just such involvements in order to become a part of the powerful identity that had become available to them.

Adult roles in constructing negative identities for youth are only now receiving the kind of focused attention they deserve. A similar construction of a youth problem was researched by Patricia O'Reilly and Thomas Fleming (2001). They examined the way Squeegee Kids, youth who for a few coins wash the windshields of motorists stopped at red lights, have been made into thugs, rather than appreciated as entrepreneurs, their preferred construction of their role. O'Reilly and Fleming posit that a moral panic created by the media has only added to the marginalization of these youth already at the fringes of society.

In situations where youth feel they have few options, access to the resources that are available skews their development. Terri Moffitt has speculated that if adolescent-limited antisocial behaviour, problem behaviour that ends abruptly as children become young adults, is related to social mimicry, then 'delinquency must be a social behavior that allows access to some desirable resource. I suggest that the "resource" is mature status, with its consequent power and privilege' (1997: 25). Such behaviours help youth cope with a maturity gap, the difference in the timing between when they are ready for sex and other forms of adult self-expression and the imposition of restrictions on them that admonish them to wait. In contrast, children who persist in antisocial behaviours throughout their lives, whose deviant and delinquent behaviour follows a steady pattern from childhood into adulthood, do not appear to suffer this same maturity gap, drawing other less committed youth who are status seeking into higher-risk activities that may be mistaken as gang related. Moffitt found that just 5% of youth persist with troubling behaviours into adulthood. Despite almost three decades of study, her explanation for the differences between persisters and their adolescent-limited peers remains as basic as this maturity gap: 'With the inevitable progression of chronological age, more legitimate and tangible adult roles become available to teens' (1997: 35).

Moffitt's observation is borne out in the lived experience of the teens in the present study as well. Only here, coping with maturity is a discursive activity that can lead youth of all ages to seek a plurality of personal and group identity constructions and invest these with sufficient power to sustain a healthy self-definition. Rather than pathologizing persisters, one might speculate that Moffitt is simply identifying youth who are comfortable with their achieved identity, and for any number of reasons, are stuck or choose not to abandon the powerful and adultlike identities formed through problem behaviours during their adolescence.

Such a hypothesis fits well with findings from the Seattle Social Development Project (SSDP) which examined the mechanisms that predict violence at age 18 based on children's socialization pathways. Todd Herrenkohl and his colleagues (Hawkins et al., 1998; Herrenkohl et al., 2001) on the project question Moffitt's theory that the etiology of life course persistent offending is to be found early in a child's life. Herrenkohl et al. (2001) point out that, while patterns exist between early acting out behaviours in childhood and later delinquency and violence, children may begin these behaviours later in life and persist with them if they encounter social influences that reinforce problem behaviours. Findings such as theirs add credibility to what is proposed here, although researchers with the SSDP have not adopted a constructionist interpretation of their data. The way social influences act to sustain healthy self-constructions should become clearer when youth account for their lives themselves.

Case Study: Brodie

Before I ever met Brodie I had heard a great deal about him from unsolicited accounts of how difficult he was to manage inside custody. Jokes and tell-tale guffaws could be heard all around the institution the morning Brodie was to arrive with his police escort for yet another period of incarceration. He was 17 by this point and had a lengthy history of perplexing behaviours that had won him the strange admiration of the staff. He was one 'messed up kid,' 'a sexual deviant,' 'a mean little fart,' or so I was told. He was also, according to the last youth worker he had had, extremely bright, motivated, and ambitious. Brodie prided himself on being the kid who liked to take on the role of leader. Although not a fighter, and on the short side for his age, he had looks, charm, and a quick wit that kept him one step ahead of his peers and always a favourite of girls his own age. Female staff found his sexualized behaviour disturbing. The male staff laughed at Brodie's constant attempts to play the stud, swaggering and recounting in detail his sexual exploits.

The morning Brodie arrived, no one meant to be malicious, but the staff were in their own way letting off steam, preparing themselves for a difficult six months with a kid they wanted to like, but did not. It only added to Brodie's reputation that he had worked with his legal aid lawyer to develop his defence. He had spent hours in the courthouse law library researching what he thought his lawyer should know to properly defend him. The community worker who phoned the facility to warn us of Brodie's arrival gave the two of them full marks for a wonderful performance that had successfully convinced the judge to give Brodie a lighter sentence than he might have otherwise deserved for 11 break and enters. Although Brodie frequently got caught, he more frequently got away with his pimping, drug dealing, theft, and violence.

It was not that Brodie was dangerous physically when he came into custody: he was dangerous psychologically. He had a way of poisoning a housing unit with his defiant attitude. His behaviour was no surprise. It was how he survived on the outside, a nice enough kid at first glance who tried to rule the few city blocks surrounding his home. His mother and stepfather, recovering alcoholics and chronically unemployed, had little capacity to do much with their son. Brodie mostly raised himself, surviving as best he could. At least that was how he explained his life, if one took the time to listen.

Within an institutional culture that already had decided who he was, Brodie had little room to be anything else but the delinquent. Perhaps because I had not yet met him, it struck me that the problem for Brodie inside custody had less to do with Brodie, and more to do with the staff who surrounded him. They were like those funhouse mirrors, full of twists that distort what they reflect back. Brodie encountered among his caregivers only images of himself as a problem youth. He was told more frequently than most residents that he was headed nowhere in life except maybe to an adult jail. Whenever Brodie heard these prognostications it was his turn to guffaw, a dismissive gesture that he had perfected and that was his way of disarming any aggressor. It was as if staff opinions were beneath Brodie's consideration. 'Who were they anyways?' he would say, 'Just a bunch of mainstream "losers" earning next to nothing and going nowhere.'

We tried a variety of interventions to help Brodie while he was incarcerated. None worked terribly well because Brodie liked his lifestyle, and he was happy to keep being who he was. Upon discharge, left to survive on his own, Brodie found it was easier to take up most of his previous patterns of behaviour. This was especially evident when interacting with his family. Although Brodie had great potential to go on to university, in his family even graduating from high school was exceptional. Brodie's drive towards a sustained sense of himself as healthy and powerful naturally led him back to his previous self-definitions as the delinquent.

Resistance

As both Brodie's and Cathy's stories show, pathologizing discourses are embedded in material practices. Discourse is not a private act, nor is discursive resistance. The articulation of discourses about problems takes place in a political arena (including among family and community members, institutional caregivers, and peers) in which discursive and material actions have mutual effects. Deconstructing the meaning of the labels that attach to problem youth raise the possibility that the young person's family, behaviour, and community norms will be seen as adaptive rather than problematic.

Lyn Mikel Brown (1998), in her study of early adolescent females, discusses ways the girls resist negative constructions of themselves through expressions of invulnerability found in tales of drinking, swearing, and fighting. In their performance of these tales, Brown says the girls distance themselves from the expectations that others have of them to be a certain way. As a study of two cohorts of teenaged girls aged 12 and 13, Brown's research specifically examined both the differences and similarities in how young white women grow up in different class contexts. Brown found among her participants the knowledge required to perform in different settings, to please others, and to negotiate multiple realities. And yet, the girls from more privileged homes are more confined in their expression of their bossy, smartassed, and oppositional selves. Brown comments, 'Few people want to know this lively girl; most, adults and peers alike, prefer not to hear what she has to say' (1998: 150). We live unconsciously with the myth that teens who express themselves too much will become caught in the storms and stresses of adolescent development without questioning the inevitability of this or any evidence to the contrary (Arnett, 1999).

Such tensions between who our children are and who we think they are necessitate a closer look at their experience of health from their own perspective. Michelle Fine has stated, 'Research that breaks social silences fractures the very ideologies that justify power inequities' (1994: 221). To study problems while ignoring their social construction is shortsighted at best, and potentially violent to those whose realities are being objectified. In other words, discourses on adolescent health are constructed through linguistic rules and social practices that reflect the politics of knowledge-producing activities. A cartoon in a recent edition of a popular children's magazine shows a sad young boy dressed as a clown being disciplined by the principal of his school, who is dressed the same. The caption reads: 'I understand you're not clowning around enough in class.' We see the humour because we realize that the connection between what we know and how we came to know it goes largely unquestioned in the arena of human services.

How do high-risk youth and children protect themselves? What roles do their dangerous, deviant, delinquent, and disordered behaviours play in enabling them to cope with the chaos around them? Surely, we reason as adults, the serious consequences that these adolescents encounter because of their persistently troubling behaviour should be enough to deter them. And yet, a large number of youth like Brodie, despite our interventions, and sometimes because of them, choose to behave in ways that appear to increase their exposure to risk. Counter-intuitively, high-risk youth find their health enhanced through conduct that is problematic for their caregivers. To hear youth tell it, these behaviours are their salvation. It is strange, in listening to these youth speak, how one is reminded of the same factors, which appear in the literature on resilience, that typically include lists of characteristics correlated with health amidst adversity. Researchers like Patricia and David Mrazek (1987) have for decades been identifying dozens of personality variables of abused, but resilient, children. Many of these variables are relevant to this discussion, including information-seeking behaviour, formation and utilization of relationships for survival, decision risk-taking, idealization of an aggressor's competencies, altruism, optimism, and hope (see also, e.g., Jew & Green, 1998, Wolin & Wolin, 1995). These personality dispositions and personal competencies contribute to the likelihood that a child will survive a high-risk environment. What the Mrazeks do not specify is the relational or behavioural context in which these qualities are enacted. Lives lived in chaos may express these characteristics of self and relationships in antisocial ways when resources to do otherwise, or the power that attaches to normative definitions, are absent.

The views of youth that we can find in studies that leave it to youth to speak for themselves (Caputo, 1999; Dryden et al., 1998; Ensign & Gittelsohn, 1998; Ladner, 1971; Spira et al., 2002; Taylor et al., 1995; Totten, 2000) are consistently contrary. Thus, we are ill advised to trust middle-aged adults, and the policy-makers they represent, to understand what is good for teenagers today, any more than parents of these power brokers understood the rebellion of the late 1960s and early 1970s. If we go searching, we can locate an alternate discourse hidden in our popular consciousness, sitting there scarcely recognizable for what it is, a challenge to our understanding of what youth are supposed to be.

One need only pay close attention to the popular press to see that all is not as it appears. Margaret Wente (2000), in an editorial piece in a national newspaper, compared Eminem (Marshall Mathers) and Britney Spears. Eminem is one of those bad boy performers that shouts profanity, misogyny, and hate from the stereo speakers in our teenagers' bedrooms. Britney Spears, in the unlikely case one has not heard, is the sexualized pop star 6-year-olds listen to when their Spice Girl

CDs start skipping. Wente wonders, 'Who scares you more?' There is reason to believe Britney Spears and others like her are the representatives of evil forces in our culture far more insidious than the overtly rebellious Eminem. We adults do not want to see it. Having attended an Eminem concert in the predominantly middle-class white suburbs of Toronto, Wente writes, 'An Eminem event cuts through the banality of everyday life in Thornhill. It also addresses a major problem in Western culture, which is how to channel young men's natural aggression now that war and hunting are obsolete ... I honestly think [Eminem] and his ilk are far more wholesome than Britney Spears, an invitation to pedophilia if I ever saw one.' Anyone who has seen Spears's album cover of a pubescent girl on the floor in a position that invites fellatio knows what Wente means: 'Our eight-year-olds are in thrall to a hypersexualized, hyperinfantilized overage nymphet who sings "I was born to make you happy." Yuck.'

So why all the fuss over Eminem? Constructions of delinquency make us hypervigilant to threats from young males. We do not want to acknowledge that not all young men can or want to fit willingly into our society's expectations of them to act 'properly.' But then, sexualized teenagers, especially girls, have never received our attention in the same way. Eminem is a gift to politicians who have a hidden agenda to scare us into believing that youth are a problem. Britney is just entertainment, or so we say. One of these two discourses, that of police chiefs who pontificate about crime and kids, is powerful and pervasive. The other discourse, that of 'politically correct feminists,' a dismissive and marginalizing label, is far less a part of our national agenda.

Just as we can detect in the popular press an alternative discourse that explains why kids act out in ways that trouble us, we can also find empirically sound proof for the same phenomena in academic discourse. Take, for example, work by Jo Ensign and Joel Gittelsohn (1998) studying the perspectives on health of 15 street youth in Baltimore. They found that teens fully appreciate many of the risks to their health. Using qualitative methods, which sought to empower the youth through the research process, Ensign and Gittelsohn observed that it was important to capture the broader social context of these youth's lives in order to understand what they needed in regard to health resources. Ensign and Gittelsohn's study shows that even unconventional youth have important coping strategies and awareness of their need to maintain their health despite their apparent failure to do so:

'Many of the youth included in this study are surviving and even thriving despite significant negative socioeconomic pressures. Instead of focussing on the pathology of inner-city youth or street youth in particular, it would be beneficial for health researchers to begin examining the youths' strengths and what is working with these populations' (1998: 2098). We know from a number of studies that street families, no matter how threatening to a youth's well-being and security, offer youth an escape from unpleasant family lives (Gordon, 2001/ 2000; Novac, Serge, Eberle & Brown, 2002).

Similarly, the Cambridge Study of Delinquent Development, which has followed 411 south London males from age 8 to 32, has produced some surprising results that need a better explanation than the ones provided by its researchers. In his look back over the study, David Farrington notes, for example, that the peak age of offending (between 17 and 18) coincided with the height of affluence for convicted males: 'Whereas convicted delinquents might be working as unskilled labourers on building sites and getting the full adult wage for this job, nondelinquents might be in poorly-paid jobs with prospects' (1995: 936). The relationship between success (even by conventional standards) and certain behaviours is evidently not straightforward. Such complexity was also found in the way being a nervous, withdrawn child with few friends was found by the Cambridge researchers to protect children against becoming delinquent. I find it odd that they conclude that such characteristics are 'protective' when these vulnerable youth, while less likely to grow up to be delinquents, were also the most unsuccessful later in life – most of them did not own their own homes, lived alone in squalid conditions, had large debts, were employed in poorly paid and low status jobs, and had never married. While some childhood characteristics might make for 'well-behaved' adults, one might question if these individuals would not have preferred delinquent lifestyles and the status and short-term success that such behaviours bring.

Ethnocentrism

Our tendency to overlook the competencies of high-risk teens should not be a surprise. John Ogbu (1981) argues that competence is most frequently defined by white middle-class standards. Proponents of theories that explain how competencies are developed are often times blind to their inherent cultural bias. Ogbu looks at the way parents prepare their children for life, noting the clash in cultures inherent in the research. His point is particularly relevant to this discussion, as it opens up to scrutiny what we deem to be healthy functioning. Ogbu writes: 'I suggest that the research model of dominant-group developmentalists ... is ethnocentric. Rather than being truly universal, it is merely a pseudouniversal rooted in the beliefs of an ethnocentric population. It is false because it looks at the origins of competence from the wrong end of the relationship between childhood experiences and the competencies essential for functioning in adult life. It decontexualizes competencies from realities of life. As a result, it confuses the process of acquiring and transmitting adaptive, functional, or instrumental competencies with their causes, or origins, which are the reasons for their very presence or absence in a given population' (1981: 425).

Children growing up in inner-city ghettos are led to believe that they will achieve success if they develop a degree of competence as defined by mainstream society. As we have seen, this ignores these children's lack of power to define for themselves competent behaviour as well as the barriers they experience in accessing mainstream health resources such as employment, counselling, financial stability, education, and well-funded health care. Ogbu argues that the parents of these children are doing what they need to do to prepare their children to succeed at adult cultural subsistence tasks that differ from those of white middle-class norms.

Ogbu proposes a model of competence that is cultural–ecological, meaning that competencies are not simply the property of individuals, but of social groups. He argues that society teaches its children how to succeed at the tasks necessary for each culture's subsistence. These tasks are, therefore, culture specific and the skills necessary for their completion are held in trust by each successive generation. Of course, over time, competencies change as cultural values change. A marginalized cultural group will adopt more mainstream values if those values are instrumental to their success. This will only happen, reasonably, when the marginalized group can benefit from behaving like the dominant culture (Gooden, 1997). Ogbu gives the example of recent immigrants to the United States adopting the parenting patterns of the mainstream culture to ensure that their children succeed in school. This cultural–ecological model, if applied here, would help researchers better understand that even cultures of poverty include skills (sometimes referred to as 'street knowledge') that ensure survival outside mainstream culture.

If we return to Moffitt's notion of a maturity gap, and view this as a problem unique to different cultures, we can see the complexity of the pathways that high-risk youth may follow to health. It has been two decades since Ogbu gained notoriety for his work, and three since Joyce Ladner did her famous study of black girls. Yet their lessons are still vibrantly current. Ladner wrote in 1971: 'In addition to attempting to break the close ties with parents in the area of sex, [the girls] also engaged in other forms of prohibited behavior. Smoking, drinking and breaking curfews were some of the problematic areas. They seemed more willing to be rebellious against their parents and to engage in those activities which, to them, symbolized being a mature woman. Sexual involvement just happened to be one of such means of self-expression' (1971: 205). It is refreshing to read (and controversial to share) a non-pathologizing account of young women's sexual expression. Even more so where their ambivalence towards marriage is explored.

In her concluding remarks, Ladner offers us a well-grounded and critical explanation for why things are the way they are. She attaches blame not to the girls but to the broader white middle-class society that limits the choices of black girls for an identity as mature and respectable: 'The dominant intellectual perspective on the Black family and the Black woman is still one which views them as pathological and an aberrant of the white middle-class model. However, it has been the overt and covert malignancy of institutional racism which has produced the alleged deviance and pathology. The behavioural characteristics of Black women which assumed these negative dimensions (when judged by the larger society) emerged as adaptations to a pathological society. It was the institutionalized structures and processes of racism which caused the so-called family disorganization, matriarchal society, high rates of juvenile delinquency, "illegitimacy," violence and homicide' (1971: 266).

When cultures collide, the less powerful one will devalue previously held beliefs about which skills and talents are most useful. Enhancing individual and group power allows people to define for themselves their notion of competence. As David Miller (1999) has noted, in the case of urban African-American adolescents, racial socialization and racial identity can act as protective factors by buffering these youth against the harmful effects of a discriminatory environment. Clearly, aspects of health rely on powerful self-constructions from within cultural contexts that influence social discourse (Strickland, 1999).

Youth as a Cultural Minority

Viewing teenagers as a homogeneous group is a ridiculous reduction of diverse patterns of social interaction. And yet, we see this occurring just as often as for any social, ethnic, racial, or gender group. All are subjected equally to the limits of essentialism. Chris Smaje (1996), in his discussion of the ethnic patterning of health, begins with a discussion of how arbitrary ethnic distinctions are. His point can be useful to this discussion of high-risk youth, if the concept of ethnic distinctions is liberally applied to the distinctiveness of youth culture when an adolescent group's construction collides with the more powerful classification schema of adults. Smaje makes the point that in regard to health experiences, we have not paid enough attention to the nuances of difference in the way we create explanations for health along complex ethnic lines. Nor have we paid enough attention to the way structure and identity interact to produce health. It is not enough to measure what we think we measure, without understanding that the health of a particular group depends on structural (e.g., economic, geographic, political, racial, and body) variables that interact, through the filter of daily meaning and activity, with the identities that people create.

Troubled youth enjoy little of this power to define themselves as either healthy or resilient. Instead, they, like cultural minorities, are judged by norms established by the dominant group, usually adult professionals, who, for the longest time, were white and predominantly male from middle- and upper-class homes. Constructed within a discourse of privilege, our understanding of individual vulnerability has been skewed. What case can be made that vulnerability is a construct of language and not an objective fact? 'Dangerous,' 'deviant,' 'delinquent,' and 'disordered' youth display a range of behaviours that are troubling to adults but that support *their* mental health. This is not an argument for relativism, a common critique of constructionism. On the contrary, it acknowledges the discursive power and definitional certainty one group imposes on another. As discussed in the previous chapter, Peter Leonard (1997) has theorized that there are truths we hold that are 'universal by consent.' My purpose is to deconstruct the truth claims of youth with regard to risk and resilience without necessarily arguing that we accept total anarchy in our children's behaviour just because some (though not all) propose it as a path to health.

· Robert Stebbins has made a career of examining how society copes with deviant behaviours and of the fluidity in the definition of 'tolerable differences.' Specifically, his work on tolerable deviance (1996) provides one way to understand the social construction of resilience. Unitary understandings of what constitutes deviance are not adequate to explain the complex way in which society interacts with individuals who behave outside social norms. Deviance, according to Stebbins, can be justified by the one so labelled as one of three things: leisure, work, or adjustment. Of particular concern here is deviance as adjustment, although disenfranchised youth might also find through their behaviours in their impoverished environments opportunities for work and leisure resulting from problematic behaviours. With a paucity of choices, the deviant behaviours of high-risk youth are highly intelligible: 'The main condition distinguishing tolerable deviance from intolerable deviance is the presence or absence of tolerance: the former is passively endured, the latter actively scorned. These reactions constitute the perception of the dominant majority (or the powerful minority) within the community of the threatening extra-institutional behaviour taking place within it. However, they often do not comprise the perception of the deviants themselves. Many who engage in tolerable deviance argue that their values and activities are merely different, and they readily offer views of and reasons for doing what their community regards as wayward behaviour' (1996: 7). Stebbins gives the example of someone with a sexual orientation other than heterosexual who enjoys sexual contact. While that person's community may see his or her behaviour as an example of deviance that is tolerable, it is an absolutely necessary form of adjustment for the person himself who has a non-heterosexual sexual orientation and wishes to engage in fulfilling sexual activity.

Specific to this point, youth who are gay, lesbian, bisexual, or transgendered are at heightened risk for suicide and other adjustment problems because of the intolerance (or grudging tolerance) of them by their communities, and not because of their sexual orientation per se (D'Augelli & Hershberger, 1993). The social context in which their identity is constructed is the problem. In the case of these youth, they have little or no power to create a positive identity construction of themselves that incorporates their sexual orientation. Instead, we tend to dismiss their sexual identity as a 'phase,' when in fact, research shows clearly that youth are aware of their sexual orientation during adolescence (Steiner, 2001; Williamson, 2000).

Similarly, high-risk youth find through their behaviours opportunity to satisfy basic needs for power and control, as well as leisure and employment, all health resources that are in short supply in the environments in which many of these youth live. Brenda Robertson (1999) has observed that delinquency is a satisfactory choice for some youth who are trying to meet their need for social connection, a physical or psychological rush, or release of stress. Families of such youth, and especially fathers, were, according to Robertson, poor substitute sources for activities that would similarly meet their children's needs. As with sexual orientation, what society calls deviant behaviour is not always a choice for youth at risk: sometimes it is a personal, social, or cultural imperative.

Seeking Health through Status

This is not to imply that it is easy for those enmeshed in conventional discourses to accept youth as they want to be seen. Mark Totten's (2000) qualitative study of young males, their group behaviours, and their abuse of girlfriends introduced earlier, underlies the problem with tolerance. Where do we draw the line? While many studies have pointed to the connection between health in adolescence and comfort with both masculine and feminine characteristics, Totten finds in his purposive sample of 90 young males a stereotypical interpretation of masculinity as power. All the participants were between the ages of 13 and 17 and were either clients of a youth services agency or street youth. Some of what Totten finds is disturbing for its graphic content. These youth describe a process of identity construction that is supported by an account of male power and privilege suppressed in popular 'politically correct' discourse. Take, for example, one of the study's participants, Marty, and how conforming with the norms of his gang turns a 'scared shitless' loser into a powerful young man. Marty explains:

At the time, it was a high. A power high. It was a feeling of being king shit – no one could touch you. It was like niggers were to blame for everything and we made them pay for everything. They were the reason we had no money, no jobs, no decent place to live. Being a part of the gang [white supremacist] gave us a sense of belonging. We felt like we were accepted and someone cared for us. They told us we had an important job to do. We felt really important – because we were white – because we were guys. I mean skins don't exactly respect females either. A lot of them pounded on their girlfriends too. It wasn't just blacks. And gays as well. People think skins just hate blacks. It's not true. They hate gays, women – you name it. I think I was part of it because it made me feel good as a guy – respected. I had status. It was like I was a member of some very important club – doing really important work ... Most of the guys into it were losers – stupid, no money, no place to stay, addicts. It's like we didn't want anyone to see that side of us – a guy who really has no balls pretending he's got the biggest prick in the world. It's all about fear and status. I was scared shitless inside – I felt like shit, a loser. But as soon as people knew I was a skin, that all changed. I had power.

Interestingly, Marty is now an ex-skinhead, perhaps having grown past whatever it was about this identity construction that he needed. While it is problematic exporting qualitative data from one study to another, the patterns observed by Totten are also found in the lives of the youth with whom I worked. Framed within the meta-constructs of discursive power and identity construction, the way in which the young men in Totten's study find their masculine identity is more understandable. Unfortunately, for some males, under the tutelage of fathers and others, this pattern of male hatred and violence is offered as an effective way to find status when other paths may be blocked. Most of Totten's participants had little else except their 'balls' and 'pricks' to convince the world that they were something other than losers.

Martin Gooden (1997) takes a different approach, but arrives at similar conclusions about the relationship between delinquency and enhanced self-concept. In his review of the relevant literature, Gooden tries to make sense of the contradictory evidence that self-esteem is linked to delinquency both as a cause and effect:

It appears that the findings from both lines of research, those supporting the idea that low self-esteem leads to greater delinquency, and those proposing that involvement in delinquency may enhance subsequent self-esteem, find empirical support. At first glance, this may appear inconsistent ... however, both findings may be correct, in that under some circumstances low self-esteem may be a precursor to delinquency *and* delinquency could be a precursor to later high self-esteem ... The relationship appears to be a bi-directional one which varies in valence as a function of initial levels of self-esteem. Specifically, those with initial low levels of low self-esteem are likely to exhibit the following pattern: low self-esteem leads to greater delinquent involvement, and delinquency leads to greater subsequent self-esteem. Among those with initial levels of higher self-esteem, delinquent involvement is presumed to be less likely overall. (1997: 19)

Gooden hypothesizes that not only do youth seek out delinquent activities because these activities bring them greater self-esteem, but these youth are motivated to seek affirmation outside normative social behaviours because of threats to self from failure to achieve in these domains. Persistent threats from poor performance make children dis-identify with the activity that threatens them. This dis-identification, then, makes success or failure less important to the child's self-concept.

Reasoning that young African Americans experience routine threats to their self-esteem in school, and that as a consequence of racial oppression, fewer expectations for success from academic performance, and differential income rewards, Gooden hypothesizes that African Americans who perform poorly at school would disidentify with academics in favour of delinquent behaviours. Specifically, Gooden reanalysed data from two studies, the longitudinal Youth in Transition study of 2,213 Grade 10 students, begun in 1966, and the National Youth Survey first administered in 1976. What he found was that a combination of race and academic performance played a role in determining whether youth conform with normative values and goals. Gooden's work shows that there is a positive relationship between delinquency and self-concept among African-American youth who do poorly at school. The whites in the studies did not show this same pattern, perhaps, Gooden speculates, because they still had access to socially acceptable sources of self-esteem. Gooden concludes, 'Successful academic experiences that lead to identification with school can operate as a deterrent to delinquent interests' (1997: 73).

Gooden's work is particularly relevant to the theory being put forth here. Racial, cultural, and other social factors provide a context for identity constructions by youth. Discursively, we can see in Gooden's study a marginalized group of young African Americans who have rejected academics in favour of other forums in which they are less oppressed and which afford them power and prestige through patterns of behaviour that the dominant culture calls delinquent. Youth, white or otherwise, who participate and experience power in the dominant discourse, buy into the belief that if you 'study hard, you'll be rewarded.' Many high-risk youth like Brodie, as products of the same culture as their mainstream counterparts, hold this belief as well. However, in the finely woven stories that these youth tell, we see that they also participate simultaneously in alternative discourses as a way of coping with the threat of failure at school. Combining Gooden's work with a social constructionist perspective allows for a deeper understanding of these observable patterns. It is not just that high-risk youth dis-identify with one set of norms; they construct powerful alternatives through associations with other delinquents who have similar life experience. When this process of adaptation is seen discursively, we can better understand how to intervene.

Klaus Hurrelmann and Uwe Engel (1992) studied 1,717 students in Germany who were between the ages of 12 and 16. They had expected to find that adolescents' strong orientation towards success and status in both their academic and social lives contributed to the high rates of delinquency among this age group. Their study confirmed the hypothesis. Youth who fail or at risk of failing at school are the same youth who are most likely to be delinquent. While these findings are useful to the present discussion, they require some elaboration.

It comes as no surprise after listening to youth themselves speak about their social constructions of resilience that failure in one domain leads to a search for status resources in another. In the case of school failure, it makes sense that teens seek out delinquent behaviours where they have a better chance to excel. Anecdotally, we all remember our school days and the way that children who did not fit in were teased. Frequently these were the children who performed poorly academically, although sometimes those who excelled but lacked social skills were treated poorly as well. In either case, youth who are excluded from social standing at school are likely to choose peers who can buttress the harmful effects of their academic performance. In other words, children look for youth who can give them status. For socially disadvantaged children, especially those who are doing poorly at school, these are frequently delinquent youth who have established other benchmarks of success (see Moffitt, 1993, 1997). As Hagan and McCarthy (1997) have found, among criminally oriented street youth street families can provide them with the much needed resources of criminal capital, including the skills and knowledge necessary to succeed at unlawful activity. Thomas Dishion, Joan McCord, and Francois Poulin (1999) observe a similar sharing of knowledge among delinquents that they term 'deviancy training.' In both cases, learning happens in much the same way as for pro-social youth who might engage with their peers to learn much needed skills such as how to get a job.

Case Study: Jason

To understand deviant behaviour as health-seeking activity, and explain the actions of problem adolescents, we must appreciate the context in which it takes place and the way meaning is constructed. Jason's life, which is typical of many of the males with whom I work, has been a long saga of disempowering experiences, followed by experiences of power shared with the other dangerous and destructive youth in his neighbourhood. The constellation of risk factors and opportunities for discursive power that manifested themselves in his life was typical of what I find confronts other high-risk male youth.

It was Jason's sole-parent mother, Dorothy, who originally came in for counselling, a therapeutic relationship that lasted for over a year. She was asking for help to manage Jason, her 15-year-old son, in the hope of feeling better about herself as a parent. Dorothy complained that her son was out of control at home and that he had recently 'trashed' his sister Amanda's room. He was intimidating everyone in the family, breaking things, and demanding that Dorothy and Amanda do his chores. Outside the home, his behaviour was even worse.

By this time, Jason had seen many social workers and psychiatrists because of his anger. He was born with congenital absent fibula and had his foot amputated when he was a year old. All through his childhood Jason had repeated operations and constant problems with his artificial leg. By age 15 he had become very good at hiding his physical disability, although he admitted that it was awkward to have to wear long pants all summer.

Jason thought everyone made too much of his physical challenge. He refused to acknowledge it as an issue that was at all linked to his 'problem' behaviour. He had been getting into a great deal of trouble around the housing complex in which he lived. The police had come to see Dorothy several times and had accused Jason of everything from throwing rocks at trucks to shoplifting. At the time he was interviewed, Jason had so far avoided detention. He presented himself as an angry young man and talked often about neo-Nazis, Hitler, and

Satanic worship. He had few friends and, in fact, was often being chased by other kids whom he taunted.

Jason had very little contact with his father, although he had gone to live with him for four months, two years earlier. His father had insisted that Jason leave when he was verbally abusive to his step-mother and was blamed for ruining his father's second marriage. At age eleven, Jason also lost contact with a Big Brother whom he had had for several years.

Despite previous repeated attempts by Dorothy's social workers to meet with Jason, he had refused all contact. Work with Dorothy had therefore focused on helping her reassert control in her home. This approach enjoyed some limited success, and Dorothy and Amanda had begun to feel safer. However, home life remained chaotic. It was not just Jason who had problems. The house was dark and dirty. Newspapers covered the windows, so Dorothy could sleep during the day. The kitchen table was full of boxes and garbage; evidently it had not been used in weeks. This was a strange and eerie home to visit when I went to interview Jason for the purposes of this research.

Jason said he felt that neither his family nor society treats him fairly: 'We have a stupid government because like I probably won't get my [driver's] licence. I'm probably going to get a graduated licence, just because I'm younger they think I'm going to have an accident. They treat us like we're idiots.' Given such feelings, it is not surprising to hear that Jason thinks Hitler was a great leader, that he holds racist attitudes, or that he likes the philosophy espoused by what he terms a Satanic cult. The following is part of an interview in which Jason was asked who he idealizes and how he sees the world:

My friends [the Satanists] aren't evil, believe it or not. I've read their bible. It's not you don't sacrifice cows or anything. You just survive. Their law is just to survive. It's like selfish. You kill someone else if you have to. Like there are lots of rules like don't steal stuff only if you need to steal stuff, and don't kill unless you need to kill. I don't know how they could have gotten evil out of that. It's just common sense really. And like my friend's a genius. And he failed school. So like he doesn't like the system either. Nobody does ... I'm not a Nazi either, at least by their rules. I like black people. I don't find anything wrong with black people. I just don't like Arabs. I like Chinese people, although I wish there weren't so many of them here. It's after all our country. Like the black people and us and the Indians were here first. I don't hate Jews. I don't even care about religion ... I just don't like the way black people have all these organizations and want all these rights ... Or feminists, I don't like feminists. It seems to me they don't want equal, they want more rights than we have. Like my uncle says if you're a Canadian citizen you should just be a Canadian citizen when you're getting a job. Not a black man or a woman or a white man.

It was not surprising that Jason had found a powerful identity through these hateful and unconventional means. Jason has little power, is accepted by few other teens, and worries that his disability will be discovered by people at his school. He often gets beaten up because he lacks social skills. He fails school even when he tries. As objectionable as his comments were, the longer he talked, the more he showed that he wants to be accepted, but has found nobody but other social outcasts who will take him in.

Delinquent Pathways to Health

Delinquent pathways to a powerful identity such as Jason's are not unique to this present work. Problematic and socially unacceptable behaviour appears as successful adaptation in a number of studies including that of Thomas Simon, Clyde Dent, and Steve Sussman (1997), who examined predictors of in-school weapon carrying among 504 students from seven high schools in southern California. Youth who felt vulnerable to attack reported carrying weapons as a form of self-defence and personal protection. Simon and his colleagues also found that vulnerable youth experienced carrying a weapon as a way of bolstering their sense of self-worth. The weapons allowed them 'to show off' and 'to feel powerful.' Typical of many such studies, Simon et al. highlight the positive aspects of delinquency but ignore the full implications of their findings. 'Perhaps prevention efforts could attempt to encourage the norms that are incompatible with weapon carrying. Specifically, weapon carrying could be portrayed as an *ineffective attempt* to show off and to compensate for other weaknesses' (1997: 286: emphasis added). This strategy would likely be unsuccessful. It would start from the wrong premise, namely, that the behaviours of high-risk youth are problems to be challenged. Acknowledging the benefits of weapon carrying, *and then* finding other more acceptable ways to achieve the same sense of personal power and security might be a more effective intervention strategy. But it would depend on whether the interveners truly understood the intelligibility of the teens' delinquent behaviour.

When health appears intertwined with deviance, it creates unsettling results for researchers, clinicians, and the families of high-risk youth. Eileen Yellin, Mary Quinn, and Catherine Hoffman (1998) for two years tracked 100 youth, each of whom had a history of incarceration in Arizona. They found that those who were successful in making the transition back to their communities and those who quickly returned to the juvenile corrections system as a result of new offences and parole violations were not perceptibly different. Wondering what then made the difference, Yellin and her colleagues interviewed four of the successful youths whose lives they found demonstrated the complex relationship between risk and protective factors, between deviance and health. Two of these youth would, before publication of the findings, return to jail, although the investigators remained at a loss despite their research to predict which youth would succeed and which would not. In fact, one of the youth, known as Natas (Satan spelled backwards), a racist neo-Nazi, was one of the youth who did best! Yellin and her colleagues wondered, 'As shocking as Natas's current behavior may seem to us, what does he have that allowed him to remain arrest-free?' (1998: 8).

Other researchers, in the field of adolescent addictions, frequently have published results that demonstrate the positive aspects of substance abuse among youth (Michell & West, 1996; Pavis et al., 1998). Rather than embracing these findings as accurate accounts of subjects' experiences, the tendency has been to avoid deeper explorations of the benefits of substance use and abuse by adolescents. While it may be preferable that youth not abuse alcohol and other substances, it is important that we understand how such risk-taking behaviours act, paradoxically, as protective factors. For example, through a study of 57 adolescent–parent dyads and their argument styles, John Caughlin and Rachel Malis (2002) found a pattern to their interaction. Specifically, making demands on parents or alternately using drugs and other antisocial behaviour as a form of withdrawal are ways teenagers successfully mimic parental withdrawal and cope with excessive parental demands.

Further support for the utility of substance abuse among some youth comes from Carl Ziervogel and his colleagues (Ziervogel et al., 1997). In a qualitative study of South African adolescent male binge drinkers, they found that participants preferred the identities conferred on them that included an 'adult/manhood status' when they drank to excess. Ziervogel et al. evidently see this as problematic and interpret their data in ways that construct this status attainment as a weakness – without appreciating that excessive drinking among some males is a purposeful display that impresses their friends and potential sexual partners. Have we missed something here? What is it about each of these cultural and social contexts that makes some young people choose these behaviours above others to enhance their relational status? These questions have yet to be fully explored from the point of view of adolescents themselves. According to Lynn Michell and Patrick West the notion that adolescents are 'socially incompetent and vulnerable' does not hold true: 'individual choice and motivation need to be put back on the drug use agenda' (1996: 47).

Understanding these patterns to the health-enhancing deviance and delinquency as one way disadvantaged youth negotiate for a sense of well-being requires attention be paid to the relationships in their lives. Peers, families, and communities are intricately involved in constructions of health among youth from marginalized social locations. However, new research is demonstrating that many of our assumptions about these relationships and their influence on a teenager's health are not always correct. In a well-received, but controversial work, Judith Rich (1998) conducted a review of hundreds of studies on children and their peer relations. Although Rich is not a social constructionist, her work demonstrates the power of group socialization, a characteristic that others have found important in recent cross-cultural studies (Decovic, 1999; Stanton-Salazar & Spina, 2000). Rich shows that family factors are less important to a child's health than extra-familial factors like a teenager's association with peers and the resulting externalizing and internalizing behaviours. Findings such as this support a view of the peer group as a holding environment for the child's growth and development. If this is the case, it seems reasonable that the group culture and norms encountered in those peer groups will influence a child's behaviour. While Rich recognizes that this occurs, she never enters the discursive debate to which her work leads. She assumes that adult norms are the benchmarks of successful adaptation even though her review of the literature shows that the behaviour of youth is influenced more by the culture and expectations of each other than that of their caregivers. If peers are so influential, then it makes sense that for the child who turns to peers for clues to normative behaviour and acceptance that the peer group itself would establish, and more importantly, support alternate constructions of health (such as binge drinking, reckless driving, drug use, and criminal activity).

Despite Rich's argument, there is abundant evidence that the family remains an influence on how children access resources and what resources children access, including their peer groups. As we have seen in the lives of youth like those discussed so far, and based on published evidence, all significant relationships, peers, families, and communities, exert an influence on the way health discourses are constructed.

Take, for example, a study by Gregory Pettit and his colleagues, including developmental psychopathologist Kenneth Dodge (Pettit et al., 2001), who teased apart the relationship between behavioural problems and the nature of parents' styles of supervision of their children. Monitoring, which usually means parents' supervision of children's whereabouts, activities, and friends (Dishion & McMahon, 1998), especially in middle childhood and adolescence, may be accomplished through a pro-active parenting style that anticipates children's needs or through psychological means. Monitoring may either demonstrate tolerance for children's choices (a preferred method) or, more negatively, attempt to control children emotionally and keep them dependent on one or both of the parents. These patterns change over time as children grow, although Pettit and his colleagues show that parenting styles are best understood as resulting from the broader context in which families are embedded. No one style over the life course of a child has yet to be shown as the best, with a complex set of exchanges typifying most parent–child relationships. The more that parents treat their teens as mature, however, the more likely they are to develop mature and intimate relationships with their peers (Updegraff et al., 2002).

Those who have examined similar aspects of family life from a symbolic interactionist point of view, such as Albert Farrell and Kamila White, have found that the meaning attributed to parent–child interactions is an important aspect of the observable activity. Farrell and White find that a youth's relationship with his or her father is a significant 'resiliency factor' (1998: 255) in determining the likelihood that an adolescent will, or will not, abuse drugs. The presence of the male parent appears to offer children a positive influence that buffers the potentially negative influences of peers. While studies such as Farrell and White's do not explicitly look at the way resilience is socially constructed, they do demonstrate that relationships are pivotal to resilience and that contact with significant others, including family members and peers, present forums in which children discover ways to protect themselves from risk. If we were to look beyond the statistical correlation between a caring father and drug use by teens, and examine the qualities of the relationship that inhibit drug use, we would likely find evidence for resilience as a social construct. As I will show in Chapter 5, youth explain that a positive relationship with a parent provides them with acceptance for their construction of a healthy identity and opens up a wider range of possible other self-constructions. Their subsequent resilience is indicative of their participation in a discourse of health that is co-authored with the parent. It is not that dad encourages a child to not use drugs: it is that dad offers a teenager an opportunity to create a healthy and powerful identity that does not depend on drug use for its definition.

All this begs the question of which comes first, the delinquent group and its powerful identity construction or a group of wayward kids lacking attention from caregivers and looking for an identity? Terrie Moffitt's (1993, 1997; Moffitt et al., 2001) work, discussed earlier, offers an interesting hypothesis that points to a resolution of this dilemma. Moffitt notes that by age 20 the number of active offenders drops by 50%. By age 28, of former offenders 85% have stopped their criminal behaviours. Looking backwards, we now know that most chronic offenders show very early signs of disordered behaviour, although disordered behaviour during adolescence is on its own a poor predictor of future delinquency, unless earlier problem behaviours are also considered. As noted before, the empirical work reviewed by Moffitt shows that there is a core 5% of offenders who persist throughout their lives with heterotypic continuity, a phrase Moffitt uses to 'extend observations of continuity beyond the mere persistence of a single behaviour to encompass a variety of antisocial expressions that emerge as development affords new opportunities' (1993: 679). Moffitt's point is that delinquent behaviours change in their manifestations depending on the individual's environment and life stage as each affects the possible expressions of an underlying orientation to problem behaviours. This is significant in two regards. First, it makes the case for a ready group of delinquent peers who, already by adolescence, are well along in their development of a criminogenic lifestyle. Second, it makes clear that the choice of criminal behaviour depends on the context in which the individual lives and the individual's access to resources (including peers) who can sustain the individual's self-construction as healthy.

Even risk-taking behaviours like early sexual activity must be similarly contextualized (D'Augelli & Hersherger, 1993; Graber et al., 1998; Lesko, 2001; Lonczak et al., 2002; Robinson, 1994). Kathleen Rounds notes, in her discussion of the prevention of sexually transmitted infections among adolescents, that the very risk-taking behaviours that teens engage in are also part of normative development and, to adolescents, signs of healthy functioning: 'It is critical to keep in mind that although early, risky sexual behavior clearly can have negative consequences, adolescent sexual behavior in itself is not necessarily negative and may serve many developmental functions ... For example, by engaging in sex with others, adolescents may seek to enhance their sense of intimacy and connection with others, elevate their status in their peer group, and challenge authority or assert their autonomy. Moreover, adolescents may believe that the initiation of intercourse marks their transition to adulthood' (1997: 175). Interestingly, Rounds also notes the paucity of discussion about protective factors in the empirical literature on risky sexual behaviour among teens. 'More research on protective factors is needed to develop effective interventions for adolescents' risky sexual behaviour' (1997: 185).

David Gregson (1994) talks of 'normally very abnormal' youth. In his work with addicted children and youth, he questions our partializing and pathologizing discourse that sees youth at risk as individuals with individual problems. Instead, Gregson takes an explicitly constructionist approach to his work, encouraging counsellors to understand that the map is not the territory: 'If Johnny is abused at home, or living with the consequences of institutional racism, or the victim of unattended learning challenges, he may understandably become involved in high-risk behaviours. In the 1990s in the West at least, his "abnormal" behaviour may be seen as perfectly normal; not socially acceptable, but perfectly understandable' (1994: 33). Gregson muses on the meaning of sick and delinquent and finds little support for either distinction in his work with at-risk youth. Adolescents do not construct meaning for their experiences this way. Instead, they construct stories of themselves and their behaviours as health-enhancing.

In a study of 30 adolescents between the ages of 16 and 18, Cynthia Lightfoot (1992) examined this constructionist interpretation of development more rigorously. She conducted personal interviews with each youth providing the teens with scenarios related to group cohesion and risk-taking delinquent behaviours. Her findings are very similar to those of the present study, even going so far as to explicitly support a postmodern understanding of youth culture as socially constructed out of personal narratives in sociohistorical contexts. Specifically, Lightfoot found that adolescents placed great value on 'the importance of sharing a novel experience' (1992: 237). These experiences, even when deviant, accrue benefits to participants. Adolescents who participate in risky activities, like smoking marijuana, say the activity affects the developmental course of their interpersonal relationships. Such activities help to maintain social cohesion in groups and more clearly define the children by giving them a forum in which to say, 'This is me' or 'This is not me.'

The Problem with Interventions

Further evidence for this alternative discourse comes from many different sources. It is even found among the professionals who are mandated to intervene. Many of these interveners are questioning the way in which they manifest their power in the clinical relationship and how that power disadvantages high-risk youth seeking health identities. Adding an analysis of power to the relationship between youth and their care providers makes much clearer the differing needs expressed by each party. Professionals play an important role in creating health, not just through interventions, but also through their participation in the health and illness discourse. In a text that promotes relational diagnosis (see also, Kaslow, 1996), rather than the individualizing assessments more typical of the mental health profession, Kenneth Gergen, Lynn Hoffman, and Harlene Anderson (1996) offer a constructionist counterpoint to the demands for accurate objective diagnostic categorization of problem behaviours. In their carefully orchestrated discussion, Gergen et al. note how professional labels gain legitimacy through discourse:

> As the terminologies are disseminated to the public – through classrooms, popular magazines, television, and film dramas they become available to people for understanding of self and others. They are, after all, the 'terms of the experts,' and if one wishes to do the right thing, they become languages of choice for understanding or labelling people (including the self) in daily life. Terms such as depression, paranoia, attention deficit disorder, sociopathic, and schizophrenia have become essential entries in the vocabulary of the educated person. And when the terms are applied in daily life, they have substantial effects – in narrowing the explanation to the level of the individual, stigmatizing, and obscuring the contribution of other factors (including the demands of economic life, media images, and traditions of individual evaluation) to the

actions in question. Further, when these terms are used to construct the self, they suggest that one should seek professional treatment. (1996: 103)

Later in the study, they contend that diagnosis is explicitly a discursive act committed within a professional culture: 'A diagnosis is an agreement in language to make sense of some behavior or event in a certain way. But a social constructionist perspective warns us that this kind of agreement may mislead us into holding the diagnosis to be true. Is it the diagnostic reality we should be treating in therapy?' (1996: 105). In addition, according to Gergen et al., diagnostic categories give helpers the illusion that they and their colleagues are all working on the same issue, when the labels themselves are differentially constructed across individual helping contexts. What paranoid or depressed mean to the psychiatrist are not the same as what they mean in the working environment of the social worker.

When professionals intervene and what they do adds to the problem-saturated self-descriptions of those with whom they work, it is the helpers who become a threat to the mental health of their clients. There is growing evidence that more and more professionals share a 'reluctance to diagnose psychiatric disorders owing to fears about the adverse effects of medical labelling and stigmatization' (Kurtz et al., 1998, p. 551). As Freeman and Dyer explain, 'Intrapsychic definitions of children's problems may predetermine how their behaviors are assessed, leading practitioners to define the behaviors as pathological rather than as manifestations of coping skills or strengths in troubled families' (1993: 422).

Interventions with high-risk youth that disregard their constructions of resilience can become similarly iatrogenic. In what is a rare instance in which those intervening admit to the problems that they cause, Carolyn Simmons and Ruth Parsons (1983) show that a 'life choices' program for adolescent girls helped to develop competence in working-class youth, but resulted in decreased measures of competence and self-esteem for an underclass group. Experiencing one's self as competent is frequently cited in the literature as one of the cornerstones of resilience and mental health. Simmons and Parsons recognized at the time the mistake they had made, but they had no theoretical frame with which to explain their significant negative results. They speculated that the underclass girls may have perceived themselves as competent before the program because they valued their street knowledge. It is likely, the programmed intervention de-valued the expert knowledge of these youth and negatively connoted their survival strategies, leading to threats to their self-esteem. As Simmons and Parsons provide no detailed qualitative data, one can only speculate that this is true for the program participants. From the perspective of social constructionism, however, exposing the girls to all the possible options for their future, and trying to build their self-esteem by emphasizing preconceived notions of health, would be expected to devalue the knowledge base of underclass children. Feelings of competence, as an outcome of interaction with the environment, have as much to do with the value that society places on an individual's skills as the personal sense of satisfaction derived from their usage.

One need only think of little Frankie in Frank McCourt's (1996) Pulitzer Prize–winning autobiographical novel *Angela's Ashes*. Like other tales of children who beat the odds and succeed in life, McCourt's protagonist is a small boy growing up in extreme poverty, in Limerick, Ireland, during the Depression. Frankie and his ilk must either figure out how to survive or die of starvation and disease. Remarkably, Frankie lives and escapes his home and family, but not without having developed an impressive array of skills. He steals and lies, but most of all, he learns that he must break with the conventional norms of his class. For wanting something more than the job of a postman, or a labourer, he is told by those in his community and church that he is acting wrongly. McCourt's book is a poignant tale because of its contrast between the utter hopelessness of Frankie's family's situation and Frankie's capacity to thrive on his own terms. The antagonism of his community makes Frankie's voyage to health all the more inspiring. Ultimately, he escapes Limerick because he puts his talents to use in ways thought unconventional by all but a few people around him.

What McCourt demonstrates through autobiography has also been shown through research with similarly disenfranchised youth. In a study of youth participation in communities done for Health Canada (Caputo, 1999, 2000), it was clear that youths' most pressing concerns are that they have nothing to do, few job prospects, are hassled in public spaces, and are constructed in the popular media as a group of troubled individuals. This marginalization of our youth contrasts with what they say they need, which is to be involved in real and substantive ways in their communities at all levels, including, politically. They resist being pigeon-holed into increasingly lengthier periods of nascent development that make them less than fully contributing members of society.

Similarly, Forrest Tyler and his colleagues (1992) interviewed members from two groups of street youth, one in Bogata, Columbia, and the other in Washington, DC. In part of their study, they looked at the impact that self-definitions and labels have on the children they observed: 'We forget how much the words we use to express our thoughts also shape our thoughts. For example, when I refer to "my" children, I am using a shorthand way of indicating which children, but I also suggest ownership and property. Without recognizing this dual meaning, I do not keep my meaning clear. When I use the words *street youth, delinquents,* and *alienated kids* to describe these youth, I am also separating them from society by words that become labels. Such labels are often inaccurate, stigmatizing, and damaging not only to the children's self-esteem, but to their survival' (1992: 206; emphasis in original). Tyler and his colleagues used their findings to support a primary prevention model of intervention that recognized that children must be given power over the personal, vocational, and educational resources that they need in order to grow. And they must be given the power to challenge the dominant discourse that defines their lives and their health status: 'It is our contention that to attain a sense of personal integrity, we must all acquire a personal code that at times differs in important ways from society's conventional standards' (1992: 207). The youth in Tyler et al.'s study challenged adult perceptions of them as passive victims and, instead, showed that they were actively involved in making choices for themselves.

That street life may solve home-based problems is self-evident and documented, but rarely acknowledged as a sign of health. Kimberly Mitchell and David Finkelhor (2001), for example, provide evidence that family and home-based violence affects children in three ways. Using data from the National Crime Victimization Survey from 1996, 1997, and 1998, which was an annual panel survey of 50,000 households across the United States, Mitchell and Finkelhor demonstrate that youth are at heightened risk of being victims of crime when they live with an adult who is also a victim. Perhaps taking to the streets is a rational choice for many of these youth? Tyler et al. conclude, after all, that 'adolescents who develop early autonomy and choose to live outside the realm of adult authority are capable of making rational choices in their lives' (1992: 208–9). John Hagan and Bill McCarthy (1997) observe, in their look at 390 street youth in Toronto and Vancouver, that youth choose the street as a logical solution to problems. Although they do not often find a better life there, at least, they argue, the challenges they encounter are different. A focus on competencies or the street as a solution to problems acknowledges aspects of children's lives that are evidence of their resilience, a resilience that may be invisible to adults who view street life as an expression of failure.

Summary

Although the evidence is abundant that some teens use a pattern of deviance to bolster what they argue are health-enhancing identities, little of our research or clinical work proceeds with this construction of resilience in the foreground. In this chapter, I have strung together an assortment of research and narratives that address the problems and solutions that high-risk youth find in resource-poor environments in authoring identities that are powerful and health-enhancing. I began with a discussion of postmodern youth and the competing discourses that tell us about their health status. My hope has been to show that youth today are offered a plurality of possible identities, even as we insist they are unhealthy and more at risk than ever before. I then presented research from the fields of criminology, developmental psychology, social work, and education that shows that good things happen for some youth when they behave in dangerous, deviant, delinquent, and disordered ways. Gang activity and other forms of antisocial behaviour were discussed to discern what we know about pathologizing discourses and the material practices that support them. I also examined how power and status are conferred on youth as a result of these same activities and the role that professionals, communities, and families play in these constructions of health and illness.

Perhaps comic singer-songwriter Nancy White captures best the patterns discussed in this chapter. White pokes fun at the resistance that girls raised by feminist-oriented mothers show to the values of their parents, even when those values are supposed to be more progressive than those of the mainstream. What White observes among her friends and family is oddly reminiscent of youth like Allison and Cathy. In a song called *Daughters of Feminists* White sings:

Daughters of feminists love to wear pink and white short frilly dresses
They speak of successes with boys
It annoys their mom
Daughters of feminists won't put on jeans or the precious

construction boots mamma found cute
Ugly shoes they refuse
How come? ...
Daughters of feminists curtsey and skip
Daughters of feminists flirt
They say, 'Please mommy, can I do the dishes,' or, 'Let's make a pie for
    my brother.'
Are they sincere?
Are they crazy?
Or are they just trying to stick it to mother?

The review of the research in the preceding pages demonstrates a thread of thought in the literature that foreshadows the postmodern interpretation of the behaviours of high-risk youth discussed throughout this book. Propping up the youth's self-constructions as healthy requires power: not just power in the social discourse that bandies about competing definitions of experience, but also the power to access the very real health resources that support the attainment of experiences that nurture and maintain health. This power and the process of empowerment as it relates to mental health outcomes will be examined in the next chapter.

Chapter Five

From Experiences of Power
to Mental Health

This chapter is concerned with the material and psychological manifestations of power in the lives of high-risk youth and the pivotal role
that power plays in how teens nurture and maintain a mental health
discourse of resilience. The following discussion will argue that discursive empowerment is a protective mechanism. The theory presented
is grounded in the narratives of the youth with whom I have worked.
In this chapter, the experiences of these youth will be discussed in
relation to peer, family, and community relationships to explore the
patterns of discourse participation and the drift between spheres of
relationships inherent in the complex lives of high-risk teens. These
teens' experiences of power, and the manner in which they acquire,
maintain, and challenge discursively constructions of themselves as
either vulnerable or resilient is my focus.

   'Sticks and stones may break our bones, but names will *really hurt
us.*' That is how adolescents who participated in this study explained
the threat to their well-being that comes from a lack of discursive
power. They argued that their capacity to experience power in the
social discourses that define them is the most important determinant
of their ability to overcome adversity and the risks posed to their
mental well-being. Naively, and with no knowledge of postmodern
interpretations of language and power, these adolescents provided
new insight into old beliefs forced on them since their childhood nurs-
eries. Regardless of the way they behave, delinquent or scholarly, youth
acquire and maintain a sense of well-being by 'drifting' (a term indigenous to this study) towards social discourses in which they exercise
some degree of power over the self-defining labels attached to them.
This patterned drift between discourses is the process by which ado-

lescents, their peers, family members and communities co-author a youth's personal narrative of resilience. These narratives are more than stories youth tell about themselves; they are the way the self constitutes its identity through intersubjective experiences in sociohistorical contexts (Gergen, 1991, 1994, 1996). According to the participants in this study, when the stories youth tell about themselves are invested with sufficient power to be widely accepted, mental health is maintained. When youth feel they lack the power to influence the way they are viewed, their mental health becomes threatened and troubling behaviours and symptoms follow.

Case Study: Pam and Sophie

Not every disadvantaged child makes what might appear to be self-destructive decisions to achieve health. In fact, there is an incredible variety in the pathways that the 43 youth in this study followed towards health. Even among siblings we can see differences, largely, they explain, as a result of their unique constellations of strengths and vulnerabilities. Any two teens might approach the problem of discursive power and resulting acceptance of a chosen identity very differently. Pam and her fraternal twin Sophie each presented with their own unique ways of surviving and thriving. While Pam turned to the street, Sophie looked elsewhere.

Initially, when referred to the study, it was assumed that Sophie would be selected as an example of a resilient child, while Pam would offer an interesting contrast as a vulnerable sibling. As discussed in Chapter 1, this dichotomous thinking may be useful to professional helpers, but it serves no purpose to the youth themselves. Although Sophie is certainly doing better in life by conventional standards, her sister's pattern of resilience is just as viable, given Pam's constellation of personal, social, and environmental risk factors. In getting to know Sophie, one discovers that she has had a few more conventionally acceptable attributes with which to work. Although still frequently on the street and into petty crime, vandalism, and exploring her sexuality, Sophie distinguishes herself from her sister because she does well at school, plays sports, and needs to take fewer risks to feel mature. For reasons that she could not at first articulate, Sophie has been less traumatized by the abuse that both girls suffered. In fact, she has reacted to it by doing what she can to be sure her mother, and both she and her sister, are kept safe from further harm.

At the start of one interview with Sophie at her home, she was observed cursing at her mother, ordering her around like a child. Her mother apologized to the interviewer, saying that she could do nothing about the 'mouth' on her daughter. Yet, later during the interview, without her mother present, Sophie explained how much she needed her mother, and how much she wanted to protect her: 'I won't let my mom have boyfriends ... My sister and me were hers for so long. We were here first. And no guy is gonna come in and take her away.' No guy was also going to ever again get in the door to abuse Sophie, Pam, or their mother, as long as Sophie had something to say about it.

Power

Power, as currently defined by Western society's dominant discourse, is 'the ability to control others.' When used this way, the word *power* reflects the individualistic ideology of our society that promotes competition and blames those that fail for their failure. Nietzsche (1968/1889) described this type of power best as an individual's 'will to power' over others. In the constant struggle for domination, we look for victims to subjugate to our will. In the case of mental health and illness, those with power convince those who are judged 'normal' that it is in their best interest to exercise their will by separating and interning those who are different. For Nietzsche, the moral universe that might temper these acts of domination is nothing more than a 'psychology of error.' The emotion of calm contentment that we experience when we live in accordance with divine rules is a false consciousness. In other words, Nietzsche argued, we create God to convince ourselves that we are living a moral existence, forgetting that the divine was our own creation from the start. Thankfully, there exists another view of power which, when put into practice, is less hegemonic and more health-promoting.

Foucault's (1982, 1994/1977) work, as an example of an alternative view of power, sees power as capillary, rooted in the everyday actions of ordinary people. To Foucault, power is a productive force. By productive, he means it results from a process by which individuals internalize social values and thereby legitimate dominant ideologies. Unfortunately, this power, which rests with the collectivity, is seldom used in support of alternative discourses that might challenge the internalized social constraints that control our lives. This self-defeating process by which we allow ourselves to be subjugated is related at present to our acceptance of a neo-conservative ideology and the competition it breeds in Western culture.

But what happens when we challenge this dominant discourse? What is to be accepted as the norm if, say, in the case of mental health, we reject the notion that the power to access health resources is not limited? Although Foucault does not offer a good answer to this question of norms (Fraser, 1989), the emerging definition of mental health discussed in earlier chapters clearly shows that mental health is a measure of our state of well-being, regardless of the biological and psychological illnesses that impinge on that state. Normative mental health is whatever we, in connection with others, feel is sufficient power to define it as such. It is important to note that this resource of power that individuals and groups need in order to have a say over socially constructed definitions, is not a zero-sum commodity (Katz, 1984). This capillary understanding of power helps to fortify the connection between experiences that promote mental health and the process of empowerment. This has long been shown through studies linking mental disorder to events that are outside the control of the individual (see Hollingshead & Redlich, 1958; Myers & Bean, 1968). When there exist inequalities based on gender, class, or race, inevitably those who are denied experiences of power are the ones most likely to suffer mental and emotional problems.

The power to define mental health is based on intersubjectivity experienced in our relationships with others. Although it was once widely accepted that 'Western man's' mental health resulted from 'the illusory goal of independence, self-sufficiency, and free autonomy' (Wolf, 1988: 28), this is an antiquated belief that few adhere to today. Relationships allow us to exercise our collective power, and they have an impact on the dominant social discourse, fundamentally altering how mental health and mental illness are defined. It is essential that individuals participate in a reverse discourse (Weedon, 1997), if they are to challenge the socially constructed labels assigned to their behaviour. Although motivated by the personal need to define for one's self one's state of mental health, the path to this agentic exercise of power is through communal interactions. To influence the discursive constitution of subjectivity, alternate meanings for everyday actions must be given voice communally. This process of discursive empowerment can affect individuals on both micro- or macro-levels.

At the level of the individual, Scheman's (1980, 1983) work on women's anger is an example of the battle between hegemony and a discourse focused on liberation that is still as relevant today as it was two decades ago. Scheman offers an understanding of women's anger that challenges the myth that the objects of psychology are an individual experience: 'That the objects of psychology – emotions, beliefs, intentions virtues and vices – attach to us singly (no matter how socially we may acquire them) is, I want to argue, a piece of ideology. It is not a natural fact, and the ways in which it permeates our social institutions, our lives and our senses of ourselves are not unalterable. It is deeply useful in the maintenance of capitalist and patriarchal society and deeply embedded in our notions of liberation, freedom, and equality' (1983: 226). The naming of anger and other emotions such as depression, for women and men, is governed by socially embodied norms that have tended to deny us our right to become conscious of the oppression we experience (Osherson, 1992; Stoppard, 2000). Scheman (1980) describes the process by which women rediscover their anger, justify it, and name it, as a 'political redescription' of their reality. The outcome may be that feelings of depression, alienation, and anxiety are renamed as intelligible adaptations to exploitative situations. This redefinition occurs through the fruitful interaction with others who nurture this alternate point of view.

Yet, despite some gains, it is sad to think how little has changed since Nietzsche was judged insane shortly after completing his treatise on the 'will to power.' At that time, he was labelled ill and eventually institutionalized. It is ironic that the one who most believed the individual could control others was so easily subjugated by the popular consensus on the way madness should be treated. Nietzsche may have believed he possessed individual power, but the tragic fact of his committal showed that power is collectively defined and exercised.

There are countless studies that have discussed the role that relationships play in measures of mental health without ever recognizing that the transcendental experience of mental health is illusionary and discourse based. This is not to say that conventional research on the connections between relationships and mental health does not accurately document the experiences of certain groups. It is only to say that these studies assume that what they are measuring is a constant for everyone and that all research subjects value and perceive mental health in the same way. It is more likely that the positive effects that relationships have on mental health occur because their meaning is filtered by a dominant ideology that orders people's world and the beliefs that shape that world. When people have an experience of relationship that fits with what they are told by society is supposed to be a good experience, there usually follows an emotional reaction that society also says should occur. Mental health is the predetermined result.

Two examples may help clarify this point. First, it is not uncommon for us to feel at some point, after good or bad fortune comes our way, an emotional response that is not the one expected of us. I may feel happy at the death of someone I am supposed to be grieving because, in my view, the event of their passing means something different to me than it does to others. In this case, I must either succumb to the expectations of society and grieve 'appropriately' or challenge the dominant discourse and do things in my own way. Similarly, this pattern of expectations is very easy to see when one travels within a culture different than one's own. During a recent stay in a small community in rural northern Pakistan, I lived in a family's guest house. Long into the evening people would come to visit, sitting and talking among themselves or just reading and smoking, seldom paying much attention to me with whom they could communicate very little. After a time I went to bed, which I was assured by my host, was not rude in the least. Long after I had curled up and fallen asleep in the corner, people continued their visit. It was later explained to me that in the culture of my hosts, sharing time and space with a guest is very important. They would have considered it rude to leave me to myself for fear that I would feel lonely and neglected.

Experiences of power related to constructions by individuals as resilient can be grouped into three categories. These categories are:

1 *The power that results from being in relationship with others.* Relationships serve two functions. First, they allow people to collectively define for themselves what is and is not mental health, and second, relationships are essential for social action to access the resources needed to sustain health.
2 *The power to control the physical, emotional, and social resources needed to experience mental health* (e.g., housing, food, employment, self-esteem, a say over community institutions.
3 *The power to exploit opportunities to feel competent.*

Each of these three aspects of power were found to be foundational to the process that high-risk teens engage in constructing an identity as mentally healthy. All three should be evident when one reads the narrative accounts by youth in this and previous chapters.

Relationships

The first of these, power through relationships, is the lynchpin upon which the theory of a socially constructed resilience rests. The other two experiences of power find their expression as a consequence of relational power. Other studies of personal and social empowerment have shown that experiences of power take place similarly within the context of relationships. Janet Surrey (1991a, 1991b) explains that 'relational empowerment' is dependent on a 'process of enlarged vision and energy, stimulated through interaction, in a framework of emotional connection' (1991a: 171). The relationships necessary for empowerment can range from experiences with internalized representations of significant others from our past to actual relationships we currently enjoy with family, peers, our community, and its institutions. Of course, even while enjoying relations with others in the present, internal psychological processes are believed to shape our experience of the social realm. Therefore, empowerment is an interactional process in which people are dependent on each other for activities that support feelings of well-being. This is as true for children as it is for adults.

Experiences of control and competence in relationships with significant others affect the identities that high-risk youth construct. Those experiences, however, do not fully explain the way these youth cope with the stigmatizing labels that attach to them. *Acquiring* and then *maintaining* an acceptable identity that is congruent with one's sense of self, while *challenging* aspects of one's identity that are discordant, are three aspects of a process of discursive empowerment through which high-risk youth construct resilience in relationship with others. The three are, of course, interrelated and are typically not as distinguishable as presented here for the purpose of clarity.

Acquiring Identities

As has already been shown, teens acquire health-enhancing identities through participation in a social discourse that presents them with a limited number of options from which to choose. Participants in this study attempted to maximize their sense of personal and social empowerment through their identity selection. Sociocultural, familial, and personal factors place limits on the choices available. These factors are both implicit and explicit in the social discourse and the material practices through which it finds expression.

Margie, who was 13 when we worked together at a community clinic, talked of the shame that she experienced a year earlier when she found herself in a new school without friends: 'People called me a loser just because they didn't like me.' At home, Margie is one of the more fortunate youth: she has parents who reinforce their daughter's positive characteristics. Although helpful, as vulnerable and peer-oriented as she was, Margie still relied more on her peers than on her parents for a powerful self-defining label. Contrast such name-calling and resulting identity with a teen like 14-year-old Tammy who is given labels by her friends that fit better with how she wants to be known, indicating to her some control over her identity construction. As Tammy explained, 'Everyone comes to me with their problems because I want to be a shrink when I grow up.' There is congruence between how Tammy wants to be known and is known by her peers. But significant others like her father, now divorced from her mother, are more critical. The constant interplay between peers, families, and communities in the labels made available for acquisition by high-risk youth is typical of this population. Sometimes the results are positive, but more frequently, when high-risk youth are assigned stigmatizing identities, they must work hard at rejecting them. If there is any pattern to identity acquisition, it is more serendipitous than purposeful. If one imagines a large soup pot in which a mixture of ingredients are placed, one is never very sure exactly what the flavour of the final recipe will be.

Those youth who, by their own admission, were less healthy, explained that they tend to gain power through the full expression of the identities *given* to them. Even Sophie recalls how following a recent newspaper story about her and her friends, she lapsed for a time into more delinquent behaviour: 'They called us slang and trash and they think we're no good ... We just picked up the label of delinquent and decided if they're going to call us that, why not just show them.' While Sophie grew past the negative stereotype, her sister Pam did not. Choosing from the alternatives presented to them, these teens say they adopt the most powerful identity available, even when that identity enjoys limited social acceptance beyond those who invest it with power.

It seems that the more stigmatizing the label, the more enduring it becomes. Labels that come from their communities tended to infuriate these teens the most, in part because they were given on the flimsiest of evidence. At age 16, Tommy, the persistent offender I introduced in Chapter 3, was the one who asked for counselling at a community mental health clinic while nearing the end of a one-year sentence in secure custody. Tommy gave the example of how quick adults are to see kids like him and their peer groups as problems, labelling him and the boys with whom he hung out on the street as members of a gang. Tommy insists his friends were more like his family than a group of organized criminals. For many of these youth, just being young was enough reason for their communities to think of them and their peers as trouble waiting to happen. It was these same communities that played such a pivotal role in the discourse that invested power in these youths' 'problem' identities. Paradoxically, youth who did not see themselves as 'bad' felt compelled to exploit these negative labels when assigned to them as one of the few options available for a powerful self-construction when other more acceptable paths were blocked or experienced as unattainable.

From a social constructionist perspective, this pattern in relational power makes sense. We learn how to participate in discourse and the nature of discursive power first within our families, then later within an ever-widening circle of non-kin individuals and groups. This movement outside the family does not negate the child's ongoing attachments to family supports. The older the child, the greater his or her capacity to experience intimate relationships. As Nathalie Franco and Mary Levitt (1998) found in their study of 185 ethnically diverse male and female Grade 5 students from the southeastern United States, family supports to children affect the quality of their peer relationships (competitive or cooperative) outside the home, influencing the child's well-being as indicated by a measure of self-esteem (see also Bender & Loesel, 1997). Within neither an ecological nor a constructionist framework (see Chapter 3) can we overly partialize the context of a child's development. Family, extended family, and even non-kin are all important contributors to children's intersubjective experience of their world: 'These findings suggest that parents have a pervasive influence on the nature of the friendships that children are able to establish. However, they also indicate that children may acquire the capacity to engage in supportive, intimate exchanges and to modulate conflict with friends through their association with nonparental adult family members. This result lends further support to the idea that extended family relations may provide a bridge to the establishment of close intimate ties with peers' (1998: 319).

Franco and Levitt do not, however, speculate on why supportive relationships with parents develop the child's capacity to sustain supportive friendships with others. If we accept that supportive peer relationships have an element of reciprocity (shared power) to them, then we can guess that something is being taught in the family about how to negotiate for acceptance and attachment with non-kin others. This skill is transferable and, for young people, an important ingredient in their building more widely accepted and powerful identity stories through participation with others. The better parents are at teaching children these negotiation skills, the more likely it is that the children are going to be able to equitably participate in empowering exchanges beyond their homes. Dependency on others does not mean that individuals subjugate themselves to the dominant culture's definition of them or their health status.

Relationships that function to support individuals' personal and social power counter a tendency by people to blame themselves for the oppressive situations they confront. Michael Lerner (1986) has called this pattern of self-blame 'surplus powerlessness.' By building empowering relations with others, it is possible to change a feeling of personal helplessness into universal helplessness, as one realizes the non-contingency of one's life situation (Abramson et al., 1978). Awareness that attempts by others in similar circumstances have not been able to change an oppressive situation is a far less debilitating attribution than one that leads to a perception of helplessness as a personal problem. Obviously, a change in attribution does not lead to an alleviation of oppression. However, because such an attribution helps to bind people together around a common perception, it facilitates the building of relationships that are required to experience discursive empowerment. The shift that occurs from heightened awareness to social action is indicative of the praxis inherent in the empowerment process. Without the group, and in particular the intimacy of a family or familylike substitute, the individual's potential experience of power is limited (Cochran, 1988, 1991; Dunst et al., 1988; Fick & Thomas, 1995; Hawley, 2000; Micucci, 1998; Oglesby-Pitts, 2000; Walsh, 1998).

Maintaining Identities

A second aspect of youths' search for discursive power is their maintenance of the health-promoting identities that they acquire. Maintaining an identity requires engagement in an ongoing process of construction that, in turn, depends on a continuous stream of intersubjective experiences that sustain a coherent self-construction. Each label that is acquired becomes part of the teenager's life story, and maintaining it, just another chapter in his or her personal narrative. Creating an identity is as much about the relative degree of power that one asserts with others who must accept one's self-definition, as it is about the bringing together of diffuse elements of one's personal story into a coherent whole. Frequently, high-risk youth report that attempts to maintain powerful identities lead to spiralling episodes of problem behaviours. As Mark explained, 'I've always been the outcast, the scapegoat' and acted accordingly. He offered no resistance to these constructions of him by others until his behaviour became so destructive that new resources were made available to protect him from himself. Ironically, when he finally attempted suicide, he says he felt like he had found a way to re-author his personal story from that of the 'abused child who got what he deserved' to someone who could take control of his life.

These youth found many creative ways to express themselves despite the opposition of the institutions, communities, families, and professionals who would have them remain stuck in their subjugated roles. Allison chose to become one of the worst, rather than best, group home kids as a way to carve out for herself an identity in the system as someone who would not be pushed around. And Pam explained, 'If you're gonna be a leader you've got to be top in everything or else you feel like dirt. If you're in a race, you have to win.' There's a lot riding on success among peers for teens like these who have no other way to define themselves as healthy but as leaders among their troubled peers. Through their oppositional behaviour, high-risk teens frequently appear to be choosing self-destructive or compromising activities, rejecting what adults in their lives think are viable alternatives for health.

It is exactly this dynamic that can be seen in a child's selection of clothing. Just like their caregivers, they too need the trappings of appearance to maintain a sense of themselves as powerful. As 15-year-old Tammy said, 'Makeup is important to me. Clothes is important. I don't want to go around looking like crap. Like if you took off all the makeup off all the girls in my school our school would look like Grade 6s. Like everyone except maybe the geeks wear makeup and even they wear some gloss ... I just like myself better that way.'

But not all these youth found comfort in conventional expressions of dress and appearance. There is a tension between what they should be and what they want to be. Fourteen-year-old Tanya explained, 'I have fit in. I used to be popular. But I'm not really any more. I want to be me. I want to be normal. I want to be different. I don't want to have

to dress the same, act the same, think the same. I want to dress my
way, talk my way, think my way. Of course, sometimes you can't do
that because I have this tendency to do what other people want.' The
trouble, from the point of view of the parents of these teens, is that
high-risk youth frequently take the message 'dress for success' and,
instead, dress outlandishly to maintain their status on their own terms.
This same belief system has been found in other studies that document people's use of body art and piercings (Blose, 1999). Through
dress and physical adornment teens successfully maintain their powerful self-images.

The relationship between what the individual does and what his or
her peers do is, however, more complicated. The relationship has both
agentic and communal aspects. The power derived from self-constructions is enhanced through affiliation with, but not subjugated to, the
dress codes of peers and cultural icons. Within a communal context,
being different *in the same* way others are different, allows high-risk
teens who prefer status outside conventionality to experience the comfort of being in fine company: alternatives all wear black, skaters wear
baggy pants, skinheads shave their heads. Collectively individuals assert a stronger identity than when they go it alone, but the choice to
participate in an identity story remains the individual's.

Maintaining an identity means strategically convincing others of the
acceptability of one's self-construction. Specifically, high-risk youth
identify two relational experiences of power that they consider pivotal
to maintaining a health-enhancing identity amidst the chaos in their
lives. The first is the power to control the physical, emotional, and
social resources needed to experience mental health (e.g., housing,
food, employment, schooling, self-esteem, a say over community institutions, and peer groups). The second is the power to use these resources to demonstrate competence and be recognized for one's talents. Bill Henry and his colleagues from the Dunedin study in New
Zealand (Henry et al., 1999) have provided evidence that supports a
similar conclusion, although for different reasons. They found that for
girls – but not boys – school attendance predicted a lower rate of
antisocial behavior. Henry et al. speculate that girls are constrained in
how they express themselves by social influences at school where they
encounter both authority figures and a wider peer group. Girls may
be directed away from externalizing behaviours in favour of internalizing ones that do not appear as antisocial. Boys from similar backgrounds do not experience the same constraints. According to my

findings, teens who are likely to act out use the school setting and the opportunities it presents to be oppositional to authority. Boys who attend school may also experience greater variety in their negotiations with different peer group subcultures through which they assert a powerful identity. These others become an audience to the performance of overt displays of deviance. Lacking access to academic constructions of success, these male youth are reasonable in choosing to be antisocial. The one caveat to this gendered pattern to exploitation of resources is that Henry and his colleagues may have missed the hidden aspects of girls' relational violence that typically has been overlooked in studies of adolescent behaviour (Simmons, 2002; Crick, 1997; Crick & Bigbee, 1998; Crick et al., 1999). Girls may be every bit as antisocial at school but we have not yet asked the right questions to talk about it.

While there are many more studies of boys than girls in the risk and resilience literature (see Brame et al., 2001; Farrington, 1995; Loeber, Green, Lahey, Frick & McBurnett, 2000), an emerging trend is to look specifically at girls' experiences and, like Ogbu's work on culture and race, understand the unique ways that gender determines coping. In Rachel Simmons look at the hidden culture of aggression in girls, she found a disturbing pattern in which the girls she interviewed viewed the ideal girl as the one who holds back from life, choosing to manipulate others rather than assert herself: 'The ideal girl is stupid, yet manipulative. She is dependent and helpless, yet she uses sex and romantic attachments to get power. She is popular yet superficial. She is fit, but not athletic, or strong. She is happy, but not excessively cheerful. She is fake' (2002: 126). Our culture, and I include teen culture in this as well, supports this mimicry of a life more fully lived. Girls who assert themselves may quickly find that they get into trouble when they fail to live up to these neutered expectations. In such a context, what is and is not problematic or normal becomes difficult to discern. This is nothing new. In A.S. Neill's (1960) presentation of a radical approach to child rearing, *Summerhill*, he spoke of the conspiracy of a culture that places children at a dull desk in a dull school in hopes that they take their place in an even duller factory or office. We seek in our children, both boys and girls, a fanatical desire for them to be conventional without attention to their (and our own) discourses of resistance.

Efficacy in social relations that give voice to this resistance is closely linked to experiences of competence, whether that competence is expressed prosocially or problematically. 'I get accepted by showing what I'm good at,' is how 14-year-old Christopher put it. This statement is deceptively simple. The problem is that within the dominant discourse, the talents of high-risk youth are seldom valued when they are displayed. Take, for example, a youth like Tammy, who not only maintains power through her choice of dress, but also through the help that she offers her peers. She has taken her own experience of sexual abuse and turned it into a source of strength:

> I get calls from people in my class. Like this guy who's in my class and his dad beats him. Everyone phones me with their problems. They yell 'Tammy,' and I just go, 'Calm down, calm down.' It pisses my mom off because I will help everyone else but I won't do anything about my own problems ... It makes me feel good to solve others' problems. But my problems are still there. I don't know how to solve them. My friends can never think how to solve them because like I'm the counsellor person in the group ... Like I've had so many people disclose to me. A whole bunch of people from my class and everywhere. I swear I've had 15 or 16 people disclose to me. It's gotten all around the school. I've got sexual abuse books in my room and when a friend just disclosed to me a little while ago I gave her a piece of paper and a pen and had her put down her feelings, maybe some poems or something. And just comfort her and everything ... I love helping people.

While laudable, Tammy's strategic use of her abuse experiences as the basis for an identity as resilient has meant that she spends more time helping others than helping herself. Those around her take her 'resistance' to treatment and her continuing association with 'problem kids' as signs of persistent psychopathology.

It has surprised me that helping others is one of the most common talents I find among both female and male high-risk youth. Robert's experience is not unlike Tammy's. A troubled and out-of-control 16-year-old who has had numerous run-ins with the law, Robert explained, 'Like my parents think I'm not good for nothing. They just don't realize what I am good for. I don't really know what I'm good for but there are things ... I guess I'm easy to talk to. I always help my friends out when they have problems and I give good advice.' It is not often that these problem children get to be so visibly in control, and so competent at finding solutions to the problems that they and other youth experience. This is not a view of high-risk youth that we typically hold, but it is an image that they certainly hold of themselves.

While helping is a reasonably benign expression of power, teens also find that expression of destructive talents brings them equally important experiences of power and control, including control over their self-definitions. Margie, whose parents were in the midst of a messy divorce when she joined the study, explained that following the break-up of her parents' marriage and the subsequent diagnosis of her mother with chronic fatigue syndrome, her survival strategies unnerved those around her: 'People say I am really pushy and make a big fuss if I don't get what I want. I don't like being told what to do. People say it comes with an artistic mind. I like to make decisions for myself which I'm usually not allowed to do because I'm only 14.' Despite signs of emotional disturbance elsewhere in her life, Margie maintains a semblance of well-being. She accomplishes this by controlling many aspects of her life, including deciding which parent she lives with, if and when to be sexually active with her boyfriend, what she eats, her choice of peer group, and how she behaves in her community.

Margie also takes advantage of the power that comes with being seen as an 'artist' and the positive connotation it gives to her erratic, even suicidal, behaviour. In this way she resembles another girl in the study, Cathy, who also shares this talent. These girls' self-definitions as artists is reinforced through the opportunities they access at school and with friends to display their abundant talents. And yet neither girl was able to fit in during conventional art classes. Although apparently failures, seen in the overall context of their lives, their obstinate and oppositional behaviour has been far more of a help than a hindrance to their survival, even if, when viewed out of context, their behaviour appears problematic. Cathy explained, 'I've had art lessons by two different teachers but when you go to art lessons you have to draw what they tell you to draw. And they are like "This isn't good enough" even if that's the way you want it to be. It's not really your own. It's like I'm here to learn to draw the things I want to do, not what you want me to do.'

Although I have focused on expressions of powerful identities that are problematic for those who care for these teens, many participants also became active members of church groups, air cadets, community centres, took part in extra-curricular school activities, and held down jobs where they could feel like adults. These conventional expressions of power were surprisingly abundant among a sample of youth chosen for their problems and illnesses. Assumptions about what talents high-risk youth have and how these will be expressed can obscure from view their health. If resilience is to be understood, then the complexity of the localized constructions of disadvantaged teens need attention.

Challenging Identities

The challenge high-risk youth face is not simply to maintain an identity of their own choosing, but to assert some degree of personal agency in the construction of that identity from the resources they have at hand. The process of challenging a dominant discourse that gives a high-risk youth an unacceptable self-definition is the third aspect of the process of discursive empowerment leading to mental health. While this sounds straightforward, high-risk teens find that controlling the self-definitions which attach to them demands a curious blend of active resistance to the labels given and the purposeful adoption of powerful but socially unacceptable identities that serve to modulate the effects of the stressors in their lives.

All the troubled teens in this study, however, made great efforts to convince others of their personal power and control. Working collectively with their peers, these 'dysfunctional' teens sought to make adults see them as, in Allison's words, 'just a bunch of kids trying to get through life.' She explained: 'Adults look at you like you're just teenagers. Like a lot of people just look at you and say "That's why they do that, they're just teenagers. They're in that phase." You hear that from adults all the time. I want to say "Shut up!" It bothers me 'cause not all teenagers are the same. They should look at how you act and who you are, not just that you're a teenager. That's like a stereotype.'

Challenging negative identity constructions frequently involves desperate attempts by participants to exercise control over the people and institutions in their lives. Feeling like one is in control of one's life and that decisions are one's own responsibility results from opportunities to exhibit competencies such as sound judgment, good social skills, and the practical management needed to control mental health resources. These feelings of control have a profound affect on how high-risk youth perceive themselves and contribute to their power over self-definitions. Put simply, feeling like one has a say over one's world helps one feel valued for who one is.

Feeling this way is a starting point for a teenager's vision of himself or herself as worthy of respect and, according to these teens, leads to mental health under stressful life circumstances. The teens were very specific on this point. They feel good about themselves and feel like they have a clear concept of who they are when they feel in control of the world around them. These feelings of control, combined with experiences of themselves as competent, and their talents as unique expressions of their identity, secure for high-risk youth powerful self-definitions and enduring feelings of well-being.

A clearly defined identity and sufficient power to feel in control of that identity gives high-risk teens the confidence to make decisions for themselves. Being able to say 'This is who I am' gives them permission to grow in directions that enhance rather than threaten their self-esteem. They made decisions relating to sex, drug use, school attendance, and other issues by seeking congruence between the consequences anticipated from each decision and individual self-definitions. This congruence is seldom appreciated by those outside teen culture. Instead, adults in the lives of high-risk youth want to blame peers, bad genes, almost anything, to avoid recognizing the sensibility of teens who, while facing enormous obstacles in life, muddle through as best they can. High-risk teens spend a great deal of time thinking about the congruence between who they are and what they do.

It is not possible, however, to make sweeping generalizations about how much power one particular teen will need over self-defining labels to establish health. High-risk youth vary in how much control they want over their lives, largely depending on their level of maturity, as defined by them, and the context in which they exercise control. At one end of the continuum is Cathy, who was adamant that she wanted 'total control over [her] life.' This attitude, however, was more often tempered by teens and expressed as a desire to control as much of their lives as possible while still tolerating the benign rule of their caregivers. Although many parents would imagine otherwise, these teens do not mind advice: they just do not want to be told what to do, nor be expected to do as they are told. As 15-year-old Callum put it, 'It's not that you solve problems by yourself. But if you decide to do something you decide it by yourself.' It is this perception of choice, any choice, that underpins constructions of resilience. Decisions, good or bad, offer an opportunity to author an identity. As outsiders to these decisions, caregivers are seldom good judges of how particular actions by individual teens will affect their trajectory through life. Sadly, choice is often denied teens when their behaviour is misinterpreted as requiring interventions that only serve to further restrict their self-determination. It is a vicious cycle that, as will be shown in more detail in Chapters 7 and 8, need not occur.

For example, in the secure facility where a portion of these youth were housed, a determined effort had been made to be less punitive and to use lock-down rooms and other forms of restraint less often. The result was a calmer population of residents, fewer incidents, and more secure attachments between residents and staff. The staff said the changes had obliged them to make better use of their relationships with the youth. They worked hard investing youth with the power to control themselves, while recognizing in the youth in their care the agentive aspects of their personalities. The residents noticed the difference in their treatment and knew they were being seen as competent to make good decisions for themselves.

This is a quite different way of thinking about youth from how we conventionally construct them and their choices, in particular their sexuality. As has been highlighted several times already, sexual expression is frequently used as a way youth (most often in this study the young women) construct adultlike identities. In relation to this finding, Karen Budd, Kristin Stockman, and Elizabeth Miller (1998) note that there are numerous antecedents of adolescent motherhood, including a lack of access to and negative attitudes towards birth control. But attributing early pregnancy simply to accidents or carelessness ignores what Budd et al., found to be another explanation. Among poor urban teens early pregnancy outside of a committed relationship may be viewed as an accepted career option in the face of a dearth of other life opportunities and a lack of eligible partners for marriage. The resulting identity that a young single mother acquires is not necessarily experienced as problematic, but instead brings with it acceptance as a mature and contributing member of one's communities and a challenge to the label of disempowered teen.

As the above examples illustrate, and as unbelievable as it might sound to many caregivers of high-risk youth, these teenagers want to participate in relationships with those concerned for their well-being, most especially with their families of origin. The angry outbursts of teenagers and their demands to make their own decisions blind caregivers to the true nature of what teens are asking them to provide: acceptance and nurturance for the self-defining labels they themselves choose. In the pitched battles for control that occurs between teenagers and their parents, this need for power-sharing contorts into the need for power and control over others. This change reflects the social construction of power in our competitive, hierarchical, and patriarchal society where someone is right at another's expense. Take, for example, the bickering most families experience over household chores. Time and again, it was striking to me how little importance high-risk teens actually place on having a say over housework. It was as if these youth could accept their responsibilities to their families (although they still did their chores grudgingly) if more fundamental rights are granted. In other words, their need to argue and take control of household duties is more a reflection of a lack of power-sharing by adults throughout the home than a specific example of control-seeking behaviour on the part of children. Clinically, and in parent training courses, much is made of how to get kids to do mundane tasks. Yet, the teens in this study talked more about the acute discomfort they experience inside and outside their homes when they are denied opportunities to participate in defining themselves as unique individuals. Once teens are sharing in this discursive power, other less important battles over chores are seen as inconsequential.

It was discursive disempowerment that was explained as the root cause of most of the problems these teenagers experience at home. Robert talked at length about his mother and stepfather and how little control he felt when with them: 'The only thing I can't control, I guess, is the way my parents have their attitude towards me. Right now I think they think I am a bum because I'm always getting into trouble. And I could have helped that by not getting into trouble, but now it's too late and they've already started looking down on me. You know? ... It makes me feel like dirt. It almost makes me feel that they don't care about me. I know they do but it makes me feel that they don't.' At times it seems that these teens are cast to play a part in a drama they did not choose to be in. Yet, they cannot exist separately from their families and communities, either. As Cathy said, 'It's like if you're not really part of a crowd, you're nobody.' These youth experience great emotional pain when they are told by others who they are supposed to be. This is the real issue from the perspective of problem youth. They are more than willing to concede power to their caregivers when their personal self-definitions are tolerated.

For many youth, being denied opportunities to define themselves also means being denied the basic resources that they need to sustain health. For example, Lorraine had to tolerate her mother's boyfriend being invited to the family's Christmas dinner *after* Lorraine had disclosed that she had been sexually abused by him. Although the charges could not be proven, that made no difference to Lorraine, who felt betrayed and hurt that her mother would show so little regard for her daughter's feelings. 'I was really angry,' Lorraine exclaimed. 'I don't know how she could have kept seeing him. It's disgusting.' In this case, along with the lack of a strong attachment to a parent came the stigma of being unloved and devalued.

The most common way this particular type of loss occurs is when a child is denied access to both parents following a separation. Christopher's father avoided contact with him for many years after his parents' divorce. He said, 'It felt pretty bad 'cause I couldn't see my dad. I needed a father in my life and I didn't see him.' Even when there is access, teens are seldom consulted as to when and how much time they can spend with the absent parent (Kelley, 1995). When Tammy's mother decided to move in with her new boyfriend Michael, it meant moving to a rural part of the county, 45 minutes away from where Tammy considered home. Tammy had no say whatsoever over the decision and was forced to distance herself from her natural father because of the move: 'I just found out we're moving to Michael's for sure and I don't want to live in the country. Like I need my friends, but she's the mom and she wants to be there and there's nothing out there for me. Like she never thinks about what I want ... So I said, "I want to go to a foster home," and she said, "No you won't." And she won't let me go live with my dad.' Teens respond to moments such as this when they are denied power with an array of problematic behaviours. Unfortunately, in many cases their solutions merely exacerbate their already disempowered position tainting them with more negative labels. When viewed from the dual perspective of discursive power and the search for resilience, it is striking how symptoms that are identified in high-risk youths' clinical records seem to mirror the precipitating experiences of disempowerment in their lives. Tammy lost power over her body during a sexual assault, then loss control over her time spent with parents. Her ensuing anorexia allowed her to exert her personal agency in opposition to the will of her caregivers. Although her behaviour appeared to cause her to lose more control through the threat of forced treatment, from Tammy's perspective, she had gained the upper hand.

This example bears out an interesting pattern among the youth in this study. While both boys and girls experienced the same disempowerment, their acts of resistance leading to discursive empowerment were typically gender specific. More girls threatened suicide, became anorexic, or talked of their sexual behaviour as an expression of personal agency; more boys chose socially unacceptable ways to cope with their powerlessness, finding power through delinquent, violent, and risk-taking behaviours. However, this pattern was not universal. It is interesting that Moffitt and her colleagues (2001) speculate that girls in the peri-pubertal period around ages 14 and 15 are more likely to affiliate with older males who may reinforce their criminal capacity. These relationships may be chosen by girls who go through puberty, especially early puberty, because they feel more comfortable and more mature among an older peer group.

To understand high-risk teens, whether boys or girls, one must also understand how they cope with painful experiences of helplessness. High-risk teens appreciate some limits on their behaviour, especially when they maintain a feeling that they have voluntarily subjected themselves to external controls. There were many examples in this research of this willingness to subject one's self to another's authority without threat to one's own power. Accepting voluntarily to abide by another's rules gives a teenager space to grow, avoiding the unpleasant feelings of being overwhelmed and hurried in their growth. Decisions that teens want to make, whether they are conscious of these desires or not, always remain within the teens' power because the choice to submit to another's will is perceived as being within their control. When caregivers take appropriate amounts of responsibility for a child, the child is presented with opportunities to experience competence in the assigned tasks he or she is told to carry out as a member of that family, group, or institution: 'It's just good to have someone show they love you. Like someone cares about you. That's different than taking control,' Lorraine explained. Pam talked about one of her teachers in the same way: 'She'd give me crap for showing up late and goofing off and not doing my work. She didn't even give me a very good mark, but I still liked her. I have respect for people who stand up to me. People who I can't boss around ... I don't have respect for my mom.' This need for control is evident in a clinical case note found in Pam's file: 'Pam appears able to manage with fair and consistent controls in place, but if community support is withdrawn or her mother becomes more ill or impaired, Pam lacks the inner resources to maintain acceptable and age-appropriate behaviour.'

One can hardly blame Pam for this lack of internal or external control. Poverty, abuse, divorce, and a lack of community supports all contribute to creating a difficult environment for her to grow in. Kathy Weingarten (1998) has offered a similar challenge to our shallow understanding of parenting. Although principally concerned with mothering, her work in this regard rings true for fathers as well (Osherson, 1992; Oglesby-Pitts, 2000; Updegraff et al., 2002). Our discourse concerning parenting insists that adolescents be left alone, that parents not thwart their independence, and that caregivers can be a threat to a young adult's development. This has left parents uneasy and lamentably detached from their teens, mourning for more contact but admonished from reaching out. Research on parental monitoring, not unlike the qualitative work done here, demonstrates empirically that teens want and need help with self-control (Dishion 2000; Dishion & McMahon, 1998; Lonczak et al., 2002; Stanton-Salazar & Spina, 2000; Stouthamer-Loeber et al., 2002; Weingarten, 1998). Teens want a parent to get involved in their lives, but not to dominate the child's own choices. Even a young man like Tommy, whom I introduced in Chapter 3, whose reference group was his delinquent peers, wanted a parent to take the time to notice him and offer some instrumental support and guidance.

Fifteen-year-old Laura-lee articulated this pattern well. Her mother was jailed for assaulting her in full view of neighbours on a city street. When asked by social workers and police about the incident, Laura-lee willingly described what had happened. Incredibly, given this history, Laura-lee talked about what it was like for her to have too much control in her life:

LAURA-LEE: I just wanted to be able to do whatever I wanted.
INTERVIEWER: Being able to do that, how does it make you feel?
LAURA-LEE: Like I have power over myself. Like my mom's not controlling me. It makes me feel almost like an adult. Like responsible, it's not responsible, but in a way responsible for myself.
INTERVIEWER: Do you want that much control over your life?
LAURA-LEE: Well, *not really*. Having total control gets me in trouble, like with the police, with my dad, with the family. Because a lot of the stuff I do is illegal, like drinking ... It doesn't have to end up like that. It's just that it's exciting.
INTERVIEWER: Are you telling me it's better to have someone have some control over you in some ways?

LAURA-LEE: Yeah. In most ways, yeah (she laughs). Like when I was doing really good was at my aunt and uncle's. And my aunt was really strict with me and my uncle was laid back and whatever. So it was basically my aunt being strict with me. I don't know, it just made me totally turn around. I'd just laugh at my mom. I didn't care what she said to me.

INTERVIEWER: When you lived at your aunt's and she took control of your life, how did you feel?

LAURA-LEE: I was mad. 'Cause I still wanted to do what I wanted to do. But after a while, I don't know. I felt better about myself when she did that. When someone has control over me there's not as much that I can do. And when the more stuff I do the more I tend to get in trouble. So when I can't do as much and I like I have to divide up my time because I only have a certain amount of time to be out, then I don't get into trouble.

INTERVIEWER: So actually giving up some control to your mom could actually make you feel better about yourself?

LAURA-LEE: Yeah (she laughs). But don't tell Mom I said that.

Numerous times during my clinical work and research, I have encountered troubled teens who describe similar positive feelings when someone they choose exercises limited control over them. They feel better about themselves because they succeed at the tasks that they are left to perform, relying on the power of others to tend to aspects of their lives with which they are unable to cope.

The challenge for caregivers is knowing when to take control, and when to leave high-risk youth in charge of their own lives. As Tanya explained: 'Basically it's always hard when someone makes a decision for you. But it depends what the decision is. If it's something easy and I know I can handle it and I know the answer and someone else makes a decision for me, then I don't like that. Like when my mom at Christmas time makes a decision for me when I'm going to go to my dad's and visit him, and I know how to make this decision, then I don't like it. I hate it. I feel hopeless. Like I can't do anything and that I can't solve anything. Then when someone solves it for me it makes me feel even worse.'

It can be confusing trying to understand high-risk youth when they can report feeling their mental health threatened when denied power, but at the same time say they feel increased power and acceptance in other instances when they choose to have caregivers exercise power over them. At the heart of this paradox is a constantly changing and complex set of attributions each teen uses. Participants in this research seemed to be assessing whether they could handle a situation, and how their anticipated success or failure would affect their feelings of competence and control. Success in this regard demands negotiation skills and opportunities to practise using them with family, friends, and community members. Conformity, submission, assertion, and anger are all used interchangeably to create the most power-enhancing experiences possible.

The Power to Control Mental Health Resources

Experience of personal and collective control over mental health resources is the second component that links the constructs of resilience and discursive empowerment. This control is dependent on the robust matrix of relationships discussed above. Control of resources refers to one's ability to access the emotional (e.g., sense of self-efficacy, self-esteem, and coping strategies), physical (e.g., housing, employment, and health care), and sociopolitical (e.g., social support, the right to vote, to participate, and to challenge) resources necessary to sustain health. This broad range of resources from the personal to the political are interwoven: any advances made in one area are both dependent on, and exert an influence over, access to others. This exercise of agency is a principal motivation in life leading to feelings of self-efficacy and a healthier sense of self.

But positive outcomes from experiences of power are complicated by personal control beliefs, perceptions of control in specific situations, and attributional styles. For example, it is generally believed an internal locus of control (Nowicki & Strickland, 1973; Rotter, 1966) is associated with a greater sense of empowerment (Zimmerman & Rappaport, 1988; Zimmerman, 1990; Zimmerman & Zahniser, 1991). The work of Philip Brickman and his colleagues (1982) showed 20 years ago that the preferred helping modality is one that encourages people to attribute the cause of a problem to others while attributing control over the solution to themselves. Although this pattern holds true in most instances, locus of control beliefs are framed by motivational and attributional factors. In other words, people's actions will depend on whether they believe they can both really change things and whether they attribute the responsibility for that change to themselves. This attributional process is as relevant for individuals as it is for communities that are involved in collective social action (Craig & Maggiotto, 1982; Davidson & Cotter, 1991; Lerner, 1986; Wallerstein, 1992).

A related and growing body of literature on learned helplessness has looked at the negative consequences of experiences of non-control. Lyn Abramson and his colleagues (1978) reformulated their learned helplessness theory in the 1970s to take into account the complicated relationship between attributions, control perceptions, and control beliefs. In their reformulated theory, Abramson et al. made the useful distinction between personal helplessness in which individuals believe the non-contingency of outcomes is a result of personal failings and universal helplessness in which people perceive the non-contingency of their actions and outcomes to be generalizable. Although internality is generally preferred in cases where people have the resources to change their environment, universal helplessness, one aspect of an external locus of control, is less damaging to people's self-esteem when there is objective non-contingency.

These patterns of control and non-control can be demonstrated in natural settings when the choices youth make in terms of risk-taking and delinquent behaviours are examined. Even when outsiders perceive a youth has pro-social options to sustain powerful self-definitions, the children themselves may experience powerlessness, if the only choice offered is opting in to the value system of adults. North American suburbs are typically places where apparently healthy youth struggle for rites of passage that resist their commodification by advertisers and their communities as passive disciples of social norms.

Those who have wrestled with these issues include Daniel Monti (1994), who spent a great deal of time looking at gang activities among youth who live just outside the inner core of a large American city. These are youth who have access to some of the resources that we typically want our children to have. Many know the value of an education and intend to go on to college or university, if they can find the money. Many live with families who have a strong work ethic and who try to do well for their children's sake. And yet, the youth Monti studied still found the power of a gang affiliation seductive. Monti recounts at length his interview with Tyrone, a member of one gang who explains, ironically, that his income from drug dealing is his way of financing his future college education. Tyrone's solution to his impoverished status reflects an odd mix of socially deviant and socially acceptable expressions of power. He is a teen seeking the American dream through deviant behaviour, empowering himself on the streets with his peers in order to escape that very same world. Monti uses Tyrone's story as an example of the complexity of gang affiliations: '"ganging" is a reasonable expression of sociability and a way to acquire a measure of security. At the same time, [Tyrone's] conversation revealed the tentative and brittle character of the social bonds developed in many gangs and the limits imposed on the personal freedom or financial security achieved through them' (1994: 17). We frequently misunderstand the expedience of a marginalized teenager's search for resilience.

When individuals experience successful environmental mastery and believe that past success predicts future positive outcomes, a sense of 'learned hopefulness' results. Marc Zimmerman coined this term in contrast to the work on learned helplessness. Zimmerman defines 'learned hopefulness' as 'the process whereby individuals learn and utilize skills that enable them to develop a sense of psychological empowerment' (1990: 73). Empowering experiences which help develop positive expectations about the future contribute to a sense of control over that future and good mental health. However, as Christopher Peterson and Albert Stunkard (1992) explain, just because one has a general belief that one can control one's environment, as in how one handles a job interview, one may still choose a set of efficacy expectations (e.g., 'Am I good enough to get the job?') and an explanatory style (e.g., 'My getting the job will depend on the mood of the interviewer more than my behaviour') which can actually contradict an overall positive orientation towards one's personal power. It should, therefore, not surprise us that some youth, despite what caregivers perceive to be abundant opportunities to succeed and control health resources, will still seek out deviant and delinquent peers. How a teen experiences more acceptable trajectories through life may not be as their caregivers hope they do.

Drifting between Discourses

In looking to antisocial peers, or any other source for non-conventional resources to sustain health, high-risk youth describe their lives as a drift towards health. Challenging negative and disempowering views of one's self within one's current discourse, as discussed above, is not the only way to construct a more desirable and health-enhancing identity. High-risk youth frequently seek out new discourses rather than stay and challenge the meaning-generating systems in which they have grown up. This movement between discourses is another aspect of the process of discursive empowerment employed by teenagers to challenge the way that others see them, and exercise a more powerful voice in the construction of their identity as a resilient high-risk youth. Drifting between discourses that support different self-constructions, rather than negotiating for power within one's current discourse, is akin to the difference between first-order and second-order change (Watzlawick et al., 1974). The availability and accessibility of different discourses is, of course, circumscribed by the barriers that block access to mental health resources such as class, race, gender, sexual orientation, physical challenges, and academic ability.

This indigenous concept of drift that emerged during this study has some qualities that are different from those typically associated with it. David Matza (1964) was the first to talk of a youth's drift into subterranean subcultures, characterizing adolescent drift as negative, downward, and lacking in personal agency. In the vernacular use of the term, *drift* is often taken to mean aimless wandering that leads to no good. However, drift does not mean undirected movement; it refers to the act of being driven or carried along by forces outside one's control. High-risk youth explain that as they drift through life they encounter both good and bad fortune. Thus, serendipity combines with personal agency and motivation to determine the experiences a young person chooses for piecing together an identity story.

In many cases, high-risk youth are like sailors on a voyage of discovery. Challenging self-definitions means putting back to sea when the identity they co-construct with the people they encounter during their travels is experienced as oppressive. Adults, however, may not always approve of the discourses that teens choose to drift towards. Tommy, the 'delinquent,' admits he chooses to be in detention because he makes a far better 'delinquent' than a mediocre 'school failure.' Such reasoning should not come as a surprise. Michael Newcomb and his colleagues (Battin-Pearson et al., 2000; Newcomb et al., 2002) have shown through their analysis of data from the Seattle Social Development Project, which is a study of 18 elementary schools in neighbourhoods with high crime levels, that among 808 students tested in Grades 5 and 12 deviance and academic competence acted as mediating factors between structural strain factors (e.g., gender, ethnicity, and socioeconomic status) and high school failure, truancy, and drop out. Rather than being a sign of vulnerability, however, Tommy's choice to leave school, although related to the factors Newcomb and his colleagues study, is for Tommy a reasonable way to access resources to sustain a more powerful identity than he can find in school.

Substance abuse and other forms of delinquency, like early school leaving, is similarly explained by some youth as other resources they use to bolster their sense of personal control. Fifteen-year-old Amanda does not become an alcoholic like her mother. Instead, she becomes involved in a different relationship to alcohol and dugs, one that brings her respect from her peers for the way she handles her consumption and for the way she looks after others when they abuse. Alcohol and drugs became a resource through which Amanda created a sense of herself as powerful, but in ways unique to her. In another expression of control over available resources, 15-year-old David spends most of his time on the street and is suspected by his parents, teachers, and the police of being a thief. However, he talked at length about how he purposefully stays out of trouble and has in the past refused to help his friends break into the homes of people he knows. Like his peers, David takes advantage of opportunities to define intersubjectively a new and more powerful identity for himself by drifting into association with problem peers and accessing lifestyles through which he learns about himself. While adults frequently may wonder why youth do not chose more acceptable options, it demands a lengthy and rigorous investigation of youth's lived experience to engage them in an account of their lives that makes sense both to them and their caregivers (see Brown, 1998; Ensign & Gittelsohn, 1998; Ladner, 1971; Lightfoot, 1992; Taylor et al., 1995; Totten, 2000; Whyte, 1955).

Among the stories told by high-risk youth are to be found two different concepts of drift: (1) accidental, as when a family moves or a child otherwise encounters new resources; and (2) purposeful, typified by decisions that the child makes such as adopting a new group of friends or other significant changes in the structure of his or her relationships. In both cases, however, high-risk teens emphasize the process of the drift more than the specifics of where they arrive. Any change in circumstances, negative or positive, has the potential to offer a new, more powerful self-construction. This randomness of events became a key factor in understanding why some teens apparently succeed in more socially acceptable ways, while others appear to slip into problematic behaviours. Melissa's discomfort with traditional female roles, combined with her interest in mechanics, and the availability of an automotive course open to both boys and girls at her school, led her into a very successful redefinition of herself as the brightest student in her class, beating out all the boys in the course for the top mark. The randomness of circumstance opens doors to opportunity.

Even more important for sustaining resilience, however, was the ability of teens to purposefully drift to labels of their own choosing. While these labels appeared at random in each participant's life story, teens would, when possible, select those self-constructions that best served their need for a powerful identity. Paradoxically, some teens talked about enchanted latency years during which time they were good students and very likeable. The teens' drift into troubling behaviours was explained as their attempts to free themselves from the shackles of conformity and powerlessness that these early labels forced on them. Compliance did not always support well-being, unless, as shown earlier, it was the young person's choice to tolerate another's power over him or her. For some teens, newly encountered problem identities brought with them 'excitement,' 'success,' and 'safety.' Pam moved from passivity to downright defiance in her life as she grew into her adolescence. Somehow, for her, the new story she constructed as a scrappy foul-mouthed teen worked, both on the street, and strangely, at school too: 'I don't usually want to fight actually. I never ever when I was playing sports got into a fight. But people are always talking, like they go "Pam, you're so tough," and they want to fight. Actually, sometimes I stand up and tell my class to shut up. Like sometimes when everyone is fooling around and the teacher can't do anything, I say, "Shut up or I'll beat you in the head" ... This year I get along with all my teachers.'

Different encounters in each relational sphere of their lives give high-risk youth the opportunity to develop the talents they need to construct powerful health-enhancing identities. The drift they experience is usually felt to be successful if, to the teen's mind, the result is more skill at discourse participation. To return again to David's life for an illustration, it is worth noting that he has survived on the street by impressing an older group of peers with whom he hangs out in between periods living with one or the other of his divorced parents: 'If I'm hanging around with my older friends it takes some skill to know what to say and what not to say ... Like when I talk to them I can't say hardly anything wrong or else, because, like they won't beat me up. But talking to them makes it easier for me to talk to my friends [my own age]. Talking with them I realize how far I can go. Being with my older friends helps a bit with adults, but I don't like to talk to adults very much.'

Teens who drift like this are well positioned to acquire the skills necessary to competently negotiate an identity privileged in more than one sphere of their lives. A similar pattern has been found by researchers who are interested in the transfer of pathological behaviour, especially between home and school environments. Work by Elizabeth Stormshak and Carolyn Webster-Stratton (1999) has shown that children as young as ages 4 to 7 years follow a predictable pattern of development in their behaviour. A sample of 75 boys and 26 girls, all clients of a parenting clinic at the University of Washington, were examined to understand their relationships with peers and parents and their behaviour both at home and at school: 'In early childhood, some of the behaviour problems that children have at home appear in the context of peer relationships before they generalize to school. Peers at this age may serve an important developmental function in providing the relationship context for the transfer of behavior problems from home to school. That is, as behavior problems develop in the context of parent–child relationships, children learn these patterns of interaction and begin using them in their other close relationships' (1995: 311).

While the teens in this study demonstrated less determined patterns in the transfer of behaviour from one setting to the next, it is important to note that they too used their peer groups as a place to develop the skills needed to privilege an individual and collective identity of their own choosing. Seen from outside the peer group, it can appear to parents and other caregivers (including educators) that the peer group exerts a corrupting influence (peer pressure) when, in fact, youth themselves say that peer groups offer them a forum in which to practice behaviours that they view as health-enhancing. Success in one forum supports the transfer of behaviours (and identities) from one forum to another. Thus, teens will try to bring home new behaviours and associated self-constructions in contrast to the children in Stormshak and Webster-Stratton's study, who did much the same but in the reverse direction.

Illustrative of this pattern, 16-year-old Leslie, despite numerous problems in her life and her parents' frustration with her defiant attitude and reckless sexual behaviour, had held a job at a fast food restaurant for more than two years. The sense of personal responsibility that she maintained through her work was key to her mental health. Armed with this view of herself, she said that she was much better equipped to challenge her parents, who wanted her to be responsible at home so that she could assume many of the responsibilities of her mother who had recently returned to paid employment outside the home. To cope with the pressure to assume this role as parent, Leslie confidently played at being the irresponsible child when at home without ever threatening her self-construction as the responsible young woman she had so convincingly proven herself to be in her role as an employee. Clinical work to resolve this pattern focused on inviting Leslie's construction of herself as responsible into the family home, something she was willing to do when she stopped feeling threatened that she would be exploited if she acted responsibly.

Power and the Peer Group

Of all the forums in which teens experiment with constructing an identity as resilient, their peer groups figure most prominently. Peer groups offer teens a place where they have more say over labels and greater opportunities to explore personal competencies through personal relationships. Peer groups are particularly important as forums in which to assert both an individual and collective identity. Far from problematic, peer groups offer teens the chance to exercise both agentive and communal aspects of discursive power. They borrow from their peer groups each group's identity status to bolster threatened individual self-constructions. When viewed from the perspective of high-risk youth, interaction with peers is health-enhancing. Peer pressure is a myth that adults use to explain the troubling behaviours of youth, but it does not reflect the grounded experience of high-risk teens. Power is a commodity that teens share between them through peer relationships, maximizing their limited access to personal and social empowerment through collective action. This understanding of power is similar to that of Foucault's (1982, 1994/1977) description of power as 'capillary,' infused throughout the group and evident in its contribution to and internalization of, discursively based rules.

Typical of this study's participants, 14-year-old Jessica emphasized the tolerance that peers show towards each other in their constructions of unique and powerful self-definitions:

JESSICA: I'm my own unique person and nobody is like me and nobody will ever be just like me. I don't like it when people are the same. People should have their own identity and know who they are ... I don't let nobody see me as something that I'm not. Like somebody could call you a slut and you're not at all like that. Like people are like that in my school. I've been called a slut, but I'm definitely not a slut. They just say those things 'cause they've got nothing better to say ... I'd just rather get along with people and have nobody be higher than another person 'cause that's not right.

INTERVIEWER: Is it important you find other people who think like you?

JESSICA: Yeah, 'cause then you know if you say something they're not gonna find it offensive. I tell my friends what I like about how they act, and they tell me the same thing. But they don't take it as criticizing. It's better that way. They're just trying to help you. They're not trying to put you down for who you are ... I just stay with my friends who like me and believe in the way I do things and don't believe in what everyone else says. I usually ignore when other people try to change me 'cause I like the way I am now.

Jessica argues that her individuality is not compromised by her relationships with her peers, although her parents and community are convinced otherwise. Teens like Jessica insist that they choose who they associate with and how they behave when with peers on the basis of which relationships and behaviours enhance their sense of self.

Clothing is frequently used as an outward symbol of how a child constructs his or her identity among peers. Negotiation for the power to have one's personal style accepted helps teens practice the skills necessary to negotiate other aspects of their self-constructions that they perceive as health-enhancing. Pam offers an interesting case study of these skills under development. Even though she is a leader in her community of troubled teens, and is appearing to conform to all the standards of her peer group in dress and behaviour, Pam emphasizes how much she differs from her peers: 'Everybody knows this about me, that I dress for me. Nobody else. Like one day, I'll be wearing docs [a high-cut leather boot], then the next day I'll be wearing these [she points to high cut army boots]. *That's a big change.* Like one day I'll wear nice preppy clothes, then the next I'll wear big huge jeans that fall off my butt. Like if I think a big long skirt is neat, and if my friends don't like it I'll say, "Don't look at it then."' What observers mistake for hegemony is, in fact, a mosaic of subtle differences in personal expression.

Teens use their peer groups to practise the skills that they need to individuate themselves from social norms. Kevin, a 15-year-old delinquent, sees himself as different from other delinquents because, as he says, 'I always help my friends out when they have problems and I give good advice.' And Stephanie, age 16, who has problems with truancy and violence, just like others in her peer group, insists that she is different from her closest friends because she does not drink and does not want to be an alcoholic like her mother or her aunts and uncles. Apparent conformity hides the more important power that teens experience within their peer groups in defining themselves as different. This same dynamic search for power is discernible in children's relationships with their families and communities.

The Power to Experience Competence

The third component of power that influences mental health is the power to explore and manipulate mental health resources. From these experiences, we derive competence, our capacity to interact effectively with the environment. Robert White (1959) was the first to show that competence was the result of our motivation to make changes to our environment through exploration, activity, and manipulation. He believed our motivation to experience competence comes from our need for sensory and motor stimulation that is manifested as an endless search for 'differences-in-sameness' in our interactions with our environment. White added that this search for competence is related to our desire for feelings of self-efficacy. As such, competence and self-efficacy are inextricably linked with experiences of competence resulting in 'mastery, power, or control' (1959: 320).

Control experiences allow us to change our environment to better suit our needs: competence is related to the power to exploit the environment that we control. This power to exploit resources is different from the power to control the availability of those resources. In other words, access to a good education is important as a control experience, but in and of itself does not guarantee feelings of competence as a student. For example, an adolescent in an apprenticeship program will have the power to explore many latent talents by making good use of his or her placement. Being competent at a trade can also make the young person feel a personal sense of control over the materials of production (e.g., wood, steel, or information) and over his or her relationships with others at the workplace. But competence in technical and social skills learned during an apprenticeship seldom leads to increased control over the structure of the apprenticeship program itself or over the occupation into which the young person enters. High-risk teens argue that they need to experience both levels of competence, the personal and political, to sustain self-definitions as resilient. They not only need skills that make them employable, but also the support of institutions to provide educational experiences that respect their indigenous knowledges and tailor programs to their informal lifestyles.

Most often, our dominant discourse on mental health, of which competence is one well-studied component, places little or no emphasis on the differential impact that relative personal, social, and political power have on an individual's state of well-being. The nexus of responsibility for disorder and health is typically located within the individual, or some medical condition beyond the individual's control, but still within the individual's sphere of influence. This social discourse results in our implicit (and at times explicit) blame of the victim for his or her state of poor mental health (Ryan, 1976). Development of competencies, according to high-risk youth, takes place in a highly charged political context in which they are frequently denied access to health resources and opportunities to assert publicly their paths to well-being.

These youth explain their interaction with peers, as well as their families and communities, as forums in which they hone the competencies required to construct a positive identity and access the experiences and resources necessary to acquire and maintain such an identity, while also offering an effective challenge to the degrading and stigmatizing labels that attach to them. Youth talk of three distinct approaches to these tasks, with each dependent on the resources available: staying stuck, playing the chameleon, and assuming acceptance. All three depend on varying degrees of competence in exercising power in social discourse. Although these approaches are presented as distinct for purposes of illustration, teens move back and forth between them as they cope with the multiple risks present in their lives.

Staying Stuck

This first approach is used when high-risk teens feel they are stuck with one self-definition. Although youth say they exercise some choice in their selection of this singular identity, they acknowledge that they become stuck when they have few alternatives from which to choose. The one self-definition chosen usually demands vigorous maintenance in every sphere of the child's life. These are typically the repeat offenders whose talent is getting into trouble, the suicidal youth who has few other coping strategies, and the children who sacrifice their needs for the needs of others.

In and out of custody, a youth like Tommy explained that he copes with his lack of options for a healthy identity by presenting a singular persona of the tough kid who stands up to every challenge when among his peers, family, or out in his community. Those around Tommy accept him in this one way and reflect back to him his status as a long-time troublemaker. Not surprisingly, even when Tommy tries to be something other than a delinquent he remains stuck with this one self-definition. He gave the example of how he uses bullying tactics with other youth in an attempt to act in pro-social ways. In one poignant account, he explained, 'There are small kids in jail and the bigger guys will end up starting a fight with them and I'll be like, "If you touch him I'm going to kick your face in."' Unable to construct an alternate self-definition, Tommy turns the label of delinquent to his advantage in all spheres of his life.

Playing the Chameleon

The second approach teens use to experience the competence that underlies healthy self-constructions is to become chameleons. Some high-risk teens adopt the labels made available to them by different groups with whom they interact. These youth are the ones who do fine in school but are violent to themselves or others when at home, or they act confident when in leadership positions but surprise us with their lack of self-esteem.

Chameleons take advantage of the serendipitous discovery of their different talents experienced during encounters with others. From these experiences come new self-constructions that are maintained through participation in alternative discourses. The life histories of this study's participants show how chance encounters with new groups of peers and adults, although circumscribed by the socioeconomic forces present in their young lives, offer opportunities to construct new identities. In their search for acceptance, chameleons knowingly share their power of self-definition with others by conforming with superficial standards in dress and behaviour. Conformity brings a modicum of acceptance within the social group and allows a vulnerable youth to borrow a group's identity to appear more powerful than he or she feels when alone. By adopting strong group identities like punk, prep, rocker, or alternative, the chameleon gains status among peers, family, and in his or her community.

Tanya's behaviour typifies the chameleonlike coping strategies of many high-risk youth. Tanya is a pleasant young woman, plain in her features and not very popular with her peers. She and her 4-year-old brother, Brian, live with their mother, Samantha. Tanya sees her father, Grant, every second weekend. When I met Tanya, her parents had been divorced for three years. At first Tanya and Brian lived with their father because of their mother's emotional instability. She was under psychiatric care for 18 months. During that time, Tanya took over Samantha's role with regard to her younger brother and acted 'as a wife' for her father. She was responsible for all the housework while also attending school full-time.

Tanya has done well in school and has become involved in the local politics of her low-income housing project. She was very proud of her recent appointment to the board of the recreation centre. She makes a good impression on adults, although she has only a few close friends her own age. Tanya tries desperately to fit in with her peers by adopting the mannerisms of different groups, but she is seldom accepted by them as much as she is by adults. Tanya has once been caught for shoplifting, having stolen a few cosmetics that she says her family could not afford.

Tanya's ability to fit in with adults and her constant efforts to make new friends with peers helps her to avoid feelings of alienation and depression. She has created a large network of relationships that sustain many different identities, although she asserts little influence, especially with her peers, over the labels she is given in each setting. Tanya explained: 'I change, when I'm in a particular environment. How I'm talking here is not how I talk anywhere else. I'm a totally different person here than I am with my mom or my dad. I'm never the totally same person in every spot. I don't want people to know me totally, just a little bit about me. Feels better that way ... I want to change everything. I want to be different, totally different. And I will be different.' This lack of consistency is not simply a function of her age or the moratorium associated with a teenager's search for identity. Tanya changes who she is with each group of peers and adults that she encounters because she lacks influence over how the labels given to her are constructed. She would like to say, 'This is who I am,' but she does not have the skills necessary to participate equitably in the discourses that define her. Therefore, she purposefully moves between discourses, discovering new labels. Playing the chameleon helps teens like Tanya learn and practise the social skills they need to eventually negotiate a self-definition of their own choosing.

What, then, breaks this pattern of constant change evidenced by chameleons? Teens in this study say that they become less willing to fit in everywhere when they have sufficient resources of personal and social power to assert an identity that differs in some respect from the dominant discourse in which they participate. These moments of divergence occur when the teen's personal moral limit is transgressed by his or her peer group, family, or community. Instead of simply changing with whom he or she associates, the teen has by this point the skills needed to challenge what others are doing and offer an alternative meaning to the behaviour under consideration. For example, David's chaotic life included bouncing back and forth between a verbally abusive and alcoholic father and a battered and depressed mother, neither of whom could control him. His moral limit was reached when he learned that some of his peer group were planning to burglarize the home of one of David's closest friends: 'I don't want to live with myself breaking into my friend's house stealing everything and then having to confront him a few days later ... If I decide not to do what everybody else is doing sometimes I'll feel good, but sometimes I'll feel like I regret not doing it. Most of the time, like if it's drugs or something like that I'll just completely walk away from it all. I guess it's all how much you feel.' As the chameleon, David had appreciated the escape that his peer group offered him from the degrading labels he had experienced at home. His individuation from his peer group is not a separation from his peers, but a more equitable sharing with them in the way the group defines its world and invokes its tolerance for difference.

Assuming Acceptance

The third approach that high-risk youth use to experience competence and develop the skills to construct healthy identities is to assume that they are accepted by others and assert an identity construction that is indicative of a cohesive sense of self (see Antonovsky, 1987). Typically these are youth who say they have the control and competence necessary to construct self-definitions of their own choosing that are accepted by peers, family, and their community at large. For them, members of their community provide a pathway to wellness even under extreme conditions of adversity (see Cadell et al., 2001). These are children most often seen as resilient self-assured individuals. They steadfastly proclaim to the world, 'This is who I am. Accept me.' They use the peer group, their family, and their community to assert unique aspects of their identity. However, while some of these youth fit the stereotype of the healthy child who is gifted at sports or in school, many others act out socially. For example, as has been shown, some delinquents show an incredible ability to survive and thrive by getting themselves placed in jail, some victims of physical and sexual abuse run away from home in order to cope with their abuse, and some teens whose parents have significant problems act up until attention gets focused on the larger issues confronting their families.

Once well rehearsed in the skills necessary for discourse participation and identity formation, youth are ready to take advantage of opportunities to share in the construction of one or more chosen identities. For example, watching a friend cope with a pregnancy made 15-year-old Melissa both more cautious and assertive about the choices she is making concerning the expression of her sexuality:

MELISSA: It's like if you're sexually active you have to worry about getting pregnant and getting diseases. Like my friend is now 4 months pregnant. I guess everyone just goes with what you agree with and do what you wanna do. If you wanna be safe, be safe. But a lot of people I know don't bother with it, which I think is real stupid. It doesn't make sense.

INTERVIEWER: How do you cope with boys and pressures around sex?

MELISSA: I don't know. I went out with my boyfriend for a year and a half. We just broke up a few weeks ago. So I knew him. I don't do anything with just anyone, like I knew him for a long time before we did anything. It was easier that way. It was my decision. Anything he didn't want to do he told me and anything I didn't want to do I told him. That was good ... We definitely used protection. It was my decision. You just hear about everything going on now and it's not something I could deal with happening to me right now so it was the best decision I can make right now. It's weird, 'cause everyone thinks you shouldn't be thinking about that, especially adults.

Teens like Melissa relish these opportunities to make their own decisions that demonstrate personal competencies and maturity. Through this exercise of their power they explain that they gain a sense of personal worth that contributes to a more positive self-definition. Consequently, experiences of powerlessness affect these youth profoundly.

Other participants showed this same capacity to exercise control over the labels placed upon them. Johnny, a former addict, organized a Narcotics Anonymous group in his community for youth. Previously in custody, he had used that time to get himself cleaned up, creating a new identity for himself as a reformed drug addict. Troy, meanwhile, talked about how he had confronted his abusive father about the emotional and physical abuse he suffered as a child, saying that he was tired of living with the pain and depression that came with being identifying as an abused child. At the same time Troy changed peer groups, nurturing friendships with boys he had known years earlier, before the onset of his depressive symptoms. Beth is an ecologically minded young woman with a passion for social justice. The self-esteem she gains from participation in these social causes gives her the strength to support and encourage her friends to deal with their problems, just as she dealt with the chaos in her own home. These are just a few of the paths that high-risk youth follow as they construct identities that bring them feelings of competence leading to acceptance and discursive power.

Constructing Alternative Discourses

As they try each of these three approaches to developing the personal and social competencies necessary to participate equitably in social discourse and the resulting co-constructions of themselves as healthy, youth seek to establish alternative discourses that support a view of themselves as resilient under stress. Teens say they both actively and passively engage in behaviours that resist pathologizing discourses and promote salutogenic ones. Therapists who think along similar discursive lines have demonstrated that even problem behaviours lead to innovative and effective solutions when resources to sustain health are scarce. Alan Jenkins (1993) uses a technique based on the work of Michael White (1988, 1995) to help families change the way they view their teenagers. To help a child move from the label of 'delinquent' to 'responsible young person,' Jenkins recommends purposefully leaving money around the home where theft has been a problem. When the child is counselled not to take the money, the family's story about the child is challenged (see Chapter 7 for a fuller discussion of clinical interventions). In a similar way, high-risk teens are constantly engaged in efforts to control the labels that are placed on them. Jenkins's example shows a passive approach to recreating a label: the teen simply stops doing what he or she was doing before. High-risk youth say that they employ both passive and active strategies to achieve these same ends.

Most significantly, when verbal challenges are unable to change labels, high-risk teens frequently resort to violence. Seen in this context, youth violence becomes far more intelligible. When Margie was called a 'slut' because she dated an older boy, she responded first with words and then with physical force: 'I beat up a lot of girls that said it to my face.' For Tommy, a large intimidating-looking youth, using violence or the threat of violence was the only personal resource he had to challenge how others saw him. His walking up to people on the street who, he feels, look at him oddly, and confronting them, brings him a sense of personal control, even while it limits his experience of social acceptance. Teens like this intuitively know they pay a price for the strategies they employ to maintain a singular and powerful identity. Consequently, they prefer to seek out other ways to achieve the same discursive power when resources are available. For example, Melissa enrolled in a vocational automotive program. No longer the below average kid from a dysfunctional family, she was able to show others a unique competence that had the added benefit of challenging gender norms. Equally effective was Leslie's experience of holding down long-term employment. Eventually, her peers, parents, and community had to admit that she was both a responsible young women and independent. As she put it, 'Though my family doesn't have much money, I'm not a charity case.'

Once a dominant discourse is successfully challenged, however, the next task is to construct a new alternative discourse. An episode that occurred between 16-year-old Robert and his stepfather Martin illustrates the unique way that these constructions take place. Robert and

Martin had been arguing for years. Fed up with the constant fighting, both verbal and physical, Martin seized on the idea suggested by a counsellor that he and Robert do something together to build their own relationship apart from Robert's mother. The two decided that the most effective way to challenge Martin's view of his stepson as 'nothing but a kid who doesn't deserve respect' was for them both to go to a bar and get drunk. Although a unique solution that was not quite what was prescribed, this time together gave Martin and Robert an opportunity to change their relationship from hierarchical to more egalitarian:

INTERVIEWER: When you both went out and got drunk, what did it change?
ROBERT: Well, I noticed we could relate to each other but I guess we were getting along better. We could communicate better. We could basically talk about anything. Usually if I tell him something he puts me down, but that changed. And I don't put him down usually, either.

Robert found this episode an opportunity to spend time with his stepfather in a role that contributed to an adultlike identity for himself. Robert was quite clear that he could see this new identity growing, although it should also be noted that, at times, he was hesitant to be an adult because of the responsibilities that came with that self-definition. He explained: 'I see myself as someone who is trying to prepare himself as an adult, to be an adult. I guess I want to be an adult, but I want to enjoy my adolescence at the same time. Like I'm kind of mixed up between the two.' The more Robert felt accepted in his new role, the more it helped decrease the tensions at home. Evidently, the specifics of the solution Robert and Martin found are a problem for a society that does not condone fathers taking their underaged sons to bars to get drunk. It is, nonetheless, one way that Robert addresses the maturity gap that Moffitt (1993, 1997) identifies as contributing to pathways into delinquency. Ironically, a delinquent act with an adult may mitigate Robert's need for association with more persistently delinquent peers. Teens like Robert move towards a state of well-being by engaging in never-ending challenges to the dominant discourses that define them. Constructing alternative self-definitions means teens must make the best use possible of the structural locations (Sampson &

Laub, 1997) in which they find themselves and the associated health resources available to challenge the oppressive stories that skew their development.

John's interaction with his mother exhibits similar elements of this battle for control over one's identity story, but succeeds in ways quite different from that of Robert and his stepfather. What might sound like disrespect to the reader was 13-year-old John's attempt to find what little power he could in a very dangerous and disempowering home: '[My mom] thinks I'm a bad kid. She uses other words but I can't use it right now. I don't really care. Like she's not any better than I am, at least the way I think anyways.' Because therapists, teachers, and other adults tend to hear the voices of adults over those of teens, teenagers like John sometimes find themselves in therapy when it perhaps should be their parents in therapy. The therapist working with John, whose mother Pat had instructed to 'fix' her son, found that, in fact, it was John's resilience that was exacerbating his mother. John no longer submitted to her violent attacks and now either ran away or yelled back at her the same 'foul-mouthed' things that she said to him. Pat experienced this as a personal loss of control over the boy and was certain that John's lack of respect was *his* problem and that she had played no part in making John behave as he did.

No matter how these alternative self-definitions were manifested, they relied on a matrix of others to sustain them. For John, this meant teachers, coaches, and friends who knew him as something other than as a bad kid. High-risk youth like John say they value most experiences that share power with others rather than experiences that bring power at another's expense. This may surprise adults who believe that teens want to dominate and exploit any power they are given. Instead, toleration of others and mutuality in relationships are seen by teens as signs of maturity and are characteristics related to feelings of well-being.

Individual teens share their power with others as they themselves share in the power of the groups to which they belong. Developmentally, this power-sharing allows them to access the discursive and other health resources that they require to establish resilient identities. As has been shown, high-risk teens take three approaches to negotiating favourable self-constructions. Teens with few resources tend to remain stuck with singular self-definitions; more adept youth become chameleons, moving between discourses but exercising little control over the identities constructed in each. A moral crisis is usually explained as the catalyst whereby chameleons change and assert a more individual identity. As a consequence of such turning points, and when resources are plentiful, teens may adopt a third approach, that being to assert their self-constructions as resilient in a number of different social spheres. These strategies take place through group interaction and ensure that youth labelled 'vulnerable' acquire and maintain healthy identities while successfully challenging the negative labels others place on them.

Summary

This chapter has explored the link between experiences of power and a self-construction as mentally healthy. High-risk youth overcome adversity when they successfully negotiate for a healthy identity within the social discourse that shapes their personal narratives. This link between health and power has been explored by looking at how power is manifested in the lives of a sample of high-risk youth. These youth argue that they understand themselves as resilient and creatively pursue activities and relationships that sustain this self-construction, by drifting either purposefully or haphazardly between different social groups. Each occupies distinct positions within the dominant health discourse. In this understanding of power and health power, as Foucault has demonstrated, is capillary, residing in the everyday actions of people themselves. We all play a role in defining health for one another, although Foucault has shown that over the past number of centuries, we have progressively handed over more and more of our power to medical, judicial, and political elites.

Building on this view of power, I have recounted stories from the lives of youth that demonstrate that three types of power sustain health. First, power is experienced through relationships that provide us a forum in which to acquire and maintain health-enhancing identities, while mounting a collective challenge to pathologizing discourses that emphasize weakness. Resilient youth successfully negotiate for powerful identities through their interactions with others. Second, high-risk youth say they require control of mental health resources to bolster their self-stories as healthy. They find through their drift between different peer groups, interactions with family members, and through time spent with other caregivers and in the broader community, access to health resources. Third, once they achieve this access, high-risk youth who construct an identity as resilient are those who successfully find opportunities to feel competent. In particular, youth employ a number of strategies to bolster their feelings of competence leading to health. They stay stuck with one identity and carry it everywhere they go, rigid in its application. They play chameleons, participating in any number of different discourses, adopting the identity each provides, but exercising little influence on the meaning attributed to labels. Or they assume acceptance and participate more equitably in the discourses that define their health status. Each of these three approaches contributes to an alternate understanding of who high-risk youth are and their strengths. In the next chapter, the nature of this drift towards resources and discursive power will be examined within the context of institutional placements that are common to many of the youth in this study.

Chapter Six

Constructions of Resilience in Out-of-Home Placements

In the previous chapter, the ways in which high-risk teens manoeuvre within and between discourses to sustain health-enhancing self-definitions were examined. High-risk youth construct the marginalized discourses that define them as resilient by nurturing, maintaining, and challenging identities within a single discourse, or drifting between discourses in search of empowering experiences that bring acceptance. High-risk youth say that their capacity to navigate within and between these discourses develops over time depending on the personal and social resources available to them. The complexity of these youth's pathways to resilience and the nature of their co-constructions of health-supporting labels, can be explored more thoroughly through an examination of their behaviour in one sphere of interaction. In Chapter 5, teenagers' interactions with peers, families, institutional caregivers, and their communities were examined to identify aspects of a process of discursive empowerment. This chapter will look at this same process, but in the context of institutional and community-based out-of-home placements. It will be shown that identity constructions as resilient require *continuity* in a child's discursive power across interactional spheres. Institutional and community placements are forums in which one can clearly discern how the different intersubjective spaces teens occupy compete for control of the child's self-definition. As many high-risk youth are placed in group homes, foster homes, treatment centres, and custodial facilities, these relational contexts play an important role in the construction of youth identities. Within these institutional and community care settings youth must nurture, maintain and challenge identity constructions. The strategies they employ, that can so beguile their caregivers, are indications of where these youth are developmentally in their capacity for discursive participation.

These constructive efforts resist the problem-saturated identities imposed upon them while they are residents/clients/wards/patients. That this is the case should not surprise us. Irving Goffman (1961) found that much of the behaviour of psychiatric patients is intelligible and reflects the norms socially constructed by the patients and staff of the institutions in which they reside. Many of Goffman's observations are still useful today for understanding how power is expressed by patients attempting to maintain a semblance of mental well-being: 'From the patient's point of view, to decline to exchange a word with the staff or with his fellow patients may be ample evidence of rejecting the institution's view of what and who he is; yet higher management may construe this alienative expression as just the sort of symptomatology the institution was established to deal with and as the best kind of evidence that the patient properly belongs where he now finds himself' (1961: 306). That the behaviour of the patient functions to maintain a sense of discursive power is evidence of a healthy response to a disempowering situation.

Case Study: Allison, Not Katie

Allison, the abused young woman introduced in Chapter 1, who insisted on choosing her own foster placement, was first placed in foster care at age nine and shortly thereafter made a permanent ward of the court. Looking back over her life, Allison explained the role of those around her in creating and sustaining a personal self-definition that either threatened or supported her mental health: 'If you're living with people who are putting you down all the time and don't give a crap about you then it's going to be hard for you to keep yourself happy 'cause you won't feel good about yourself 'cause other people don't feel good about you. You can try, I know other people do, like they say I like myself and I don't care what you think, but inside I think they really do care. I don't think you can do it by yourself.' She eventually found the supports she needed. However, when first placed, she proved too much to handle and by age 11 she was being transferred from one group home to another every few months.

Even then, Allison knew that her mental health needed a sustaining community of concern to help her celebrate her many strengths. These strengths, on which youth like Allison pride themselves, are often the same characteristics treatment providers seek to extinguish: mouthiness, defiance, a 'bad' attitude, sexual promiscuity, emotional dependency, addictions, self-injurious behaviours, and various forms of risk-taking.

While certainly problematic, these behaviours were reflective of Allison's determination to remain in control of her life when she so evidently had been denied that control. As she explained, there were few other choices available to her for construction of a powerful identity once she was removed from her abusive family.

Allison didn't find sufficient affirmation inside the group homes to undo the harm of placement. Instead, she found an identity as a troubled 'group home kid' that only served to further stigmatize her. Her being made a ward placed her in association with a narrow range of people whose health-enhancing behaviours included exploiting their roles as problem youth. Allison's first survival strategy after being placed was to accept the mirroring of her group-home peers to bolster her self-concept. With time, however, she became disenchanted with their problem-saturated lives. She broke free after meeting her friend Becky, whose family she later adopted as her own: 'Before I was well "I guess this is who I have to hang out with," but then I felt better about myself and I thought "No, I don't have to take this any more. I don't have to be friends with these people. I can grow and find someone new and still be friends with the others on the side." So if you don't feel good about yourself you're gonna be like they probably won't like me so why should I try. I've come a long way! I'm not just another group home kid. I'm Allison!' Allison had, developmentally, mastered being stuck with the singular self-definition of the group home kid. Growth meant learning to successfully navigate back and forth between the different groups of youth who helped her construct multiple identities. Allison said it was difficult to get the social workers and group home staff to accept her choice of home, and even more difficult to get them to have that choice approved given the problems Becky and her mother had experienced before Becky's mother divorced her abusive drug-addicted husband. Typical of high-risk resilient youth, Allison showed that as social skills are developed, there is more purposeful drift towards associations which support self-constructions as resilient.

Allison went so far as to change her name from Katie, to her middle name, Allison, as a way of asserting control over her identity. In the foster placement with Becky and her mother, Allison adopted her new name as a symbol of her newfound sense of control:

I can act how I want to now. I can act according to how I want to act, not how people want me to act. Like before I had to like act this way, and with my mom I had to be on my best behaviour. And I felt people would stare at you. But now I feel that I can tell a joke and don't have to worry about it. And with my friends I don't have to act a certain way to be accepted. And now I can act how I want to. I wanted to be accepted by them so I could be one of the cool people. Now if people don't like me for who I am, it's their loss, not mine ... It feels good to not worry if they're going to accept me whether I dress like them or not or if I have different hair than they do, or if I wear the right kind of makeup. Feels good, feels real good.

While Allison's association with other problem youth inside placement was defined by her as a threat to her well-being, youth in other placement settings, like Mark, also introduced in Chapter 1, report finding support for a more powerful identity among the treatment resistant kids they meet. Still other youth report finding in placement adults who offer them opportunities to co-construct powerful identities. When adults share their power and act to bolster weak identity constructions, they offer youth in their care an opportunity to share in the discursive power of caregivers, just as youth in care share among themselves the power of resistance in order to sustain a positive image of themselves. Chapters 7 and 8 will discuss how informal and formal caregivers can integrate this understanding of resilience into their practice with high-risk youth.

Institutionalized Youth

The identity constructions of youth who are living outside their homes, but institutionalized, are complex but explained by them in terms of power and control. The fact of their institutionalization is a factor in how they behave and the resources they encounter to support or deny their constructions of health. There have been few studies with institutionalized adolescents that have examined the meaning of their problem behaviours. Such is not the case in the movies. The recent Wynonna Ryder film *Girl Interrupted*, based on the book by Susanna Kaysen (1994), took a very intimate look at what 'crazy' behaviour means for young women who are placed inside treatment facilities. A less popular film, but one far more brutal in its portrayal is *Little Criminals*, a National Film Board of Canada production that examined the life of an eleven-year-old street kid both inside and outside treatment facilities. Both films show the intelligibility of the behaviours of troubled youth when confronted with the powerlessness of their placement.

There is little empirical work that has taken a serious look at the iatrogenic effect institutionalized placement and contact with social services agencies have had on the negative identity constructions of high-risk youth. This postmodern understanding of mental health as a social construction has remained theoretically sound, but poorly authenticated in the lives of those it seeks to explain. We seldom investigate the experiences of youth within the service delivery systems designed to meet their needs.

A number of studies, however, have provided indirect support for this constructionist position. Hutchison, Tess, Gleckman, and Spence found that there are more similarities than differences between clinical and nonclinical groups of at-risk youth. Their study of 187 institutionalized youth 'wished to determine if, indeed, the adolescents who comprised the sample were as psychologically at risk as might be surmised given their current placement situation' (1992: 345). The youth, who were all institutionalized in an Indiana state facility, presented with a range of emotional and affective disorders. Many had histories of abuse and neglect while others carried significant co-morbid conditions such as diabetes and cystic fibrosis. Based on results from the Adolescent Health Inventory and the Beck Depression Inventory, the authors found many similarities between their sample and adolescents in general. More than half of the youth studied had working fathers, and just less than half had working mothers. As in other populations, females were more likely than males to be depressed. They also resembled the adolescent population at large with 'normal' mood fluctuations and similar levels of overall life satisfaction. Of course, in other respects the sample population showed characteristics typical of other at-risk youth such as a higher than average incidence of strained relationships with peers, low self-esteem, poor self-concept, and the mistreatment of others.

Hutchison and his colleagues caution that stereotyping youth by the fact of their placement is counterproductive to good treatment or prevention work. Their findings point to the need for more research. But their work also opens the door to questions about why at-risk youth are so frequently thought of as different from their peers? Hutchison et al. urge others to examine closely the 'complicated and multifaceted causes of many at-risk behaviours and outcomes' (1992: 353).

Distinctions of who is mad, bad, or sad, and the necessity for certain institutional placements can also be thought of an issue of the fit between the individual and the classification schemes we use to categorize them. As Hilary Ryglewicz and Bert Pepper (1996) explain in their look at young people with dual disorders, this fit is crucial to puzzling together explanations for the youth's behaviour. How an individual is dealt with often has as much to do with social policy as psychology. This can be demonstrated by examining the criminalization of mental illness that occurs when state funds are transferred from mental health care beds to prisons, with a concomitant shift in the population of institutionalized individuals. These transinstitutionalized people encounter social control in prison, but little treatment. If such a redefinition is possible when politically expedient, then one might also wonder if the notion of who is and is not a patient of the mental health care system is not also fluid.

Residents and patients of these systems of care wonder as well. Studies that have examined the way adults cope with transitions between their communities and institutional life have noted the discursive dissonance that occurs as people juggle identities. The shift from the community to the hospital for people with mental illness signifies, according to Shulamit Ramon and Deborah Tallis, changes 'in personal responsibility and initiative, control over one's life, how suffering is managed and interpreted, types of support available, expectations of others and of oneself' (1997: 38). The person who has been locked away and is in the process of returning to his or her community needs to understand and foster effective strategies for re-building threatened identities. While recognizing the individual agency in such strategies, Ramon and Tallis point to the importance of the availability of community support, the relationship between individuals and their families and friends, and the relationships between service providers, as factors which affect this reintegration.

The processing of youths as young offenders subjects them to the same kinds of threats to their identity (Dodge, 2001), as it raises questions about, and alters the labels that these youth use to describe and define themselves. The placement of these youth in an institution and the disengagement from their communities reinforces this identity threat. Coping with that threat explains, in part, why young offenders choose delinquent identities when they return to their communities following their incarceration (Matsueda & Heimer, 2001). Delinquent youth select powerful and troubling roles as these are the ones most readily available to them when excluded from their communities. Clearly youth in care run the risk of developing their criminal capital (Hagan & McCarthy, 1997), becoming more skilled at delinquent activities. As Ross Matsueda and Karen Heimer explain: 'Individuals lacking qualities or skills that social roles require will be unlikely to be selected into such roles. Through the interactional process of being denied entrance into various roles, the individual is likely to adjust by externalizing failure, devaluing the role, or internalizing failure, and blaming himself [sic]. They may have no alternatives to less desirable positions, and may also develop a preference for such positions' (2001: 117). Institutions can, however, provide opportunities for youth to assert desirable social roles by facilitating and maintaining contact between the community and institutionalized young people. Strategies to accomplish this will be discussed in Chapters 7 and 8 where the focus of this work shifts to treatment.

This need for community building as part of a continuum of care has been highlighted by Gerald Smale and his colleagues (1995; Darville & Smale, 1990; Smale et al., 1988). They argue that agencies are inadequate to meet the challenge of providing for people's social welfare needs. Similarly, Ken Barter (1996; Graham & Barter, 1999) argues for collaboration between professionals and the community in order to address the root causes of the problems presented by at-risk individuals and families. These community-institution links do not just provide support to workers in the design of treatment plans. Case studies of high-risk youth show that the ongoing community responsibility for a youth who is placed in an institution offers the youth a powerful and health-enhancing identity both inside the institution and when he or she returns home. The community adds its voice to the construction of an alternative identity for the displaced young person, we hope offering the child and his or her caregivers, a way of thinking about the young person as something other than just another delinquent. A community or institution that offers a child an identity that is more health focused simultaneously offer a child recognition as healthy. Sometimes, this is all it takes to stimulate well-being: the belief of a few in the child's potential. This positive therapeutic relationship is also known as a therapeutic alliance.

Control and Placement

Contrary to what caregivers believe, youth see themselves as exercising a great deal of control (but not exclusive control) over several aspects of the placement process. They argue that they consciously influence when they get 'put inside,' the way they 'survive inside,' and the way they cope when they are 'going home' after discharge. At each phase of the placement process, high-risk youth explain their behaviour as purposeful attempts to optimize their health status and nurture and maintain discursive empowerment in ways similar to that demonstrated by Allison (see also Ramon & Tallis, 1997). Placements, like families, peer groups, and communities, become settings in which to experience power over self-constructions leading to an identity story as resilient.

Identities for survival nurtured inside institutional settings may or may not transpose themselves well when high-risk youth return home. Similarly, surviving and thriving frequently requires that identities nurtured on the street are brought with the child into placement, much to the chagrin of caregivers who had hoped to exert a 'positive influence.' Continuity in the power and acceptance accorded a particular identity between intersubjective spheres is critical to the child's healthy development. Identities nurtured and defined as healthy inside institutional settings may enjoy very little status when that child is moved back, or in cases when discharge planning is poor, drifts back to his or her community. The institution must understand its role as an extension of the community, rather than the community as an extension of the institution (Ungar et al., 2001). The distinction is more than semantic. Institutional treatment and out-of-home placement has tended to be seen as a cure that will then carry over when a child is returned home. Instead, we would do better to understand the institution or out-of-home placement as an extension of a community's continuum of care. Continuity in self-constructions and definitions of health are necessary between a child's home environment and his or her place of treatment.

Two distinct patterns emerge in the way high-risk youth move between home and placement-based identities: either the teen vigorously maintains continuity in both positive and negative identity constructions throughout the placement process, or the teen experiences discontinuity in the social discourse that defines him or her through placement, resulting in new identities replacing old. Supporting new self-constructions requires continuity in the child's discursive power across interactional spheres. As will be shown below, even when new identity constructions are nurtured, these are chosen on the basis of the power they bring, and not for their social acceptability with caregivers. Continuities, and discontinuities, in a child's developmental path will likely frustrate parents and caregivers, as high-risk youth choose identities that ensure their survival. By way of illustration, time spent in institutions sometimes provides high-risk youth with health-enhancing labels that caregivers inside and outside placement view negatively. Likewise, placement can act as a forum in which the negative labels youth bring with them are maintained and enhanced rather than challenged. But institutional and out-of-home placements can also offer the resilient child options for new identity constructions that are positive and challenge the stigmatizing identities that burden them in their communities. With support, these can be transplanted back home. In either case, the institution is an intersubjective space where both youth and caregivers compete for discursive power. Contextual barriers to health demand that identity constructions bring sufficiently high status to address the very real lack of resources that high-risk youth experience. When high-status healthy and socially acceptable self-constructions are under-resourced, or unavailable, teens turn instead to dangerous, deviant, delinquent, and disordered behaviours. Although these may appear to be undesirable, they are frequently successful at maintaining for the youth a healthy self-definition as an empowered, attached, and accepted individual in a limited number of interactional spheres.

Getting Put Inside

There is a lot of power which comes from being placed. Placement, when understood from the perspective of high-risk youth, is an opportunity to enhance their self-definition. Many of the youth in this study chose to 'resist' treatment (a phrase ubiquitous among their caregivers) and persisted in the problem behaviours they showed before placement. In those cases, placement was experienced as being supportive of problematic self-definitions. Others chose to participate in treatment, nurturing powerful identities that built on their capacities. In both cases, high-risk teens' accounts of being placed demonstrate that placement is used by them as a personal strategy to sustain their well-being through the enhancement of their discursive empowerment. Whether their behaviour is viewed by their caregivers as negative or positive, the process by which they negotiate for power over healthy self-definitions is the same. Frequently, their reasons for being placed are at odds with the treatment goals of mandated services, which want to deter children from needing placement, especially incarceration.

The Benefits to Giving Up Control

David, the street-wise 15 year old introduced in the previous chapter, who bounces back and forth between his divorced parents, experienced only short periods of incarceration, but knew he needed the structure provided through these occasional placements. What's more, getting caught and jailed is one way he knows he can get his parents, especially his alcoholic father, to notice him: '[Dad] didn't like really, at the time, it didn't seem he cared very much about me, and he just let me do whatever I wanted to do. And it got under my skin a bit 'cause I like to be treated like with discipline once in a while. So like when I went out there stealing with my friends, I thought "Hey, if I get caught my dad will realize I was here." That's the way I felt, like I wanted him to realize I existed and then he'd just try and care about me a bit more. And if I didn't get caught then, hey, something for nothing.' Placement which gets a child attention from his or her family and community provides discontinuity in what are ofttimes unhealthy self-constructions for these children. Professionals have examined the benefits to youth from treatment when inside, but have not looked at the positive effects the fact of getting placed has on high-risk youth.

Such was the case for 16-year-old Jeremy who showed a remarkable ability to find trouble and stick with it. In his role as delinquent, Jeremy got himself placed in a secure custody facility serving a one-year sentence for stealing a car while high on drugs and then totalling it in an accident that almost killed him and a passenger. The accident had occurred while he'd been on probation after serving time in open custody for a similar offence. When asked about his escalating pattern of problem behaviour and the apparently reckless way he lived his life, Jeremy just shrugged. Custody was not a problem for him, but a solution to life on the outside: 'I think it's good that I'm in here for the time I'm in here. 'Cause I'll get a lot of stuff done here that I want to get done.' Inside, Jeremy succeeded at school and sports and stayed away from drugs and alcohol, all things he knew he needed to do, but which were beyond his capacity to control when left on his own in the community.

For another youth, Campbell, time spent on a forensic psychiatry unit was described as an important part of his personal health maintenance plan. Addicted, and a diabetic, Campbell found his time in a secure setting afforded him an opportunity to get his physical and mental health problems under control. He always seemed to find his way back inside just as his physical health was deteriorating. As he explained, he'd do something 'stupid' and purposely get caught for selling drugs or a minor property offence: 'Not that I like to come here [to custody], but every once in a while I need it. It's my "little rehabilitation spot" I guess.'

To see Campbell, Jeremy, or David locked up is to appreciate the benefits of incarceration or other placement. Often youth like these arrive at an institution's doors dangerously close to the edge of permanently harming themselves, underweight, addicted, out of control, and frequently depressed. They feel unconnected and, consequently, lost socially. They come into placement to reconstruct for themselves a healthy identity (and a healthy body) through connections with other youth and their caregivers.

Stan, like clockwork, puts himself back in custody every few months. There he dries out and hits the weight room. He, like Campbell, hates the way he looks when he's on the outside too long, his physique emaciated by the effects of an unhealthy lifestyle and drug abuse.

INTERVIEWER: You said you really didn't care if you got caught or not.
STAN: Right. Whenever I was out getting high and stoned and stuff like that, you know, when I didn't have a place to stay, a place to live, walking the streets in the middle of winter, then custody was all right.

Even something as important to Stan as bodybuilding evades his control when outside: 'I can't stick with it and work out when I'm outside.'

Sixteen-year-old Samantha, who also had a long history of involvement with corrections, said much the same as her male peers: 'They throw you in and they expect you to learn stuff and everything. This is great! Like, you're putting me here for a punishment? I get my education. I have a roof over my head and everything for the winter. I'll get my body back in shape and cleaned out and healthy. It's not really a punishment.'

Interestingly, it goes against our 'get tough on youth crime' rhetoric to think that youth choose the identity constructions offered them through incarceration. High-risk youth who experience custody find they actually enhance their sense of themselves as capable of coping with the high-risk environments in which they live. For vulnerable youth, placement makes use of formal institutions as a strategic resource to cope with the risk factors they face even as it threatens aspects of personal control. As noted in Chapter 5, high-risk youth will purposely choose to give up control to a benign caregiver when they feel the decision to do so was theirs.

Finding New Identity Constructions

In this study, Alexander typified this use of incarceration as a health-enhancing resource. He committed an armed robbery of a bank in a small village just a few kilometres from his home where he was easily recognized. This desperate act was his way to escape from a troubled home life.

INTERVIEWER: How do explain what you did?

ALEXANDER: I was just irrational. I didn't feel like doing anything else. So, I thought I may as well do something worthwhile. Yeah, because I wanted to leave home. I was high and I was all depressed all the time. I didn't care about nothing.

INTERVIEWER: Why a bank, though?

ALEXANDER: Because I needed some money ... to run away.

INTERVIEWER: What were you running away for?

ALEXANDER: I wanted to get away from my parents and everyone around ... Like with my mother and father fighting all the time and things. They'd never stop. My father beat up on me and stuff like that. But he couldn't help it, he was sick, mental illness, crazy ... I wanted to get away from them.

INTERVIEWER: How did doing the robbery get you 'away from them?'

ALEXANDER: Because, I could get money and get going and go live out West or something.

INTERVIEWER: Is being in jail now helping you to get away from them?

ALEXANDER: A little bit.

INTERVIEWER: So is this a solution you wanted?

ALEXANDER: No. I wanted my freedom too.

INTERVIEWER: Do you think you'll be back in jail ever?

ALEXANDER: Probably. I just think I will.

INTERVIEWER: What makes you think that you will keep coming back to jail?

ALEXANDER: I don't know. It's just the way I am, I guess. I don't like myself too much. Because I'm a loser. Just someone who loses. I don't like myself at all.

While psychological explanations of Alexander's behaviour as indicative of depression might ring true for diagnosticians, this explanation
is likely to lead to the erroneous conclusion that Alexander is acting
irrationally. This 15-year-old knew that he was not the street-hardened child capable of running away and surviving alone on the streets
of a large city. Although he idealized that image of himself as resilient,
his clinical case notes show that he knew that time inside custody was
the more accessible solution. As a result of the clumsy way he did the
robbery, he found a little of the help he knew he needed more readily
accessible. In custody, he stopped seeing himself as a loser. Among his
peers he enjoyed the status that came with having committed an armed
robbery. With staff, he stood out from the other incarcerated youth
because he was a 'nice' kid, and he was intellectually a big fish in a
small pond, more gifted academically than most of his peers. Both
capacity definitions, the so-called negative one nurtured with peers
and the typically positive one found among caregivers, had evaded
him while at home. Certainly, Alexander wanted complete 'freedom.'
However, a more realistically attainable goal was the freedom to define himself as competent, which was made possible through an out-
of-home placement.

Mental health settings serve this same function for high-risk youth
like Mark, the large brooding 14-year-old introduced in Chapter 1. His
six months on an adolescent psychiatric ward following a pattern of
violent outbursts and a suicide attempt, allowed him to construct an
identity that he explained had evaded him in his community. In hospital with other adolescent patients, he found his first genuine experience of acceptance. There he could be an angry, disturbed, and suicidal youth. Unlike the delinquents discussed above, though, Mark
would not say he chose this experience because he had no idea how
much to his advantage it could be. Once exposed to an institutional
setting, however, the experience in hospital helped Mark to co-author
a marginal but powerful discourse of himself, in partnership with the
other youth whom he met inside. That discourse promoted his self-
description as a 'crazy patient.' One doubts this was the intended
outcome of his caregivers' interventions. Mark said that the defiance
he and his peers showed toward staff in the institution was the most
healing aspect of his placement. He left with the supportive friendship
of other disturbed kids, having formed a cohesive group through their
struggle against authority. Mark liked this newfound identity as a

patient and, ironically, the status it brought him. It was, he felt, a licence to be himself. Deviance has tremendous payoffs for under-resourced high-risk youth, whether they manifest troubling behaviours in psychiatric or custodial settings. Better to be a good delinquent or mental patient than just another problem child, invisible and vulnerable to the labels others force upon you.

Differences in the Meaning of Placement

An important and often overlooked aspect of this process of label construction is the cultural milieu from which these teens come. In some instances, a child's placement and its potential stigma is not the same symbol of failure as it is for more mainstream families and their communities. While institutional caregivers will seek to create discontinuity in identity stories, many high-risk youth explain their choice of 'problem' identity as part of a culturally appropriate set of behaviours. Placement is a normative experience, one seen by some youth as a necessary right of passage. It might be exciting, allow them to spend time with friends, or provide a travel experience, while almost always adding to a powerful self-definition. As Allen explained following his incarceration for breaching his probation, drinking in public, and uttering threats, time inside was not a problem for him, his family, or his immediate community:

INTERVIEWER: What does your family think about your being in here and about the crime you committed?
ALLEN: I'm not sure. Oh, they said it was a mistake and stuff. Other than that, they didn't say much.
INTERVIEWER: What do they think about the crime you committed? How do they see it?
ALLEN: They probably don't see it as all that bad of a crime, I don't imagine. It's pretty common from people who come from where I do and drink.

Fighting, drunk and disorderly conduct, even violence, is not beyond the norms for some of the communities in which these youth grow up. As noted in other studies, some parents give their children direct and indirect messages that deviant behaviours such as these are tolerable (see Totten, 2000). The institutional placements which result are seldom sufficient sanction to deter a set of behaviours that find their support from family, peers, or communities.

Sixteen-year-old Jessie explained that the 'family' and 'community' with whom he identifies when living on the street are supportive of his self-construction as a delinquent in ways his caregivers at his group home and wider community are not:

JESSIE: When I was in need, all you people out there that are good people didn't give a shit, but the people you call 'scum' and all, they gave a shit. It wasn't just to see a young kid they could hook on drugs, it had nothing to do with that. They offered me a warm place to stay and food to eat ... didn't even offer me drugs. But the police kept picking me up, taking me back to the group home.

INTERVIEWER: What was the group home like to live in?

JESSIE: The pits. It sucked, too many rules. They just thought they could run me. When I'm on the outside I'm doing a good job and I hate people telling me what to do. I hate it.

Sustaining a defiant attitude while in placement, and being a problem for his caregivers enhances Jessie's power when he returns to his street family. When inside either a group home or custody setting, Jessie's strategic promotion of his anti-authoritarian and threatening persona makes him a potential danger to other residents and staff. Evidently, Jessie did not want to be placed, nor to be back with his natural family. Still, he did recognize that he had done a poor job of running his life on his own and needed occasionally some structure. He just wasn't ready to concede the power and acceptance that he found as a delinquent to those with the mandate to change him. Time in institutions was grudgingly tolerated as simply a place to embellish his identity as a delinquent and learn from other residents more tricks of his trade.

Surviving Inside

Just as the fact of getting placed offers high-risk youth opportunities to enhance their discursive power, strategies used to survive while in placement are targeted toward the same goal. Participation in the social discourse of other youth and caregivers encountered inside either builds on previous self-constructions, or authors new ones that are made more accessible through time spent away from family and community. It is difficult, however, to predict how this identity development will proceed without understanding the risk factors a child faces and the meaning of the placement experience to the child. Behaviour manifested inside is intelligible when understood contextually as a search for a self-definition as a resilient youth.

There were many different ways that high-risk youth find discursive power when in placement. Of particular note are the participants who had been placed by the child welfare system. Almost all experienced the placement as a threat to their sense of personal control, and reported that sustaining an influence in the social discourse that defines them is particularly difficult when they are in foster homes, group homes, or emergency beds. Youth placed in the child welfare system experience less say over the placement decision than incarcerated youth or youth in in-patient treatment settings. Those youth feel they can control whether or not they are placed, whereas the child welfare client is frequently a victim of the behaviours of adults or the paternalism of the state, which insists the child live outside environments he or she considers home. In either case, these children say they suffer as the innocent victims of their adult caregivers. In contrast, their formal and informal caregivers earnestly believe that placement can be beneficial.

When placed, these youth say the adaptive strategies they used previously to maintain their resilience in high-risk environments, become dysfunctional. Youth in care are forced to find a different way to construct a sense of themselves as resilient. Similar to the youth already discussed, conventional forms of treatment found inside child welfare settings are seldom reported by these youth as the medium through which they heal. Instead, youth in care argue that it is their relationships with peers and adults with whom they share discursive power that most influences their health status while in placement. The national youth in care networks that build community among displaced youth is a good example of how this discursive empowerment can promote identities that are viewed positively. More typically, however, high-risk youth report that their associational life inside the child welfare system fostered identity constructions that are saturated with problems.

J.R., an Aboriginal youth, had shown for years an escalating pattern of drinking, car theft, and vandalism, which had finally landed him in secure custody after probation and diversion programs failed to change his behaviour. J.R. said of the white worker who was his primary caregiver inside custody, 'He always wanted to help me and stuff. He said he wasn't going to give up on me, no matter where I went. I believe him.' Mentoring relationships such as this can exert a tremendous influence on youth in care. Within the relationship, a youth can discover a different construction of himself or herself from that which is otherwise available. The child hungry for an alternative identity finds, through these institutional relationships with adults, a pathway to a more resilient story. This was J.R.'s experience. Custody was a solution, because it saved him from further harm and offered him, through his relationship with his worker, an opportunity to open space in his life for a new story about himself other than that of a criminal. J.R. resisted that label, and in fact, when returned to his community, at the urging of his worker, joined a youth drumming circle, and began a search for role models in his community. For J.R., time inside broke a cycle of delinquency and offered him, through his participation in the discourse of his caregivers, greater access to the resources necessary to sustain a powerful self-definition. Through his time in custody, he developed the skills necessary to negotiate a new identity for himself as other than the troubled child his community saw. J.R. noticed and valued this change: 'It seems like when I first broke the law it was, well, people, every time something was missing or something like that, they would all look at me and accuse me first thing. I just didn't want to be that any more.'

In J.R.'s case, successful identity construction inside placement translated into a new experience of intersubjectivity when he returned to his community. But J.R., like most of his peers, understood the danger of having to rely on the discursive power of institutional caregivers and the other youth met while inside, to sustain a healthy self-definition: 'This is not a place you should get used to. Because if you get used to places like this, you're going to end up right back in the same spot.' When given alternatives invested with sufficient discursive power and resources, teens will participate in the construction of identities that offer more widely accepted self-definitions.

Discursive Put-Downs

Viewed as a contributing factor to discursive development (see Chapter 5), out-of-home placement can play a role in whether a child sticks with a singular identity, behaves like a chameleon, or assumes acceptance for who he or she is by negotiating with others for discursive power. Although the above examples show that youth like Mark, Allison, and J.R. find through the serendipity of placement new and more powerful identities, many high-risk youth do not survive so well. Frequently placement becomes a forum in which their discursive disempowerment is reinforced and the stigma of being a troubled or at-risk youth further accentuated. Sometimes, the put-downs these youth experience are a wake-up call that raises their self-awareness of their limited power. Other times, the put-downs simply calcify already fixed identity constructions that hold limited power or appeal.

Most youth bring with them negative self-constructions when entering facilities, nurtured over time in environments devoid of caring and concern. Patricia, while remanded in custody, explained: 'I read my predisposition report and it said how I assaulted a person and all that. And I look at somebody else and think that person's cool but deep inside I know that person's a retard because they're just messing up their life. Like I look down on myself for all this.' Inside custody, Patricia did nothing to change her identity story, except perhaps to perfect it. With nothing positive reflected to her about her or her survival strategies, she held on to the one identity she had, the delinquent, which guaranteed her some status.

Similarly, Nicole, a 16-year-old repeat offender who was sentenced to two years for her role in the kidnapping and armed assault of another youth, found time inside custody a serious threat to her self-concept: 'I wish I wasn't a part of here, really. It makes a person feel pretty weak, pretty small. It makes me feel that way, kind of. I think it would take a long while to build that back up, again. Just being in custody makes you feel really small, just like everything else. It's going to take a while. People are always looking down at you or I think that's how they look ... I think they think I've become like a rotten person. Maybe not my whole self, but I think anybody that knows me could hardly believe that I could do something like that. 'Cause even myself, I didn't believe that I could do what I did.' An intelligent, charismatic young woman, Nicole could have been anything she wanted. Instead she is comfortable with being nothing more than what she is already. Her muted dreams remain just that, voiceless:

INTERVIEWER: Do you think you'll ever get help?
NICOLE: I don't know. A lot of people say that I have a talent and stuff to make something of myself, but it doesn't mean anything to me. Like, I just want to be able to have, like even if it interests me to be like a teacher or something, or to be a youth worker, you know, you go to school for that and you learn ... I'd just be happy to have a job that supports myself and keeps me alive, rather than making something of myself.

Nicole's behaviour in custody put her at considerable risk. She ran away twice when out on temporary absences in the community. Other times she threatened to run, making it necessary to scuttle any reintegration plans to get her back to a normal life. She made several suicide gestures, scarring herself with objects as benign as plastic forks. She managed to barricade herself in a storeroom with another youth whom she terrorized for 15 minutes until staff forced their way into the room with the help of police. These behaviours repeated over and over patterns she had used to sustain herself throughout her life. While evidently this was her path to resilience, inside the institution Nicole never found any other way to define herself. She was stuck with a singular self-construction and the more she persisted int her behaviour, the more stuck she became. Staff stopped pushing her to explore her many talents. They too were forced to concede that Nicole would likely 'graduate' to an adult correctional facility later in life.

Cognitive Distortions as a Health-Enhancing Strategy

Many of these youth resist therapeutic interventions in order to maintain a singular self-construction. Sixteen-year-old Paula was emphatic that her problems had little to say about her as a person. When interviewed, she had returned to a forensic psychiatry unit for a second time, sentenced to six months for burning down a neighbour's house. Inside, she maintained her personal integrity and a powerful self-definition by minimizing the seriousness of what she had done. The more she minimized, the more staff tried to address her cognitive distortions and force her to take responsibility for her actions. However, as Paula explained, her minimizing behaviour was not a sign of psychopathology, but instead, a strategy she employed to maintain an identity as other than an offender while incarcerated: 'I'm not a bad person. I just do some things and, I don't know, it just gets me in here.' Paula did not resist treatment as much as challenge the stigmatizing discourse of her caregivers: 'Anybody could have went into somebody's house, you know, and just not really been thinking and, you know, done something. Like, even, you know, people joke around or something and they light something up, you know. Like people light papers up, you know, or something like that, or something. You know, somebody's sitting there lighting a paper up and stuff, and it burnt their fingers or something and they dropped it, and there is something flammable, like the rug or something, and it started flaming or something, you know. It was only an accident that that fire started.' Rather than faulty cognition, Paula's resistance opposes a system that she experiences as offering her a one-dimensional label.

Seen this way, very different therapeutic conversations are indicated if those intervening in Paula's life are to be experienced as helpful (see Chapter 7). In the absence of these conversations, youth like Paula find their own ways to heal: 'Not that I want to be in here or nothing, but I know why I'm in here [secure treatment]. I'll help myself out because I've got lots of time to think and you know, it does help a person out a bit. Like if a person was all troubled and, you know, and everything like that, and they came in here for like, you know, a week or two, like I think they could help themselves out because they could think about their problems and stuff.' Resistance to treatment can be health-enhancing from the child's point of view.

High-risk youth placed for treatment or care may perceive little hope of constructing positive self-definitions when removed from their homes by authorities. After all, what advantage does Paula derive from admitting the 'accident' was intentional, or even indicative of a pattern of irresponsible behaviour? How would such an admission build for her a stronger identity in the relational sphere of her community or institution? In fact, her chosen construction of herself may be more healthy without the admission of guilt. At least then, she can be something other than just another problem kid in a neighbourhood full of them.

INTERVIEWER: What do your friends think about your being in here?
PAULA: My friends, I don't know. I guess it's just natural to them now. 'Oh my God! She's going back in,' and they're just like, they're always saying, 'Stay out of that place. Don't screw up,' you know. And, then it's just like, well, 'Guess what guys? I'm going back in,' and they just think, 'You stupid dummy,' you know? ... They think it's sort of cool that I've been in a place like this, but they think it's really not so cool, too, because you know, 'I'm screwing up my life' and I'm like, 'Eh?'
INTERVIEWER: What's cool about it?
PAULA: I don't know. They just think you know, 'Wow!' I don't think its' cool. Some of them, you know, go around, 'Oh, gee, watch out for her. She just got out of jail, you know, she's tough.'
INTERVIEWER: It can get you a reputation for being tough?
PAULA: I'm not really, but some people think that. I don't know. I'm

tough with some things. And, some think it's cool. Like, my friend Tammy, she goes up to me one day and she's just like, you know, 'I'm going to court some day and I'm going to be going to juvy, too.' And she's got a great, big smile and everything like that. And, you just want to slap her because it ain't that great and it ain't something you really want to do with your life, you know?

High-risk youth like Paula survive placement by creating powerful identities through negotiation with their caregivers for an equitable role in the social discourses that define them.

Going Home

Despite rhetoric to the contrary, in practice institutions seldom act as extensions of the communities they serve. Instead, they imagine their role as one of fixing children, then helping children accommodate to the exigencies of their home environments. Institutions exist beyond the community, often situated many miles from residents' homes, often leaving back-door reintegration planning to shortly before a child is discharged. The transition from institution to home can be very perplexing for a youth who has made changes in his or her identity during placement, either through treatment, or through association with other youth in care. Coming home means integrating new self-stories into old plot lines. The processing of youth as mental health patients, young offenders, or children in need of care poses a significant threat to their identities. A shift from the community to an institution creates changes 'in personal responsibility and initiative, control over one's life, how suffering is managed and interpreted, types of support available, expectations of others and of oneself' (Ramon & Tallis, 1997: 38). Recognizing this threat, Ramon emphasizes the importance of a well thought out process to return people to their communities and the need to understand and foster effective strategies for rebuilding their threatened identities. A similar concern has been expressed regarding young offenders, who frequently choose to carry the delinquent identities they build inside institutions back with them to their communities following their incarceration (Farrington, 1995; Hagan, 1998; Hagan & McCarthy, 1997; Tolan & Gorman-Smith, 1998), and older youth, whose foster placements end before the youth are ready to care for themselves (Kerman et al., 2002). Youth in such circumstances select powerful but troubling roles, because these are the most readily available to them when they are excluded from their communities.

For high-risk youth who were thought by their communities to be vulnerable, 'successful' treatment of their behavioural problems may further complicate their lives after discharge. Lacking any continuity between one setting and the next, youth find little support for new self-constructions that fit normative definitions of health back home. Instead, high-risk youth find their new identities burdensome and diminishing of the power and acceptance they experienced previously. The high rates of recidivism and persistence of psychological problems following treatment, apprehension, or incarceration, support these findings.

Take for example 17-year-old Coady, who had spent much of his adolescence in and out of jail. Coady left school at age 15 and consequently had few prospects for work that would have brought him anywhere near as much money as he made from criminal activity. He is a hard-drinking, sombre young man who explains his alcohol abuse as the way he finds social acceptance and recreation. His criminal behaviour has provided a steady stream of funds to buy the alcohol and drugs that allowed him to keep his friends 'liquored up' and 'high.' His role as provider ensures him a high-status position among his peers. During an interview four months into an eight-month period of incarceration, Coady demonstrated a surprisingly high degree of self-awareness:

COADY: I just, I like it. I like the effect it has on me ... I can't really explain it. Now that I'm dry, I realize that I shouldn't be drinking, 'cause it's not doing me any good – I know that. But, it's easier said than done – to just get up and quit.
INTERVIEWER: When you were drinking as a younger teen, how did the drinking fit into your life? Why did you make those choices?
COADY: Whenever I started drinking, I started going out a lot more, associating with more people, you know, around.
INTERVIEWER: You mean the drinking made it possible for you to be with more people?
COADY: Yeah. Like I fit in, you know? I fit in better whenever I was drinking than when I was sober ...
INTERVIEWER: What do you expect to happen when you leave custody?

COADY: I don't have a clue. I'm hoping not to go back to drinking, but I can't say that until I get outside 'cause that's what the plan was last time and it didn't take long for me to get back to it.

Coady's drinking did not stop, nor did his association with the same peer group, who provided him with the recognition he previously enjoyed as someone who knows how to party. Booze permeates the lives of his peers and the lives of the adults in his community. By his participation in this lifestyle, he has secured for himself an identity as one of his community in opposition to the values found among outsiders, especially his caregivers in the sanitized institutional setting in which he was housed. Coady intended to be the same after discharge as he was before and during his time in custody.

A Role for Institutional Caregivers

Understanding the experience of institutionalization from the perspective of teens themselves makes visible the resilience they exhibit through out-of-home placements. While troubled youth may appear to resist treatment, or need institutionalization, they clearly feel more in control of the process and their responses to treatment than caregivers suspect. Treatment that seeks discontinuity in problematic self-definitions, and attempts to discredit the marginal discourses of high-risk youth through the introduction of normative definitions of healthy behaviour, overlooks the positive ways teens connote what they do.

The varied evidence presented above suggests that our decisions about which children need help and placement are not as objective as once thought. Treatment decisions are based on the way high-risk youth are seen by the systems that service them. Furthermore, interventions that seek to help these youth may actually limit their opportunities to access forums in which they can co-create a health-promoting discourse. Placement decisions are negotiated outcomes between service providers contingent on implicit rules governing the ownership of clients (Baldwin et al., 1997; Kurtz et al., 1998; Teram, 1999). Typically, placements occur with many constraints imposed by mandated agencies on the length and quality of care (e.g., foster placements ending at age 18) that may result in services inadequately meeting the needs of young residents/clients/patients (Kerman et al., 2002). Furthermore, care providers add to the pathogenesis of high-risk youth by labelling their behaviours in ways that say 'these children need help.' Problems are thought of as residing in individuals and not the communities or systems that co-construct the problem's meaning. The result is that children are removed from communities of concern and 'treated' in placements that exclude them from the power-enhancing relational webs they enjoyed at home. In excluding the community, we force children to look to other institutionalized youth for discursive resources with which to build identities that protect their mental health. Of course, we expect high-risk youth to look to their caregivers for their self-constructions. However, many youth report experiencing their caregivers in these settings as oppressive in the way they construct the child's identity as ill, weak, or needy. As I will show later, this can all be very different.

By way of illustration, Lawrence Frey, Mara Adelman, and Jim Query document an alternative institutional communicative context that is instructive for the purpose here of understanding high-risk youth in institutional and out-of-home placements. Frey et al.'s interviews and long-term engagement with 43 residents and 11 staff at Bonaventure House in Chicago, an AIDS residence, sought to understand 'the collective communication practices that shape and constrain people's understanding and experiencing of physical health and illness.' They explain, 'Rather than examining these processes decontextually, we ground our analysis within the specific interactional context of a residential facility' (1996: 387–88). Frey et al. found that the institution actively sought to enhance the value placed on people who were otherwise devalued through patterns of communication that build powerful and health enhancing identities for residents. Although as a population, people with AIDS are different from high-risk youth, the stigma attached to each, often for reasons beyond their control, is remarkably similar. As Frey et al. note: 'Illness, in general, can lead to being stigmatized, but this is especially true when an illness encompasses physical disfigurement, character shortcomings, and/or normative deviations' (1996: 387). Many of the activities in the AIDS residence celebrated the residents and their lives, and reconstituted an identity, in life and in death, as passing onwards and upwards beyond problems. It is a remarkable testimony to the health of the very ill and the power of the collective in recognizing the personal resilience that stigma hides. Frey et al. conclude that we cannot separate the experience of health from the 'important webs we spin through the interpersonal and group communication practices in which we engage' (1996: 394). To understand health, we must see health as a construct constituted within language. A residential facility, like all institutions, is a microcosm of discourse and can either add to or diminish personal conceptualizations of wellness:

Summary

Institutional settings may potentially be a forum in which to construct healthy and empowering identities for high-risk youth and their families, if patterns of resilience that are labelled deviant are instead given discursive value. Doing so does not encourage development of further problems, but instead instructs youth in how to negotiate for acceptance of healthy self-definitions.

This chapter examined data from the case studies of 43 youth with experience in child welfare, mental health, and correctional settings and how resilience is socially constructed by participants and their caregivers. The deviant behaviours have been shown to be strategies they use to successfully cope with the risk factors they face. Placement in institutions and community-based residential programs offer high-risk youth forums in which to create continuities or discontinuities in their identity stories. Getting placed, surviving inside, and going home are experienced by high-risk youth as opportunities to enhance their discursive empowerment in the social discourse that defines them as either vulnerable or resilient.

Collaboration between service partners can have a negative or positive impact on the development of healthy identities in high-risk youth, depending on whether care providers participate in the construction of problem-saturated or health-enhancing identities. Professional and lay staff are encouraged to acknowledge the resilience of troubled youth who survive by relying on deviant behaviours to enhance their feelings of well-being. Devaluing 'deviant' behaviours is bound to be counterproductive. A more effective intervention strategy would be to acknowledge the mental health benefits of such behaviours through an empowering dialogue. The onus is on caregivers to find ways in which institutionalized youth can achieve power in the mental health discourse in a more socially acceptable manner. These interventions are the focus of the next two chapters.

Chapter Seven

Professional Interventions to Build Narratives of Resilience

Most high-risk children and youth survive and thrive without professional intervention. Volunteers, informal guides, mentors, and para-professionals sustain a continuous stream of positive relationships in these children's lives that, when combined with family resources, nurture these youth throughout their teenaged years. These relationships, and their impact on high-risk youth's constructions of resilience, will be examined in Chapter 8. In this chapter, I look at what professional therapists can offer when families and communities are unable or unwilling to help a young person who is experiencing problems. Sometimes the problems that these youth manifest are overwhelming; at other times these teenagers have simply exhausted the capacities of their caregivers to intervene. These are the children whom we are told have 'burned all their bridges.' Professional interventions are then necessary while also being less likely to produce unintended and negative consequences in the course of treatment. This chapter examines a constructionist therapeutic approach that is both appropriate for, and effective with, high-risk teens in need of clinical interventions. A case illustration is included at the end of the chapter to demonstrate the approach in detail.

In my clinical practice, I have always been reticent to intervene in the lives of troubled youth for three reasons. First, the baggage I carry with me in the form of credentials, public perception, and the obligations I have towards the settings in which I work means that any youth referred to me is instantly identified as either bad, mad, or sad. A referral says that the child is beyond the coping capacity of his or her family and community. Professional interventions are frequently seen as the last possible option to remedy a hopeless situation. As such, children come with their personal stories of resilience already battered. I prefer that families and communities understand that most cures happen because of what *they* do, not the supposed magic of a weekly hour of contact.

The second reason I hesitate is because most times these youth come to me with files bursting with prior assessments. Teens walk in expecting nothing more than another label to add to their pile. Assessment after assessment is completed, but there are seldom resources (except when placed) to see that recommendations are acted upon. Far better, I reason, to save the money that will be spent on another professional intervention and provide a youth with a one-on-one worker who can help manage many different aspects of the child's day-to-day life.

Third, the perception of caregivers is often that once a child is attached to a therapist, the caregivers can withdraw from their role as informal clinical support, confident that the weekly contact will fix the child. Instead, counselling should be seen as work generating. Good clinical practice stimulates change that demands flexibility and responsiveness from a child's environment. The child who comes to see himself or herself as resilient is going to challenge caregivers to do likewise. School programs may need changing, advocacy work will be demanded, and new resources sought to support the child along his or her personal trajectory to health. Counselling, when effective, demands more support, not less, from parents and the formal systems that service youth. If this commitment is not there to increase resources, clinical interventions are bandages over deep wounds that do more harm than good. When counselling is well supported, and is in concert with the work of other caregivers, professional interventions can be a catalyst for growth in a child's personal construction of resilience.

This chapter explores a model of critical constructionist practice that can guide professionals who seek to help youth nurture and maintain resilience. While most of the techniques are meant for use by professional therapists, families, community members, paraprofessionals, and even a youth's peers should be aware of what a therapist is doing and why. As will be shown in the next chapter, these significant others are the most important part of a continuum of service.

A Failing System

Increasingly, we appreciate that we need to better hear the voices of youth if we are to understand their experiences of problems and identify solutions that fit their constructions of reality (Brown, 1998; Caputo, 1999, 2000; Steinhauer, 1996; Stoppard, 2000). Clinically, there is evidence that encouraging this self-expression is an important component of treatment. Lynn Focht-Birkerts and William Beardslee (2000), for example, have shown that when a parent is suffering from an affective illness, opportunities for children to express their experiences of their parent's illness are helpful and healing. This appreciation for individual and group constructions of experience resembles as much anthropology as psychology. Not surprisingly, Michael White, who along with his colleague David Epston, pioneered the first comprehensive applications of narrative to therapy (White, 1988; White and Epston, 1990) had completed doctoral-level course work in anthropology. The nature of inquiry in narrative therapy resembles the naive and sensitive exploration of an unknown culture more than the objective study of disorder that is typical of the health professions. Narrative therapy and other models of constructionist therapies, in privileging local accounts by individuals of their lives, is overtly political, with treatment understood as something individuals and their communities have the capacity to do for themselves. Therapists simply facilitate processes and add to health discourses already at play in people's lives. Treatment is decentred from the role of the therapist to the contributions a community of concern can make, meaning this approach fits well with interventions that emphasize primary prevention as a complement to clinical care (see Hallenbeck, 1998).

Although there is a growing emphasis on building the capacity of communities to look after themselves, a large portion of our human services remain committed to secondary and tertiary levels of care (McKnight, 1995; Graham & Barter, 1999). Most of these resources go to fund interventions based on the work of those outside the community care networks of natural helpers. I suggest, instead, that we reposition therapy as a small part of the treatment continuum and commit resources back to communities themselves. In practice, this means fewer institutions, and more community-based supports with secure funding.

For many high-risk youth and families the unfortunate consequence of a system that tries to intervene directly, without making resources available to strengthen the social fabric which surrounds a child, is children who are burned out on treatment. How many of us would want to tell our personal story to 10 or 20 strangers, each coming and then going from our lives without committing to helping us? Kids themselves say that there is little the formal system can do to make their lives better (Ungar, 2002).

A short while ago, in preparation for a training session for social workers on counselling angry kids, I gathered a group of youth together from inside an institution and asked them what they thought professionals could offer them that would be helpful. The conversation took place during a regular unit meeting, with 10 slouching youth sitting looking bored, ball caps over their eyes, their legs stretched out in front. Not surprisingly, though, when I asked them this question, apathy gave way to an animated exchange. What they told me was that if professionals really wanted to help high-risk kids they should rethink what they have been trained to do. Specifically, the teens advised professional caregivers:

- 'Do nothing'
- 'Get the kid back with his natural parents. That's the real problem.'
- 'Give up on the kid.'
- 'If the kid is doing drugs forget trying to help. If the kid is not ready to give them up nobody can tell him [or her] to.'
- 'It's all up to me no matter what I'm offered.'
- 'You can't stop a kid from doing anything.'
- 'Kids have to reach bottom before they change.'
- 'I never heard any advice given to me, so why would anyone else.'
- 'Nothing could be done for me or anyone like me.'
- 'Group homes are a joke, they drag kids down, the older kids teach the younger ones how to be delinquents.'
- 'If you are going to help, you need to really listen to kids.'

There is nothing on this list, except the final comment, that would predict that professional interventions have a lot to offer these youth. Sonia Jackson and Pearl Martin (1998) found much the same in their study of youth in care: 92% of their respondents said social workers had been no help to them during placement. We might want to believe otherwise, but little of what is offered through treatment is experienced by these youth as helpful. This does not, however, mean that interventions are not wanted. Work by Steven Asher (2002) has shown that of children in school who feel rejected and lonely more than one in three want help and would self-refer if an individual was available to work with them to develop the competencies to be a better friend and game participant. This finding held for both boys and girls.

The approach to treatment outlined below resembles other conventional therapies in many ways. Youth are still seen individually and in families, often in an office-based setting. The difference between what is proposed here and other therapeutic models is that constructing narratives of resilience explicitly attends to the needs of adolescents for discursive power to define their mental health status. The popularity of such an approach is growing, although there has been little work that explicitly links narrative therapies and the building of resilience. One exception is Sandra Turner's (2001) exploration of interventions that build resilience in adults by creating an alliance that resists dominant perspectives of illness. In Turner's work, therapists are encouraged to become part of the collective voices of resistance expressed by those with whom they work. Resilience-enhancing experiences affirm the less privileged position of clients in social discourse, helping them to get in touch and name their pain. Turner's approach also emphasizes the discovery and description of personal assets, highlighting their usefulness as self-protective strategies and matching strengths with external and internal resources.

Constructing Identity through Narrative

A youth's identity is the culmination of the story the young person tells about his 'self' or her 'self' in relationship with others (McAdams, 1993; Ruth & Kenyon, 1996). There is no transcendental self structure that exists to be measured or experienced by another (Gergen, 1991, 1994, 1996; Madigan, 1996; Saari, 1996). Identity formation is part of the process of discourse participation. Kenneth Gergen (1994; Hoyt, 1996b) calls this postmodern concept of identity the 'relational self.' Self construction takes place within a politically charged cultural context. As Stephen Madigan writes, *'a person's identity is viewed within the politics and power plays of a culturally manufactured and constituted self.'* (1996: 50, emphasis in original). This book itself exists as a challenge to the dominant discourse that pathologizes the identities that high-risk youth construct. While it has been assumed that the delinquent is somehow 'dysfunctional,' research reviewed in previous chapters shows that some youth may choose incarceration, drug addiction, gang affiliation, or other forms of what we term 'conduct disordered behaviour' as a way of bolstering a fledgling identity story. Interventions depend on whose account of a child's behaviour is most privileged. Scott Okamoto (1999), for example, looked at interagency collaboration with high-risk gang youth and found that the language that professionals use to describe troubled kids creates a spiralling cycle of more and more restrictive interventions and placements that further exasperate children's individual efforts to sustain health. Okamoto's work shows that children's health status and identity are constructed through the records kept about them and that these records create personae that push potential caregivers away, making youth whose disruptive or violent behaviour is only episodic, contextual, or utilitarian appear too dangerous for informal placements. Seldom, it seems, do these records reflect alternate stories that teenagers tell about themselves which explain their actions differently.

Unlike other therapeutic approaches that describe the self in very physical terms similar to the brain, heart, or nervous systems, the approach here argues that there is no transcendental self that exists to be measured or experienced by another. Our identities are constructed inside the social narratives that we co-author with others. The stories that youth tell about themselves are culturally specific and politically charged. We do not want to think about kids' sexuality so we deny that part of their self story. We do not want to see the hypocrisy in our social attitudes towards drugs and alcohol, so we arbitrarily decide that marijuana is bad, but alcohol is good. We allow 16-year-olds to drive, but not to vote! Children as young as 10 can use a gun. An 18-year-old can vote, but not go into a bar. We contribute to youth identities through these political acts just as we do through the micro-politics played out in families and between the child and members of his or her community.

If our identity exists anywhere, it exists in the stories we tell collectively about ourselves. When a diagnosis is placed on a child, that diagnosis becomes part of the plot of the child's life. To the extent that the diagnosis fits with the child's view of the problems or challenges that he or she is confronting, or the world view of the child's caregivers and peers, the meaning and impact of these diagnoses will vary.

Nothing in this approach, however, privileges all constructions of meaning as equal (Dickerson & Zimmerman, 1996). Some narratives that are constructed socially give power to one group at the expense of another. The therapeutic approach discussed here addresses the real consequences of the actions of high-risk youth such as violence, sexual exploitation, and drug addiction. By attending closely to the teens' constructions of their personal narratives, therapists are in a position to collaborate in the deconstruction of the meaning that certain 'deviant' acts have for the youth who perpetrate them.

Treatment as Meaning Construction

Narrative therapy in formal settings is most often a series of conversations through which new meanings for everyday events are co-created and then put forward as explanations for what people experience. This all takes place within a larger social discourse that forms the 'personal baggage' that both client and therapist bring into the clinical encounter. To nurture these narratives of resilience, the therapeutic context must be one in which certain principles apply. Narrative therapy, because of its close attention to language and power, is arguably the most synergistic with the needs of high-risk youth. Narrative therapy grew out of postmodernism, which as a field of thought refutes essentialism, the notion that there is an underlying truth to what we accept as reality (Freedman & Combs, 1996; Gergen, 2001; Madsen, 1999; Smith & Nylund, 1997; White & Epston, 1990). Instead, narrative therapy, follows the lead of postmodernists like Michel Foucault (1980/ 1972), Kenneth Gergen (1991, 1994, 1996) and M.M. Bakhtin (1986), who argue that people's identity and experience are dependent on interactions with others and the language that is collectively generated to describe that experience. The postmodern therapist identifies the discursive elements of the language we use, looking closely at how problems are internalized and experienced through social interaction. Successful therapy generates new meaning for everyday events and, in the process, challenges the dominant discourse through the construction of an alternate one.

Treatment is as much about story generation during sessions as about nurturing and maintaining health-enhancing self-narratives in the resource-challenged environments in which high-risk youth and their families live. One might think of it as a community-building approach taking place in a clinical setting. As such, it demands of the clinician both the skills of a therapist and the critical awareness of the community organizer. The boundaries between what happens in treatment and life are more permeable than typically found in other talking cures (White, 1997). The therapist is reliant on the expertise of community helpers, even as these same individuals are turning to the expert knowledge of the clinician to help them help a child.

Individuals and communities who are described as being at risk or high risk invariably understand how these descriptions stigmatize them. Traditional therapies attempt to promote health by first making people acknowledge problems, a paradoxical process in which goals and practice contradict. In a narrative approach people come to understand how problems exist in language, not in individuals themselves (Andersen, 1996; Anderson & Goolishian, 1992; Freedman & Combs, 1996; Hoyt, 1996a; Madsen, 1999; Monk et al., 1997; Rosen & Kuehlwein, 1996; White, 1988, 1995; White & Epston, 1990). Power relations between people and the institutions they create decide which definitions of self are privileged. Nurturing narratives of resilience depends as much on the discursive power youth exercise collectively as on individual therapeutic technique.

Long before the clinical interview, particular meanings for particular words have been codified and given meanings to which we all tacitly agree. Occasionally, in therapy, these meaning systems are broken down and examined for what they are: mutually agreed upon constructions with no substantive base. Think of the word 'red' and what it describes. What the word red means to one person is not the same as what it means to another. For one individual, it is the candy red of a sports car, for another it is the deeper maroon of blood. While we do not tend to fight very passionately over whose idea of red is right, and whose idea is wrong, we do get into an uproar with children when they start challenging the dominant discourse around the meaning attached to activities that adults call deviant. A constructionist therapy works with these discursive differences, giving the less vocal expressions of youth a measure of credibility in the discourse of adults. Doing so is not simply a therapeutic technique that makes kids feel better and behave. Conversations such as these give youth control over the description of their mental health, and it is this control that is critical to their well-being. As we have seen in earlier chapters, when a child exercises some control over what he or she defines as healthy, then health is more likely to result.

There are, of course, limits to this practice. We cannot as therapists side with teens and argue that dangerous or self-destructive acts are health-promoting. While the onus is on those intervening to understand the alternative discourses of youth, we need not act to empower these discourses further if we find them personally in conflict with our own beliefs and values. Nor can we, in good conscience, allow youth to define activities as power-enhancing or healthy that are good for them but harmful to their community. In such cases, it is incumbent upon helpers to join youth in a search for other ways of constructing similarly powerful identities, but ones which do not risk harm to themselves or others. In a constructionist therapy, however, it is not simply that the therapist denies the articulation of these deviant pathways to health, but the therapist deconstructs the relative power of conventional and unconventional understandings of what is acceptable in a particular social context. I may not like what a teen is telling me, but I will give him or her space to speak. From this dialogue comes negotiation for an identity story that is sufficiently resourceful to allow the young person to get from it what he or she hopes to achieve, while possibly decreasing the threat that the young person's former self posed. Narrative therapy encourages the active deconstruction of the therapist's position of privilege as much as it does the marginalization experienced by those with whom they work.

Narratives of Resilience

I have called the stories of health that high-risk youth co-author 'narratives of resilience' (Ungar, 2001a). Contrary to patterns inherent in traditional models of treatment, a constructionist approach to therapy does not demand that a child acknowledge that he or she has a problem for treatment to proceed. That paradoxical situation has more often than not made high-risk youth who survive through dangerous, deviant, delinquent, and disordered behaviour 'resistant' to treatment. As understood here, the construct of resistance says more about the care provider's inability to engage youth than about youth themselves. There is no need to focus on problems exclusive of solutions.

Often, troubled teenagers come to a first clinical meeting telling me, 'My parents say I've got a problem,' 'My parents say I hang out with the wrong crowd,' or 'Everyone thinks I need help.' Conversations that begin like this seldom advance very far unless the teenager's own story is given equal weight to the problem-saturated identity constructions imposed on them by others. Ironically, the stories youth tell about themselves are more often survival stories full of health, coping, and adaptation. But they are not stories privileged with the same power as the stories of illness, neglect, and failure that others construct for them.

While there is always a story of resilience to be excavated from beneath the debris of damaged lives, not all of these stories bring with them happy endings. Sometimes children are so stuck that no matter how much this story of resilience is privileged, and their capacity to survive acknowledged, they cannot stop doing the same troubling thing over and over again. A young woman, Yvonne, with whom I worked for several years, reappeared in custody at age 16 only to be released, re-offend, use drugs, become involved in violent altercations with other youth, and then find her way into a highly abusive relationship. For those of us who had worked hard to help up to that point, it was difficult to watch Yvonne slip back into a lifestyle that would keep her permanently at risk. She had never bought into any vision of herself except as the streetwise and fiercely independent youth who could survive just about anything that life brought her. In a grudging sort of way, we caregivers came to accept her for what she was, and although sad that she returned to the street each time she was discharged, understood that this was the best Yvonne could do at the time.

Predictably, Yvonne's life kept getting worse. By the age of 17 Yvonne had developed a serious addiction to alcohol and drugs. Her previously hefty 5'9" frame was ravaged by the effects of her unhealthy lifestyle. She had only made things worse when she became anorexic. A one point while in treatment, she exploded at the people in her housing unit, requiring five staff to physically restrain her and bring her to a secure holding cell where she could be monitored and kept safe. It was a sad moment for us all to watch this child crumpled on the floor of the cell, sobbing heavily, her tattooed arms and wrists scratched and torn from her own nails, her long curly hair in disarray, her clothing stained with grime, urine, blood, and sweat. There was not much any of us felt we could do except sit with her and wait. In that moment on the floor of the cell, all of Yvonne's vulnerability was there to be seen and she was forever after embarrassed for having shown us that side of her. She would never recover from the shame and the hurt that she carried with her. The only identity that she had managed to salvage for herself from a life of abuse was going to kill her, but it was also the only identity she had found that sustained her sense of personal power. Yvonne came out of the cell a few hours later, showered, and returned to her life in the housing unit, her identity as an incredibly unruly teen intact with her peers. 'It took five of them that time to drag me up to the f–ing room,' she told everyone. She was released a few months later and began the cycle of addiction, delinquency, and abuse again. Last I heard of her, she had moved across the country and 'graduated' into the adult correctional system.

Given the tenaciousness of the destructive stories that cling to high-risk youth, it can seem impossible to interrupt them. Although not every child can be helped, treatment does work when it begins with these stories of resilience and survival. Whether it is interventions by professionals, paraprofessionals, community members, families, or peers, the common element in all successful interventions is nurturing a new self-story that is powerful enough to replace an old one. A therapist is potentially no better or worse than anyone else at creating these stories. When stories are complicated, however, and a child stuck, a therapist can be a resource to move the child along a little more quickly towards a new identity construction that fits with the child's strengths. Good therapeutic work finds and builds upon narratives of resilience, helping children avoid unnecessary drift into problem-saturated discourses.

The remainder of this chapter uses clinical material to elaborate upon techniques I have found useful in constructing these narratives of resilience. The following is a story of one young woman, Trish, with whom I worked for 8 months. The case history demonstrates what a self-constructing therapy looks like in practice.

Case Study: Trish

It was Trish's mother whom I first met. She came in on behalf of her 18-year-old daughter insisting that the young woman needed help, but that she was 'fed up with counsellors.' Trish, her mother told me, had been sexually abused at age 13 by an older boy. Charges were laid, but he was found not guilty when Trish's friend, because of her own embarrassment, lied about what had happened just prior to the assault. Trish eventually agreed to meet with me after first talking on the phone. As a condition for her coming to see me, I had agreed that I would not try to convince her she was 'ill,' nor would I insist that the assault was a 'problem' with which she had to deal.

Trish is a bright young woman who was a compliant and quiet youth growing up in a white working-class family in an east coast urban community. When younger, she always felt she was overweight and socially unpopular: 'When I was 10 or 12 I wanted to stand up and say no to people, not be so shy. I didn't want to look like me. [I'd think] I'm not beautiful, I'm not popular, I don't like my body. I decided I wouldn't show how bright I am. I figured I don't measure up.' She remembers being called names like 'pig,' 'bitch,' 'loser,' and 'tubby' by her peers and people in her extended family.

When Trish reached junior high she skipped a grade, which resulted in her being further ostracized by her peers because of her academic success. To cope, Trish says she started seeking out the friend-ship of a group of girls at the school who were very outspoken and into drinking, drugs, and boys, a group that she called the 'rough people.' When Trish and I explored this choice it became apparent that becoming part of that peer group was a simple solution to her problems: 'With my friend Cindy, I was the shadow. But I fit in. I could be who I wanted to be with them. I could be loud at times.' Trish explained that conforming with the behaviour of her new friends solved several problems in her life: she was accepted as part of a group she perceived to have status and this, in turn, prevented her from being further stigmatized for her talents and looks. She met the boy who sexually assaulted her while with her friends at a pool hall.

Throughout the 20 months of legal proceedings following the as-sault, Trish began using more and more alcohol and drugs, especially after she started dating her boyfriend, Glen. Glen is a very large young man who has a history of school problems and is still known among his peers for his fighting and drinking. Trish, in her words, 'chose the biggest guy I could to make sure nobody messed with me.' She ex-plained: 'I was trying to find people I could fit in with. I'd met these new people. I thought they accepted me. I didn't like myself. Glen was funny, always laughing. He was one of the top dogs; he's a really big guy. [Glen and his friends] would tell anyone to f–off. Glen would show me off because I was brainy!' By the time Trish went to court she had lost a great deal of weight and was smoking heavily. Possibly anorexic, she looks back with amazement that she ever survived at all.

Remarkably, Trish says her real problems began with Glen. She feels the impact of the sexual assault was far less traumatic than the physical and emotional abuse she suffered for 4 years with her boy-friend, much of which she has never told her parents. Trish and Glen would get into fist fights during which he would punch and threaten her, even in the presence of her friends: 'Everybody stopped inviting us to parties because we were always arguing.' She stayed in the relationship, fearing that he would hurt her if she left, but also reas-sured by the status her affiliation with him brought her among her peers.

During the 8 months that Trish and I met, she slowly changed the story that she tells about herself. At first she emphasized how similar she was to her delinquent and abusive group of friends. Now she sees she was, in fact, very different from them: 'I always had one foot outside that life.' We talked at length about how she managed to succeed academically despite the chaos in her life and the lack of recognition for her talents: 'When I graduated high school, that was really for me.' There were also other relationships she pursued outside her regular peer group. For example, she made friends with a 'preppy' boy named Ross. The threat of violence from Glen, however, made her afraid for her and Ross's safety so she reluctantly stopped seeing him.

Trish eventually left Glen and changed her group of friends. As Trish says, 'Someone turned on the lights. I could have stayed with them other people, but I know I was different.' As Trish and I reflected on her past, she came to see how disempowered she had been in her relationships with others. Her search for power and a voice all her own carried her into high-risk situations, which ironically, helped Trish to find a sense of personal power and control: 'I'm not putting the blame on anyone anymore. Where else was I going to go [when I was being abused]? Glen's parents couldn't do anything and mine were just letting me roam wild ... Glen just stuck up for me. I was used to listening to people in every situation. I'm not so much big on listening to what people tell me to do now.' When I met Trish she had committed herself to going to college but was having serious problems staying motivated and feeling like she belonged there. With her leaving Glen, connecting to the college community became easier: 'I wanted college more than I wanted Glen, so I decided to go.'

Trish now asserts herself better in all aspects of her life except with her mother, who continues to see her daughter as unable to make good decisions for herself. This was explained in part because Trish's mother suffered her own physical and sexual abuse at the age of 18 during her first marriage to an alcoholic. Trish says that her mother needs to stop worrying about her: 'This all will affect me differently. I was more prepared than Mom.'

Trish has now completed her first year of post secondary studies and works as an assistant manager in a retail chain store part-time. She continues to excel academically and shows a strong entrepreneurial spirit. She has a new boyfriend, who is 23 and works in the fishery. She looks back now at her relationship with Glen and thinks: 'It's the most unreal thing I've ever done.' Trish is trying to quit smoking, uses drugs rarely, drinks seldom, and is not sexually active with her boyfriend. These are all decisions that she has made that she says enhance her well-being. Trish once told me, 'I want a new start ... I want my sexuality back!' With the new story she tells about herself and her past, Trish is experiencing this new beginning. She has been able to remember her life differently, not as a series of mistakes, but as a search for resilience that, even when it created problems, was still a defiant challenge to the story of the withdrawn and 'brainy' child she loathed to be.

Three Phases of Therapy

Eliciting and nurturing narratives of resilience involve three phases of questions and exercises woven together into therapeutic conversations that enhance the power of one's personal narrative. I call these phases of work reflecting, challenging, and defining (see Figure 7.1).

Reflecting

Reflection with high-risk youth means exploring the context in which their life story is written. It is important to consider how different relationships affect this story development and become critically aware of who exerts the most power in the process. It is also important to understand the real barriers in our lives that shape and limit the stories available to us. Poverty, abuse, physical limitations, family disruptions, social unrest, immigration, racism, gender politics, and a whole host of other factors limit the power any one individual child will have and how much his or her experiences will be valued. For example, Trish and I discussed who told her she was 'fat' (her uncle who called her 'porky' and her friends who called her 'tubby'); what was her experience with the girls whom she perceived as popular (they brought Trish a feeling of belonging and status at school); what was it like for her as a girl to succeed academically, and what was it like growing up in her community (she shared in a feeling of inadequacy because of her family's limited financial resources)? Each question examines important aspects of the youth's life now and looks backward to see where ideas and accepted truths come from. I take a positive and curious attitude towards another's life, humbled to know that, really, I understand very little about their experience until I ask. I base my questions on a comprehensive understanding of the potential risk factors that are predictive of developmental problems.

GENOGRAMS AND SOCIOGRAMS WITH AN ATTITUDE

To help organize all of this material, I borrow the structuralist techniques of genograms and sociograms but employ them with a twist.

Figure 7.1 Constructing narratives of resilience

Reflecting

Conversations that:
1) Contextualize past events
2) Deconstruct memories
3) 'Externalize' problems
4) Highlight exceptions to narratives of vulnerability

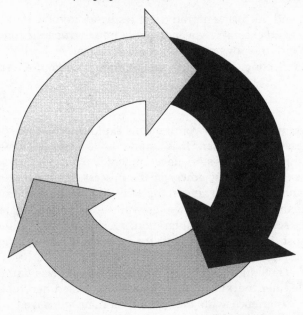

Defining

Conversations that:
1) Explore ways to demonstrate resilience
2) Locate support for a new identity
3) Review progress
4) Anticipate future growth

Challenging

Conversations that:
1) Thicken description of narratives of resilience
2) Invite 'audience' participation
3) Explore talents

Building on the solution-focused approach to genograms discussed by Bruce Kuehl (1995), I use these tools to record 'voices' across generations and the relative influence each voice has in the discourse that defines the young person. Retooling Kuehl's model, I use these genograms to help those with whom I work draw family trees that I like to describe as having 'an attitude.' These diagrams are not just a genealogy, but the tracing of power relations, ideas, problems, *and* solutions across generations. In my work with Trish, the graphic depictions of her life that we created together were a chaotic blend of lines, figures, and quotations, representing her relationship with the people most influential in her life and the way their voices have helped co-construct her identity. Beside Trish's name on the genogram was a cluster of words her mother used to describe Trish, such as the 'business person,' the 'university student' and 'my little girl.' Next to these were the words and phrases Trish has used to describe herself over time such as 'rough,' 'brainy,' 'entrepreneur,' and 'gambler.' We charted both individual and family strengths as well as the dominant narratives of different family members across generations. Similarly, the sociogram identified group and individual narratives which have imposed on Trish the labels she either accepted or challenged. I often add a time line to these diagrams, noting how different identities fit for the individual at various points in his or her development.

When I construct these images and stories, I am particularly attentive to whose voice is relating historical facts, as often much of what we remember is a construct of our experiences filtered through the interpretations of others (Madigan, 1997). These constructions of our past recognize that our memories are not ours alone. What we remember about the past is negotiated with others and filtered through their interpretations, as much as our own. How many of us think we remember something from very early in our lives? These remembrances are often tinged with what others have also told us about how we behaved at that time. Do I remember my grandfather holding me at age 2, laughing, just days before his death, because I really remember it, or because it has been talked about so frequently over the years? It is important to go back and find out how it is someone knows what they know. Where did the story start that said this child is vulnerable, unhealthy, a problem, destined to be in jail, likely to be as bad as his father, or unlikely to ever succeed? Sometimes, therapists have to help children excavate stories all the way back to the point of their conception. As one young woman told me, 'I was a fix-up baby,' meant to save her parents' stormy marriage, while a young man was told in a family session that his birth, and therefore he himself, was 'an accident.' These aspects of a child's story are still just one part of the plot that becomes their lives, no matter how pivotal they may seem. Stories of resilience are also there, as they were for Trish, buried but not entirely forgotten. Therefore, it is important to ask about people's conception, birth, and preschool years. The information uncovered is useful, not as part of a pathologizing discourse, but as elements in a reconstruction of a story of health. If we are to discern resilience we need to find its plot line amidst the chaotic stories that we hear most often when we talk to high-risk youth. These early experiences are almost entirely constructed for the person and begin narratives of resilience or vulnerability.

DECONSTRUCTING MEMORY
In deconstructing these narratives from the past I ask, 'Who told you about this?' 'How is it you remember what happened?' 'Do you remember it any differently than you have been told?' and 'Did anyone else tell you something different about what happened?' I ask similar questions about each period in a person's life, identifying the dominant voices that have had the greatest impact on the young person's identity story. I attempt to help those with whom I work to see the complexity of their lives and that the problem that brings them to counselling is only one aspect of their total life experience. Frequently, high-risk youth tell me that the labels that attach to them define them singularly by their coping strategies and that the multiplicity of self-identifications that they experience are hidden beneath words like 'delinquent,' 'conduct disordered,' 'promiscuous,' and 'depressed,' which are used by others with more power in the social discourses that define them.

These conversations, aided by a visual representation tracing story development, can start a process of putting a child's experience in context. Sixteen-year-old, Serge, whom I recently interviewed, was referred to counselling for alcohol-related problems. He had breached his probation when he refused to stay sober and then, while drunk, had driven a car recklessly and without a licence almost killing himself and a pedestrian. He insisted he did not have a problem with alcohol. He insisted he had chosen to drive drunk, that he liked drinking, and he did not mind being in jail. He would get out and do it again. There was no point talking about it.

To look at Serge, one would wonder why he was persisting in making his life more difficult. He was a popular youth who made friends easily. He did not appear to need to maintain just one identity as the local 'drunk kid,' and he had enough talents and academic abilities to do something important with his life. At least that was how we adults saw him. But the story of 'alcohol' had a persistence all its own in Serge's life. From early on he had been told about his great-grandfather who had died frozen in a snowbank after a drinking binge. He had been 62 at the time. The boy's grandfather had drank well into his 50s, abusing his wife and children, who had eventually left him. At 58 he gave up drinking and, at the time of my conversation with Serge, had been attending Alcoholics Anonymous for 5 years. Serge's father had continued the pattern and been a heavy drinker with a history of incarceration and petty crime. He had also abused his wife and children, just like his father. But at 36 he had given up alcohol. Although he had suffered relapses and voluntarily placed himself in a rehabilitation program in the 2 years since he quit, he had managed to stop the cycle of addiction in his life earlier than had his father or grandfather. It struck me that if one stopped to think about it, each generation was doing better than the one before and that even at age 15, Serge was not off course. The question was not whether he would drink anymore after he got out of custody (that was certain), *but when he would quit*. Would he wait until his 20s? How many intimate relationships would the drinking ruin and how much abuse would he inflict on his future children? There was no way to deter Serge from abusing alcohol. But together we could predict a better future based on the lessons of others who had given him his past. Interestingly, when Serge's mother and father came and met with Serge and me, and these thoughts were shared with them, they were both very supportive and optimistic for their son's future. Instead of there being the sense of despair that Serge would repeat the mistakes of his elders, there was a story in development of Serge doing them one better.

In interviews such as this, singular adaptive story lines can be interrupted by finding in the past other stories that may be less well remembered or seem less powerful. Often these are the exceptional stories, the ones that breed success.

EXTERNALIZING
Another helpful way of reflecting is to use what Michael White (1988, 1995, 1997) calls 'externalizing language.' This language distances high-risk youth from the problem-saturated identities that they have constructed by separating the problem from the child. Having children talk about the problems that challenge them in the third person is an

empowering experience. As a history of the problem is taken, focused exclusively on when the story of the problem began, who helped to construct the problem story, and the rules that one must follow when living with the problem, children discover that their problem identity is only one aspect of who they are. I like to place on a flip chart aspects of a person's life that give the problem strength and those that weaken it. Together we develop a rule book about the problem. Because risk factors frequently occur in clusters, it is my experience that conversations such as these help young people see the interweavings of the myriad of forces at play in their lives that have put their mental health at risk. In Serge's case, we talked about how alcohol was a force to be reckoned with in his family. But we also talked about who had had the most, and least, success controlling alcohol.

Similarly, an 18-year-old young woman I saw some time ago, Marcy, struggled with depression and had experienced numerous psychiatric assessments, as well as spent time on an inpatient psychiatric ward. She was also on several medications to control suicidal feelings related to her diagnosed condition. When we looked backwards we found that depression had been a powerful force in her mother's and father's lives, but had gone largely untreated. From an early age, she had not been able to allow herself to enjoy her accomplishments, of which there were many both academically and on the sports field. This depression, we discovered together, had hung around her life like a 'darkness' for years. When she left home, it had followed, packed in her suitcase with her other belongings.

I was curious about what made the 'darkness' stronger and what weakened it. What made Marcy better able to control the depression? Again, on a flip chart, I constructed a rule book that we added to week after week as the problem and its solution became more clearly defined. The challenge in this work is to understand the context in which a problem persists. Psychological factors may have only a small part to play. I am frequently amazed at how much the non-organically based aspects of mental and emotional illnesses can be controlled by the people who cope with them. While depression and alcoholism certainly have a biological component, a problem that is so universal to the human condition cannot be explained with a singular etiology.

For example, in one of our regular interviews over a period of 6 months, Marcy told me how depressed she had been during the past week. She had thought of putting herself back in hospital. She had thought about calling me. And she had thought about suicide. But she had done none of these things and had remembered that she felt better when she looked after her dog. In her near collapsed state of mind, she had found the strength to control her depression and take her pet for a walk. She was close to tears the whole time, except when an acquaintance from a few doors down passed her and stopped to chat, pat her dog, and share some pleasantries about the weather and their mutual landlord. The whole conversation took only a few minutes, but during that time Marcy says she pushed aside the depression that hovered over her. She had shown her neighbour a healthy and happy person. Neither one of us knew exactly what happened to the depression, but we did know that through that spontaneous contact, Marcy was able to control the depression momentarily and author for herself a different identity. This was one of many instances where Marcy gained control of the depression in her life and asserted a new more preferred construction of herself. Her interaction with peers was particularly important in this regard. By practising a new identity in her peer group, Marcy came to know that she was not just a depressed and suicidal young woman, as she had come to believe. Our work together offered a series of conversations that helped her bring another identity construction with her into more and more spheres of interaction and eventually back home where she had grown up. She focused more intently on her academic and physical abilities. She began to see that she had a network of social supports. Marcy also recognized how different she was from her family of origin.

Reflecting on the past to trace the way stories are constructed helps to bring into the clinical setting the social context in which people live. It is an overtly political act when part of this reflection looks beyond individual factors to social factors that add power to some stories and takes power from others. Trish did not on her own come to believe she should be thin, nor invent anorexia. Thin is a cultural value, and 'sizism' is consumer manipulation directed at young and old. There is one acceptable body shape. Who can blame a teen for wanting to have the power associated with such a self-defining image? Being thin, or in the case of boys, muscular, means being powerful. Alcohol use, and at times abuse, is constructed in much the same manner. There are powerful social forces which say that to drink heavily is a sign of masculinity or maturity (see Chapter 3). Cigarette use among young women continues to rise because it is associated with images of independence, maturity, and helps to control weight. Deconstructing these social phenomena through a contextually sensitive therapy is necessary to unravel the social aspects of psychologically constituted problems.

Reflecting on old and new stories means asking questions about the social voices that populate our heads and the discourses that control us. When creating the rule books referred to above, I am very interested to know what television programs, what advertising, what experiences in shopping malls, what experiences with adults, at school, in the workplace, with peers and families, support a problem-saturated identity.

Challenging

The deconstruction of social discourse that occurs in the reflecting phase lays the groundwork for the construction of an alternative health-enhancing narrative. Building narratives of resilience requires that the now deconstructed old story be challenged by a story of resilience. To find support for this healthy narrative, I review the same territory already covered, except that this time I target the inquiry to periods in the youth's life when he or she resisted the problem and successfully confronted risk. Through our conversations, I focus on elaborating a new narrative.

When these alternative stories are visually represented on the same problem-saturated genograms and sociograms used previously, these graphic representations of life can become quite cluttered and chaotic, with the abundant use of symbols to identify both the externalized problem and alternative resources for health. This visual chaos is intentional, and represents symbolically the complexity of these new identity stories. In my work with Trish, we together found ways to represent the 'storm clouds' of depression, and the 'craziness' of generations, alongside the 'determination' to survive, and the 'brainy kid' who wanted to stay in school. The clinical tone is purposefully upbeat in order to stimulate a sense of power and excitement about the discoveries being made. As stories of resilience emerge, we spend more and more time discussing these, thickening their description.

The audience, comprising myself as the therapist and others who are brought into the therapeutic process, witnesses these performances and becomes particularly important in the task of meaning construction. Families are almost always a resource in this process, even with children as out of control as Serge or Yvonne. Susan Stern and Carolyn Smith note: 'The current empirical research on reciprocity in families underscores the importance of an interactional approach that explicitly recognizes youth and parent influences in both the development and treatment of delinquency' (1999: 179). Even in what are typified as highly dysfunctional homes, inclusion of family members in treatment still brings with it great benefits. White and Epston explain: 'The endurance of new stories, as well as their elaboration, can ... be enhanced by recruiting an "external" audience. There is a dual aspect to this enhancement. Firstly, in the act of witnessing the performance of a new story, the audience contributes to the writing of new meanings; this has real effects on the audience's interaction with the story's subject. Secondly, when the subject of the story "reads" the audience's experience of the new performance, either through speculation about these experiences or by a more direct identification, he or she engages in revisions and extensions of the new story (1990: 17).

In Trish's life there were teachers, a boyfriend, a distant aunt, and her parents, who saw her potential to be more than a drug-addicted and abused youth. It is important to include in therapy as many people as possible in order to address the complex social, political, and environmental factors that are present in the lives of high-risk youth. Often, with enough digging, there is someone, an aunt or uncle, a cousin or grandparent, who followed a different path in life. These are the experts on how to solve problems. Their expertise is especially relevant because it originates close to the child and family. It is much more likely that whatever it is that worked for that individual will also work for the child who is in treatment. A solution that comes from within a family is more likely to be accepted and inform change than a story brought into the family by an outside therapist. Constructionist clinicians invite people to participate in sessions that offer them a forum in which to co-construct discourses of resilience. The process in the therapy room looks much like what happens for teens naturally in their peer groups, communities, and families. However, it is orchestrated with care. New stories that may emerge through trial and error in less structured encounters are brought more quickly to awareness and practical realization through the intense process of the interview. In institutions, too, it is important to assess a young person's behaviour in real-world settings prior to discharge. This means drawing into treatment the child's family, friends, and peers (Hollin et al., 1995). It is these others who form a young person's audience and act as forces for or against the construction of healthy identities.

We know from efforts like the Seattle Social Development Project that the most effective prevention efforts are those that intervene in multiple domains. When Heather Lonczak and her colleagues (Lonczak et al., 2002) looked at the effect that the project had on sexual behavior among high-risk youth, they found that interventions that foster cooperation and build communication and competencies in both home and school environments provide the best protection against problematic development leading to sexually risky behaviour. It would appear that consistency in a child's audience (those encountered at home and school) made it easier for participants in the project to carry their identities from one sphere of interaction into another. The typical scenario of academic success or problems being ignored or unappreciated at home or parents lacking the training and open lines of communication to support the school in its efforts (and to have trained teachers appreciate their struggles at home) were avoided. Instead, youth received consistent mirroring of who they could be and the support to achieve a more powerful identity in front of multiple audiences. The impact was that much larger because in combination this audience provided youth with the resources necessary to define themselves as healthy in ways that did not require as much risk-taking.

In this example from Seattle we see that treatment can be targeted towards the broader social institutions that sustain narratives of vulnerability. In residential settings, I have worked as much with interdisciplinary staff teams and their story about a resident as with the child who has the problem. Working with family members has an added advantage. With families, it is often possible to identify in their collective past the same themes of resistance to the dominant discourse that are now defining the young person as deviant or disordered. As we explore how other family members have dealt with the same risk factors, we can borrow plot elements from their stories to help in the construction of the youth's new narrative. In practice, this means that it was as important to talk with Trish's mother about her early pregnancy, her loss of dreams, her fears, and her path to resilience as it was to explore these themes in the life of her daughter.

Through these conversations, I spend a great deal of time discovering talents, even when those talents are socially unacceptable (e.g., adeptness at stealing cars, bullying, being able to drink more than others, knowing how to hide one's depression). These conversations look at the functionality of the behaviours that are typically pathologized as symptoms. For example, for Trish, doing drugs became a way of 'numbing out' and minimizing the overwhelming effects of emotional pain. For other youth with whom I work stealing becomes a way of gaining status in a group or of finding a way into custody and the sense of order and 'security' that being incarcerated brings. Slashing becomes a way to 'let the pain out.' Refusing to take prescribed medications becomes a way to assert 'independence.' By acknowledging particular behaviours as functional, I do not validate them as appropriate. In fact, questions about who gets hurt, how effective the behaviour is, and contextualizing the behaviour in terms of relationships of power and responsibility have the effect of engaging youth in a thoughtful discussion without the therapist creating resistance.

These conversations co-construct a story about the youth's actions as health-seeking. Teens engage in these constructions much more willingly than in pathologizing conversations. The process deconstructs the dominant narratives in a person's life, highlighting themes of powerlessness that are associated with vulnerability. Stories that people tell about themselves as 'violent,' 'delinquent,' 'insane,' 'depressed,' 'worthless,' or any of a host of other signifiers are juxtaposed to stories that emerge about themselves as 'struggling,' 'resisting,' 'functioning,' 'surviving,' 'growing,' 'learning,' 'status-seeking,' and 'coping.' Nurturing health-enhancing narratives means identifying the sustaining qualities of what youth have been doing given their limited access to health resources, while looking for alternative strategies that achieve the same ends with fewer negative consequences. These new stories, because of their coherence and complexity, are by their nature healthier and more integrative (Saari, 1996).

The process is at once divisive and constitutive. As we reflect on past and present stories we open up opportunities for deconstruction of the old and construction of the new. Forces for and against change are calculated and questioned. Perhaps change is not even desired. But with stories taken apart, it is now possible to construct a new alternative health-enhancing narrative that details the child's strengths while challenging old stories of vulnerability.

GROUP WORK

Similarly, one can use groups of people to accomplish the same types of interventions used during individual and family therapy. At times group work can even be more effective. In a group, the audience is real, and the opportunities to practise the skills necessary to negotiate a new meaning can be rehearsed until they are honed razor sharp and ready for the street.

For example, I co-facilitated a group for parents with young teens who were 'out of control' and into a number of problem behaviours. Five families participated in the group, two of them sole parents (mothers), two blended families, and one family with the married biological parents of the children attending. Getting both adults and youth to the group took much convincing. There were real worries on the part of the parents about their kids embarrassing them. The teens were actually a bit easier to entice to the group. Once we promised that they would have a chance to tell their parents and other adults how things really are for teenagers today, they became much more interested in attending. The parents agreed to participate when they realized that they would have a chance to share their struggles and get some advice from other parents who were coping with the same issues. It was not long into the 16 weekly sessions that we managed to get everyone engaged. Part of each meeting broke the group in two with the parents and teens meeting for 30 minutes in separate rooms. This worked well, as it made each group very interested in what the other group was discussing. For the teens, it was a chance to compare parents and be heard. For the parents, it was a chance to get some support in making tough decisions about how to handle their children. The emphasis throughout was on the indigenous knowledge and expertise the parents and teens brought to the group. As facilitators, we simply structured exercises in which that experience could be shared and heard.

Another group in a very different setting and with a very different structure provided these same opportunities to challenge negative identity stories and collectively construct new ones. A colleague of mine, a youth worker, and I working together in a closed custody facility for delinquent youth noticed that many of the youth were hesitant to participate in formal expert-driven therapy groups. We also found, time and time again, that the youth were actually a source of emotional support to one another. In many cases, as we got to know the residents, we could see that they showed a great deal of maturity about their situation and had much good advice to offer one another. Often, their decision to be in jail was exactly that, a choice made to solve problems they encountered in the world outside.

Based on these observations and familiarity with 'positive peer culture' models of group practice (Gottfredson, 1987; Kuchuk, 1993), we teamed up to facilitate a group where the youth themselves could help each other and advocate for one another's rights. We held group meetings twice a week for an hour and a half each afternoon. While this gave the group a structure, the content was largely up to the youth to decide. The group was open, meaning that as youth finished their time in custody and left, new group members joined. Group membership never exceeded more than 10 participants. The only criterion for inclusion was that group members had to agree to maintain the group's confidentiality. They could talk about their own experiences in the group outside the group, but not about what others said. Group members who broke the confidentiality of the group were brought to the next meeting and sat in a chair in the middle of the group and asked to explain themselves. Other group members then had the chance to confront the member with how what he or she had done had affected them personally. On the two occasions that this occurred it was remarkable to see how seriously the youth took the contract they had made with each other. The group then decided if the group member would be allowed to join the group again. Interestingly, the group leaders, too, were obliged to keep the confidences of the participants, except when it breached their professional ethics (the facilitators would not keep confidential any disclosures by the youth relating to abuse or criminal behaviour).

Each session began with a lengthy check-in where members could talk about whatever they wanted. With time these conversations became the heart and soul of the meetings as the youth grew comfortable enough to challenge each other on behaviours they saw as avoiding real issues, or minimizing a group member's responsibility for events in his or her life. I will not say this level of open and constructive confrontation was achieved quickly. At first, it took a great deal of the facilitators' genuine use of self to confront and cajole participants to look critically at the issues before them. But with time, and as members of the group stayed on, this role of group leadership was adopted by the youth themselves. What had started as gripe sessions on everything that was wrong with the institution, the police, and their families, eventually became a forum in which the teens could talk frankly about the real issues in their lives. The youth loved it. This was the only time in their day when they could relax and tell it like it is and be heard. During more formal therapy, they felt they were expected to fall in line with a professional discourse that defined them as troubled youth. But the group was their space, and it allowed them to say what they liked and define their world in the ways they experienced it.

The group grew in credibility with those who were not attending, as group members began to advocate for rights for residents. On numerous occasions, issues raised in the group were brought to the attention of the facility's management, sometimes with results, other times not. In each case, it was the youth themselves who went forward to present their concerns. Some of the ideas were serious challenges to staff authority, such as visits between girlfriends and boyfriends who were in custody at the same time in different housing units, or requests to take in community events when residents felt that their behaviour merited such privileges, but staff did not.

The group took a special kind of facilitation. It was not therapy. It combined the talents of paraprofessional and professional staff. Interestingly, participants in the group showed a marked decrease in the number of serious 'incidents' in which they were involved while in custody. Even when youth were being disciplined with lock-downs or other consequences, they were still allowed to participate in the group if they were not a risk to themselves or others. Within the group, confrontation between members was often more effective than any clinical work that could have been done with the youth by their caregivers.

Whether in groups, or through contact with peers, families, or a community, each audience for whom high-risk teens perform offers them a different opportunity to co-construct their personal story. In treatment, as in other relational spheres, the plot elements of a teenager's story are available to be borrowed, rejected, contrasted, and criticized through therapeutic conversations that open space for children's voices to be heard.

HEARING OTHERS' VOICES
The challenge when doing this work intergenerationally is that it is difficult for the adults in the room (and this includes the therapist) to discover the abundant talents of many of these youth when these talents are manifested in socially unacceptable ways. Teens who are adept at stealing cars, bullying, drinking to excess, or masking their depression are more likely to earn DSM-IV (American Psychiatric Association, 1994) diagnoses than accolades. A therapeutic conversation that explores the world from the vantage point of the teens will look at the functionality of their constructions of their behaviour rather than judging that behaviour by predetermined criteria. Is doing drugs a way of 'numbing out' and coping with emotional pain, as it was for

Trish? Is custody a safe haven from the ravishes of abuse and neglect?
Is being oppositional the only way a street kid can survive on his or
her own?

There is always a fear among professionals and the parents of these
teens that approaching these behaviours in this way gives problem
youth the message that what they are doing is 'just fine.' I have heard
this same argument used against allowing young mothers to continue
their education by funding day care facilities in schools. I have also
heard adults say that we should provide no birth control to youth as it
encourages them to be sexually active. In all such cases, adult misunderstanding causes misinterpretation of juvenile realities. Adult assumptions fail to recognize that our kids are more intelligent than we
think. They have been raised in the same culture as their parents, and
they are acutely aware of the social gaze of others. If we take the time
to ask, we will find that high-risk teens know that theft is bad, suicide
harmful, jail stigmatizing, and early pregnancy a threat to one's future. But they will also tell us that, sometimes, each of these behaviours
is a strategy for personal salvation.

This alternate discourse on health is just as evident in research conducted by allied health professionals as it is in the work of progressive
family therapists, social workers, and psychologists. Patricia Flanagan
(1998), a pediatrician, counters the myths we tell about teen mothers
by first debunking the belief that early unplanned pregnancies are
increasing as a social problem. Teen mothers have always been a part
of the social landscape but are actually lessening in numbers overall
(Federal Interagency Forum on Child and Family Statistics, 2002;
Tyyskä, 2001; Vanier Institute of the Family, 2000). While the problem
of teenage pregnancy persists in many people's minds, it has become
less of a problem among some teens who perceive their roles as young
mothers positively. Basing her findings on qualitative interviews with
100 young mothers, Flanagan explains, 'Through listening to, watching, and interacting with these young women, I began to understand
early pregnancy not as a dysfunctional behavior or part of a constellation of dysfunctional behaviors but as, sometimes, an alternative
developmental pathway: sometimes a rational option, sometimes a
shifting of life course, but always a complex, individually experienced event' (1998: 239). Childbearing raises a girl's status quickly,
making her like her mother, sisters, or other women in the community. This is one creative way that marginalized youth have found to
bridge the maturity gap discussed by Moffitt (1993, 1997), but in ways

that are seen in some communities as less problematic than more destructive solutions common to deviant, delinquent, and disordered youth.

I encourage validation and acceptance of teenagers solutions to life's challenges, although affirming those behaviours need not say that they are the best ones, or even that I personally would make the same choices. I avoid saying, 'This is a better solution' or 'I like your solution' unless that is what I sincerely think. But I do say, 'It's tough for me to understand, but it seems like your behaviour is working for you.' From this position of acceptance a clinician is more likely to have a conversation in which shared goals can be discussed. Both the therapist and the child want to promote health, to stop emotional pain, and to make the child safe, accepted, and loved. The role of therapy is to add to the shallow pool of resources that impede the growth of high-risk youth towards these goals.

I never encounter resistance when using this approach: not among drug addicts, abusive parents, incarcerated delinquents, males who abuse their partners, or adolescent sex offenders. When I am open to hearing the localized truths that explain these offending behaviours, I encounter a willingness on the part of others to educate me as the clinician. Our conversations are respectful, with me freely sharing what I believe, and then, together, searching for other ways for the person that I am working with to solve personal challenges in ways that are more widely accepted and empowering.

When professionals take the time to listen, we are privileged to hear stories about health-seeking behaviours and identity constructions that emerge as a consequence of life circumstances and difficult choices that maximize the utility of health resources. Powerlessness is masked and then transformed by acts of power. Vulnerability succumbs to narratives of resilience through the discursive challenge offered by alternatively constructed stories.

Defining

Once personal narratives are reflected upon and pathologizing discourses challenged through the construction of new identities, therapists and those with whom they work can begin the process of sharing these new and defining narratives of resilience. This third stage of treatment depends on individuals exercising a measure of control over their personal stories of health. The task therapeutically, then, becomes having this new defining narrative more widely accepted than the problem-saturated identities by which the child has been known. Sharing an alternative discourse means telling others both a new story about one's life and a new-old story about one's past (Hewson, 1991).

The process is both dialogical and experiential. Therapists can encourage youth to live their new story in different contexts generalizing it to a number of spheres of social interaction. Reflecting on these new defining experiences, youth are then asked: 'Who accepts this new way you see yourself?' 'Who does not?' 'After living with the problem for so long, what is it like to watch it change (or disappear)?' 'Who do you need in your life now to help you be more healthy and resilient?' 'How are you now different from the people who see you as vulnerable in your family, among your friends, and in your community?' These questions, and many others, about new ideals, new mentors, other possibilities for peers, work, recreation, and intimacy, are all investigations to identify the forces for and against change.

The artefacts of treatment are particularly useful in this regard. We know from the work of other constructionist therapists that certificates of progress, letters, token gifts, and artwork can all stimulate a reflective process that encourages change (see White & Epston, 1990). These artefacts also provide significant others with whom they are shared further proof of the child's growth and development. In the treatment settings where I frequently work, clinical case notes and assessments are particularly troublesome to this constructive process. Most frequently, the discourse of professionals is pathologizing, hidden from direct view of patients or clients, but nonetheless a debilitating force in their lives.

I had an unfortunate experience some years ago in meeting with 16-year-old Steven who had acted out criminally for many years. He was sexually promiscuous, violent, and a drug addict. He had a history of sexual abuse and seemed both unable and unwilling to change. Before meeting with him during one of his many stays in a youth custody facility, I spoke, with Steven's consent, with his mental health counsellor from another institution. She explained that Steven's behaviour was the result of his past abuse and a 'narcissistic personality disorder.' I was troubled by such an untreatable diagnosis being given to a child whose personality was far from formed. During a meeting with Steven, I tried to explain that his pattern of behaviour was causing him to be labelled in very negative ways and that I did not believe that he was as 'disturbed' as everyone thought. To his credit, Steven did not think he was all that crazy either, and he asked me who had labelled him and what 'they' had said. In hindsight, I realize now that I betrayed the confidence of a colleague, by sharing with Steven the diagnosis of his other therapist who had never told Steven that this was how she saw him. But I was also troubled by the supposed privilege that the other therapist had taken in talking to me about Steven, without conceding his right to know every detail of our conversation. Was his life a commodity for us to discuss? While I should have explained to my colleague that I felt obliged to share anything we discussed with Steven, I instead let Steven know what professionals were saying about him unbeknownst to the other therapist. Steven was quite upset once I explained what the term 'narcissistic' meant, and he went back later to confront his former therapist (who then called me). Although it was bad practice, the incident highlights the power of labels and the way in which teens will mount a discursive resistance if given the opportunity.

Since then, I have tried to make case notes user-friendly, confident that when they are shared with those with whom I work they further the defining work of constructing new health narratives from positions of illness. There are other benefits as well. Anderson (1996) talks about her and her colleagues' dislike for reifying professional-therapist language that imposes jargon on the lives of those with whom they work. Instead, an alternative treatment discourse that celebrates the self-descriptions of clients is preferred: 'When we talked with our colleagues and trainees about clients, we used the clients' descriptions and explanations, their words, and phrases, and not our professional vocabulary. When we talked about our cases, we shared the clients' self-told stories. We found that telling the clients' stories (or fragments of them) as they had told them to us captured more of each client's uniqueness, the interest of each client's situation, and the essence of the way each client viewed him- or herself' (1996: 28).

A 14-year-old boy, Anthony, growing up on a Native reserve, and with whom I worked for many years, had just been interviewed by me after his return to custody following a spree of break and enters. My case note, purposely meant to be shared and used by his family, youth workers, and the boy himself (with some help), included the following comments:

> I had a good chat with Anthony and I think I can offer some helpful hints
> as to where to proceed in our casework together ... Anthony, in some

ways, resembles his siblings and relatives, and in other ways, shows unique strengths that may give us clues as to how to help him. He has an alcohol 'problem,' no doubt, although the way he talks about it, it sounds like he also has some sense about what the alcohol does to him. His story about himself in this area is of a less than frequent user who does not like the hangovers, nor the trouble it gets him into. In fact, to hear him speak, he seems to differentiate himself from patterns in his family, and instead is more interested in identifying with positive patterns like his father's sobriety, and quiet ways. At least this is the picture I was getting.

There are many other positives here as well. He has shown the courage to change peer groups at least once, and holds in his mind the idea of 'smartening up' like many others in his community. When exactly he decides to make this change entirely is still to be seen. Yet he does have a vision of himself stopping his criminal and substance-abusing behaviours.

Working against his changing is a personal philosophy of living one day at a time. He added that he has no expectations of what his future will be. He says he has none so that he won't get pissed off if he 'fails.' How much of this is the result of the oppression he has experienced culturally, or the result of other environmental factors, is difficult to say, but it does mean he will be unlikely to discuss at length anything but immediate concerns.

One other area really caught my interest and it is worth some exploration. Anthony talked about his admiration for the members of Native Warrior societies, their determination to fight for their rights, and other aspects of his cultural heritage. He perked up when we started talking about the struggles of Aboriginal peoples and he said he practices his rights whenever he can. He tells stories of fishing with his uncles despite the presence of Department of Fisheries officers or his band council's agreement to stop unlicenced fishing. He is a fighter and comfortable with this label in its political, non-physical sense.

The only troubling aspects of our conversations were Anthony's isolating behaviours, such as leaving school, spending days alone, drinking alone, and playing chess alone on a computer. Clinically speaking, he may be mildly depressed, but I am hesitant to give this label to behaviours that might make a great deal of sense and be adaptive for him. It would be up to others closer to his family and cultural milieu to interpret what I am observing and comment with authority.

All this makes me hopeful, however, that we can help Anthony. Anthony would like things to change, but not through formal talking cures alone. Instead, I would hope we can build on his past success at staying out of trouble, at changing peer groups, at being a fighter, and at limiting his substance abuse. He has adapted quite well to some very difficult situations, and it is this adaptation that needs further reinforcement.

I am also impressed with the number of people he says come to visit him and are still in his life. Are we connecting to this informal community of concern? Are they all invited to his case conferences, and can these meetings be used to help Anthony find the resources he needs to regain control of his life? Quite frankly, in this case I do not see we staff are the agents of change. These supports already exist in Anthony's life and can be marshaled together to mount an offensive against Anthony's problems. Our real task is to engage Anthony in a dialogue of resistance and power. This will be what is most healing for him.

More often, clinical case notes on children like Anthony become lengthy discussions of pathology, measuring how well a child fits with institutional norms. Labels become easily attached, and the context in which the child lives outside the institution all but ignored. It takes time and sensitivity to write about a child's life from the child's perspective. These notes, like the interviews that produce them, can be steps in a process of building a new salutogenic story about a child in which the cultural basis of his or her strengths come to make sense. Peer and family experiences become intelligible when seen as ways in which high-risk youth maintain coherence in their lives. These artifacts of treatment can also become resources which the child uses to maintain health, rather than barriers to well-being.

REVIEWING AND REFLECTING

As gains are made in a child's discursive power, both clinically, and in the wider social context, it is important to review clinical progress, reflecting back on the original contract and speculating on future developments. What started as a new story about the present, and then grew into a new-old story about the past, now becomes a story of resilience that predicts a different future from that previously anticipated. At this point in the therapeutic process, youth are asked about people and experiences that they may want to bring into their lives and strategies that need developing to accomplish this phase of intervention. As people begin to notice the differences between themselves and others, and can identify the resilience evident in their behaviour, it is my experience that they seek out new relationships, confident in their capacity to adapt. Furthering the clinical exploration of this new future, youth are asked, 'Are there still more ways you can make yourself feel healthy?' and 'How will you continue to show people how healthy you are?' The same individuals who were invited in to therapy earlier may now attend again and, in the same way that a reflecting team works (Andersen, 1991), provide the individual being worked with an updated picture of how his or her story of resilience is perceived by others.

Of course, personal growth is seldom as linear as presented above. More often, old narratives compete with new ones, and people experience temporary and cyclical returns to outdated stories that they used to tell about themselves as they confront conditions that put them at risk. When narratives of vulnerability return, high-risk youth need to be reminded that the original problems that brought them to counselling were powerful forces. Conversations about how tricky problems can be are useful tools. Equally important is exploring how lonely children can feel without their old stories and those who supported them and about how tiring it is to make changes. Sometimes it is worth recommending that problems be given back space in children's lives for a short time. In this regard, the process is similar to mourning any loss: at times there is the need to feel despondent, until the adaptive qualities of former behaviours are seen as generative and that which was discarded is remembered for its place in a process of growth. A problem like depression may have helped one cope with one's family, drug addiction may have been a way to break from isolation or feelings of powerlessness, and time in an institution may have brought with it a sense of belonging.

Trish had to take her new way of seeing herself, as a survivor and a brainy entrepreneur beyond the therapy room, back to both her friends and her family. She had not only to tell them this is how she wants to be known, but she also had to help those close to her realize that she has been this person all along, hidden beneath layers of expectations. In remembering her past, Trish was reminding others of the seeds that were planted early which foreshadowed who she would become.

Manifesting these changes is crucial to the change process. Trish had to get to university and sit down beside other 'bright kids' to prove that she could hold her own. Another youth, Saël, who was in custody for drug-related charges, decided that he no longer wanted to be an addict. Unlike previous times when he 'tried' to quit, this time he made the serious decision that the identity of addict no longer served his needs. He was 17 at the time and aware that his next serious criminal charge would land him in an adult facility. Creating a new self demanded participation in a landscape of action (Freedman & Combs, 1996) in which Saël purposefully placed himself in front of others so they could witness his new story. In custody, he organized a Narcotics Anonymous group specifically for teens and brought in the resource people to launch it. He talked it up with other residents, and although many attended just to visit with youth from other housing units, Saël and the few others who clustered around him were there with a sincere wish to change. The functionality of the drugs was no longer the only option Saël had for defining himself. In an odd reversal, the identity of recovering addict was even more powerful and brought him more recognition than being just another addict.

A SPIRALLING PROCESS

This phase of the work is necessarily reflective. Making progress through the three stages resembles a spiral circling upwards. Much time is taken when defining a new identity construction, creating experiences that help to nurture the young person's alternate story, then reflecting on the success or failure of these new plot elements. Sixteen-year-old Leslie successfully brought home the identity she had constructed for herself as an independent and responsible young woman outside her home, but not before the chaos of her parents' lives had seriously impeded her growing into the responsible young woman she wanted to be. Her mother insisted that, along with assuming responsibility for many of the household chores, Leslie attend a fundamentalist Christian church each weekend. When she refused to toe the line and do everything she was expected to do, her mother called her 'irresponsible' and labelled her a 'problem child.' She did this while ignoring the fact that her daughter was the only one among her peers to attend school full-time, hold down a 20-hour a week job, and make good grades. The mother could not get past her daughter's refusal to do as she was told. Leslie's two older sisters, aged 19 and 21, had either run from home or visited frequently with their own children, making the house more chaotic and more work for Leslie to keep tidy.

It took some negotiating but we eventually managed to untangle this web of complicated expectations and stories. Here was a young woman, similar to Melissa introduced in Chapter 2, who acted very responsibly outside her home, but was being cast into the dual roles of caretaker and child when at home. Leslie was not being treated as an adult or a child, but a fusion of the two without the respect afforded to either. In conversations with the family, what was discovered was not that Leslie hated going to church, but that she did not see the need for church at this point in her life, and that she wanted to make the decision to attend or not herself. What we also found was that this very responsible worker and student would be willing to bring home those identities if space was opened at home for others to see her for who she was. For Leslie, defining herself in front of her parents meant her showing them through responsible behaviour what she could do, while also challenging their story of her as irresponsible. But she would only bring this responsible self home if her family offered her the right to be treated more fairly and adultlike. Happily, these therapeutic conversations worked. Leslie found her way back home and negotiated a reasonable distribution of work between all the adults living there. As a young adult, she was also given the choice whether to attend church or not, and allowed to make other important decisions in her life regarding boyfriends and curfews.

When working with youth on the public definition of their resilient selves, therapy becomes a forum in which new identity experiences are documented and the plots of these alternate self-stories thickened. Through treatment, characters are given richly textured personalities as each chapter in a youth's life leads to a new understanding of what he or she can be. As these new stories are enriched, they come to predict different futures. While risk factors change the trajectory of a child's life, therapeutic conversations that help to redefine the child can also change a child's pattern of growth. Sustaining change means building on each sequential shift in perception. As high-risk teens more forward, new experiences and relationships become available as empowering and health-enhancing resources. The therapist, looking forward, asks about future coping capacity: 'Are there still more ways you can make yourself feel healthy?' 'To who else do you need to show your new self?' and, 'How else will you continue to show people how healthy you are?'

Understanding Setting

The setting in which this work takes place is important. The social construction of identity occurs within specific contexts in which both human and physical geography play a role. Treatment, therefore, must be attentive to the contextual complexity in which interventions are carried out. Such contextual specificity frequently threatens the fidelity of intervention programs that target high-risk youth (Mercy & Hammond, 2001). While unavoidable, flexibility in the delivery of programs is more akin to a constructionist approach to treatment that recognizes and affirms localized constructions of reality. For this reason, it is necessary that clinicians know where their clients live, work, and play. I prefer to vary the settings in which I conduct interviews. I enjoy the opportunity to travel to the homes of the children with whom I work so I can see their personal spaces (or lack thereof), their neighbourhoods, and interact with their friends and families in more relaxed settings. There is much to be learned about teens' construction of health when one is having a cup of coffee with them and their parents in their own kitchens.

Note the differences in the homes of two boys, both aged 15. Both Jeffrey and Callum had run away from home and then purposefully committed property crimes to have themselves placed in jail. During treatment both said they did not want to return home. Prior to participating in the research reported on throughout this book, both boys were in treatment with me for several months. Jeffrey lives in a well-maintained bungalow in the suburbs. The linoleum on the kitchen floor is new, the home is bright and evidently well cared for. His father had taken time off work to attend one of our in-home therapy sessions, although he checked his watch frequently while waiting for us to finish up. Jeffrey's mother was relaxed and played the hostess, having put on a fresh pot of coffee before Jeffrey's one-on-one worker and I arrived. Jeffrey has his own room, a panelled section of the basement he helped to fix up 2 years earlier so he could have privacy. It is an orderly scene, but one which Jeffrey has time and time again run from, lured by the unpredictability of the street and a lifestyle of drugs and criminal behaviour. Jeffrey said he has never felt at home with his parents. He said he felt like he was adopted and that he belongs with another family.

Callum's mother and stepfather live in a low-rent district on the outskirts of town. When Callum's social worker and I went for a scheduled visit at 11:00 one Tuesday morning there was no answer at the door. We phoned 15 minutes later and woke up his mother who said she had slept in but would be ready to see us in half an hour. Callum had stayed home from school for the meeting. When we returned we were shown into a small smokey two-bedroom basement apartment.

The television was on. Callum's stepfather glared at us from the couch, where he sat without a shirt, and a can of Coca-Cola. Another fellow was there as well, having slept on the couch after drinking with the stepdad into the early hours of the morning. Callum was having a bowl of Cheerios with powdered milk, while his mother made coffee. We were not exactly invited in, but found a place to sit around the small kitchen table. Eventually we got dad to leave his friend and the television to join us for a few minutes of conversation. We even got to see Callum's room. There we found a mattress on the floor. The boy's few belongings were in boxes in the corner of the room, while the stepdad's work tools were scattered everywhere else. He is unemployed, the stepfather later explained, and needed a place to put them. There were no posters on the wall, no blinds, nothing that said a 15-year-old boy lived there.

Both boys were in treatment at the same facility at the same time and frequently in the same groups. What drove them each to leave home, however, was very different. Callum says he enjoys his time inside. Jeffrey knows it does him good, but would rather be out.

These home settings and those who reside there form the backdrop to the stories youth act out as they sustain resilient identities. Without an understanding of the context in which a child constructs meaning, it is unlikely the therapist can know the meaning of a child's behaviour. For clinicians working in settings where office visits are the norm, an alternative approach is to invite in as many of the informal supports a child has as possible. Although therapists are sometimes shy to ask in to sessions boyfriends and girlfriends, roommates, close friends, concerned teachers, one-on-one workers, or whoever else mirrors support for the emerging identity of a youth, these significant others can contribute greatly to the contextualization of the child's experiences of discursive power.

Seldom is confidentiality a concern for the child who welcomes the opportunity to introduce his or her therapist to those who see the youngster as healthy and those who are perceived as threatening to that health. If anything, youth find that the inclusion of their friends, family, and community in clinical sessions counteracts the potentially stigmatizing effects of treatment. 'See,' they can say, 'it's not so weird going to see a therapist.' I do not, after all, work in a city like New York, where, as Woody Allen would have us believe, psychoanalysts are apparently as common as plumbers. Instead, in the conservative communities in which most professionals like myself practise, people mystify the work of therapists. Making the boundaries between the clinician and the world outside therapy more permeable challenges the stigma that comes with misunderstanding. It also conveys to communities the message that these youth are still *their* responsibility and that they have the potential to co-construct a child's healthy sense of self.

Case Study: Cameron

A detailed clinical history of Cameron provides a case study based loosely on a youth I worked with at length over several years. This recounting of our work together highlights the way the three stages of therapy flow together. Of course, although the specifics of Cameron's life are presented in great detail, the individual upon whom I have based this case study is different in many ways from the child presented here. To keep the real Cameron's identity confidential, like all the other youth who appear in this book, substantial details have been changed, and case material amalgamated to create a story of a boy typical of many with whom I have worked.

Cameron's life and treatment illustrates the integration of therapy with social context. While included in this chapter, Cameron's course of treatment really reflects the way that *formal and informal* community and institutional caregivers, including myself as his primary therapist, worked together (see Chapter 8 for more on this). Mentors and volunteers, families and paraprofessionals were not just there to support intensive clinical work, but were themselves offering Cameron clinically significant interventions that contributed as much or more as my work with him to his construction of a personal and social identity as resilient.

Cameron is now 18 years old. He has spent his entire life in a small urban centre on the eastern seaboard. There are many things remarkable about this young man, not the least of which is that he is *not* in jail, but lives in the community in which he grew up, relatively free of problems. Cameron attends school three half-days a week. When we last met, he had been employed at his most recent part-time job for 2 weeks washing dishes at a local restaurant. He found that job with the help of his former one-on-one worker, who still maintains contact with him. Cameron does, however, remain on probation under the terms of a youth court order that specifies where he must reside. He takes no medications, but he admits to using soft drugs occasionally.

He says he has given them up entirely since he started working, although he continues to drink heavily on weekends.

Cameron resides now with his Aunt Tanya, his father's youngest sister, and her 4-year-old twin boys. Tanya has been Cameron's primary caregiver for the past 3 years, although he also frequently stays overnight with his paternal Grandmother Betty. Betty and her late husband John, legally adopted Cameron at age 2 and kept him until he was removed by Social Services staff and placed with Tanya at age 15. For Cameron, this is a surprisingly stable and positive life, given earlier expectations expressed by many who know him.

Growing Up at Risk

Cameron's mother Cheryl was 18 when she gave birth to Cameron. She and Cameron's father, known to his friends as Buddy, had been going out for over a year. Six months into the pregnancy they moved in together. Cheryl describes the relationship as extremely violent with her having to go to a shelter when in a drunken rage Buddy fired a shotgun at the wall behind her. Cameron was asleep in the next room. Cheryl describes Buddy as always having been 'a little crazy.'

Neither parent, according to Cheryl, was ready to look after Cameron, and he was left for long periods in his crib. Following an incident where he fell down a flight of stairs while in a child's walker at the age of 18 months, Cameron was hospitalized and then removed from his parents home by Social Services. Previously, Cameron had been brought to the emergency department after ingesting lighter fluid, and with a variety of bumps and bruises. He returned only briefly to Cheryl's care before she had him placed permanently with Buddy's parents, both of whom were recovering alcoholics. Cheryl left to look for work in another part of the country. Buddy ignored his son, visiting his parents rarely even though he lived only an hour away. Despite the return of their drinking problems shortly after Cameron's placement with them, Cameron's grandparents were able to maintain a relatively stable home for their grandson until Cameron's grandfather died when he was 9. At that point, Betty's drinking became uncontrollable and Social Services was forced to make Cameron a permanent ward, although he returned to live with Betty for varying lengths of time until he was 15. He saw his mother once a year when she came home for a visit, but he rarely saw his father. It is believed that sometime during the years at his grandparents, Cameron was sexually assaulted by a member of his community who is known to have molested several of Cameron's friends. Cameron has no memory of the incident.

When younger, Cameron's behaviour at school was particularly difficult for authorities to cope with as it endangered other children. In one report, made when Cameron was 11, his elementary school principal wrote: 'Cameron has been involved in a number of incidents on the playground where the rights and safety of other children have been violated. The latest incidents included pushing a girl into a puddle such that she sat in it and became soaked. That happened yesterday. Today he and another boy had a rope which they wrapped around the neck of a third child, then pulled on it, choking and terrifying that child.' By age 13 there is mention in Cameron's file of at least 6 different psychiatric and psychological assessments being completed during his childhood. Among the different diagnostic labels that were assigned to Cameron by the time of his early adolescence are reactive attachment disorder of infancy and early childhood, attention deficit hyperactivity disorder, and oppositional defiant disorder. In general, Cameron was described as a youth with attachment problems, low self-esteem, poor peer relations, and problems with aggression. These behaviours were, according to one report, believed to 'reflect Cameron's low self-esteem and difficulty achieving lasting acceptance from peers.'

Even before he went into custody at age 13, Cameron had been assigned the constant support of a one-on-one worker, usually for 10 hours per week. This person was meant to provide Cameron with 'basic life skills training,' accompany Cameron on various outings and act as a 'big brother,' provide 'support and respite care and control' allowing his foster parent time to 'recharge her batteries,' and provide transportation and logistical support to get Cameron to his many clinical appointments. The one-on one worker who cared for Cameron a year later described him as requiring 'clear boundaries' without which his behaviour would always be 'unpredictable.'

Cameron had also begun scarring himself, carving deep lines into his forearms and chest. He had repeated violent episodes at both his foster home and his grandmother's, including one where he punched numerous holes in the walls and pushed Betty over the back of a couch. Cameron's physical and sexually aggressive outbursts, his past physical and sexual victimization, his emerging pattern of delinquency, his lack of a stable home environment, and lack of attachment to school made him one of the highest-risk youth in his community. It was becoming apparent that the available resources were quickly being exhausted and that there was little to offer him. The alternative school program that he attended kept having to suspend him, time in custody was becoming more and more frequent, and mental health facilities such as group homes and psychiatric units had trouble coping with the risks Cameron posed to himself, other residents, and staff.

Numerous case conferences were held. At the first one I attended, there were 21 professional, paraprofessional, and family supports people all gathered to discuss Cameron's problems. At this one meeting there were representatives from management and staff of secure and open custody programs, probation services, the director of mental health, a psychiatrist, a sexual deviance specialist, educational alternative program administrative and teaching staff, staff from special services for the department of education, Cameron's grandmother and aunt, social work supervisors and front-line workers from Child and Family Services, representatives from community groups such as the Boys and Girls' Club, and two one-on-one support workers who had had recent contact with Cameron. Interestingly, the only person who reported success with Cameron at the meeting was a young female one-on-one worker who was able to highlight Cameron's cooperative and helpful nature when properly engaged. Her acceptance of him and willingness to work with him at a pace he could handle had resulted in Cameron making some progress in his studies (her gender and caring attitude may reasonably have contributed to his willingness to cooperate as well).

Case conferences such as these tended to focus on Cameron's urgent need for help and the frustration with each system's inability to effectively intervene. While placement outside the region was discussed, several people, including Social Services staff, one-on-one workers, and Cameron's extended family, preferred that he be maintained in his community, despite the risks. Periods of incarceration were forecast as a way of setting limits on Cameron's behaviour. Respite and alternative placements were proposed to help Betty cope with Cameron, and increased resources were to be put into providing one-on-one supports. Local community groups also said that they would help to integrate Cameron into their programs as long as he attended with supervision. Despite this plan, Cameron soon had to be placed in a residential adolescent mental health facility after becoming violent on several occasions with Betty.

Cameron was at the facility for 6 months on a course of medication to stabilize his behaviour. He received both Clonidine, an antihypertensive, and Dexedrine, an amphetamine used for ADHD. Academically, Cameron received extra support with educators noting that 'due to Cameron's short attention span, plus his problems with sequential thinking and information retention, Cameron still needs a lot of work on his cognitive skills.' Despite the interventions, Cameron was soon charged with breaching his probation order after uttering death threats to his uncle, damaging Betty's home while on a visit there, damaging property at the treatment facility and carrying a concealed weapon. A predisposition report done at the time described Cameron as 'hyperactive, immature, easily distracted, unpredictable, impulsive and an individual who requires an appreciable amount of direct supervision, guidance, structure and encouragement.' The report also noted Cameron's 'capacity to exhibit positive characteristics, i.e., kindhearted, respectful, communicative, likeable, intelligent, honest' and the hope that if placed in a 'normal, stable and safe home environment' he would do better than being returned to custody. Surprisingly, the court followed these recommendations and continued Cameron's placement in the community, fining him, putting him under the supervision of his youth worker, and ordering him to attend counselling and live where directed. Despite the effort, though, Cameron's behaviour continued to deteriorate, and he found himself in secure custody for 3 months when he failed to comply with the conditions of this second probation order. Within days of his placement back at the treatment facility he had caused further damage to property, started a fire with barbeque lighter fluid, and been physically aggressive towards other residents. The director of the facility noted, 'We have tried many interventions to turn Cameron's behaviour around. Constant care, moving him to our crisis bed apart from other residents, having staff members who he trusts spend extra time with him, but nothing has stopped this boy from continuing his direction downward.'

Even though Cameron was returned to custody at the time and stayed there for most of the next year, several aspects of a collaborative multisystemic and institutional response helped to stabilize Cameron's behaviour. A one-on-one worker, who was employed both at the custody facility and who had worked with Cameron in the community, maintained contact with Cameron providing continuity in the case planning process. As the one-on-one worker noted 8 months into Cameron's sentence, 'the knowledge that I would remain with Cameron, allowed for more concrete long-term planning. It was much easier to focus on long-term tasks and goals when one knows that there will be someone there to facilitate their completion.' Although a large number of people had become involved in Cameron's life, efforts were made to maintain consistency in the one-on-one workers and other Social Services' staff. Interestingly, up to this point there was little emphasis placed on the interventions of professional staff who conducted the assessments. In reviewing Cameron's file, there appears to be a greater reliance on the supports that came from the paraprofessionals who helped Cameron and his family cope with the challenges they faced. These supports helped Cameron make the transition back into his community.

First Contacts

It was during this period of incarceration when Cameron was 14 that I finally became involved with him and his family directly. That involvement would last several years, with contact occurring periodically as Cameron cycled through episodes of calm and chaos. This pacing of my work with a youth like Cameron is fairly typical of my practice. Because these youth grow along irregular paths, and their identity constructions change and are challenged frequently, I find brief spurts of treatment followed by periods during which I watch from the sidelines to be the best strategy for clinical interventions. These youth can be further stigmatized by treatment that does not respect the fact that, at times, they will be well adjusted and not want or need to see a counsellor. Having additional supports in the community and open lines of communication can ensure that when help is needed, it is readily accessible. Such was the case for Cameron, as his behaviour and identity changed over the ensuing years.

When I start working with a youth like this, one who comes with a file already chock-full of diagnoses and a lengthy history of involvement with people like me, I start by reviewing past interventions and finding out what, if anything, the child experienced as helpful while working with professional clinicians. In Cameron's case, he told me emphatically that nothing that had been tried had been the least bit useful to him or his family. I try to learn from what did or did not work in the past, then start my own exploration of the child's history, attentive to the potential failures that children like Cameron expect from therapy. In the first interview or two, besides looking backwards, I also begin a series of drawings and externalizations. In Cameron's case, the exercises we started when he was 14 would be revisited numerous times in the coming years.

It was not long into these first conversations that I felt it necessary to pull out a flip chart and markers to try and organize all the different people in Cameron's life. Using a genogram as a structure for our conversation, we explored the history of Cameron's family and the various problems he had encountered. I was looking for clues as to what would help this boy build resilience amidst the chaos he faced.

MICHAEL: All these details are sort of getting me confused. There's a
  lot that's happened to you. If it's alright, I'd like to just draw out
  what you talk about, so we can both see what's going on here.
CAMERON: (shrugging) Makes no difference.

Over the next half hour Cameron talked about his family and some of the important events in his past. The interview was purposefully kept at a quick pace to avoid losing his attention. We would have plenty of time to go back over this same territory later on. I learned much about his family and that he had always had a reputation for being 'bull headed' and the 'Number One Bad Kid' in the family. But we also discovered that there were times when his Grandmother Betty and Aunt Tanya told him he could be 'sweet as gold.' We wrote all these descriptions of him, along with descriptions that he volunteered for others in his family, on the flip chart. As we carried on, I realized that he was confused about much of his family history and knew little or nothing about why he was removed from his mother. Incredibly, he was even a little unclear whether his grandmother and grandfather with whom he was placed are his father's parents or his mother's. We ended that day agreeing to meet again to talk some more.

The next time we sat down to talk his primary unit worker Shane joined us. This would become typical of many of our meetings, with invitations extended to any number of significant people in Cameron's life. During this second meeting we negotiated a contract to work together to help Cameron have what he described as 'fewer break-outs,' referring to the violent displays of his explosive temper. He wanted to be able to continue living with his grandmother, and he wanted out of custody. These all seemed reasonable goals, and with the help of his primary worker, it was easier to help facilitate a discharge plan that reflected the gains made during treatment.

In the following weeks, Cameron, his caregivers, and I worked on developing a new language that he could use to describe himself. One of the words indigenous to the therapy was 'crazy.' It just kept coming up as the best way Cameron could describe his behaviour and the way most others who were tasked with caring for the boy thought of him.

CAMERON: When I'm out it's like I keep going crazy. And then I do wild things like punch holes in walls. My room has all these big f–ing holes all over the place. And my door too. I kicked it off the hinges and my Uncle Ricky had to come over to Mom's [grand-mother's] to fix it.

MICHAEL: How often does stuff like that happen?

CAMERON: A lot. I think I must have been like that when little too 'cause I have all these memories of Cheryl having to hold me and rock me. Like I'd just be freakin' and like she'd have to get down on the floor and do that. I'd smash toys, everything. I was a mean little f–er.

MICHAEL: Do you remember these things yourself, or have people also told you about them?

CAMERON: What?.

MICHAEL: Well sometimes what we remember is also told to us by others, so our memories and what we are told get all put together.

CAMERON: No, I can really remember what Cheryl used to do. But they talk about it. It's like a bit of a joke now.

MICHAEL: So what else do you do that's crazy?

CAMERON: I guess I've always been that way. Like even the shrinks keep giving me this medication shit and it's supposed to calm me down, but it makes me more like a friggin' zombie or something. I'm used to always be freakin' when I'm not on it, especially in school. Everyone thinks I'm like this spaced-out kid, but it's the meds that do that to you. Except when I'm not on them, then I sometimes drink and all that so then I'm just as spaced, and some-times if I'm doing both at the same time then it really gets me all messed, right? So I know I shouldn't, but what do you expect?

MICHAEL: Are you still this crazy when you're in here, in custody?

CAMERON: Maybe.

SHANE: Like maybe should be definitely. What about on the unit yesterday? The kicking, mouthing off, all that stuff?

CAMERON: We were just joking around, but like the staff thought we shouldn't be kicking each other under the table. They didn't un-derstand. And then we get sent to our rooms for a loss of free time. And all because we're havin' a little fun. That's all. Really.

MICHAEL: Seems like in here everyone knows you as the 'crazy kid' and that's how they're going to see what you do. No matter what. What do you think?

CAMERON: Maybe. I'm not crazy, but they all think it just because before I did a few things, and like everyone says it's because I was abused as a kid and all that, but I don't remember none of it.

SHANE: He can also be a great kid when he's in here. Outside too, but outside you just run us all nuts trying to keep up with you and keep you from getting into trouble.

CAMERON: (laughs)

MICHAEL: So lots of people know you as the 'crazy kid.' Is that how it is? Are you always like that or are you ever not crazy too?

CAMERON: No most times I'm like that.

MICHAEL: Do you want to change that? Be any less crazy, or more?

CAMERON: No f–ing way. When I'm the crazy kid it's great. At parties I'm the one everyone looks at to start some fun. I'm like that. I'm always up on things.

MICHAEL: Do you want to be crazy all the time, though? Say we could make you less crazy. Like when you were threatening that kid with the knife, how crazy were you, 10%, 25%, 50%, 100%?

CAMERON: Maybe more like closer to 100%, but not exactly. I didn't actually hurt him.

MICHAEL: Okay, so how crazy would you like to be, if you could choose?

CAMERON: Twenty-five %. That way I could still have fun at parties, but I wouldn't get into trouble the same.

MICHAEL: And what word would you use to describe yourself when you're not the crazy kid?

CAMERON: Probably normal.

MICHAEL: What would normal be like?

CAMERON: Just doing what I'm supposed to be doing. Going to school, no more meds, acting like everyone thinks I should, not punching holes in walls. I don't know.

MICHAEL: And would normal be better than crazy, or would it depend on who you were with?

CAMERON: It would depend, like, I like being crazy sometimes. But not like when I don't want to be.

SHANE: I can think of lots of times when he's normal. There was another time when I was on shift and Coady was on Cameron's case all day, but he didn't do anything. Just walked away. No big deal, no consequences.

CAMERON: He's an asshole anyway.

MICHAEL: That's not my experience of Coady, but I can understand that living on a unit can get pretty tense sometimes. So it might be yours. I don't live with him I guess. Still, it's nice to see that people notice when you're not the crazy kid, eh?.

Both Shane and I thought that we should work on getting others to notice how frequently Cameron was 'normal.' It was a hard sell at first, but became easier as people paid attention. Eventually we would even convince the judiciary that Cameron was more normal than crazy.

From that point on we worked to get the 75% of Cameron that he did not want to be crazy in control of the 25% that he did. Cameron played along making sure that the crazy part always had some time and space to express himself. That 25% was what made Cameron tick, kept him positive about life, and made it possible for him to have friends. Otherwise, he would have found himself on the street, alone, and invisible. He said his girlfriends also liked him better as the crazy kid, because they were all crazy themselves.

A New Cameron Emerges

A few months after we began building Cameron's discursive power over this self-definition, and towards the end of his fifteenth year, Cameron was again preparing for discharge as he had done several times before. By this point, he had been transferred for a short period to an open custody facility. From there he was discharged first back to the mental health facility from where he had come, and then to his aunt's. During the following few months that he stayed out in his community, Cameron did not break the law and, for the most part, remained well behaved at his aunt's. Respite visits back to his grandmother's helped to ease tensions. Nevertheless, Cameron's time in the community lasted but a few months, before he was returned yet again to custody for breaches of his probation order including being intoxicated in a public place and driving under age and without a licence. While for those of us caring for him it felt like another failure, to Cameron it was just more of the same. He was actually quite pleased that he was returning to custody and that he had successfully lived with his aunt for as long as he had. Reports in his file showed that one-on-one workers, probation officers, and social workers had provided continuity in his case management during this period until he returned to custody. Close attention was paid to developing four aspects of Cameron's life in order to ensure a consistent set of expectations and structures for the next time that he was discharged. Case managers were tasked with ensuring that Cameron's place of residence, day programming, evening programming, and counselling would all be kept in place. Given that his sentence was for only 3 months, discharge planning began immediately. The one-on-one worker at the time wrote: 'I feel that Cameron would benefit from the stability of knowing who will be involved with him after discharge.' There was a realization that 'this plan involves a great deal of interagency cooperation and spending of resources.' Although the one-on-one workers who were with Cameron changed when he turned 16, the transition was smooth and done with the previous one-on-one worker's full cooperation and support. At that point, there were two one-on-one workers providing a total of 20 hours per week of support to Cameron to help maintain him in his community. Formal treatment continued, focusing on both Cameron's 'crazy' and 'normal' behaviours as he went through these transitions.

It was while he was back in his community, just before he turned 16, that we started focusing much more on the path, or trajectory, that he wanted to travel into adulthood. This time, I met Cameron in the community at Betty's home, where he was staying for a few weeks while his aunt was ill. It was the same home that the family had lived in for years, a 70-year-old wooden structure in a older part of the city. It needed a coat of paint and a bit of yard work, but the inside was neat and decorated with religious curios. A large console television sat in one corner of the living room, a glider rocker in the other with his grandmother's sewing on a table next to it. The house smelled of stale cigarettes and faintly of alcohol. The King Cole tea that was served had been boiling all day on a back burner of the stove and was dark and bitter. I was passed Carnation canned milk to dilute it. As Cameron, his grandmother, and I sat around the kitchen table, I began to hear recurring patterns to what was happening in Cameron's life and the life of his family.

MICHAEL: It's like Cameron, you can be anything, even a mechanic, but somehow all that early stuff that happened got you off track.

Just like it did for your mother, maybe your father too (I pull out a sheet of blank paper and a pen, and as if plotting a rocket's trajectory, draw two large arcs up the page. Cameron had seen the same sketch before. I take a few minutes to explain it to Betty. It's like all that stuff you remember and are now finding out about yourself bumped you off course, when you became the crazy kid. But I'm impressed that the normal kid has hung around and is doing all right. Or maybe I should say is *now* doing all right. That crazy kid keeps appearing.

CAMERON: He hasn't been around much since I got out. I haven't done nothing bad since I got out. (He looks to his grandmother.)

BETTY: He's actually been quite good, really. Though I get tired of the swearing and he won't turn the music down. The filth in that stuff is all a bit much! But he's mostly a good kid.

MICHAEL: You're noticing he's getting better. That Cameron's more normal than before?

BETTY: Oh my yes, for sure. But we're not out of the woods yet, are we? My no, not quite. I wish that were so, but no, not yet.

CAMERON: It's not like before though. And I've been out a while. Even Shane and Greg (his new one-on-one worker) think I'm doing all right. And he should know. Like he's with me every friggin' time I turn around, and then there's all the piss tests. Like it's not like I can screw up?

MICHAEL: So you're not quite back on track but you're getting real close? (Pointing to the picture I'd drawn)

CAMERON: Yeah, somewhere there in the middle I guess (he, too, points to the drawing). Like I'm not in jail, I'm not down at friggin' [he names the regional psychiatric facility]. And my uncle said he'd help me get on at Frizzle's next summer pulling parts off wrecks which means I can get for free all the stuff I'd need to fix something up. That's what I really want, to have my own car.

BETTY: You don't have no licence and you won't go get it either, will you? Will he? (She looks at me.)

CAMERON: I don't need no licence to just fix a car up or drive it around some field.

As we continued talking, we compared patterns in Cameron's conventional and unconventional behaviour. Cameron could get a job at an automotive wrecker, but he was not sure enough of himself to go through a driving test and legitimately get his licence. That step would have to wait. Thankfully, he never could quite afford to get a car of his own and therefore avoided the inevitable problems associated with Cameron again driving unlicensed and uninsured.

Gaining Control

The multiple short placements in custody when Cameron was 15 going on 16 had succeeded in stabilizing his behaviour without significantly damaging his connection to his caregivers. He had maintained contact with them and built a more positive relationship with his Aunt Tanya and his Grandmother Betty. Cameron also made several attempts around this time to contact his father, who was dying of cancer. These attempts failed because his stepmother refused to allow Cameron to see his father, fearing the stress would upset her husband's condition. Cameron's natural mother, however, became more active in his life, sending him expensive birthday presents, and eventually she agreed, while home for a visit a few months later, to meet with her son and me. Through these sessions Cameron came to better understand his personal history and the abuse and addictions problems his mother faced. Cameron wanted to go live with his mother, but Cheryl was both unable and unwilling to take her son back.

Between custodial dispositions Cameron was in school with his peers, and he even managed to return to a regular school environment, although in a special needs classroom. Cameron's intimate peer relationships around this time showed the same chaotic pattern as his relationships with his caregivers. He had several girlfriends throughout his adolescence, at least two of whom were themselves suicidal or self-mutilating and who required hospitalization. Several others had drug and alcohol problems. It was believed for a time that Cameron might have contracted AIDS as a result of one of his sexual encounters, although he later tested negative for HIV.

At the age of 16 Cameron asked to return to his grandmother's to live. It was felt, however, that this would pose too many risks to Cameron and his community because of the lack of supervision that would result. As a second choice, and with some convincing, Cameron agreed to continue living with his Aunt Tanya but wanted time away in a respite foster home. This time, his placement with his aunt was seen as a permanent solution to his residency needs until he turned 18. Arrangements were made to ensure it worked as well as it could. The supports and respite care Cameron requested were put in place.

As well, during particularly difficult times, Cameron was removed for a night or two and placed in an emergency bed at the regional mental health facility to help diffuse the tension at home.

The more we followed Cameron's lead, the easier our job as caregivers became. I can remember vividly, watching him during one case conference at his high school, squirm and fidget the whole time. He looked anxious. I had heard that day from his aunt that tensions at home and school were building, again. During a break in the action, I turned to Cameron and asked him one simple question.

MICHAEL: What do you need right now to hold it together?
CAMERON: Some time away.
MICHAEL: All right then, I'll see what I can do.

Rather than sit and talk about the problems at school or plans for greater integration with the student body, I left the meeting, made a few calls to some colleagues of mine asking them to find Cameron a short-term, out-of-home placement. His regular foster placement was unavailable. His grandmother's would not work. The team pulled together and found him something. He was quite happy to hear an hour later that he would be going for a couple of weeks to the Andersons, an elderly couple who took in problem kids. Cameron was surprisingly well behaved for the time he was there. Tensions calmed. He had a bit of time to think. He was pleased that he had not had to break the law to be heard. Systems cannot always respond like this, but my experience is that they can more often than they do, but choose not to. As workers, we get caught in our rules and procedures as surely as kids get caught in cycles of violence or truancy. We tend to do things when they are convenient for us, not when they are necessary for the kids and families that we serve.

Although I met with Cameron twice while he was in placement that time, it was his maintaining contact with his other workers that ensured this period of respite was effective. His worker with Child and Family Services who, thank goodness, kept close tabs on the boy, informed me that he was anxious about plans that he attend school more often. He also had just had a friend killed in a motor vehicle accident. And his girlfriend had spent some time back on a psychiatric ward after threatening suicide. Little wonder that with all this, Cameron was reporting being distracted and finding it hard to settle down at school or play by the rules at home.

Fortunately, it was shortly after he had returned to his aunt's, where he was then residing permanently, that his mother came back for a longer visit during which she agreed to meet Cameron and me together. She and Cameron spent a few days shopping and hanging out and then came in twice in one week to talk at my office. It was a rare opportunity to help Cameron find out more about his past and about what he could expect for his future. His mother Cheryl is a small woman, who has herself achieved much more than her past would have predicted. The eighth of eleven children, she suffered much abuse, physical and sexual, while growing up. Her relationship with Buddy was just one more sad episode in a life of disappointments. But when we met, she, like her son, had a different story to tell alongside this tale of vulnerability. She had landed on her feet, although it had taken years of bouncing in and out of detoxification centres, and now regular Alcoholic Anonymous meetings, to keep her stable. Cheryl cleaned houses for a living and had recently become involved romantically with an elderly man for whom she worked. During the first of these meetings we talked about Cameron's life history, with Cheryl filling in the pieces that her son did not know. It was an opportunity for Cameron to sit back and listen as Cheryl unfolded her life story, and his. During our second meeting, I returned to a discussion we had had of a number of themes that were by then grafted on to Cameron's original genogram.

MICHAEL: I was thinking that, Cheryl, you had to cope with much the same craziness that Cameron has had to deal with. And so did Buddy. Like this craziness, he comes by it honestly, and it shows up all over the place. (I take a marker and added to the genogram constructed earlier a bunch of stars, prodding both Cheryl and Cameron to help me identify who else in the family has had to deal with 'craziness' and to tell me a bit more about them and their experiences.)

CHERYL: There's a lot of it in the family, for sure.

CAMERON: But not everyone ... But Buddy, he used to be crazy. Like everyone says it. There's even people back at custody who knew him. They all say that's what he's like.

MICHAEL: I'm curious, though, Cheryl, you've gotten mostly over this craziness. You're doing well now. Not drinking, not in another abusive relationship, you have your own place you said. So how did you survive it all? Keep the craziness from taking you over?

CHERYL: I don't know. It sort of took some work. I'm not really sure. When I left here that was a real tough decision, but I knew I couldn't be here no more, like I had to get away from here and my family and Buddy and all the stuff we'd done. Then when I got out west I just sort of didn't do much at first. And then, I don't know, a few things changed, I went back to school for a bit, did a home care course, and like it all just sort of started going together. I lived with this guy, Amil, for 5 years. He helped. He kept me away from the drugs and alcohol, but he was all right about it. He knew about Cameron, and that was okay too ... It all just sort of happened.

MICHAEL: But something in you made it happen? Do you think you could teach your son to do that, too? I can't help but think you're the expert here on surviving.

CHERYL: I don't know, really. Expert at nothing, I'd say. I could just tell him what I've done if it helps some. I haven't really been around much to do anything else ... I sort of regret that. I've told him that before.

CAMERON: (after a pause) I'd really like to see Buddy, but I can't. That's what I was wondering if you could help with. Every time I call him Tabatha [Buddy's wife] won't let me talk to him. She keeps saying that's because they're all afraid I'm gonna upset him or something. Like he's not dying right away or anything. He's sick, but like I should be able to see him. He's my dad. Not just her husband, the bitch.

CHERYL: Yeah, Tabatha's like that. She just won't let none of the family near him. Like it's her God-given job or something stupid like that, to keep him away from his son.

MICHAEL: Does he know how well Cameron is doing?

CHERYL: Probably not. There'd be no one to tell him. Maybe Tanya might be able to get a call through. She's his sister. That might work. They're all right screwed up, that's for sure.

MICHAEL: I must say I don't really know what will work here, but I like your idea. It would be good if Buddy could see what his son's grown into. Maybe we could ask Tanya to help. Could you do that Cameron?

CAMERON: (shrugs)

MICHAEL: Well, maybe Cheryl, then, could you ask Tanya to help? This keeps coming up. I think Cameron needs to see Buddy, if only to show him he's doing okay.

CHERYL: Yeah, I can do that for him. Tanya will probably do it.

MICHAEL: Are there other people who might need to notice the way Cameron has managed to put aside his crazy kid stuff? Be normal?

CAMERON: My school needs to. And my grandmother, though she's right crazy with the drinking and all that too. My girlfriend likes me crazy so I don't tell her I've changed. And most of my friends, they just say, don't go back to jail, that's all. So I guess it's really the school and maybe the guys back at the front desk at the jail who need to know. Maybe I should just set up a chair outside the door of the jail and let them see that I'm not inside any more. I could kind of sit there laughing at them. They all thought I'd be back sooner and would never get out.

MICHAEL: Not everyone. Shane still talks about you and tells everyone how well you're doing. (Turning to Cheryl) A lot of people are proud that Cameron has gotten himself off his meds, and hasn't been back in custody for a while. They all liked him.

CHERYL: He's a great kid (she smiles and grabs Cameron's hand and gives it a squeeze). Really, he is.

Conversations similar to this took place with Cameron and a number of his different caregivers. Tanya frequently dropped in, and then there were case conferences at the school and with Cameron's one-on-one workers and social workers. Each meeting was an opportunity to share Cameron's struggle against the craziness in his life and find ways for him to perform more 'normally.' As long as we were respectful of Cameron's need to 'go crazy' now and again, he willingly played along, enjoying the attention and the control he experienced over how others saw him.

Positive Outcomes

These coordinated efforts allowed Cameron to continue in school part-time making some gains in his reading and social skills. Academically, he still functioned at an elementary school level, but he was making progress. Unfortunately, it was also at this time that he began using drugs more frequently and that his drinking pattern changed. Addictions counselling was started to help Cameron make better choices. His counsellor succeeded at least in helping him put the brakes on an escalating pattern. Cameron showed that he could stop his abuse of soft drugs and prescription medications, although continued to abuse alcohol.

That there was a consistent team of supports for Cameron also led to some unique outcomes in terms of placements. For instance, Cameron was caught shoplifting a pair of jeans while under the supervision of corrections staff who had taken him out of secure custody to buy new clothes. However, rather than being charged with the offence, Cameron was placed on a 3-month undertaking by a youth court judge who warned him he would have his time in custody extended if he committed any other crimes. The strength of the case plan and recommendations by all those involved had persuaded the judge to view this latest episode as a plea for help and a problem related to Cameron's mental health, not a criminal act. Another incident shortly after discharge had a similar outcome. Cameron was alleged to have chased a small child in his neighbourhood down his block while wielding a knife. Again, because Cameron was maintaining an attachment to school, and following through on all aspects of his probation order including maintaining a residence with his aunt, addictions and personal counselling, regular contact with his one-on-one workers, and a part-time job, he was again warned of the seriousness of his actions, but left in the community for a trial period. Six months later, a third incident occurred in which Cameron shook his 4-year-old cousin, knocked his grandmother out while she was heavily intoxicated, stayed out far past his curfew, and broke his aunt's television. Surprisingly, no charges were laid by those involved. All felt that Cameron's progress, despite these episodes, showed promise and that a period of stability in his behaviour would follow. This is, in fact, what occurred for many months. However, at age 17, Cameron was again in secure custody, this time for a series of breaches of his probation order involving abuse of drugs and alcohol, repeatedly not obeying the residency clause of the order, carrying a concealed weapon, and another alleged assault on a child in his community.

During that year we met periodically, sometimes weekly, sometimes monthly, depending on how 'crazy' Cameron was acting, and the anxiety level of his formal and informal caregivers. During one of these interviews, after he had been inside for 2 months and completely dried out, we talked about what had happened just before he came back in.

MICHAEL: How did the craziness get so strong, just before you got yourself back in here?

CAMERON: It comes out with the drugs. I was doing a lot. I was back in again with some real bad-asses. My new girlfriend didn't like what I was doing either.

MICHAEL: Do you miss her, now that you're in here?

CAMERON: I think she's more attracted to me when I'm 'normal.' Like so is Tanya, everybody. Except my mom. I don't think it matters much to her.

MICHAEL: Have you heard from Cheryl in the last while?

CAMERON: She was supposed to send me some big-assed gift for my birthday, but then said she couldn't afford it or something. I'd asked her to send up some tools so I could work on cars. Like I'd been talking about. Becoming a mechanic. You know? But they never showed up, and when I called she was like 'I'm sorry,' but I still didn't get them. I guess the drugs just helped. I was pretty sad and f–ed up. Sort of tamed down my emotions.

MICHAEL: That's interesting that you see that. Congrats. But I'm sorry about the gifts not showing up. Cheryl's got her own crazy stuff to deal with, doesn't she?

CAMERON: I suppose she must. Living with some old guy just to get his money.

MICHAEL: So what's it like now being back in here?

CAMERON: It's all right. At least it makes Tanya let go a bit more. And in school I don't mess up. I have to go, do my homework, all that. I'm not near as crazy as I was before.

MICHAEL: (pulling out the picture we'd drawn together months before of his different trajectories through life) It's like those tools were part of this path, to becoming a mechanic. But you're not really the crazy screw-up everybody expected, even if you are back in custody. The judge kept you as long as he could in the community like a normal kid. Is that how you see it?

CAMERON: Yeah. I don't think I'll wind up in adult or on some psych ward drooling gobs of spit down my chin or anything like that. And I'm not on any of those friggin' pills that messed me up. So things could be worse, but they're not. I'm still somewhere there in the middle (pointing to the drawing), like not really nowhere yet.

MICHAEL: Do you think people see that, that you're actually doing somewhat okay? Even though you're here?

CAMERON: Maybe. I saw Shane on his shift last night and like he was friendly and all. I don't think he thinks I screwed up. He probably thinks I wanted to be in here again. To dry out and all ... But I don't think my aunt likes it. She was pretty angry at me for going back in. And Darcy [one of Cameron's nephews] was crying. I took him for a walk before I went to court just to go sliding or something, but he was like 'I don't want you to go' and all that. I get to see him a lot in here. But frig, this is no place for a little kid to be in. I don't get no TR's (temporary releases) home for a while so I got no choice if he's gonna see me.

Conversations like this offer circular explorations of different aspects of the lives of high-risk, but resilient youth like Cameron. We would keep returning to the artefacts of treatment that we had created over the years as a way of anchoring our conversations and creating continuity. Much of the content of these conversations was about enhancing Cameron's identity construction as a normal kid in control of a crazy one. Despite his incarceration, he is still less 'crazy' than anyone expected. He is more attached, more self-aware, and less dangerous to himself or others. The discursive empowerment that results from these techniques provides youth like Cameron with a language to explain their worlds, even to adults. Interventions with Cameron sought to acknowledge his localized discourse and to strategize ways to share it beyond the therapy room. Doing so helped Cameron to authenticate his voice and experience. Even his natural mother's 'craziness' that had so affected his life became intelligible to Cameron when he could see her story as the first chapter of his own.

In Cameron's Words

To meet Cameron now, at age 18, one would be surprised at the pleasant young man who presents himself proudly before adults. Cameron takes pride in how different he is from his peers. For one thing, he keeps himself tidy, his hair combed, and he loves designer label clothes. Among his rag-tag group of friends, he stands out as the valedictorian, the one who looks the most likely to speak up for them. No matter how far he drifts these days from his caregivers, or from school, or from his family, one always has the sense that he is casting the occasional glance behind him to see where we all are. As committed as he appears to an occasionally delinquent lifestyle, the adults in his life know that he still holds a great deal of love and compassion for them. His vulnerability is not his entire story. It just took time to understand how Cameron survived in his world.

During one of our last contacts together, I asked Cameron if he would like to share his life story as part of the research for this book. He willingly agreed, wanting others to know what he had been through. An interview was scheduled while he was back in the community, on probation and living with his aunt. During our hour and a half together discussing this work, he said he felt certain that things could have been done differently by those who had tried to help him over the years. 'Hell, it was hell,' was how Cameron described his experience growing up. He was not sure what exactly would have helped, but the interventions he had received had left him feeling that less would have been more. The placements he experienced, the numerous assessments that he was subjected to early on, and the frequent case conferences that were held to deal with his problems had left him feeling confused and his sense of well-being threatened: 'It's totally out of control ... you got people talking at you ... you don't got no idea what they're saying ... they ask you too many big words ... half the time it's like you're not even there. Everyone's looking at you ... asking you stupid questions like why do you want to go to school? Why do you think? It's just stupid.' Listening to Cameron, one wonders if perhaps he is right and that fewer interventions would have amounted to more success. When asked whether any of his many placements helped, Cameron responded, 'I didn't want to be there. I didn't want to be anywhere. There was nothing they could have done. They never done squat. I wouldn't have been in custody if they done nothing.' Cameron went on to say, 'If Cheryl had raised me, I just have this feeling that I wouldn't have all the shit going on. Kids should be kids.'

Cameron believes it was the system that failed him and made his life worse, instead of better. He made several specific points in this regard. First, in reference to his being treated with medications from the time he was young: 'They shouldn't have put me on medications. I was right slow. I was on so many frigging pills ... and they wonder why I'm a drug addict. Jeez, you get me on all these pills then you want me to take counselling. You're the guys who put me on stuff.' In regards to his placements, Cameron said, 'My aunt wanted me home. But my social worker wouldn't let me go home. But they wouldn't listen to me ... Nobody wanted to listen to me. I know I wouldn't be here in jail if they had listened.' Although most of Cameron's placements were in his community, the closest treatment facility was a 2-hour drive from his grandmother's home. 'When I was in ... it was hell. I'm used to being in ... But my family doesn't have any gas to get there. It's just hell. The 72-hour room there doesn't work. It's all booked up. People need a roof over their head. We need a big-ass house just for the people who need shelter.' Cameron also explained that as he got older, he learned to manipulate the system to get what he wanted. While his case managers were hesitant to return him to his aunt's home or his grandmother's, Cameron said he purposefully acted out while in placement to breach his probation order and return to custody, knowing that after a short sentence or period on remand, he would be discharged to his family having exhausted the capacity of the community residential programs to care for him: 'There were a couple of times I would have come back to jail for a long time but I didn't. But they put me in a foster placement to see how I get along for a couple of months. They said they'd send me home but it didn't happen. So I quit school, came back to jail, then went home ... It was a long road. My only choice.'

It is unlikely that the system that sought to care for Cameron would ever have left him to survive on his own. Certainly, from Cameron's point of view, he believes he would have been better off to have remained with his natural family. Cameron told me his life would have followed a different course if that had happened. He fervently believes a different story about his past, one denied by his caregivers, but one in which he was taken from a home that offered him a more secure and loving environment than what he experienced over the years, despite the best efforts of his caregivers. Whether he is right or wrong is immaterial. The fact that Cameron still holds to the belief that he could have had a normal childhood, and risen above his family's problems, is what stands out therapeutically as the best indication of Cameron's now empowered narrative of resilience. He confidently proclaims to those who take the time to listen that he is not a crazy kid. Despite his chaotic behaviour, he maintains a strong sense of himself as a victim of the system and a resilient and capable young man who could have coped with the risk factors that challenged him. That is the way he remembers his past now. We just never gave him a chance to prove himself, something he has begun to do in more recent years.

If Cameron's story teaches us anything, it is that formal and informal therapeutic interventions have the potential to provide high-risk youth with the resources they need to prove themselves resilient. Periodic misbehaviour, and more appropriate normative behaviour, must be seen for what they are, discontinuities in old problem-saturated stories and the beginning of new health-enhancing narratives.

Summary

The postmodern clinical approach detailed in this chapter addresses the impact of multiple risk factors on the mental health of high-risk youth and is ideally suited to engage young people in the construction of health-enhancing narratives. The youth I have worked with have shown me that when these narratives of resilience are given discursive power, and challenge narratives of vulnerability, youth experience improved mental well-being. A three-stage process has been discussed that includes reflecting upon the dominant stories of a child's life, challenging old stories while constructing new ones, and finally defining one's self in front of others in order to perform a new identity as resilient. In all three phases, setting and the broader social and political location in which therapy takes place require special attention.

Maintaining improvements in mental health made in the therapy room requires that narratives of resilience be recognized outside the therapeutic milieu. Gergen notes: 'It is insufficient that the client and therapist negotiate a new form of self-understanding that seems realistic, aesthetic, and uplifting within the dyad. It is not the dance of meaning within the therapeutic context that is primarily at stake. Rather, the significant question is whether the new shape of meaning is serviceable within the social arena outside these confines' (1996: 218). The real challenge for high-risk youth is taking their new story about themselves back home and into their communities. As has been shown through the lengthy case study of Cameron, postmodern therapeutic techniques coupled with systemic change to mitigate the impact of risk factors in the lives of young people have the potential to strengthen youth constructions as healthy. In the next chapter, I will examine the role that non-professional and paraprofessional resources can play in helping youth achieve the same gains as achieved in formal therapy. Unlike clinically based interventions, these individuals provide a more social arena in which to perform identities as resilient.

Chapter Eight

Volunteers, Guides, and Paraprofessionals

Understanding resilience of children as socially constructed obligates us as formal and informal caregivers to examine our own roles in the construction of health among high-risk youth. Chapter 7 dealt explicitly with the role of professional helpers who want to promote the health-enhancing effects of discursive power. This chapter is intended for other caregivers who occupy special places in the lives of high-risk youth and who are intimately involved in their self-constructions. As adults, we are not only caregivers to our own children, but also a resource to all children in our community. Volunteers with organizations that reach out to marginalized youth, informal mentors who earn the respect of youth, non-professional support staff in the many formal and informal institutions that service youth, and of course, paraprofessional helpers such as youth care workers, homemakers, family resource workers, outreach workers, church workers, and other people whose role is to help, can all be tremendous resources to troubled youth as they discover and assert their resilience.

While some developmental theorists believe youth primarily reference their peer group during adolescence (Rich, 1998), this assumes that a child's capacity for attachments remains constant during these formative years. In fact, a more likely explanation is that as youth move through their adolescence their capacity to care for others increases and with it the complex weave of relationships in their lives. High-risk youth say they need adults to supplement the power afforded the health discourses in which they participate among their peers (see Madden-Derdich et al., 2002). Teens seek opportunities to perform their identities in front of as wide and diverse an audience as they can find. This has been shown empirically in work by educators such as Carolyn Webster-Stratton and her colleagues (Stormshak & Webster-Stratton, 1999; Webster-Stratton et al., 2001), who have demonstrated that in prevention efforts with children who are disruptive at home and school, programs that work with both sets of caregivers, formal and informal, creating a consistent and positive experience for the child, will have the most effect on a child's behaviour. Although it is intuitively obvious that children need people who can aid them in their construction of a healthy identity and help to advocate for health resources, professionals and paraprofessionals frequently work with families or in community settings in bureaucratic silos that prevent them from providing a sufficiently large audience for children to practice their identity constructions.

While the previous chapter examined the role of professionals in nurturing health and resilience in high-risk youth, this chapter looks at what can be done by those who are frequently closer to these youth and immersed in their communities. All too often the work of these significant others remains invisible.

These ideas are not new. In every community the role played by these non-professionals has been woven into the fabric of our social order. The University of Calgary, for example, pairs university athletes with children in need of positive role models. Both parts of the dyad benefit. In a story of mismatch and hope from that program, 13-year-old Ryan was paired with a 6-foot-6 middle blocker from the university's volleyball team, named Sol, who says of his experience: 'The best thing about it is helping someone. Plus, it's an affirmation about the good in people. This child is such a good guy. If he's at that pivotal stage in his life, maybe I can make a difference in which way he falls as an adolescent' (Maki, 2000). There is something special about this recognition of the good in a troubled child like Ryan. After all, he was referred to the mentoring program because his teachers had been giving dire predictions about his future for years. While there are different theories which explain the positive things that take place in a program like this, few have looked at how the child accounts for the experience. Youth like Ryan would likely argue that the time spent with a mentor like Sol gives them an opportunity to explore an alternative identity construction. The older male becomes a hitherto unavailable health resource. Ryan, we were told, already had an interest in sports. Putting Sol in his life may just have been the right resource at the right time for this child from a sole parent home, whose mother earns a low wage and has little time to tend to anything but meeting the basic needs of her three children. In the discursive space created by their relationship, Sol offers Ryan a powerful alternative to the stigmatizing identity of the poor troubled kid disadvantaged by race, poverty, and family circumstances.

Adrift in life, high-risk teens are searching for groups of people who can mirror back to them their uniqueness and offer support for healthy self-constructions. In the absence of a community or family that will fulfil this role, teens will turn exclusively to their peers. However, when an alternative is presented, in the form of an empathic adult, high-risk teens say they are happy to flock to that person and engage with him or her respectfully. This respect is not demanded or cajoled. It is a respect that grows from the youth's freedom to choose or not choose to avail himself or herself of the resources provided by the adult helper. The youth is able to get to know the adult sufficiently well to make an informed decision as to whether he or she can be of help.

The sense of competence and personal control that these mentors instil in youth helps them to assert themselves in all spheres of interaction, including with their peers. A particularly poignant example of this was captured in the film *American Generation X* in which a young neo-Nazi reaches out for help from a former teacher while in detention. The young man had been sexually assaulted by other skinheads he met in jail who he thought were his friends. It is a strange film in that it both glorifies the lifestyle of these kids and offers a challenge to it. Perhaps that is as it should be, as youth who are in these gangs know they are doing something that is socially unacceptable (Monti, 1994). In other words, they know what is socially normative behaviour. The main character in the film eventually comes to realize that his life has 'not added up to much' and decides to leave behind his gang affiliation. It is his relationship with his former teacher and mentor that offers him a different experience of himself that he brings home when discharged.

The Non-professional Volunteer Helper

As community members, we all play a role, passively or actively, in this process of identity construction. When we get on a bus and a group of youth are gathered at the back and we avoid them, we contribute to who these youth think they are. Their identity is reflected back to them through our response. Similarly, but more positively, the community guides, volunteers, and paraprofessionals to be discussed in this chapter reflect back to young people positive constructions of themselves.

Family friends, aunts and uncles, neighbours, tradespeople, Big Brothers and Big Sisters, coaches, among others, all have the potential to become significant players in an adolescent's pursuit of well-being. John, a 13-year-old introduced in Chapter 5, talked about how he purposefully seeks out the company of a friend of his mother's, Andrea, as a strategy to bolster his sense of himself as a 'good kid.' Andrea, like many other adults in John's life such as social workers, teachers, and youth workers, attests that he is not as bad as his mother makes him out to be. John talked about his relationship with Andrea as fortifying a threatened sense of self:

> Andrea, she's older, well not old, old ... Well she's kind of like a second mother. I sometimes on the weekends go over to her house and she doesn't say anything bad about me. Like if I've slept for the whole day, she might tease me, but that's all ... I've known Andrea since I was a little baby. She's a friend of my mom's. We go there sometimes on weekends, and we've gone there on Christmas a couple of times, and we go there for barbeques and sometimes I just go there alone ... I think her husband and daughter like me. I like them ... Like when I go to her house she sort of says I'm a cousin and like that. I'm pretty sure her husband likes me. Like he never says 'I hate you, you little ... ' They live a little far away. She sometimes comes and picks me up. I think my mom gets jealous sometimes. Like she feels like I like her more than I like my own mom. Sometimes I do.

It is simple magic like this that makes all the difference. Sometimes, in our efforts to intervene as outsiders, we overlook the easy paths to discursive power already present in these youth's lives. 'Sometimes I just forget about my problems and other times I might ask Andrea for help,' says John. With a supportive adult like Andrea rooting for him, John can feel incredibly well supported when defining himself as healthy and resilient.

The health-enhancing role played by individuals also occurs in broader sociopolitical contexts when groups of individuals open space for youth to meaningfully participate in their communities. Results from a study by Marc Zimmerman et al. show that, for a sample of 172 African American adolescent males, 'sociopolitical control moderated

the negative effects of personal helplessness on mental health outcomes ... Psychological symptoms did not vary as levels of personal
helplessness increased for youths who reported the highest levels of
sociopolitical control' (1999: Discussion, para. 1). The authors of the
study note how much more we know about what causes pathology in
this population than how or why some of these youth become well-
functioning citizens. Zimmerman et al. observe that 'community interventions that provide opportunities for involving youths in action
groups, such as church groups and voluntary and neighbourhood organizations, may help protect them from other risks they face. The
idea is to enhance perceptions of control and foster abilities and knowledge to act in sociopolitical processes through community participation' (1999: Discussion, para. 8).

Random Encounters

Few communities have a strategic plan to provide such opportunities
for the inclusion of youth in community life. Instead, the randomness
of health-enhancing relationships between adults and high-risk youth
is striking. The human services worker who tries to influence the mental health of a young person such as John would do well to keep an
eye out for whatever chance encounters might come John's way.

For Hugh, another 13-year-old boy, an unlikely but significant extra-familial contact occurred between the boy and the lawyer who was
acting on his family's behalf. Hugh, who is confined to a wheelchair
because of cerebral palsy, and his two younger brothers were involved
in a suit against their father for non-payment of support. Hugh com-
mented that the lawyer had noticed his passion for justice and his
ability to represent the interests of others. 'You'd make a great lawyer,
you've got the brains for it,' Hugh remembers being told. From that
one offhand observation, a strong relationship developed through
which Hugh sustained a much more powerful image of himself than
the one he was typically assigned by those who saw him as nothing
but a 'handicapped' child. For Sophie, the 14-year-old daughter of an
alcoholic mother introduced earlier, this same supportive role was
played by a gym teacher: 'I don't know if I'm his favourite student but
he really treats me very good,' Sophie explained.

For another youth, Tanya, her need for someone to notice her was
so acute that she would latch on to anyone who came close. When
asked specifically about who has had a big influence in her life, she

responded: 'My bus driver ... I don't remember much about him, but he was the most awesome bus driver. His name was Sparky or something like that. And because my mom worked and my dad worked and they were sometimes like a half an hour late for when I get home and the door was locked, he would sit there with the bus and wait till my parents got home. It didn't matter if they didn't get home an hour later or two hours later.' Tanya's experience of neglect following the divorce of her parents, complicated by her own inability to evoke positive attention from others, left her grasping at anyone who came near for unconditional acceptance and a positive self-story. In the absence of other sustaining resources, just about any support can produce the desired effect of augmenting a child's discursive power.

These examples emphasize the important role that informal individual volunteers or community members play as the vehicle of support for high-risk youth's constructions of powerful identities. In a more formal sense, these same individuals also play a very special role in organizing and maintaining the social fabric of a community that provides experiences for youth that bolster the narratives youth choose to privilege. However, the more formal the role of the volunteer, the greater the chances that high-risk youth decline association. Frequently, informal helpers are overlooked by professionals while individuals who conduct their work through organizations are more typically thought of as deserving the title volunteer, in keeping with our understanding of volunteerism as 'long-term, planned, prosocial behaviors that benefit strangers and occur within an organizational setting' (Penner, 2002: 448). While often positive, the planfulness, differences culturally between the volunteer and those served, and the organizational context in which the volunteering takes place can also act as barriers to participation. Some effective examples of volunteers at work with this population are to be found in Boys and Girls Clubs, midnight basketball programs, or any other recreational and social function that has the potential to offer a high-risk teen a place to practise the skills needed to relate to others and construct a healthy identity through the intersubjectivity of relationships.

Sadly, we tend to think of these programs as only 'diversions' and fund them accordingly (we have even more trouble providing funding and support to informal community helpers youth choose themselves). We fail to recognize volunteers as often superior interventions to those provided by the formal mental health care and child welfare systems. In some instances, I have found alternative programs staffed

by volunteers are more likely than individualized treatment to produce the healthy sense of coherence sought by resilient teens. These
diversions need to be viewed as construction zones, places where new
selves can be erected. Volunteers who create these opportunities offer
youth a forum in which to practise the skills they will need to sustain
powerful labels other than those they find through acting out troubling behaviours. These places, which are staffed largely by volunteers and paraprofessionals, provide a much needed resource to communities concerned with a mythic 'youth problem.' These programs
do not divert children from delinquency: they offer them a competing
discourse in which to participate. As such, they compete directly with
street culture and the power of the labels found there. When such
avenues for participation are either unavailable, or unduly demanding and restrictive in their requirements for entry, then we are more
likely to see youth finding their own community-based supports outside their own homes.

Inviting in 'Problem' Selves

The volunteers who organize sports, the arts, or other challenge activities, offer teenaged participants access to a new identity. But volunteers can also, inadvertently, push teens back to 'stuck' positions within
their peer groups when volunteer activities are too different, too formal, or demand of participants concessions that they are unwilling to
make. A frequent symptom of this clash is the teen's resistance to the
rigid boundaries that programs erect that exclude the teenager's peers
or the artefacts of a peer-based lifestyle. Alcohol, sexual expression,
liberal curfews, indeed anything that is not socially normative, is frequently confiscated or suppressed at the door to these programs. Sadly,
we insist kids park their street-smart survival skills at the door if they
are to become part of the clubs adult sponsors. For youth desperate to
find a new identity, the concessions are worth it. But for the child who
has already constructed a powerful identity in opposition to cultural
norms, there is simply no reason to compromise. Volunteers and paraprofessionals who work close to these youth, and appreciate the power
they already enjoy, are in my experience, less likely to see the need for
this negation of self as a prerequisite for participation.
    Take, for example, two different programs, both staffed by parapro-
fessional helpers and volunteers. One organization explicitly for street
youth with whom I once worked encouraged youth to participate in

activities that took them away from their street friends. To participate, the kids had to identify themselves as being in need of help and agree to come off the street and into a structured environment. There, the explicit goal by those staffing the facility was to rehabilitate the youth and help them return home. In fact, the program was run out of a homelike setting which made sense to the volunteers. Their explicit goal was, after all, to help youth resocialize and move back towards the safety and security of their natural or foster families. The peer group that remained outside was seen by workers as being in conflict with organizational goals. When a program participant slipped in his or her behaviour, allowances were made, but youth were asked to leave the centre if there was more than one incident where there was abuse of any substances, the excessive use of foul language, or a threat made to others. In and of themselves, these limits made sense and allowed the smooth operation of the program. But they also told the youth there was something inferior and morally wrong with the youth culture to which they belonged. The bias of the program was, instead, towards normative family functioning over the alternative families youth find among their peers. The result was that program volunteers and staff competed with the child's street-based social supports for control of the young person's self-definition.

In contrast, the tone and delivery of programs in a second setting in which I worked is very different. That program is run by a board of volunteers with substantial youth representation. The program has been set up in an old recreational facility close to the street scene where youth hang out. The programs that are offered are targeted at the interests of disempowered youth with an emphasis on sporting activities, cultural events such as movie nights or visits by celebrities, advocacy, health care, especially sexual health, and the informal support of caregivers at hours when they are most needed. The physical space is warehouselike, and the atmosphere very relaxed. While swearing, threatening behaviour, and drug and alcohol use is prohibited, it is policed by the youth themselves under the direction of board members and program committees. If a youth has to be expelled for some reason, outreach and follow-up through the youth's peer group are encouraged to make sure the young person maintains a connection with the program while waiting to return. The youth is clearly told, 'You're welcome back.' Of course, problems occur when an organization sets up this type of welcoming environment. Keeping the peace with the facility's neighbours is always tricky. There is the danger that the spaces just outside the centre become staging grounds for gang warfare or are used by dealers as a ready marketplace for drugs and weapons. There are no easy solutions to these concerns. But peer groups, by becoming allies with centre staff, are far more likely to effectively police these activities than adults.

While we are quick to invest in solutions that divert youth from their peers, or coerce them into changing troubling lifestyles (Miles, 2000; Archbold & Meyer, 1999), we seldom offer them viable alternative forums in which to re-author themselves. Recreation activities designed with their needs in mind are really about providing a place where teens can 're-create.' At the second facility, teens experience continuity with who they are beyond its walls, while also being exposed to something just different enough to leave an impression. In such an environment, new roles can be tried, discarded, and then tried again.

Community Guides

Non-professional helpers succeed because they expand both the discursive and instrumental resources a young person needs to sustain well-being. Sometimes these helpers assist a youth with instrumental tasks like finding employment. More often, they offer youth a mirror in which to see themselves as something special. In almost all cases, the potential of the child, rather than the dismal fact of his or her problems, is highlighted and celebrated.

Using a grounded theory approach (Glaser & Strauss, 1967), social work students and I conducted a study of non-formal helpers who were identified as having 'made a difference' in their communities (Ungar et al., 2000). Each was selected on the basis of the variability in the ways he or she provided help to marginalized populations. These helpers were much more than volunteers though. And while many held formal roles as helpers (e.g., teachers or social workers), it was their unpaid service that was studied in an effort to discern the principles of helping that are most effective with populations that typically resist interventions by formal care providers. The 35 participants included in the study came predominantly from rural parts of Atlantic Canada, although even urban dwellers identified themselves as rural in background and approach to their community. Twenty-five participants were female, 10 male, with ages ranging from their early 20s into their 60s. Some participants were raising families, some single, some had already launched families. As a group, their occupations were diverse and included mayors, teachers, convenience store owners, aid workers, retired business people, homemakers, students, government employees, recreation directors, pediatricians, real estate agents, and unemployed fishery workers. Those whom they chose to help were an equally diverse group. Many devoted their efforts to helping young children, teenagers, adults, and senior citizens at the same time, while others focused on one particular age group. For example, some of the participants helped seniors isolated because of illness or the recent loss of a spouse; others helped children with learning disabilities; some worked with delinquent youth in or out of custody; many worked through church organizations with disadvantaged parishioners and non-parishioners; others helped recent immigrants, unemployed people, single parents, school dropouts, people with intellectual challenges, as well as members of their own family debilitated by disease. The one common characteristic among all the people helped was their exclusion to varying degrees from their communities.

One way to understand the work of these volunteers is to see them as bridges to inclusion for high-risk marginalized populations, including youth. Those who worked specifically with youth said they offer, through their service to young people, a way for troubled youth to return to their community's associational life as fuller participants. The skills necessary to do this are not those commonly found among professionals, nor do parents necessarily fulfil this role. These volunteers who help to build bridges between a community and its youth do so, they explain, by avoiding titles, being immersed in the web of relationships of the community, and working invisibly. This is very different from the professional who self-identifies as the catalyst for change and maintains a highly visible, and therefore potentially stigmatizing, position as helper (see McKnight, 1995). The danger posed by professionals is that rather than adding to discourses of resilience, the outsider expert can contribute to negative labels being attached to anyone caught seeking help (Madsen, 1999).

There is no doubt, navigating an ocean of risks, youth need someone to help them find their way. Too frequently, those they invite aboard only further endanger their precarious health status. But youth who have the good fortune to encounter non-professional 'invisible guides,' the indigenous phrase used to describe these helpers during the study, are the youth most likely to succeed. These helpers are at least outside institutional settings and therefore people who have no formal relationship with the young person, but who offer the youth an opportunity to experience himself or herself differently. The community is always a backdrop during these encounters, which is perhaps why the contextual relevance of the barriers the child faces are less often forgotten by community helpers than by professionals who work alongside, rather than inside, community. To the extent that a community tolerates or celebrates what a youth expresses, his or her identity claim is either strengthened or threatened.

Community guides are much more than just volunteers. They are people immersed in the life of their communities who use the advantages of their connections with others to help those who are excluded. The concept of 'community guide' is borrowed from John McKnight (1991, 1995), who used the term to describe people who help marginalized individuals become active participants in the associational life of the community in which they reside: 'Because it is so infrequently the case that excluded people and their families are able to overcome the barriers of service and incorporate themselves into community life, we have found that the most frequently successful incorporation has taken place as a result of people who have assumed a special responsibility to guide excluded people out of service and into the realms of community life' (1991: 10). Much of McKnight's work has focused on the integration of people with mental disabilities and the way in which professional services have the iatrogenic effect of isolating and stigmatizing those already vulnerable to exclusion. Guides address the marginalization of these individuals by focusing on what they have to offer.

Motivation for their work is multidetermined. As a heterogeneous group, guides may conduct themselves based on one or more of the four motives found by Daniel Batson, Nadia Ahmad, and Jo-Ann Tsang (2002) to underlie community involvement: egoism (increasing one's own welfare – seldom a guide's sole motivation although being a guide does tend to give the guide peace of mind and ensure his or her own safety); altruism (increasing the welfare of others); collectivism (increasing the welfare of a group to benefit one or more of its members); and principlism (to uphold some moral or religious belief). Playing an audience to troubled youth and creating opportunities for their participation in community discourse was talked about by guides as the right thing to do, or something that they intuitively understood as helpful to the youth, the community, and indirectly, the guides themselves.

As a bridge to inclusion, the role of guides becomes one of opening opportunities for fuller participation that changes the position and definition of those marginalized within their communities. Guides can offer youth who act out in deviant ways a path back to community, by building on the child's capacities. These bridges help youth cross over to employment, to positions of authority, to school, to church communities, back to their families, or simply to a position of respect within a community of concern.

The work of the guide is as much attitude as it is skill. It is also quite different from that of the professional who tends to focus on the child's problems. Interventions by professionals often further stigmatize and marginalize the child being helped because of the visibility of the helper and the helping agency. It is quite different for guides whose association with a young person is seen as something positive and constructive for both the guide and the child. For example, when paraprofessional staff at a youth corrections facility were asked to identify a volunteer within their organization who seemed to do more than just offer his or her time, staff talked at length about the contribution made by Mr Bentley, a long-time volunteer at the centre: 'His work at the youth centre is looked at by all as a positive thing. They love to see him coming. He provides something for the youth to do whether it's reading the books he brings or taking part in church ... And most of all he provides opportunities for these young people to see what they can do with their lives now, and when they get out.'

Community guides work to provide youth and their families both physical and social access to their communities. Take, for example, the issue of skateboard parks now before many city councils. In my community, many well-meaning volunteers and professionals are working hard to create a physical space for youth recreation. City council has listened but is hesitant to locate such a park close to the downtown core where tourists and shoppers may be harassed by hoards of youth. In their decision to locate the park in a more industrial part of the city, which is isolated and alienating, they have neglected to consider the social access necessary for young people to feel like full community participants. The proposed site will mean kids will have to travel away from their community to skateboard. While they will have physical access to recreation, they will not be part of their community's social life. If we place the park in the shadows of the community, then youth will accept that they are shadow citizens. The park will likely become a favoured destination for drug dealers and a place children from more 'functional' homes are forbidden to go. The magic of what a youth can do atop a skateboard will be lost. There will be no broader community to witness their performance. Without an audience, youth lose a valuable opportunity to construct a powerful identity as other than just troubled kids.

A similar example is commonly seen in our city parks where tennis courts are plentiful. Occasionally, during the off-season, these courts are converted to outdoor road-hockey rinks to satisfy the needs of roller hockey enthusiasts. But I have yet to see in my travels a dedicated outdoor space of prominence for a healthy and positive activity like roller hockey. Evidently this is an issue of class and culture. In general, tennis is a game for those with financial means, more so than road hockey (and skateboarding), which requires little equipment, little structure, and tends to be youth oriented. Almost any youth can participate in a pick-up game with even a $40 pair of rollerblades and a $10 stick. Skill can be learned without lessons, the activity is socially accessible, and highly visible. Not so for tennis, where there is the need for lessons, limited numbers can participate at one time, times of play must be structured, and the resource shared with adults who are more likely to use it. Guides understand these barriers to inclusion experienced by high-risk youth and look for physical and social spaces where teens can participate in ways that are socially desirable (see Checkoway, 1998; Barton et al., 1997; Hallenbeck, 1998). Their proximity to the youth themselves makes their work far more effective than that of formal interveners who frequently offer inappropriate solutions to the problems confronting youth.

Guides work from an assumption that the community is a 'reservoir of hospitality' (McKnight, 1991) and are willing to welcome marginalized youth into associational life as contributing members. They build on the capacities of those who are marginalized and make known to the community what a young person has to offer. Guides may be uniquely positioned to do this work because their titles do not get in the way of the work they do. From the point of view of teenagers, getting formal help means having to admit to weakness or problems beyond their control. Even if a problem is not their fault, seeking help identifies them as being 'in need.' High-risk youth, it must be remembered, explain their problems as much more systemic, having as much to do with the familial and societal risk factors confronting them as personal dispositions. Guides, by their immersion in community and invisibility in a web of trusting relationships, can engage a child without the child having to admit to a problem. The guide simply says, 'We need you. Come join our community.' No official title means no need for formality. It also does not put limits on the guide's use of community resources from his or her work life, social life, family life, volunteer activities, and other positions of trust that he or she occupies within the community. A guide can marshal any and all of these resources to the benefit of a child. Finally, no titles also means that a guide is not identified as the agent of change, leaving a youth's sense of personal agency intact. The message is not, 'Come, I'll change things for you'; it is, 'Come, I believe in you, you have something to offer, you can change things yourself.'

Mr Bentley commented: 'Like any other community ... the individuals in jail are different, they all have different needs ... they all need someone no matter what sort of community they are, they need someone to show interest in them, they need to be loved, they need to belong, have a feeling of belonging.' Guides reflect back to youth their value as individuals. Another guide, Mary Smith, said in relation to the young girls who come to her home to confide secrets and discuss issues that they would not discuss with their own mothers: 'If I gave my word I lived up to it and seen it through to the end ... I got secrets I'll carry to me grave.' Paul Jones has similarly come to be known in his community as someone others could rely upon. As he explained: 'A young man in the neighbourhood came to me because his mother threw him out of the house for doing drugs. I didn't really know him ... I guess other people told him that I would help ... He had nowhere to go ... so what was I gonna do? At that point, there was no use in telling him that he made a stupid mistake ... all I could do was say, "So what do you want to do now?" He already knew what he did wrong.' All these guides share the same approach to their work. As Mr Hall said, 'I'm just a bridge, really to get [teens] over the hump of society and back into the community.'

Guides as Bridges

Specifically, there are three ways guides position themselves within their communities to fulfil this bridging function: they offer support directly to those who are excluded; they provide opportunities for others in their communities to become linked with those who are excluded; or they position themselves as one of many sources of support allowing a group or whole community to act as a bridge to inclusion.

When guides are the bridges themselves, it is their charisma and talent that entices teens to trust them. We forget in our hypervigilant world, where trust is in short supply, that there are still people willing to extend themselves for others. Mr Bentley explained: 'I saw these young people, young teenagers, girls and boys who were in an institution to be rehabilitated, and ... I feel that I am there to assist their rehabilitation ... People who have been misplaced or through no fault of their own, through neglect, or haven't been loved, or haven't been understood as far as I'm concerned. But when you sit down with them and show them that you really do care, then you will establish a good rapport.' He goes on to say that 'Even in their state of confinement they need something in life worth living for ... and you try to encourage them.' The rapport and message of hope he brings to the youth is welcomed by them. Through connection with Mr Bentley some negotiate their way back to feeling a part of a normal community upon discharge.

A more preferred position for guides is as architects of the bridges that excluded youth need to cross in order to rejoin society, rather than as the bridge itself. Guides would rather be initiators of opportunities for teens to interact with others in ways that are within community norms. They want excluded teens to feel a part of peer groups that enjoy wider acceptance in their community. But this is only possible when space is made for those who are excluded from participating in community life. Like changing a tennis court into a roller hockey surface, communities need to welcome back excluded youth. It is not enough to simply invite them. The circumstances of their joining have to position them with status in activities that challenge the critical gaze of those who see them as 'other.' There is no need to insist that these youth cut themselves off from the support of those outside the mainstream. Instead, the goal should be to help these teens acquire the skills necessary to negotiate more complex identities in different spheres of interaction. Diversion programs that seek to 'rescue' youth from gangs and other aspects of street life so seldom work unless they build these relational skills. Guides are recognized for their success because they ask youth, 'What was your strength while out on the street?' and 'How can you use that same talent elsewhere?'

The third way a guide creates a bridge to inclusion is also the one they most prefer, and it is the one which is least visible to others. Guides position themselves within a community of concern. Collectively, the community creates the bridge. Guides act as catalysts to see these organizations created and sustained. Take, for example, Tony, a 22-year-old who has worked with a youth organization called Allied Youth (AY) in a small urban centre. Tony feels he succeeds best as a guide when he works with others to provide a place where all youth can feel a part of their community. As he explains: 'One of the strengths of AY is that they just feel that they belong, we have a diverse group of people in AY: your jocks, your techies or nerds, I say these stereo-types so you know, I mean, we don't look at them that way, we have some people who would be your introverts, extroverts, we have your models, and the girls who feel they couldn't be furthest from a model if they tried, all shapes all sizes, all colours, all creeds, all religions, all ethnicities, and I think our diversity makes us who we are.' Youth respond well when they sense there is a genuine desire to include them in community. Hypocrisy, or tokenism, quickly destroys the most enthusiastic efforts to build trust.

All three bridging roles establish the guide as someone who can look at a group of kids and see past their problem-saturated identities. Guides believe in their capacity to offer excluded youth a path to acceptance. Nicholas, a small-town shopkeeper, explained that to get the local teenagers to feel a part of their community he starts by engaging individual kids in actions that show them they have a responsibility for, and are valued by, their community: 'If children or adolescents break a bottle on the store parking lot, instead of yelling at them or other such things I say, "Give me a hand to clean this glass up, I know it was an accident," even if I knows it was on purpose. They help and I don't have trouble with them after.' Lest we cynically doubt that this could ever happen in our communities, guides assure us it can if the guide has built a reputation for fairness and respect among young people. After all, youth themselves want what the guides are offering. While many adults want to believe that bad kids want to be bad, more often bad kids want to be respected and feel like they belong. We have a social responsibility to offer high-risk teens this acceptance. Guides are a repository of the wisdom regarding how to extend a community's hospitality.

The Paraprofessional

The third category of community-based helper is the paraprofessional. Unlike professionals who tend to work separate from community, and who are constrained by rigid role definitions and titles, paraprofessionals are often well positioned to work alongside youth within their communities. Like guides, the work of paraprofessionals is often invisible. They are the case aides, community workers, nursing assistants, correctional officers, youth workers, homemakers, outreach workers, shelter staff, and other such helpers who are frequently silent at case conferences where more credentialed voices speak. Yet these are also the workers who are in the trenches with youth and who know what is going on in their communities. In northern Aboriginal communities and similarly underserviced areas, these paraprofessionals are more likely to be much more important resources than the professionals who supervise them (Borg et al., 1995; Mastronardi, 1990). In rural and remote settings, or communities where cultural diversity dictates the need, paraprofessionals do most of the work of professionals, while in urban environments, or well-serviced areas, their work tends to be more specialized and complements the work of professional service providers. In both urban and rural settings, however, they are a critical link in the care of youth but are often overlooked, underappreciated, and underpaid, given the disproportionate impact they have.

Years ago I heard a story that has always stayed with me. A frontline worker in a shelter for street youth in a large city had a young woman staying there one night. This was a street-hardened child who had, as the story was told, been through a number of foster homes, some of them abusive, had experienced abuse and neglect in her own home, and finally fed up, had fled to the streets for survival. There she had found a lifestyle that involved delinquency, drugs, and prostitution. The next morning the young woman woke up and along with her friends came to breakfast. That morning the worker on duty met an angry teen with enough attitude to survive and keep away anyone who might have considered trying to help. She had not been to the shelter before, but had come in with her friends whom she was determined to impress.

Breakfast was a healthy spread of cereal, toast, some fruit, and whatever else had been donated or scrounged. The room was warm and clean, although it looked more like an institution than a home. When the young woman came to the table, she complained to the worker that this was 'some lousy f–ing place,' all because they did not have her favourite cereal. I am not sure quite what possessed that worker to do what he did, but there was something in the magic of such moments when we all know there is an opportunity to make a difference. The worker told me he looked at the girl and decided that she was right, and that it really was disappointing that her favourite cereal was not there. She deserved, at least once, to get what she wanted. He put on his coat and wandered the half block down to a nearby corner grocery store returning a few minutes later with the sugary product the young woman had demanded. He did not make any fuss about it. He just quietly placed it on the table in front of her with a bowl, a spoon, and some milk.

Whatever happened for that young woman in that moment made a difference in her life. She began to come to the shelter regularly and attend some of the programs that were meant to help her first survive on the street, and then, when ready, move permanently to a group home for youth with nowhere else to live. She even began to volunteer at the shelter. It was not therapy in the traditional sense of the word, but this 'intervention' which began with a box of cereal did privilege one young woman's understanding of what she needed. Together, she and the shelter worker had challenged the pathologizing discourse that had contributed to her marginalization. She was, after all, surviving as well as she could. Her helpers just needed to understand how she explained her behaviour. A further case illustration from my own work may help to elaborate upon the important role paraprofessionals play in nurturing healthy identity stories in high-risk youth.

Case Study: Rory

Like volunteers and guides, paraprofessionals can accomplish the same sharing of discursive power when they understand the role they play in the construction of a child's resilience. Take, for example, a youth like 15-year-old Rory who returned to custody for the third time on charges of theft. By that point most of Rory's teachers and workers had decided Rory could not be saved. Rory's obstinate behaviour and outlandish antics that kept staff always on their toes had not endeared this boy to anyone. Although he was evidently bright, Rory had a way of disgusting others by peeing in soup pots, masturbating publicly, drawing graffiti on classroom walls, and manipulating his parents to give him whatever he wanted.

There were a few youth workers, however, and myself as the consulting clinician, intrigued by Rory's tenacious will to survive and thrive no matter who tried to control him. We recognized, as I believe all the staff did, something very powerful about this young man that was going to waste, or so we thought. We decided that the greatest barrier to Rory breaking his pattern of delinquency was the way his identity as the criminal was being strengthened through the institutional discourse sustained by both staff and residents which told Rory he was stuck in one pattern of behaviour. We concocted what seemed like an outlandish plan to everyone. For three months we insisted that Rory, as part of his mandatory treatment, keep a journal in which he recorded any positive things he did. It was up to him to define what was positive. We then circulated among the institution's staff a brief summary of whatever Rory had done that *he felt* was kind, helpful, or in any other way pro-social. At first Rory dismissed this as lunacy and refused to comply. As time inside was explicitly designed for treatment, and this was his individualized case plan, we asked him on the days he would not write to take a time out and reflect on his life. It was a mild form of punishment for non-participation, but eventually, as we suspected, Rory got into the idea of telling everyone about how incredibly good he was. There was something about this record of his good deeds being passed around the centre that kept Rory as the focus of attention. Not surprisingly, Rory showed staff he had another side of himself. There was at first much teasing of Rory, 'So you cleaned your room, eh?' or 'I heard you called your mother, and how is the old lady?' But soon, two things happened. First, the extraordinary, Rory doing something kind or helpful began to pass with less notice. Second, Rory began to receive feedback from others about aspects of himself that everyone knew were there, but which had been ignored. In other words, once the old story about Rory had been deflated, a new story was available to fill the void. His team of caseworkers had hoped this would happen as Rory had many other strengths than the negative ones that were constantly reflected back to him.

Rory excelled at his school work, although he maintained his leadership position among his peers. Somehow he had reconciled the two. He was slowly learning he could support more than one identity, and he could better negotiate with others for what he needed to maintain some control over his life. Everyone began to see him as healthier than he might otherwise have appeared. Eventually, we stopped the daily advertisements, but Rory's journaling continued. He also began to think more seriously about his discharge. He would be well past his seventeenth birthday by that time and he knew that he was headed to an adult facility if he did not change. Rory even agreed at that point to look at the possibility of attending university. He was close to completing his high school and would have done well in a university environment if he ever got there. It took some work, but eventually we showed him that the money could be found for him to go. He even toured a local campus and was impressed that he could understand what people were talking about when he sat in on a couple of first-year classes. He was surprised that he looked like the other students and was very taken with the fact that 60% of the first-year class were women.

None of this alone, however, was quite enough to change Rory's behaviour permanently. At the time of this writing, he still has not found his way to university or a community vocational program for that matter. He survives, it is rumoured, by selling drugs when he is not helping an uncle with his plumbing business. You hear about him less, although, and to everyone's knowledge, he did not graduate into the adult correctional system.

Success? Perhaps. What we did not anticipate at the time was how ineffectual institution-based marginal discourses are when youth return to their home environments. Discursive resilience constructed inside one setting does not necessarily transfer to other spheres of interaction. The transferability of these discourses and the skills to promote them requires support. Rory received limited support while inside, but had very little help when back on the street. This has been one of the reasons programs that are more inclusive of community participation such as Wraparound and Family Group Conferencing with young offenders have proven successful (Latimer et al., 2001; Schmid, 2000; Sieppert et al., 2000; Van Den Berg & Grealish, 1996). Furthermore, barriers to academic excellence may also exist within the institutions themselves that are most frequently designed to provide remedial education rather than course work leading to university admission. In part this is a question of limited resources, but it is also, discursively, a problem of who the residential workers are and their own experiences in post secondary education. As Jackson and Martin observe in their study of youth in care, 'residential workers often saw it as a more important part of their job to encourage good social relations and participation in the life of the home, rather than facilitating the long hours of private study necessary for A level success. Individual care workers might be kind and supportive, but because they normally lacked education themselves, they often had no conception of what was involved in serious academic work' (1998: 580). Although this is specific to one setting in Britain, the point Jackson and Martin make is important: access to resources that nurture powerful identities are the consequence of the values and beliefs of those who mirror back to youth who they are and what they can become.

There is a tendency by help providers to perceive low status help seekers (like these youth) as less capable and less likely to succeed than members of higher status groups. Arie Nadler's work with university students in Tel Aviv raise, as he says, 'the worrisome possibility that different types of help may be offered to members of low and high status groups, not only by ordinary persons but also by professional helpers, such as teachers, social workers, and mental health professionals' (2002: 496). Similar to the argument made throughout this book, perceptions of low status groups can lead to offers of help that reinforce negative constructions of identity as overly dependent on others. Nadler finds that such helping relationships run the risk of solidifying and institutionalizing power-based hierarchies. In such circumstances, iatrogenic effects of the interventions would be likely.

Complementary Roles

Despite these cautions, most child and youth care workers are admirable in what they do with the limited resources they have. As the backbones of their organizations they maintain extensive knowledge of the youth they work with and the communities they come from. Several such workers stand out during my career. One woman, whom I will call Marion, is a wealth of information on practically every family, every business, and every child in the geographic region in which she both lives and works. Like a community guide, Marion knows how to mobilize people. A child needs a respite bed, and Marion comes up with a name of family with a spare bedroom. A child comes into custody, and we suspect that child has been sexually abused, and Marion tells us about the family, about the family's neighbourhood, and even whether the child may have had contact with the known pedophiles in his or her community. If a child has a drug problem, or is breaching his or her probation order, Marion hears about it before anyone else. She is a trusted member of her community and therefore given a degree of access denied her colleagues. This positioning of the worker close to a community is sometimes looked down upon in the discourse of professionalism that promotes boundaries and argues against dual relationships (Campbell & Ungar, in press). In actuality, the work of professionals is accomplished on the shoulders of workers like Marion who provide the networks that outsiders then exploit. As the study of guides discussed earlier demonstrates, effective engagement of youth requires proximity and an intimate understanding of their context-specific strengths. Such knowledge is frequently in the domain of the paraprofessional. It is they who are with the child the 'other 23 hours' when not in formal counselling (Trieschman et al., 1969).

In a remote Aboriginal community, the paraprofessional role is even more important. Like Marion, George has lived and worked in his community most of his life. Without even the resources of a social worker on site, George has the responsibility to look after the myriad social welfare needs of a community of 500. It is precisely because he speaks the language, understands what behaviours mean to the people who live there, and himself has experienced many of the same challenges as those he helps, that he is able to be effective. With problem youth he is a resource that frequently tempers the demands of professional staff. George helps families stay together, works with youth to help them solve their addiction problems, collaborates with educators to nudge kids back to school, and is not above offering a child a warm place to sleep for the night when all else fails. Typically, George hears about things before they become public issues. But he also suffers along with the community each time the community fails to keep a child safe or watches helplessly as yet another child commits suicide. It is here that the lack of boundaries between the helper and the helped is so obvious. While George is the one who is supposed to intervene, he is also dependent on his community for its support in times of crisis. He, like others, is an emotional link in the associational life of those with whom he lives.

When the role of paraprofessionals is well respected, there is a complementarity between their roles and those of professional helpers (see Chapter 7). One is not necessarily better than the other. Each brings a unique quality to a child's life. Paraprofessionals simply enjoy the luxury of being able to fully use themselves and the power of their personal self-constructions as a way to enhance the power and acceptance of the self-definitions of the youth with whom they work. When a youth worker who loves music sets out to make a disc jockey of a street-wise 15-year-old girl whom he meets in custody that worker is offering the youth not just an opportunity to share some tunes of her own choosing over the facility's licensed radio station, but also through the sharing of that experience, providing her with a unique place among her peers. Suddenly a troubled kid becomes a talented disc jockey and responsible for something that is important to others. The other youth have to negotiate with her if they are going to get to hear what they want on the noontime broadcast. And she, too, has to negotiate with the worker and the facility's management to decide what is and is not an acceptable piece of music. In cases like this, a paraprofessional joins with the youth during his or her care in the construction of a different self-story. This new story has a greater likelihood of being brought back home when it is sufficiently invested with the power and respect it deserves. Although not a cure in and of itself, it is part of a puzzle of meanings co-authored between the child and her institutional caregivers.

Paraprofessonals are, however, still part of the system that employs them. This is an important distinction from the work done by guides, volunteers, and mentors. For out-of-control kids, performing well with a paraprofessional staff is often the delinquent's first step back to socially acceptable behaviour. These relationships between the system and the child, mediated by the worker, offer the perfect staging ground for more acceptable behaviours that may (or as we have seen in Chapter 6, may not) be viewed positively by the broader community. In other words, the paraprofessional serves a unique function modelling to the youth how one navigates between the demands of authority and personal choice. Relationships with paraprofessionals reintroduce structure to a disordered child's life in contextually sensitive ways. The young disc jockey mentioned above has an obligation to do a show every day at noon. Even the imposition of that much structure might bring with it a surprising amount of growth in a youth's ability to function in non-delinquent ways.

Unfortunately, as paraprofessionals become more professionalized, they are co-opted into the abyss of paperwork and accountability that leaves them less and less latitude to help kids in the milieus where they are located. Rather than their expertise influencing professional discourse, the tendency has been the reverse, with the work of para-professionals, like the work of many professional disciplines such as social work, counselling, and nursing, becoming more and more rigidly prescribed. As reporting becomes more onerous and time is spent accounting for one's actions rather than doing them, a stiffness and formality enters the relationships between helpers and youth (see

Hornby, 1993). In the documenting of young lives, workers also begin to inadvertently label, producing 'truths' about kids that the youth themselves have had no say in authoring. This is a dilemma for most paraprofessionals. Obviously, accountability is necessary in order to protect children and workers from abuse of any kind. But how much is enough? And for whom is the work being done? I strongly encourage workers to show everything they write about a child to the child. These records, when properly used in the service of youth, can become another tool for re-storying a child's life. They can be a forum in which strengths are highlighted and new self-constructions begun. Too often, however, these records recount for caregivers the problem lives of youth, ignoring their stories of resilience.

Summary

In this chapter I have turned my attention to the role of non-professionals and paraprofessionals in nurturing narratives of resilience in high-risk youth. Given research previously presented that shows the important role played by audiences to the self-constructions of health among resource-challenged youth, the potential impact these less formal caregivers can have on youth cannot be underestimated. Through these relationships, youth experience themselves differently, thickening descriptions of themselves as healthy and practising the skills required to have powerful self-constructions more widely accepted. These relationships can provide consistency and coherence to personal narratives, especially when there is continuity and follow-up between institutional and community settings.

Specifically three types of non-professionals were discussed. Non-professionals such as volunteers and mentors are chosen by children to help them through periods of change. These are frequently people encountered through chance events in the children's lives and chosen in ways that may surprise caregivers. Community guides, in contrast, occupy a similar low-key role in their community but are recognized for their purposeful efforts addressing the marginalization of at-risk populations. Guides provide a bridge to inclusion or help communities demonstrate their hospitality by organizing others into activities that open doors to those excluded. Guides describe their activities as more focused than volunteers or the mentors chosen by an individual child, the role of the guide being to seek out those who may need help in finding a way into the associational life of their community. Finally, the work of paraprofessionals as an important complement to the work of professionals was discussed. Discursively, these less formal helpers, through their position close to their communities, offer opportunities for troubled youth to negotiate new identities with peers, families, and others in the community. Collectively, these matrices of less formal relationships with adults can build and sustain health resources necessary for high-risk problem youth to co-author powerful identities that are more widely accepted.

Chapter Nine

Mental Health, Resilience, and Discursive Power

An extensive review of documents conducted by Health Canada in 1999 (Caputo, 1999, 2000) of formal and informal accounts of what youth say about health identified a large list of potential areas of concern from violence and unemployment to self-esteem and family problems. Consistently, youth said that no matter what challenges they face, they want and need the resources and opportunities to participate in their communities in ways amenable to them and their lifestyles. Effective practice with high-risk adolescents requires a critical understanding of the differential power in the health discourses in which they and their caregivers participate. The practice principles elaborated upon in the previous chapters grow out of a grounded theory that explains the localized realities of high-risk youth. So-called vulnerable teens argue that when their understanding of mental health is invested with sufficient power to challenge the pathologizing discourse of their families and/or communities, they experience themselves as far more resilient to the chaos in their lives. When understood as a community-based event, resilience is the shared property of everyone who becomes either an audience or actors in the lives of high-risk young people. Community factors, like social support, introduced at any time in a child's life have the potential to skew development in ways that bolster self-constructions as healthy and capable when they add to the ability of these youth to have their voices heard (Wolkow & Ferguson, 2001).

Professional, paraprofessional, and non-professional helpers who understand the way resilience is socially constructed can work with high-risk teens to build powerful and widely accepted self-definitions from marginalized social positions. In the preceding chapters, a substantive theory generated from case studies of youth has been used to inform a postmodern clinical practice that does this. I have attempted to show throughout this discussion that youth are by their nature postmodernists, seeking respect for localized truths and marginal realities. Clinical work with them that is attentive to the way they socially construct their world is both salutogenic and engaging.

High-risk youth and their families explain the process of discursive empowerment as a meta-construct to account for the complex nature of people's experiences of mental health. Empowered individuals argue they drift towards powerful and health-sustaining identities co-constructed through discourse. Exercising a say over what is and is not a mental health outcome means exercising control over the powerful labels used to describe one's health status. Professionals, families, communities, and peers participate in these constructions with varying degrees of power.

In very real terms, this understanding of resilience has the potential to change how we deal with our most troubled youth. Take, for example, a misguided report by the U.S. Coordinating Council on Juvenile Justice and Delinquency Prevention (1996). To combat violence and drugs in schools, the report urges a 'comprehensive community oriented policing approach' that is supplemented by heightened controls placed on delinquent youth. Among the initiatives urged are: 'enhance law enforcement capacity'; 'gun and drug interdiction and suppression strategies'; 'enforcement of the Gun-Free Schools Act of 1994,' which suspends and expels youth for weapons law violations; 'target youth gangs through prevention, intervention, and suppression strategies'; 'effective curfew programs'; and 'technological interventions to reduce gun violence such as guns that are harder to conceal and have trigger safeties' (1996: 7). Combined, I believe these strategies would promote *more* violence and drug abuse. Each would only tell youth they are indeed dangerous and needing plenty of attention from authorities. Each would augment the discursive power associated with delinquency and further glamorize the power handling a gun brings. But even more, none of these strategies address adult behaviours such as gun ownership (see Hardy, 2002), nor do they offer anything beside delinquent lifestyle choices to youth seeking powerful identities. Instead, they increase the likelihood that children will seek resilience by modelling their behaviour on that of adults, who will still enjoy liberal access to both drugs and guns. If such responses worked, then we would reasonably expect that jurisdictions with the highest youth incarceration rates and the most restrictive responses to youth violence (i.e., immediate transfer to adult court) would have the lowest rates of serious offences. In fact, the opposite is true (Cayley, 1998).

The research reported on throughout this book argues for a substantially different perspective on youth violence and the discourse of alarm which surrounds it. As developmentalists like Kenneth Dodge and others (Cooper et al., 2000; Dodge, 2001; Garbarino, 2001) concerned with prevention note, 'as long as the problem of violence prevention is left to local departments of corrections, an assumption of moral failure will prevail and prevention policies will consist primarily of efforts to protect society from "evil" through metal detectors in schools, police officers on the streets, and the death penalty' (Dodge, 2001: 63). If these tactics had worked, surely we would be witnessing an even greater decrease in violence among youth than the nominal decrease we have seen. We need to better understand how our misguided prevention and intervention efforts contribute to the problems we perceive among youth (see for example, Hardy, 2002). As Kenneth Dodge (2001) explains, using the example of the Cambridge-Somerville Youth Study conducted in the mid-twentieth century, the provision of services to delinquents can actually increase the likelihood of delinquent activities. A social constructionist perspective on these same phenomena helps to make sense of the unintended outcomes from what we offer high-risk children and youth.

A Grounded Ecological Theory

Resilience as a social construct provides an ecologically and politically sensitive understanding of the factors leading to mental health that avoids problematic linear causal explanations typical of the U.S. government report just cited. For example, research on the impact of economic hardship on adolescents has shown that a matrix of factors, including economic and emotional deprivation, lack of family integration, the child's poor academic achievements, and a low level of parental education, may explain the low self-esteem and behavioural transgressions associated with children living in poverty (see Battin-Pearson et al., 2000; Gooden, 1997; Hollin et al., 1995; Lempers et al., 1989; Pilling, 1990; Silbereisen & Walper, 1988). Reading this literature, one becomes overwhelmed by the hopelessness of trying to understand the theoretical connections between the various explanatory and intervening variables, hypothesized as causes of poor mental health in vulnerable populations. There is a lack of overarching theory that might help consumers of research see the forest for the trees. How are we to comprehend this smorgasbord of factors and their interactions? At times, it seems that each study that has examined the link between economic hardship and the mental health of adolescents proposes its partialized findings as the foundation for a comprehensive explanation of the phenomena. In contrast, the present study addresses this problem by showing that the construct of discursive power is able to function as a meta-level theory that encompasses many of the factors and processes discussed in the conventional mental health and resilience literatures.

High-risk teens who were interviewed for this book showed that experiences that enhance capacities, promote self-determination, increase participation; and distribute power and justice, carry the greatest potential for a positive impact on a teenager's discursive power leading to well-being. These types of experiences allow hopefulness to replace helplessness (Zimmerman, 1990) and contribute to psychological growth.

Mental health, as defined by teens, results from their experiences of control and competence. When teens feel that they have a say over their world and the opportunities to use their talents they report feeling mentally healthy despite the adversity they face. Teens demonstrate that their well-being depends on intersubjective experiences of power. Like Goffman's (1961) and Laing's (1967) psychiatric patients, teens argue that their dangerous, deviant, delinquent, or disordered conduct is far more intelligible when seen as attempts to maintain their mental health with the little power they have.

To experience mental health, high-risk teens must have some say over how mental health (and resilience) is defined. Although this is implicit in many constructionist therapies (White, 1995; Madsen, 1999), there has been little empirical work that has shown this theory to be true for at-risk populations with minimal power in the social discourse. Participants in this research explained in practical terms that discursive power leading to mental health requires that one's self-constructions are accepted in as many different parts of one's life as possible. Equitable discourse participation demands that high-risk teens be seen as joined to family, friends, and community, as equal partners in their collective social discourse. Within this constructionist position, the *etiology of mental health* is linked to the individual, and his or her social group's power to access and control health resources.

The process of constructing resilience can be explained metaphorically as a purposeful or accidental drift towards the random resources and events that occur in the life of a teenager. This pattern of drift proceeds over time, with the process of empowerment repeating itself in an endless spiral of action and reflection. It is this praxis, with its multiplicity of different actors, and relying on experiences of control and competence, that has a profound impact on a teenager's self-definition.

As discussed in Chapter 5, this use of the metaphor of drift varies in its usage from that of Matza (1964), who first used the term in relation to youth in his discussion of a 'drift into delinquency.' Like Matza, the work here recognizes a subterranean subculture of youth who depend on the broader culture to react to them in order to define themselves. However, the use of the concept of drift towards this youth subculture need not imply that youth do not also drift towards aspects of the dominant culture as well. The work here makes no judgments that drift must necessarily be down, with its implied notion of something less than adequate, or dark and evil. Instead, in the theory of drift demonstrated here, the child is drifting with only one goal in mind: to find the power associated with acceptance of a self-definition as resilient that is manifested through participatory competence in the social discourse. When there is a dominant culture that tolerates the unique identity constructions of high-risk teens, then the they will drift towards that cultural milieu (recall Becky in Chapter 5 found acceptance at both church and through her social activism, two different groups of people who tolerated her eccentricities). When there is no such tolerance, teens may drift towards subterranean (although teens seldom see their choices as such) cultures with values different from those who disapprove of their choices.

Viewed out of context, a teenager's drift and the resulting experience of discursive power can be misunderstood. Even drift towards groups with problem definitions need not be negative. A longitudinal study of elite young males by John Hagan (1991) showed that drift into some subcultures, like the party subculture of young men while at university, may actually lead to greater success in life, even when short-term threats to academic achievement occur. Participation in a culture of deviance can be functional. However, that participation can also change young people's trajectory through life. While they may drift back to conformity, they are not always successful in doing so. Neither Hagan nor Matza appear to view the teens they study as exercising power over scarce health resources through their unconventional behaviour. Both authors imply that the youngster has an unlimited number of choices to gain social power and acceptance but mistakenly associate with problem peers. That the trajectory of delinquency or other socially unacceptable behaviour may be a better choice than suicide, hopelessness, or anomie is never seriously examined by either author. Drift, as demonstrated in this present work, is about power-seeking. Teens only drift to where they feel they can improve their lives and sustain a self-construction as resilient.

To substantiate this theory of drift, the teens themselves were asked their explanations of the words that are used to describe them. There is no singular or transcendental meaning that can be attached to words like 'bad,' 'goody-two-shoes,' 'rebel,' 'bitch,' 'slut,' 'boss,' 'leader,' or 'browner.' These words are the expression of sets of meanings constructed over time by the social events in teens' lives. The same word that leads to feelings of personal power for one teen may be experienced by another as a threat to his or her well-being. Being a delinquent or, by contrast, an academically gifted child, might enhance or diminish a youth's power and degree of acceptance, depending on the context in which the words are used.

The feelings and values attached to these words, as Scheman (1980) and Stoppard (2000) have shown with words like 'anger' and 'depression,' can change depending on their social construction. Although Tommy might not explain it quite this way, the pride he shows being a delinquent is an important political re-description of that term. Deconstructing these marginal discourses is a step towards greater conscientization (Freire, 1970).

This approach to work with high-risk youth is, partially, an exercise in hermeneutics. Language is a precursor to a teenager's ability to process experience. The signifiers one uses to explain one's experience are temporal in nature, relying for their meaning on both their historical usage and present context. Teens understand that each label not only says what the child is, but also implies what is absent, signifying by omission that which is not immediately present in the defining discourse. This is similar to the well-known picture of the vase and two faces. When we see one or the other image, the negative space in the drawing still contains an image, although it remains hidden from our immediate perception. Being called a 'bad kid' implies that there is a possibility of being something else, in this case, a good and responsible young person reflective of a particular set of expectations. Just as these labels are temporal, so too is the individual self created through this use of language. While a particular teen might adopt a self-description as a 'survivor' or a 'victim,' woven into such definitions are other very different meanings that attach to these signifiers. For example, Allison (who, it will be remembered from Chapter 6, changed her name) is still Katie and, in fact, Allison can only be Allison insofar as she recognizes that what makes her unique is that she has lived Katie's life as the abused child. Both Allison and Katie are signifiers connected to each other through the events in one young woman's life.

Although the lives of high-risk teens tend to be full of signifiers that are thought of as uni-polar, teens themselves demonstrate that even dangerous and destructive behaviours are fertile with meaning. Having control over these signifiers is fundamental to having some say over one's health status. Not surprisingly, then, how a teen understands a particular label has an impact on his or her mental health. Contrast, for example, Cathy's and Patricia's use of the word 'bitchy.' For Cathy, being bitchy was driving people away whom she wanted closer, while for Patricia being bitchy was an empowering experience, exploiting her abundant talent to mouth-off which earns her the respect of her peers. So confident is she in her positive construction of the term that she even offers to help her teacher quiet her class down by using her same loud insulting manner, yelling at the other kids to 'shut up.' Challenging a dominant discourse, or proposing an alternative one so that words mean what the individual wants them to mean, is not an exercise that takes place in social isolation. Each signifier hints at the existence of a vast number of possible labels invested with differing amounts of power.

Sometimes it seems that labels, which the teens carry with them between spheres of interaction, are just waiting to find an appropriate context. Once found, a teen tends to experience himself or herself as resilient as a consequence of the acceptance he or she encounters. Helpers must understand that if a label is being steadfastly held to, it is most likely a sign that the teen has chosen that identity, or is stuck in a particular discourse that brings some measure of power. The only way to find out which is the case is to see the world from the teen's point of view. For example, a youth like Stan who prides himself on his ability to fight hopes someday to join the army. One would hardly think that a rebellious angry youth like Stan would ever want to submit to the highly authoritarian discipline of the armed forces. Yet, this career path makes perfect sense. Stan seeks a place where his fighter persona brings with it broader acceptance. The image of a blue-helmeted peacekeeper, fleeing a battle zone with a child in his arms, which has lately been seen on the side of bus shelters, carries with it a powerful message that the role of fighter is respectable in certain contexts.

Authoring a Healthy Identity during Adolescence

While almost all writing on postmodern interpretations of identity has emphasized theory, the novel aspect of this present work is that the youth themselves directed the research towards the construct of discursive power without the theory being imposed on the data. These high-risk teens demonstrated that their identities are constructions, or stories, that they tell about themselves over time. Postmodern interpretations of identity have argued the same, although they have been weak at producing studies that detail how self-stories are socially constructed. The language we use to construct these stories grows out of the interpersonal context in which we live (Gergen, 1994; McAdams, 1993; White, 1995). Marginalized high-risk youth compete with their parents, mental health professionals, and the broader community for control of the self-defining labels from which they construct their identity.

The process of identity development is necessarily intersubjective, although individuals are both actors and audience for the story that emerges. This was abundantly clear in the experiences of institutionalized youth and youth in care. Besides the communal aspects of discursive empowerment, there is also an aspect of personal agency in these social constructions, as individuals who critically analyse their role in the social discourse may opt instead to participate in marginal discourses. For many high-risk youth, this is a sensible option given their lack of access to the resources necessary to build a health-sustaining identity. Surviving and thriving means authoring a story of one's self as resilient and having this story accepted. As shown in Chapter 6, continuity across associational spheres of life is critical to maintaining these identities and the power of self-definition upon which resilience depends.

Support for this radical view of health is embedded in much of the conventional work on adolescence and the treatment of adolescent problems. Family therapists like Joseph Micucci (1998) have noted that the isolation of children from parents and an atmosphere that lacks tolerance for youth identities contributes to problematic symptoms among youth. According to Micucci, 'Symptoms in families evolve in a context of interpersonal isolation, characterized by conditional acceptance and efforts to control one another. As family members struggle to eliminate or control the symptoms, their preoccupation with the symptoms leads them to neglect other important aspects of their relationships with each other. As the family relationships deteriorate, all family members, particularly the symptomatic adolescent, experience an increasing sense of isolation' (1998: 17). Agentic aspects of discourse participation are enhanced rather than threatened when teens participate in the intersubjectivity inherent in communal discursive interactions.

In studies of gay men coping with heterosexism and women's experiences with AIDS, Massey and his colleagues (Massey et al., 1998) noted a 'trajectory of agency' that results from a process of growth that reflects their 'decision for thriving.' Like high-risk youth, the participants in Massey et al.'s studies take issue with our tendency to overlook the agentic characteristics of oppressed individuals' lives. Objective measures of their well-being fail to recognize the subtle nuances of their health realities. A more detailed context-specific analysis of their lives reveals outcomes that are synonymous with patterns of thriving typically associated with resilience. Tolerance for these localized discursive constructions by loosely affiliated marginalized individuals demonstrates what Massey et al. term the 'biographies of agency that emerge in the face of personal tragedy' (1998: 351). The high-risk youth discussed in these pages demonstrate this same capacity to sustain their personal health in opposition to views of them as either ill or troubled. Where others have ignored these aspects of the well-being of high-risk problem youth, this present study gives these youth a voice in the pathogenic discourse that defines them.

Peers and the Myth of Peer Pressure

An example of this dynamic between pathogenic and salutogenic discourses can be found in the way relationships between adolescent peers are viewed. Peer groups are a forum in which a youth's mental

health is maintained through recognition of powerful self-defining labels. And yet, studies of peer group interaction more often make reference to the relationship between the peer group and the misconduct of
youth or the ubiquitous evil caused by peer pressure (see Brown &
Lohr, 1987; Hurrelmann & Engel, 1992; Pearl et al., 1990; Santor et al.,
2000; Simon et al., 1997; Ziervogel et al., 1997). These studies tend to
reify the power of the adolescent peer group, while ignoring the personal agency of its individual members and their struggles towards
health. For example, Ruth Pearl, Tanis Bryan, and Allen Herzog (1990)
conducted a study of urban and suburban youth with and without
learning disabilities and their response to peer pressure to engage in
misconduct. They report that girls feel less pressured than boys to
engage in misconduct, learning disabled youth are more likely to engage in misconduct, and urban students (mostly from ethnic minority
groups) are more likely than their white suburban counterparts to
anticipate negative consequences from peers if they refuse to engage
in misconduct. If these patterns of behaviour were examined without
the biased view that peers put pressure on one another to misbehave,
then questions arise with regard to why teens choose to associate with
peers who are delinquent. Furthermore, why, then, do these peer
groups collectively choose antisocial behaviours? With an understanding of resilience as a social construct, one can take a second look at
Pearl et al.'s study and wonder whether delinquent urban youth from
minority cultural groups have as many options to define themselves
as powerful and competent as their white suburban counterparts. Do
learning disabled youth find in delinquent acts the personal competence they lack elsewhere in their lives? And why are girls more
likely to create health-enhancing identities that conform to broader
social norms? These questions focus on the power-enhancing aspects
of behavioural misconduct, understanding behaviours associated
with peer pressure in the broader context of the socially constructed
values of high-risk youth and the barriers they face in expressing their
resilience.

Researchers who have taken an optimistic view of adolescent peer
group interactions find they are necessary for the accomplishment of
the developmental tasks critical for cognitive and emotional growth
(Brown, 1998; Furman & Gavin, 1989; Pombeni et al., 1990; Rich, 1998;
Selman & Shultz, 1989; Stanton-Salazar & Spina, 2000). Work by Luisa
Pombeni, Erich Kirchler, and Augusto Palmonari has shown that 'adolescents who highly identified with their peer group not only are more

inclined to ask other people, peers as well as friends, parents and other adults, for support, to accept their offers of support, and talk about their problems, but they also seem to be more often able to resolve their problems than low-identifiers' (1990: 366). Attachment to the peer group helps the young person achieve a necessary group identification and avoid the problem of alienation, even when the identification is with a group of delinquents (Hagan, 1998; Hurrelmann & Engel, 1992; Newman & Newman, 1976). Programs that use peer groups to intervene with adolescents have shown success in turning the positive aspects of peer relationships to the benefit of delinquent youth (Gottfredson, 1987; Kuchuck, 1993). Such an approach fits well with an understanding of resilience as a social construct. The generic benefits derived from association with others are acknowledged, even when the behaviour of the group chosen is beyond social norms. Children do not seek out these marginal discourses to be unhealthy. They seek them out because they are the most available and efficient pathways to resilience.

Studies that have examined the presumed negative influence of the peer group on teens have shown that influence to be greatly exaggerated. Through a careful meta-analysis of the literature, Karl Bauman and Susan Ennett theorize that peer influence on drug use is overestimated. They argue that the 'strong and consistent correlation between drug use by adolescents and the drug use that they attribute to their friends' (1996: 186) can be explained by the selection of friends and the projection by adolescents of personal behaviours onto their peers. Reviewing the methodological problems of studies that have examined peer influence, Bauman and Ennett question the validity of many of the findings reported in the literature. They hypothesize that the causal relationship between a teen and his or her peer group is opposite to that implied by the term 'peer pressure.'

These same themes of selection and projection were demonstrated in research by Michell and West (1996). Working with 12- and 14-year-olds over an extended period of time in two drama classes, the authors conducted research on smoking and peer group influences. They found that teens who did not want to smoke 'avoided particular social situations and contexts associated with smoking behaviour, or chose non-smoking friends or, if necessary, dropped friends who started to smoke' (1996: 47). They conclude: 'Data from this study lead us to reject definitions of peer pressure as one-way and coercive, and assumptions about adolescents as socially incompetent and vulnerable

... We agree that individual choice and motivation need to be put back on the drug use agenda and that social processes other than peer pressure need to be acknowledged. These may be more to do with the way like-minded young people group together as friends and then co-operatively develop a "style" which may, or may not, include smoking' (1996: 47). The research reported on in the preceding chapters provides further empirical support to this belief that teens exercise their personal power through their associations with peers and that these relationships exert a positive influence on the power of their identity constructions.

Support for this specifically constructionist view of youth and their peer interaction is found in a number of studies. Lightfoot found that risk-taking behaviours bring teens feelings of group cohesion and enhanced mental health. There is something wonderful that is experienced by teens through the novelty of delinquency: 'This would suggest a reconceptualization of peer pressure; it is less an externally located push to conform, than a socially constructed desire to participate in culture-creating experiences' (1992: 240). Lightfoot's results are useful for understanding the youth in the present study. Peers willingly participate in normative group behaviour to create culturally shared meanings. An aspect of this meaning-making exercise is the authoring of identities through group association, identities that are frequently held in opposition to broader social pressures to conform.

Robin Robinson (1994) documented the way teenaged girls use their problematic public behaviours to cope with the trauma of sexual abuse. She studied the lives of 30 girls in Massachusetts with histories of involvement with the Departments of Youth Services (corrections) and the Department of Social Services (child welfare). Her account of the ways that they cope with their abuse begins with an exploration of the way their community has viewed young women over time and maintained control over them. Linking attitudes towards delinquent girls to witch trials and the way young female workers were treated in factory dormitories in the early- to mid-1800s, Robinson shows that we as a society are more likely to have problems with young women who say 'No' to abusive situations and assert their right of self-determination. Her work echoes many of the same themes found in this work: 'girls *survive* by running away from home, and commit *crimes of survival* to live on the street or to find shelter' (emphasis in original, 1994: 79). With these deviant lifestyles comes acceptance from other disenfranchised youth. As Robinson notes in her telling of the story of

one young woman who became involved with a Satanic cult: 'Ironically, living at the margin of family acceptance led Lisa to seek power
from a group that would accept her, if she provided sex' (1994: 91).
Robinson concludes that the girls she interviewed embody feminist
theory and resistance, just as the youth whose lives were discussed in
earlier chapters here express a postmodern understanding of their
health. As Robinson explains:

> The stories I collected suggest the strength girls find, ultimately within
> themselves, to challenge dangerous and abusive situations and to leave.
> The stories also reveal the remnants of volition the girls retain in the face
> of horrendous experiences. The accounts draw attention to affiliation and
> care in the development and behavior of girls, and on the loyalty they
> may feel to others to the detriment of their own well-being. My research
> questions the widespread belief that adolescent girls are offenders need-
> ing to be controlled and reformed. The control of adolescent female sexu-
> ality – a tacit goal of the juvenile courts and the agencies that serve girls
> committed to their care – misses the mark. (1994: 91)

Robinson's findings are similar to those of other researchers who have
taken the time to ask youth questions that open space for them to
explain their worlds from their point of view. For example, when
youth, both female and male, are asked about their sexual experiences
Caroline Rankin and Angela Aguayo (2002) showed they are able to
list over 100 benefits (and an equal number of negative consequences)
to casual sexual experimentation that are seldom discussed when we
debate sexual promiscuity among youth. These benefits can be gathered into four clusters: fewer relational consequences (no commitment),
an ego boost (feeling good about one's self), fun (adventure), and
pleasure (enhanced sexual skills, stress reduction). Like Robinson,
Rankin and Aguayo suggest that policy-makers listen more closely to
what girls (and boys) say about their problem behaviours, including
their sexuality.

Although they are naive in their understanding of postmodern interpretations of language and power, adolescents argue that control
over their identity stories is the fulcrum upon which their mental
health balances. High-risk youth define themselves as healthy and
their behaviours as health-seeking even when their caregivers believe
otherwise. Coordinated interagency interventions can actually threaten

the health of high-risk youth when those efforts serve to further the power invested in a professional discourse that stigmatizes high-risk youth and their lifestyles (Baldwin et al., 1997; Ungar et al., 2001). The same can be said of interactions between youth and their parents or extended families. When powerful players in any social sphere collaborate to control the self-constructions of high-risk youth, youth typically respond by resisting that control. Goffman (1961), Laing (1967), and Foucault (1965/1961) have already partially charted this conceptual territory. We know that control over identity constructions is important to mental health, wherever and however that control is achieved.

The stigmatizing effect of a community's labels is further compounded by the addition of the diagnostic labels used by professionals. Some of the more common ones used with this population include conduct disordered, parentified, attention deficit hyperactivity disordered, depressed, suicidal, borderline, antisocial, bipolar, emotionally disturbed, dysfunctional, and resistant. Interventions by professionals and the diagnostic assessments to which high-risk youth are subjected cause more harm than good when these labels become yet another barrier to a child's healthy constructions of self. Indicative of their trajectory towards personal agency and resilience, high-risk youth challenge these negative constructions of their identity. In opposition to the stigmatizing labels their communities and professionals assign them, they prefer to construct self-definitions that reflect their positive adaptation to impoverished environments. They choose for themselves names such as 'leader,' 'tough,' 'gang member,' 'dealer,' 'sexy,' 'survivor,' 'stud,' 'street kid,' 'helper,' 'drinker,' and 'fighter.' These signifiers represent positive self-constructions that grow from the resources at hand. Although many are in direct opposition to the labels caregivers want youth to adopt, they are, nevertheless, contextually powerful.

This construction of meaning is also political. It is as important who uses which signifiers as the signifiers used. All voices may be created equal, but all are not heard equally. Understanding the dynamics of power in discourse opens up the possibility of hearing silenced voices. As caregivers we are challenged by youth to understand their need to do something unconventional when confronted with innumerable barriers to growth. As Tyler et al. so aptly note, 'It is our contention that to attain a sense of personal integrity, we must all acquire a personal code that at times differs in important ways from society's conventional standards' (1992: 207). Resilient but high-risk teens do just this, differing from normative standards with the explicit goal of maintaining their health.

Issues for Professionals

An understanding of resilience as socially constructed leads to three issues for mental health care providers when working with high-risk youth. Caregivers must ask themselves: For whom is the child's behaviour a problem? What is the etiology of health? and, How do formal and informal social institutions participate through the actions of their agents (caregivers, parents, lay and professional helpers) in the process of meaning-making within social discourse?

All three issues hinge on an understanding of the problems of high-risk youth being different from those of their caregivers. However, despite much good work that has demonstrated that 'normal' and 'healthy' are subjective constructs, we still codify the behaviours of high-risk youth in ways that reify problems where youth say there are none.

Whose Problem Is Healthy Deviance?

Salutogenic theory equates health with a 'sense of coherence' (Antonovsky, 1987). In a study of family health, Sarah Cowley and Jennifer Ruth Billings (1999) sampled 50 families gathered through a purposeful sampling based on characteristics of the principal caretakers, usually mothers. When asked about their perceptions of health, health services, and coping, respondents' answers could be grouped under the three components that constitute a sense of coherence: manageability, comprehensibility, and meaningfulness.

> Manageability refers to the extent to which people feel they have the resources to meet demands that arise in their daily lives. It includes resources under direct individual control and those accessible from family, friends or the community. The concept depends quite closely on people experiencing a practical and physical sense of self-empowerment in coping with their own biology and threats to health. Comprehensibility refers to the extent to which sense and order can be drawn from the situation, and the world seems understandable, ordered, consistent and clear. In translating an exceptional experience such as illness, disability or unpleasant symptoms into the 'normal' context of their everyday lives,

people make sense of what is happening to them and can gain strength to deal with the situation. The sense of meaningfulness a person can gain from a situation refers to their ability to fully participate in the processes shaping their future. To be fully engaged in the health creating processes of their own lives, people need to 'make sense' of events in an emotional as well as a cognitive sense. (1999: 996)

If we examine the results of Cowly and Billings study, we find that these three categories of coherence capture much of what high-risk teens express about their own experiences of health. However, the pathways to health that some individual families choose (not unlike high-risk youth) are not recognized as health-enhancing because they remain outside social norms. Cowley and Billings describe a health care system which is biased towards its own preconceived notions of health and organized to meet its own needs: 'The personal style and attitude of health professionals [are] important in either enhancing or inhibiting salutogenesis ... Some informants experienced services that were so inflexible or individually ineffective, that trying to find a way around the convolutions and bureaucracy became a stress that created a demand for resources in addition to (and possibly greater than) the original need' (1999: 1002).

Frequently, the greatest problem encountered by high-risk youth is the institutional response their behaviour brings. Left alone and immersed in their own cultural context, they will argue that their actions demonstrate coherence and that they do not have problems that require intervention. While this attitude may be labelled as 'resistance' to treatment by some health care providers (McCown & Johnson, 1993), it was shown earlier that this oppositional pattern of behaviour is part of an elaborate strategy by youth inside and outside institutional settings to self-promote their understanding of health. Although family therapist Steve de Shazar (1982) proclaimed the 'death of resistance' in his writing in the early 1980s, the myth that people act against their own best interests still persists. High-risk youth assert that their behaviour meets their need to attain power and acceptance, even if it places them in conflict with caregivers.

The Etiology of Health

Our persistence in labelling the behaviours of high-risk youth as deviant, dangerous, delinquent, and disordered says more about the power of the dominant discourse on health than about the behaviours of these youth. That the roots to their healthy functioning in unhealthy environments are to be found through these behaviours is rarely accounted for in pathogenic discourse. The understanding of youth that is being promoted here does not extol the virtues of violent or self-destructive behaviours. On the contrary, a more critical perspective on the relative power of youth in the mental health discourse and their strategic exploitation of opportunities for growth demonstrates the need for high-risk youth to enjoy freer access to health resources. These children's pathways to resilience are being overlooked because we ignore the etiological factors and processes that support their mental health. Gang affiliations can replace 'dysfunctional' families; drug and alcohol abuse are possible substitutes for other recreational pursuits; violence can be one of the few ways some youth find a measure of self-worth with the added benefit that it allows them to express deep-seated emotions; sexuality meets needs for love and strong attachments. These choices are indictments of the personal and social barriers high-risk youth face.

Understood ecologically, protective processes become necessarily multidimensional. Take, for example, the progressive view of interventions with youth prostitutes, as discussed by Bernard Schissel and Kari Fedec (2001/1999). The complexity of the risk factors at play in the lives of these girls and boys, and the demand for both individual and systemic responses to this social problem, highlights the interrelationship between different protective mechanisms. Schissel and Fedec show that because of predisposing experiences of early trauma, interventions with young prostitutes require a well thought out matrix of approaches: 'The specific types of caring intervention need to include not only safe houses where street youth can find sanctuary but also attendant counselling programs that deal with issues of health and safety, personal trauma, family problems, and financial and educational opportunity. Obviously what we are advocating here is not just token shelters but ongoing, well-financed programs of one-to-one support as well as educational and employment programs that obviate the need to prostitute' (2001/1999: 196). Such comprehensive efforts engage a number of different protective strategies indicative of much of what we now understand to be best practices with at-risk populations. Introducing complexity into our response to youth problems also promotes tolerance for the myriad of explanations teens provide for their behaviour.

The Practice of Discursive Empowerment

Language is shared and understood through its performance. Teens who face multiple barriers to health require opportunities to experience themselves as authors of their personal stories through a praxis of action and reflection. Those who intervene with youth in any setting are most likely to be helpful when they promote the performativity (Bakhtin, 1986) of youthful voices in the social discourse that defines them. Institutional settings in particular provide a unique microcosm in which to witness how continuity in the intersubjectivity of pathologizing and health-enhancing discourse affects well-being. As shown through the life stories of youth like Cameron, Allison, and Tommy, teens turn to each other for healthy constructions of themselves. It is their adult caregivers who are sidelined in this process when youth do not have aspects of their health mirrored back to them by adults. Ironically, when adults participate more equitably in social discourse there is a greater chance of influencing high-risk youth. The presence of caregivers then becomes like a drop of ink in water, shading the entire discourse a different hue. If that influence is salutogenic, rather than pathogenic, then youth are likely to accept this subtle influence.

Looking once again at out-of-home placements as discussed in Chapter 6, the process youth engage in to nurture and preserve their mental health makes evident the role of the institution as part of the child's community of meaning. Discursive power is not shared equally by everyone in that community. If high-risk youth are to discern their own resilience, then the meaning-making activities of their communities, either inside or outside, must open space for them to describe their world. Turning up the volume on youth voices is more difficult when everyone about them is shouting. By understanding the institution (or community placement) as an intersubjective forum, we radically depart from the tendency of professionals to confer on only one part of that community the power to name reality.

Of course, this us–them dichotomy is not quite accurate either. In fact, the dynamics between different professions and between front-line and managerial workers makes institutional dynamics as complex as those of the communities they serve. Workers manage their positions' power *vis-à-vis* that of other staff just like the youth in their care. It is not uncommon that workers with the least discursive power are also the ones closest to the youth and the ones most supportive of a child's health discourse. This has always been a strength of child and youth care workers as a profession, although they are seldom conferred the respect they deserve from allied professions. Cowly and Billings note in their study of health visitors working with mothers in the community that the visitors, more than the professionals they report to, value the mothers' constructions of knowledge: 'It was commonly recognized that lay perspectives could be more appropriate and useful in defining the needs to be targeted, and a number of practitioners claimed they deferred to these views in private while presenting a "public fact" of using the professionally accepted terminology and targets when reporting to their managers' (1999: 996). Institutional workers who support the health constructions of youth are likely to present and document a professional discourse among colleagues, all the while acknowledging the contextual specificity of the localized realities of those in their care.

Future Directions

The preceding discussion has examined critically social and academic discourse addressing the problems of alienation, delinquency, depression, and hopelessness that plague many youth today. The ideas put forth throughout this book are part of a growing trend in both the mental health and social development fields. This present work is ultimately concerned with influencing decisions with regard to the delivery of services to youth such that empowering processes are linked to both intrapersonal and interpersonal mental health outcomes. It has been shown that macro sociopolitical processes that enhance the collective power of teenagers will influence the degree of control that they exercise over their self-definitions and influence their state of mental health. To the degree that formal treatment accomplishes the same, it will de-pathologize the pathways to resilience high-risk youth pursue.

Counselling that is useful for teens encourages them to drift towards new identity constructions. The task of a therapist or other helper, when understanding his or her position *vis-à-vis* adolescent discourse, must be to guide youth towards an alternative discourse that brings with it the power of acceptance. This search for power is ecological in scope, and the effective intervener will be the one who most helps teenagers identify areas of competence, control, and power present in the different spheres of their lives. Establishing a base of support for an alternative discourse, which identifies youth in ways they want, is the task of both formal helpers and, within an ecological practice paradigm, the community at large (Germain & Gitterman, 1996). This search for discursive support is more typical of social intervention strategies that are often neglected by mental health care providers. The experience of therapy is simply not significant enough to promote change unless there is support for the changes in self-definition that occur from outside the clinical relationship. This conceptualization of empowerment as part of therapeutic process is not in itself new. Karl Tomm (1992), among others (Howe, 1987; White, 1995) have shown that empowerment is one of the most preferred strategies for therapy. What has been less well explored is the exact process by which empowering therapeutic interventions work.

Changes are forthcoming. There is evidence that this understanding of youth as having their own unique constructions of health is being espoused by more and more researchers and practitioners. A recent report by Carl Rak and Lew Patterson (1996) describes how counsellors in schools can target aspects of resilience in children through a 25-item questionnaire. Responses to the questions covering all the major indicators of resilience in children are then used to find ways to help children cope better. The process begins, however, with an appreciation for each youth's unique knowledge of his or her situation and the strengths each displays surviving day to day. While strengths-based counselling is not new, it has seldom been linked directly to patterns of resilience in problem children. As Rak and Patterson note:

> One example of a counsellor's use of the questionnaire presents an 11-year-old boy who was referred to the counsellor because of frequent violations of school rules and classroom disruptions. He answered yes to Item 5 stating that family members expect him to be helpful and to Item 15 saying there are rules and expectations at home. According to his report and that of his parents, he meets family expectations of helpfulness and he follows rules respectfully, with only appropriate negotiation for exceptions. The counsellor used the boy's responses to the questionnaire as a basis for investigating his contrasting behavior in the two environments, seeking the conditions that triggered his resistance in school. (1996: 7)

Approaches such as this are especially relevant to the present work as they position the child in the role of expert *vis-à-vis* therapist. Rak and Patterson, without recognizing it, have moved not just towards a salutogenic approach to intervention, but to a more profound shift in discursive power between health care providers and the children that they serve.

When we step out of our adultocentric bias and look more carefully at today's youth, we see much more than the copycat Columbines, the drugs, the media-hyped violence, and all the other symbolic representations of a valueless, immoral youth culture. Even for the most dispossessed youth, this monochromatic picture does not reflect their reality. Margaret Wheatley recently wrote of her experience getting to know 13 boys ages 15 to 20 during a week-long leadership seminar. A diverse group, these young men have a clear vision of the world they want to create, and it is decidedly better than the one their caregivers have handed to them. Wheatley recounts: 'They want less hate. They fear for the planet. They want robots to do dull work. They want schools to stop being so awful. They expect pure (electronic) democracy. They want to stop violence. They want to stop being desensitized by the media to violence, suffering, warfare. They want to be loving, supportive parents' (2000: 80). These boys are in many ways no different from the ones interviewed for this book. They come from foster homes, families who have experienced divorce, are minorities in their adopted homeland; some are poor, others are wealthy. Their message, however, is uniform. Wheatley observes that they embody optimism and have made links to others in the global world of the Internet with more facility than anyone a generation ago could have imagined. And they take care of each other. One can see that this surprises Wheatley, not expecting young men to work 'patiently and lovingly' to help each other during a crisis. But most of all, Wheatley, by listening closely to her charges, heard them express a desire to make their world better through their defiance of their parents' values. Wheatley, addressing all youth, writes: 'You walk away from disrespectful employers, boring work, uninteresting activities. As parents, we have been quick to criticize you – we fear that you have no work ethic. But your refusal to conform and comply gives me hope, for it might save you from being diminished. I see you reclaiming the freedom and respect that every human spirit needs to flourish' (2000: 81).

Young women show this same spirit. One need only spend some time with the girls who Mary Pipher introduces in her book *Reviving Ophelia*. Although far from 'healthy' in a clinical sense, most show an indomitable spirit hidden beneath a culture that threatens to steal their identity. As Pipher observes, 'early adolescence is when many of the battles for the self are won and lost. These are hard fights, and the losses and victories determine to a great extent the quality of women's future lives. While young women are in the midst of these battles, none of them look terribly strong. Surface behaviors reveal little of the deep struggles that are battles to hold on to true selves' (1994: 264). Pipher captures in great detail these girls' pathways to health, providing yet another place where the discursive power of pathologized youth is heard in counterpoint to the droning of lay and professional caregivers. Pipher goes on to explain: 'Strong girls strive to define themselves as women and adults. They are trying to break away from family and remain close at the same time. They are trying to have friends without sacrificing themselves to do it. They attempt to define themselves as moral people and to take responsibility for their choices. They are trying to make good choices, often without much help. All of this is so difficult that weak often looks strong and strong looks weak' (1994: 267).

It is exactly this type of health-seeking dialogue between youth and caregivers that is at the heart of constructions of resilience. While it is not new to suggest that teens need to feel in control to feel good about themselves, explanations of the process they go through to achieve that control have not been sufficiently explored. Take, for example, Reginald Bibby and Donald Posterski's concluding remarks from their 1990 study of Canadian adolescent values:

> Adults don't deliberately plan to deny young people pathways into the future. But well-intentioned or not, when adults overcontrol, overprotect, and overindulge the young, they stifle their development. Instead of stimulating life in the young, in the end, those excesses slow the maturing process.
>
> The alternative is to *get out of the way* so young people can become autonomous. Instead of standing in the way of emergence, wise adults will give young people room to become their true selves. They will give young people their vote of confidence and propel them into being what they are meant to be. (1992: 320)

The path to resilience must include engagement in a process whereby high-risk individuals living within a matrix of social relations experience both the competence and sense of control necessary to define themselves and gain acceptance for their differences. To the extent that caregivers promote this process, they will witness increasingly more powerful and widely accepted constructions of resilience in teens from the most challenging of backgrounds.

Appendix: Methodology

Being familiar with the literature concerning high-risk youth, developmental psychopathology, and the ecological barriers that children and families confront, I designed an exploratory qualitative study in the early 1990s to research a hypothesized relationship between the dependent and independent outcome variables found in studies on empowerment and mental health. As a marriage and family therapist with high-risk youth and their families, and a social worker with community experience, I suspected that the mental health and empowerment constructs could be used interchangeably. In other words, I had reasoned that the youth whom I met clinically who seemed to have a sense of themselves as empowered individuals would more likely be mentally healthy and cope better with the myriad of risks present in their lives. The reasoning was sound. However, as I began the study, my design proved problematic when confronted with the early findings.

Serendipity and Research Design

In the first of two studies from which the findings in this book come, a sample of 21 high-risk adolescents, ages 13 through 17 with differing mental health assessments were invited to participate. There were 12 girls and 9 boys. All participants were white and came from several small urban centres (population under 80,000) in eastern Canada. They attended both junior and senior high schools or special vocational training programs offered both inside and outside residential placements. All came from families who were eligible for and participated in subsidized counselling services. This income level was used as a convenient way of ensuring homogeneity in the socioeconomic status of the participants. The choice of a group of participants with a lower socioeconomic status reflects general recognition that poverty creates barriers to mental health (Caspi et al., 2000; Combrinck-Graham, 1995; Kramer, 1992; Miech et al., 1999).

These individuals were initially drawn from two subpopulations of adolescents. Theoretical sampling that reflected a grounded theory approach (Charmaz, 1983; Glaser & Strauss, 1967; Strauss & Corbin, 1990) to the research made it reasonable to choose high-risk adolescents who were viewed by society as both mentally ill and mentally healthy, or alternatively, vulnerable and resilient. The sample was purposeful, with letters sent to other clinicians inviting them to refer to the study youth who met the basic criteria of involvement with subsidized counselling and who had at least three other significant risk factors present in their lives: a parent with a mental illness or addiction; a history of physical or sexual abuse; multiple family dislocations; were living with a sole parent or in a blended family; displayed violent or other antisocial behaviour; had spent time in institutional settings such as group homes, young offender facilities, and psychiatric treatment centres; had a physical disability; low school attachment; associated with a delinquent peer group; had witnessed family violence; or had experienced other significant exposure to risk such as the chronic illness of a parent. Clinicians not only referred youth to the study, but also recommended many seek counselling with me as well. The result was that I had the privilege of working for extended periods of time, in some cases up to 18 months with 14 of the 21 youth who were eventually included in the study. This work became a component of the data collection. Interviews for this first phase of the actual research were conducted from December 1992 to December 1993, although, as mentioned, I already had begun working clinically with some of the study's participants. A second cohort of participants were included during data collection which took place from 1995 to 1999 (see below). While I knew many of the youth well, it was the anonymous review of each case by two senior clinicians who were not directly involved with the study that led to a judgment that participants did in fact face significant risk. The youth were then further sorted into two groups, vulnerable and resilient, based on reported behaviours and available prior assessments of their mental health. The reviewers found this to be a difficult task as it quickly became apparent that each teen showed both characteristics of vulnerability and resilience. The final categorization became a matter of consensual decision-making in which the overall balance of strengths and weaknesses in the teen's life placed him or her in one of the two subgroups. From the youth referred to the study, the final selection of participants was made based on matches between vulnerable and resilient youth with similar histories of exposure to risk.

A unique aspect of this sampling was that it also reflected an emerging understanding of mental health and mental illness as two distinctly separate, but related, continua. It has been shown that the presence or absence of a mental illness tells us little about the state of a child's mental health. The disorder does not itself predict the individual's state of well-being (Bradburn, 1969; Cowley & Billings, 1999; Health and Welfare Canada, 1988; Jahoda, 1958; Reich & Zautra, 1988; Veit & Ware, 1983). Signs of mental illness such as depression, attention deficit disorder, Tourette's, or an addiction can affect the child's self-esteem, opportunities to feel competent, social acceptance, and attachments to caregivers, but these effects are *only indirectly* the result of the disorder.

For example, studies like that of David Fergusson and Liane Woodward (2002) lend credibility to this two-factor model of health. Fergusson and Woodward looked at birth cohort data over a 21-year period for 1,265 children. They sought to identify a link between mid-adolescence and later adolescence levels of depression. While their findings indicate a clear and specific continuity in depression from one age to another, the links between the disorder of depression and deviant behaviours could not be accounted for by the depression, but instead were related far more to confounding social and environmental factors: 'When due allowance was made for social, familial, and personal correlates of adolescent depression, there was no evidence to suggest that those subject to adolescent depression were at significantly increased risk of later substance abuse, suicide attempts, educational underachievement, unemployment, or early parenthood. Rather, the results suggested that the contextual factors that were associated with an increased risk of adolescent depression were also associated with increased risk of these later adverse outcomes' (2002: 230). There is an important distinction that needs to be made here, and it is one that is foundational to my earlier attempt to design a study examining resilience in a high-risk youth population. Evidence for a two-factor model of health supports the position that biological, organic, and even social problems are not necessarily related to healthy functioning and that the way one accommodates to an illness may or may not threaten well-being. The illness, in other words, can exist largely independent of aspects of health such as self-esteem, meaningful involvement with others, internality, hopefulness, and other qualities associated with resilience. While cross-domain effects exist, illness and health exist on two separate continua (Reich & Zautra, 1988; Viet & Ware, 1983). This two-factor model was the first conceptual step I took towards distinguishing the health-enhancing aspects of deviance, although it would be my discovery of social constructionism that would eventually provide a more satisfying perspective from which to understand the data as presented by participants.

Under a two-factor model, which is more salutogenic (Antonovsky, 1987), or health focused, than a pathogenic, or illness perspective, I was able to identify signs of mental health that existed at the same time that an individual participant showed evidence of mental disorder. In other words, a child with attention deficit disorder was still found to have a measure of self-esteem, while the suicidal youth experienced self-efficacy.

Criss-crossing both continua, as in Figure A.1, provided a two-by-two matrix of high-risk adolescents with varying degrees of mental health and illness. In the first study, youth from 2 of the 4 quadrants were sampled: high-risk adolescents who were both mentally ill and had poor mental health (vulnerable emotionally troubled adolescents who come from lower socioeconomic status [SES] households and who, along with their families, are recent clients of a family therapy clinic), and high-risk youth who showed no signs of mental illness and demonstrated good mental health (resilient high-risk youth who were appraised by clinicians as coping well despite their lower SES households and the presence of problems for which they and their families received treatment in the previous year).

To locate resilient youth, youth who in the opinion of the referring clinician were doing better than expected given the risk he or she faced, and who fit in quadrant II of the matrix, youth who had come to the attention of clinicians because some member of their family was in counselling, but who may or may not have been included in treatment themselves, were referred to the study. In this way, a pool of potential participants were found. Initially, the first 10 youth, 5 from each of the 2 quadrants, were matched one with the other. Each pair was chosen for the variability brought to the sample in terms of the risk factors confronted.

Figure A.1 Theoretical sampling of high-risk youth based on two-factor model of mental health.

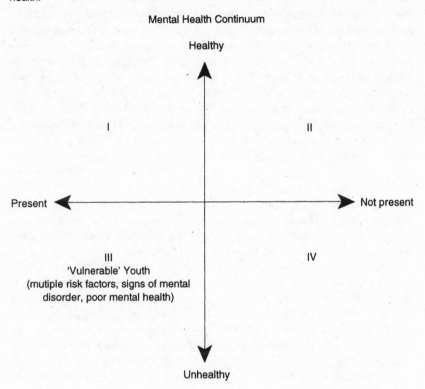

Mental Health Continuum

Healthy

I   II

Present ◄————————————————————► Not present

III   IV
'Vulnerable' Youth
(mutiple risk factors, signs of mental
disorder, poor mental health)

Unhealthy

After these first 10 interviews were well under way, it became apparent that this methodology was problematic. First, the research itself was disempowering to the teens because it categorized them before they had a chance to say where they felt they should be placed on the two continua. As a substantive theory evolved that recognized the power teens want over their self-definition, it seemed ludicrous to be categorizing the teens in advance of their interviews. What is more, as we tried to sort the teens we began to see that in many respects they were doing the best they could with the resources they had at hand. Should a teen be selected as resilient even if he or she was delinquent, but coping well with the consequences of his or her delinquency? Similarly, when is acting out after being victimized sexually a justifiable response and a sign of healthy adaptation to feelings of powerlessness? Whose accounts of the young person's behaviour were we to believe, given the myriad of assessments contained in each youth's file? While we considered conducting our own testing of the youth to ensure a more reliable sort, doing so would have predetermined the results by imposing objective standards on behaviour that the literature had insufficiently explored: power and resilience. Furthermore, with hundreds of potential variables associated with both risk and resilience, we were at a loss to decide which test protocol would produce the most reliable sort of youth into the two categories. Instead, the study remained naturalistic (Lincoln & Guba, 1985), operationalizing resilience and vulnerability as discussed in Chapter 1 in more relativistic terms and seeking variability in the sample rather than dichotomous matches. This decision to select participants by the differentness in the way they confront risk factors led to the serendipitous findings that are the basis for both the study and interventions that followed and this book. The less youth were categorized, their lives viewed from within an illness paradigm, the better able and more willing they were to explain their lived experience in their own terms.

This use of a qualitative grounded theory approach to the research was ideally suited to the study of such complex but poorly understood social interactions and the specific context of adolescents' lives (Handel, 1992; Lincoln & Guba, 1985; Padgett, 1998; Patton, 1990; Rodwell, 1998; Silverman, 2000). The grounded theory approach, as developed by Glaser and Strauss (1967), which has been employed in studies of resilience recently (Garwick et al., 1999; Gilgun, 1999; Morgan, 1998), allowed for the inductive generation of theory from data, providing opportunities for participants to generate new knowledge based on their own experiences. By encouraging high-risk adolescents to talk freely about the two key constructs, empowerment and mental health, the research process paralleled the process of empowerment as articulated in the literature. Through the interview process, participants were able to challenge old identities and begin the construction of new ones.

It is worth noting that these teens exist under the influence of the same dominant discourse that tells them they have problems needing attention. The interview process was the catalyst for many to put words to their experiences in ways that they may have thought, but seldom articulated. The interview, in other words, was an intervention. Participation became part of the construction of an alternative discourse. Reporting that discourse, first back to the participants, and now here, adds volume to previously unarticulated experience. Daniel Monti, in his look at gangs in suburban schools, makes a telling comment about the youth whom he interviewed: 'Whatever insight many of them left an interview with was constructed during the interview. They had not brought it into the room' (1994: 2). In this study, the identification of mental health amidst the chaos of the lives of high-risk teens was an immediate challenge to the way these youth's lives were socially constructed. As one parent commented, typifying the responses of many, 'You want to interview Christopher about his *mental health*? That will be *different*!'

Such unanticipated, although highly regarded effects on participants meant that they exerted a significant influence on the design of the study. That design was by necessity emergent, with sample selection changing after the first 10 interviews after it became apparent that youth, both vulnerable and resilient, accounted for their experiences of health in the same way. Even youth with the least acceptable and most disturbing patterns of behaviour talked about the same process of empowerment as their 'resilient' counterparts. Since the study aspired to look beyond the diagnostic labels assigned to the participants, and focus on their mental health, I acknowledged the contradiction introduced by the initial plan and in consultation with my colleagues accepted its rejection by the participants. It was then that I began selecting participants based on the variability in the ways they cope with the biopsychosocial risk factors present in their lives.

Data Collection and Analysis

A relative dearth of qualitative studies with this population, and the authors' own experiences with teens, made it clear that the research design would have to ensure that the participants and their parents/caregivers trusted the researchers and the research process. This provided the motivation and rationale for recruiting participants from my own clinical practice or that of close colleagues. The clinical relationships helped establish trust with the youth and their parents/caregivers who acted as gatekeepers. Although this approach is uncommon, the clinician and ethnographer/researcher roles can be merged when the boundaries between the two are clear (Daly, 1992; Laird, 1994; Noller, 2002; Schatzman and Strauss, 1973). For the first group of participants, the change in their status from client to participant was clearly evident in that all interviews were conducted after treatment had ended.

Each teen participated in two interviews of one to one and a half hours. The first interview included open-ended questions covering issues related to adolescence, mental health, relationships, experiences of power and control, competencies, and coping strategies. For example, questions in the area of adolescence and mental health included:

• What is it like being an adolescent today?
• What kinds of things help you feel mentally healthy?
• How did you become a client/resident (of the service which provides you or your family service)?

Some of the questions relating to control and competence were:

• Are there parts of your life where you feel you have control? Where do you not have control?
• How do you think other people see you? How do you see yourself?
• What makes you special?

Both data collection and analysis were guided by Glaser and Strauss's (1967) constant comparative method. As each interview was completed, the findings from one informed the next. Questions were added based on the findings, a greater emphasis placed on some aspects of the interview guide, and early formulations of a theory of resilience shared with participants for their comments. This process has been characterized by Mary Rodwell (1998) as a dialogical hermeneutic. Understanding is refined through a continual process of co-construction of meaning from one participant to the next, making participants into active members of the data analysis team.

Data were collected during the entire process of the research, and in some instances, it was my journal notes regarding roadblocks encountered to a particular participant's inclusion or systemic barriers to the research that helped to strengthen and deepen my understanding of lives lived at risk.

First interviews with the youth were usually held in an office at a local mental health centre. Between first and second interviews, completed transcripts of the interviews were sent to the participants so they could read over their comments and raise issues that they wanted to discuss in the second interviews. As well, a thorough review of each adolescent's case file with the referring agency was conducted and the material in the files contrasted with the content of the first interviews. Questions that arose during these reviews were discussed during the second interviews. These follow-up interviews took place in a quiet place in each youth's home or when the parents left the home after greeting the interviewer. These home visits proved especially important, as they gave parents an opportunity to talk for up to half an hour about their lives, the experiences of their children, and the family's history, conversations that took place with the adolescents present or, as was frequently the case, nearby. Much information was also gleaned from observation in the homes such as where the young person sleeps, how his or her room is decorated, and the natural flow of events that take place in families during two- to three-hour visits after school and on weekends. Transcripts from these interviews too were sent back to participants and phone contact was made to see if they would like to add anything to what was already said. Finally, a summary of the research findings written in accessible language was shared with each participant.

Once data collection with participants was completed a series of 6 focus groups were held with people not directly involved in the research: one with clinicians; one with parents; one with parents and teens who were participating in a treatment group; and three with different groups of youth, two in a high school setting, the third at a community recreation centre. During these groups, the findings from the study were shared and participants asked to comment and add to the theory as it had been generated. Interview guides permitted flexibility so that the order of the questions could be changed and new areas explored based on the participants' responses.

The field notes and the transcriptions from all audiotaped interviews were managed through the use of Ethnograph – a computer program for analysing qualitative data (Seidel et al., 1988). Indigenous and sensitizing concepts reflecting the themes emerging from the data were used to structure a coding and re-coding process that was both additive and divisive of categories. Individual interviews were first analysed one at a time and later subjected to cross-case analyses.

A Second Cohort

A second group of participants were interviewed between September 1995 and March 1999 and included 22 participants, 4 girls and 18 boys, attending a long-term treatment program in a forensic treatment facility in eastern Canada. Nineteen of these youth were white, the other 3 identified themselves as Aboriginal. In this group only two-thirds had a lower SES, while the others were referred to as middle class by clinicians who knew the families. Selection of participants, data collection and analysis followed the same sequence with minor variations to suit the context in which the data was collected (a research assistant helped with data collection, timing of interviews coincided with discharge plans, data collection occurred simultaneously with a discharge interview and program evaluation).

As with the first cohort, all names and other identifying information of these youth have been changed significantly and in many cases some details of their lives fictionalized. To further conform with the legal requirement to conceal the identity of young offenders, the case studies as presented have been constructed as a montage of identities. Given the vulnerabilities of this population, and the ease with which some in their communities identify them, the youth who appear in this book are character sketches typical of the study participants, but not of any one individual specifically. These efforts were necessary to protect the anonymity of participants and that of their families. For specific youth who were in placement under an order of the youth court, and whose stories I recount in greater detail in this book, permission to share these case studies (with identifying information changed) was approved by a youth court judge, subject to the conditions of Section 44.1(1)(k)(i) (research or statistical purposes) and 44.1(4) (disclosure which does not identify the young person) of the Young Offenders Act of Canada.

Additionally, to provide clinical vignettes from my clinical practice, clients gave permission for transcripts of our interviews to be used for purposes of research and training. This material too has been heavily disguised and resemblance to any particular individual is both unintended and coincidental.

Trustworthiness

In a qualitative study such as this, methodological rigour is measured by the trustworthiness of the data that are produced. Trustworthiness refers to the fit between the emergent data, the participants' experiences, and the observed phenomena. Yvonna Lincoln and Egon Guba (1985) outline four components of trustworthiness that parallel the criteria for truthfulness in the positivist paradigm: credibility (internal validity); transferability (external validity); dependability (reliability); and confirmability (objectivity). Taken together, all four ensure the best possible fit of the data with the phenomena under investigation.

Credibility

Like all four measures of trustworthiness, credibility is dependent on distinct elements of the methodology. The intent is to ensure that what I thought I observed as the researcher is an accurate account of what I was studying (Kirk & Miller, 1986). In other words, do the data that were collected help us to understand the construct under investigation? In a study of this nature, credibility is really a question of degree. As all data was filtered by my own subjectivity, ensuring credibility means being as aware as possible of my influence on the participants. The possible confusion of roles between researcher and clinician made the need to monitor the influence of this subjectivity on the study an important part of the design. Thus, the methodology selected here ensures credibility through design.

Lincoln and Guba (1985) highlight several ways in which credibility is maintained: 'We believe it to be the case that the probability that findings (and interpretations based upon them) will be found to be more credible if the inquirer is able to demonstrate a prolonged period of engagement (to learn the context, to minimize distortions, and to build trust), to provide evidence of persistent observation (for the sake of identifying and assessing salient factors and crucial atypical happenings), and to triangulate, by using different sources, different methods ... the data that are collected' (1985: 307). These elements are all evident in the methodology discussed above. In addition to these considerations, the search for negative case examples and dialogic retrospection (Kieffer, 1981; Rodwell, 1998) further contributed to the credibility of the study.

Transferability

The transferability of this study's results to other settings and populations is made possible through the thickness of the data (Glaser & Strauss, 1967; Lincoln & Guba, 1985). By providing a great deal of information on the experiences of these adolescents, other researchers will be able to judge the study for its applicability to their work. As Lincoln and Guba assert: 'It is ... *not* the naturalist's task to provide an *index* of transferability; it *is* his or her responsibility to provide the *data base* that makes transferability judgements possible on the part of potential appliers' (1985: 316).

Dependability

To ensure that the study's findings reflect what is contained in the data, continuity and trust in the relationship between the researcher and participants is essential. The combination of clinical and informal contact and the development of a trusting relationship between the participants and myself or the research assistant was designed to ensure the youth did not feel expectations to respond in ways they thought they should, but felt comfortable to relate their experiences as they saw them (Kirk & Miller, 1986; Kvale, 1996; Silverman, 2000).

Lincoln and Guba (1985) also discuss the role of the external auditor as crucial to the dependability of a study. The auditor, in this case a senior colleague of mine at the university, ensures that the data collection, data analysis, and other steps taken in the research process conform to the standards necessary to ensure an accurate *re-presentation* of the participants' experiences. This person's presence from the start of the research process ensures that dependability is more likely to be maintained.

Confirmability

Finally, ensuring that the findings are confirmable is complicated by the fact that the researcher is also the research instrument. Confirmability means accounting not only for the participants' experiences, but also the reactions of the researcher who filter those experiences. The audit discussed above helps in this regard. This study's findings will be judged confirmable if all proper steps were taken to generate the data *and* I have paid special attention to my own bias. Triangulation of the data through the use of multiple sources of data collection and personal journal notes helped to ensure confirmable results (Lincoln & Guba, 1985). These reflexive notes in particular give outside observers the opportunity to see what my relationship to the data has been and how that relationship may have influenced the results I report (Kirk & Miller, 1986).

In total, the methodological considerations discussed here ensured that the data presented are trustworthy and the substantive theory an authentic account of the experiences of participants.

References

Abramson, L.Y., Seligman, M.E., & Teasdale, J.D. (1978). Learned helplessness in humans: Critique and reformulation. *Journal of Abnormal Psychology, 87*(1), 49–74.

Abrums, M. (2000). 'Jesus will fix it after awhile': Meaning and health. *Social Science and Medicine, 50*(1), 89–105.

American Psychiatric Association. (1994). *Diagnostic and statistical manual of mental disorders (4th ed.)*. Washington, DC: APA.

Andersen, T. (1991). *The reflecting team.* New York: W.W. Norton.

Andersen, T. (1996). Language is not innocent. In F.W. Kaslow (Ed.), *Handbook of relational diagnosis and dysfunctional family patterns* (pp. 119–125). New York: Wiley.

Anderson, H., & Goolishian, H. (1992). The client is the expert: A not-knowing approach to therapy. In S. McNamee & K.J. Gergen (Eds.), *Therapy as social construction* (pp. 25–39). London: Sage.

Anthony, E.J. (1987). Risk, vulnerability, and resilience: An overview. In E.J. Anthony & B.J. Cohler (Eds.), *The invulnerable child* (pp. 3–48). New York: Guilford.

Antonovsky, A. (1987). The salutogenic perspective: Toward a new view of health and illness. *Advances, Institute for Advancement of Health, 4*(1), 47–55.

Archard, D. (1993). *Children: Rights and childhood.* London: Routledge.

Archibold, C., & Meyer, M. (1999). Anatomy of a gang suppression unit: The social construction of an organizational response to gang problems. *Police Quarterly, 2*(2), 201–224.

Arnett, J.J. (1999). Adolescent storm and stress, reconsidered. *American Psychologist, 54*(5), 317–26.

Arnett, J.J. (2000). Emerging adulthood: A theory of development from the late teens through the twenties. *American Psychologist, 55*(5), 469–480.

Arnold, M.S. (1995). Exploding the myths: African-American families at promise. In B.B. Swadener, & S. Loveck (Eds.), *Children and families 'at promise'* (pp. 143–162). Albany: State of New York Press.

Asendorpf, J.B., & van Aken, M.A.G. (1999). Resilient, overcontrolled, and undercontrolled personality prototypes in childhood: Replicability, predictive power, and the trait-type issue. *Journal of Personality and Social Psychology, 77*(4), 815–832.

Asher, S. (2002). Healthy peer relationships in childhood: Acceptance, friendship, and friendship quality. Paper presented at the 11th International Conference on Personal Relationships, International Society for the Study of Personal Relationships, Dalhousie University, Halifax.

Augusta-Scot, T. (2001). Dichotomies in the power and control story: Exploring multiple stories about men who chose abuse in intimate relationships. *Gecko: A Journal of Deconstruction and Narrative Ideas in Therapeutic Practice* (2), 31–68.

Bakhtin, M.M. (1986). *Speech genres and other late essays* (V.W. McGee, Trans.). Austin: University of Texas.

Baldwin, A.L., Baldwin, C., & Cole, R.E. (1990). Stress-resistant families and stress-resistant children. In J. Rolf, A.S. Masten, D. Cicchetti, K.H. Nuechterlein, & S. Weintraub (Eds.), *Risk and protective factors in the development of psychopathology* (pp. 257–280). Cambridge, MA: Cambridge University Press.

Baldwin, D., Coles, B., & Mitchell, W. (1997). The formation of an underclass or disparate processes of social exclusion? Evidence from two groupings of 'vulnerable youth.' In R. Macdonald (Ed.), *Youth, the 'underclass' and social exclusion* (pp. 83–95). New York: Routledge.

Bandura, A. (1998). Exercise of agency in personal and social change. In E. Sanavio (Ed.), *Behaviour and cognitive therapy today: Essays in honor of Hans J. Eysenck* (pp. 1–29) Oxford: Pergamon.

Bandura, A. (1999). A sociocognitive analysis of substance abuse: An agent perspective. *Psychological Science, 10*(3), 214–217.

Bardone, A.M., Moffitt, T.E., Caspi, A., Dickson, N., Stanton, W.R., & Silva, P.A. (1998). Adult physical health outcomes of adolescent girls with conduct disorders, depression, and anxiety. *Journal of the American Academy of Child and Adolescent Psychiatry, 37*(6), 594–601.

Baron, S.W., & Hartnagel, T.F. (1998). Street youth and criminal violence. *Journal of Research on Crime and Delinquency, 35* (May), 166–192.

Barter, K. (1996). Collaboration: A framework for northern social work practice. In R. Delaney, K. Brownlee, & K. Zapf (Eds.), *Issues in northern social work practice* (pp. 70–94). Thunder Bay: Centre for Northern Studies, Lakehead University.

Barton, W.H., Watkins, M., & Jarjoura, R. (1997). Youths and communities: Toward comprehensive strategies for youth development. *Social Work*, 42(3), 483–493.

Batey, S.R. (1999). *A case study of adolescent African-American males and factors in resiliency that have contributed to their development and school success.* Unpublished doctoral thesis, Educational Leadership and Innovation, University of Minnesota.

Batson, C.D., Ahmad, N., & Tsang, J. (2002). Four motives for community involvement. *Journal of Social Issues, 58*(3), 429–446.

Battin-Pearson, S., Newcomb, M.D., Abbott, R.D., Hill, K.G., Catalano, R.F., & Hawkins, J.D. (2000). Predictors of early high school dropout: A test of five theories. *Journal of Educational Psychology, 92*(3), 568–582.

Bauman, K.E., & Ennett, S.T. (1996). On the importance of peer influence for adolescent drug use: Commonly neglected considerations. *Addictions, 91*(2), 185–198.

Beardslee, W.R. (1989). The role of self-understanding in resilient individuals: The development of a perspective. *American Journal of Orthopsychiatry, 59*(2), 266–278.

Benard, B. (2002). The foundations of the resiliency framework: From research to practice. In *Resiliency in action: Practical ideas for building strengths in youth, families and communities.* [On-line]. Available: HTTP: www.resiliency.com

Bender, D., & Loesel, F. (1997). Protective and risk effects of peer relations and social support on antisocial behaviour in adolescents from multi-problem milieus. *Journal of Adolescence, 20*(6), 661–678.

Berger, P.L., & Luckmann, T. (1966). *The social construction of reality.* New York: Anchor Press.

Bibby, R.W., & Posterski, D.C. (1992). *Teen trends: A nation in motion.* Toronto: Stoddart.

Blose, M. (1999, May). The daughters of Lydia: Tattooed women's identity construction and encounters. Paper presented at the 16th Qualitative Analysis Conference, Fredericton.

Blumstein, A. (2002). Youth, guns and violent crime. [On-line] *The Future of Children, 12*(2). Available at http://www.futureofchildren.org/

Blundo, R. (2001). Learning strengths-based practice: Challenging our personal and professional frames. *Families in Society: The Journal of Contemporary Human Services, 82*(3), 296–304.

Bolger, K.E., & Patterson, C.J. (2001). Developmental pathways from child maltreatment to peer rejection. *Child Development, 72*(2), 549–568.

Borg, D., Brownlee, K., & Delaney, R. (1995). Postmodern social work practice with aborigianl people. In R. Delaney & K. Brownlee (Eds.), *Northern social work practice* (pp. 116–135). Thunder Bay: Centre for Northern Studies, Lakehead University.

Bowling, S.W., Kearney, L.K, Lumadue, C.A., & St. Germain, N.R. (2002). Considering justice: An exploratory study of family therapy with adolescents. *Journal of Marital and Family Therapy, 28*(2), 213–224.

Bradburn, N.M. (1969). *The structure of psychological well-being.* Chicago: Aldine.

Brame, B., Nagin, D.S., & Tremblay, R.E. (2001). Developmental trajectories of physical aggression from school entry to late adolescence. *Journal of Child Psychology and Psychiatry, 42*(4), 503–512.

Braverman, M.T. (1999). Research on resilience and its implications for tobacco prevention. *Nicotine & Tobacco Research, 1*, S67–S72.

Brickman, P., Rabinowitz, V.C., Karuza, J. Jr., Coates, D., Cohn, E., & Kidder, L. (1982). Models of helping and coping. *American Psychologist, 37*(4), 368–384.

Bronfenbrenner, Urie. (1979). *The ecology of human development: Experiments by nature and design.* Cambridge, MA: Harvard University Press.

Brotman, S., & Pollack, S. (1997). Loss of context: The problem of merging postmodernism with feminist social work. *Canadian Social Work Review, 14*(1), 9–21.

Brown, B.B., & Lohr, M.N. (1987). Peer-group affiliation and adolescent self-esteem: An integration of ego-identity and symbolic-interaction theories. *Journal of Personality and Social Psychology, 52*(1), 47–55.

Brown, L.M. (1998). *Raising their voices: The politics of girls' anger.* Cambridge, MA: Harvard University Press.

Bruner, J. (1987). The transactional self. In J. Bruner & H. Haste (Eds.), *Making sense: The child's construction of the world* (pp. 81–96). New York: Routledge.

Budd, K.S., Stockman, K.D., & Miller, E.N. (1998). Parenting issues and interventions with adolescent mothers. In J.R. Lutzger (Ed.), *Handbook of child abuse research and treatment* (pp. 357–376). New York: Plenum.

Burger, J. (1994). Risk, resilience, and protection. *Journal of Emotional & Behaviour Problems, 3*(2), 6–10.

Cadell, S., Karabanow, J., & Sanchez, M. (2001). Community, empowerment, and resilience: Paths to wellness. *Canadian Journal of Community Mental Health, 20*(1), 21–35.

Cairns, R.B., & Cairns, B.D. (1994). *Lifelines and risks: Pathways of youth in our time.* Cambridge: Cambridge University Press.

Campbell, C., & Ungar, M. (in press). Deconstructing knowledge claims: Epistemological challenges in social work education. *Progressive Human Services.*

Caputo, T. (1999). *Hearing the voices of youth: A review of research and consultation documents.* Ottawa: Health Canada.

Caputo, T. (2000). *Hearing the voices of youth: Youth participation in selected Canadian municipalities.* Ottawa: Health Canada.

Carrington, P.J. (2001). Trends in youth crime in Canada, 1977–1996. In T. Fleming, P. O'Reilly, & B. Clark (Eds.), *Youth injustice: Canadian Perspectives,* 2nd ed. (pp. 25–57). Toronto: Canadian Scholars' Press. (Reprinted from *Canadian Journal of Criminology,* Jan. 1999, pp. 1–32.)

Carver, C.S. (1998). Resilience and thriving: Issues, models, and linkages. *Journal of Social Issues, 54*(2), 245–266.

Caspi, A., Taylor, A., Moffitt, T.E., & Plomin, R. (2000). Neighborhood deprivation affects children's mental health: Environmental risks identified in a genetic design. *Psychology Science, 11*(4), 338–342.

Caughlin, J., & Malis, R. (2002). Demand/withdraw communication between parents and adolescents as a correlate of adolescent well-being. Paper presented at the 11th International Conference on Personal Relationships, International Society for the Study of Personal Relationships, Dalhousie University, Halifax.

Cayley, D. (1998). *The expanding prison: The crisis in crime and punishment and the search for alternatives.* Toronto: Anansi.

Chambon, A.S., & Irving, A. (Eds.). (1994). *Essays on postmodernism and social work.* Toronto: Canadian Scholars' Press.

Charmaz, K. (1983). The grounded theory method: An explication and interpretation. In R. Emerson (Ed.), *Contemporary field research* (pp. 109–126). Boston: Little Brown.

Checkoway, B. (1998). Involving young people in neighbourhood development. *Child and Youth Services Review, 20*(9/10), 765–795.

Chong, D. (2000). *The girl in the picture: The Kim Phuc story.* Toronto: Penguin.

Church, K. (1989). User involvement in the mental health field in Canada. *Canada's Mental Health, 37*(2), 22–25.

Cirillo, I. (2000). *The relationship of constructive aggression to resilience in adults who were abused as children.* Unpublished doctoral dissertation, Smith College for Social Work, Northhampton, MA.

Cochran, M.M. (1988). Addressing youth and family vulnerability: Empowerment in an ecological context. *Canadian Journal of Public Health, 79*(Nov./Dec.), Supplement 2, S10–S16.

Cochran, M.M. (1991). The Minnesota early childhood family education program: An interview with Lois Engstrom, Program Supervisor. *Empowerment & Family Support, 2*(1), 4–9.

Cohen, P., Brook, J.S., Cohen, J., Velez, C.N., & Garcia, M. (1990). Common and uncommon pathways to adolescent psychopathology and problem behavior. In L.N. Robins & M. Rutter (Eds.), *Straight and devious pathways from childhood to adulthood* (pp. 242–258). Cambridge, MA: Cambridge University Press.

Coles, R. (1967). *Children of crisis: A study of courage and fear.* Boston: Little, Brown.

Colwell, M.J., Petit, G.S., Meece, D., Bates, J.E., & Dodge, K.A. (2001). Cumulative risk and continuity in nonparental care from infancy to early adolescence. *Merrill-Palmer Quarterly, 47*(2), 207–234.

Combrinck-Graham, L. (Ed.). (1995). *Children in families at risk: Maintaining the connections.* New York: Guilford.

Conger, R.D., & Simons, R.L. (1997). Life-course contingencies in the development of adolescent antisocial behavior: A matching law approach. In T.P. Thornberry (Ed.) *Developmental theories of crime and delinquency* (pp. 55–99). New Brunswick, NJ: Transaction Publishers.

Cooper, W.O., Lutenbacher, M., & Faccia, K. (2000). Components of effective youth violence prevention programs for 7- to 14-years-olds. *Archives of Pediatric and Adolescent Medicine, 154*(11), 1134–1139.

Coordinating Council on Juvenile Justice and Delinquency Prevention (1996, Mar.). *Combating violence and delinquency: The national juvenile justice action plan.* Washington, DC: U.S. Department of Justice.

Cowen, E.L. (1991). In pursuit of wellness. *American Psychologist, 46*(4), 404–408.

Cowley, S., & Billings, J.R. (1999). Resources revisited: salutogenesis from a lay perspective. *Journal of Advanced Nursing, 29*(4), 994–1004.

Craig, S.C., & Maggiotto, M.A. (1982). Measuring political efficacy. *Political Methodology, 8*(3), 85–110.

Crick, N.R. (1997). Engagement in gender normative versus nonnormative forms of aggression: Links to social-psychological adjustment. *Developmental Psychology, 33*(4), 610–617.

Crick, N.R., & Bigbee, M.A. (1998). Relational and overt from of peer victimization: A multiinformant approach. *Journal of Consulting and Clinical Psychology, 66*(2), 337–347.

Crick, N.R., Casas, J.F., & Ku, H. (1999). Relational and physical forms of peer victimization in preschool. *Developmental Psychology, 35*(2), 376–385.

Cross, T.L. (1998). Understanding family resiliency from a relational world view. In H.I. McCubbin, E.A. Thompson, A.I. Thompson, & J.E. Fromer (Eds.), *Resiliency in Native American and immigrant families* (pp. 143–157). Thousand Oaks, CA: Sage.

Dahlberg, L.L., & Potter, L.B. (2001). Youth violence: Developmental pathways to prevention challenges. *American Journal of Preventive Medicine, 20,* 3–14.

Daly, K. (1992). The fit between qualitative research and characteristics of families. In J. Gilgun, K. Daly, & G. Handel (Eds.), *Qualitative methods in family research* (pp. 3–11). Newbury Park, CA: Sage.

Darvill, G., & Smale, G. (1990). Introduction: The face of community social work. In G. Darvill & G. Smale (Eds.), *Partners in empowerment: Networks of innovation in social work* (pp. 11–28). London: National Institute for Social Work.

D'Augelli, A.R., & Hershberger, S.L. (1993). Lesbian, gay and bisexual youth in community settings: Personal challenges and mental health problems. *American Journal of Community Psychology, 21*(4), 421–448.

Davidson, W.B., & Cotter, P.R. (1991). The relationship between sense of community and subjective well-being: A first look. *Journal of Community Psychology, 19*(3), 246–253.

Dean, C. (1991). Bringing empowerment theory home: The Cornell Parent-Caregiver Partnership Program. *Network Bulletin: Empowerment and Family Support, 2*(2), 5–8.

Dekovic, M. (1999). Risk and protective factors in the development of problem behavior during adolescence. *Journal of Youth and Adolescence, 28*(6), 667–685.

de Shazar, S. (1982). *Patterns of brief family therapy: An ecosystemic approach.* New York: Guilford.

Dickerson, V.C., & Zimmerman, J.L. (1996). Myths, misconceptions, and a word or two about politics. *Journal of Systemic Therapies, 15*(1), 79–88.

Dishion, T.J. (2000). Cross-setting consistency in early adolescent psychopathology: Deviant friendships and problem behavior sequelae. *Journal of Personality, 68*(6), 1109–1126.

Dishion T.J., Capaldi, D.M., & Yoerger, K. (1999). Middle childhood antecedents to progressions in male adolescent substance use: An ecological analysis of risk and protection. *Journal of Adolescent Research, 14*(2), 175–205.

Dishion, T.J., & McMahon, R.J. (1998). Parental monitoring and the prevention of child and adolescent problem behavior: A conceptual and empirical formulation. *Clinical Child and Family Psychology Review, 1*(1), 61–75.

Dishion, T.J., McCord, J., & Poulin, F. (1999). When interventions harm: Peer groups and problem behavior. *American Psychologist, 54*(9), 755–764.

Dodge, K.A. (2001). The science of youth violence prevention: Progressing from development epidemiology to efficacy to effectiveness to public policy. *American Journal of Preventive Medicine, 20* (Suppl. 1) 63–70.

Dodge, K.A., Lochman, J.E., Laird, R., & Zelli, A. (2002). Multidimensional latent-construct analysis of children's social information processing patterns: Correlations with aggressive behavior problems. *Psychological Assessment, 14*(1), 60–73.

Doll, B., & Lyon, M.A. (1998). Risk and resilience: Implications for the delivery of educational and mental health services in schools. *School Psychology Review, 27*(3), 348–363.

Donovan, J.E., Jessor, R., & Costa, F.M. (1991). Adolescent health behavior and conventionality-unconventionality: An extension of problem-behavior theory. *Health Psychology, 10*(1), 52–61.

Dryden, J., Johnson, B., Howard, S., & McGuire, A. (1998). Resiliency: A comparison of construct definitions arising from conversations with 9-year-old – 12-year-old children and their teachers. Paper presented at the Annual Meeting of the American Educational Research Association. Available from EDRS, Document ED 419 214.

Dugan, T.F. (1989). Action and acting out: Variables in the development of resiliency in adolescence. In T.F. Dugan & R. Coles (Eds.), *The child in our times: Studies in the development of resiliency* (pp. 157–176). New York: Brunner/Mazel.

Dumont, M., & Provost, M.A. (1999). Resilience in adolescents: Protective role of social support, coping strategies, self-esteem, and social activities on experience of stress and depression. *Journal of Youth and Adolescence, 28*(3), 343–363.

Dunn, J. (1988). Normative life events as risk factors in childhood. In M. Rutter (Ed.), *Studies of psychosocial risk: The power of longitudinal data* (pp. 227–44). Cambridge, MA: Cambridge University Press.

Dunst, C.J., Trivette, C.M., & Deal, A.G. (1988). *Enabling and empowering families: Principles and guidelines for practice.* Cambridge, MA: Brookline Books.

Egan, R.D. (2000, May). 'I'll be his fantasy girl if he's my money man': Negotiations of fantasy, desire, and power among exotic dancers and their regular customers. Paper presented at the 17th Qualitative Analysis Conference, Fredericton.

Ellickson, P., & McGuigan, K.A. (2000). Early predictors of adolescent violence. *American Journal of Public Health, 90*(4), 566–572.

Emery, R. E., & Forehand, R. (1994). Parental divorce and children's wellbeing: A focus on resilience. In R.J. Haggerty, L.O. Sherrod, N. Germezy, & M. Rutter (Eds.), *Stress, risk, and resilience in children and adolescents: Processes, mechanisms and interventions* (pp. 65–99). New York: Cambridge University Press.

Ensign, J., & Gittelsohn, J. (1998). Health and access to care: Perspectives of homeless youth in Baltimore City, USA. *Social Science and Medicine, 47*(12), 2087–2099.

Farrell, A.D., & White, K.S. (1998). Peer influences and drug use among urban adolescents: Family structure and parent–adolescent relationships as protective factors. *Journal of Consulting and Clinical Psychology, 66*(2), 248–258.

Farrington, D.P. (1995). The development of offending and antisocial behaviour from childhood: Key findings from the Cambridge study in delinquent development. *Journal of Child Psychology and Psychiatry, 36*(6), 929–964.

Farrington, D.P., Jolliffe, D., Loeber, R., Stouthamer-Loeber, M., & Kalb, L.M. (2001). The concentration of offenders in families, and family criminality in the prediction of boys' delinquency. *Journal of Adolescence, 24*(5), 579–596.

Federal Interagency Forum on Child and Family Statistics (2002). *America's children: Key national indicators of well-being, 2002.* Federal Interagency Forum on Child and Family Statistics, Washington, DC: U.S. Government Printing Office.

Felner, R.D., Aber, M.S., Primavera, J., & Cauce, A.M. (1985). Adaptation and vulnerability in high-risk adolescents: An examination of environmental mediators. *American Journal of Community Psychology, 13*(4), 365–379.

Felsman, J.K. (1989). Risk and resiliency in childhood: The lives of street children. In T.F. Dugan & R. Coles (Eds.), *The child in our times: Studies in the development of resiliency* (pp. 56–80). New York: Brunner/Mazel.

Ferguson, D.M., & Woodward, L.J. (2002). Mental health, educational, and social role outcomes of adolescents with depression. *Archives of General Psychiatry, 59*(Mar.), 225–231.

Fick, A., & Thomas, S. (1995). Growing up in a violent environment: Relationship to heath-related beliefs and behaviors. *Youth & Society, 27*(2), 136–147.

Fine, M. (1994). Working the hyphens: Reinventing self and other in qualitative research. In N.K. Denzin & Y.S. Lincoln (Eds.), *Handbook of qualitative research* (pp. 70–82). Thousand Oaks, CA: Sage.

Fine, M., Weis, L., Weseen, S., & Wong, L. (2000). For whom? Qualitative research, representations, and social responsibilities. In N.K. Denzin & Y.S. Lincoln (Eds.), *Handbook of qualitative research,* 2nd ed. (pp. 107–32). Thousand Oaks, CA: Sage.

Flanagan, P. (1998). Teen mothers: Countering the myths of dysfunction and developmental disruption. In C.G. Coll, J.L. Surrey, & K. Weingarten (Eds.), *Mothering against the odds: Diverse voices of contemporary mothers* (pp. 238–254). New York: Guilford.

Fleming, T., O'Reilly, P., & Clark, B. (2001). *Youth injustice: Canadian perspec-tive*, 2nd ed. Toronto: Canadian Scholars' Press.

Focht-Birkerts, L., & Beardslee, W.R. (2000). A child's experience of parental depression: Encouraging relational resilience in families with affective illness. *Family Process, 39*(4), 417–434.

Foucault, M. (1965). *Madness and civilization: A history of insanity in the age of reason* (R. Howard, Trans.). New York: Pantheon. (Original work published 1961.)

Foucault, M. (1976). *Mental illness and psychology* (A. Sheridan, Trans.). New York: Harper Colophon Books. (Original work published 1954.)

Foucault, M. (1980). *Power/Knowledge* (C. Gordon, L. Marshall, J. Mepham, & K. Soper, Trans.). New York: Pantheon Books. (Original work published 1972.)

Foucault, M. (1982). The subject and power. *Critical Inquiry, 8*(Summer), 777–795.

Foucault, M. (1994). About the concept of the 'dangerous individual' in nineteenth-century legal psychiatry. In J.D. Fabian (Ed. and Trans.), *Michel Foucault: Power* (pp. 176–200). New York: New Press. (Original work published 1978.)

Foucault, M. (1994). Truth and judicial forms. In J.D. Fabian (Ed. and Trans.), *Michel Foucault: Power* (pp. 1–89). New York: New Press. (Original work published 1973.)

Foucault, M. (1994). Truth and power. In J.D. Fabian (Ed. and Trans.), *Michel Foucault: Power* (pp. 111–33). New York: New Press. (Original work published 1977.)

Franco, N., & Levitt, M.J. (1998). The social ecology of middle childhood: Family support, friendship quality, and self-esteem. *Family Relations, 47*(4), 315–321.

Frank, A. (1952). *Anne Frank: The diary of a young girl*. New York: Scholastic Book Services.

Fraser, M. (1997). *Risk and resilience in childhood: An ecological perspective*. Washington, DC: NASW Press.

Fraser, M., & Galinsky, M.J. (1997). Toward a resilience-based model of practice. In M. Fraser (Ed.), *Risk and resilience in childhood: An ecological perspective* (pp. 265–275). Washington, DC: NASW Press.

Fraser, N. (1989). *Unruly practices: Power, discourse and gender in contemporary social theory*. Minneapolis: University of Minnesota Press.

Freedman, J., & Combs, G. (Eds.). (1996). *Narrative therapy: The social construc-tion of preferred realities*. New York: W.W. Norton.

Freeman, E.M., & Dyer, L. (1993). High-risk children and adolescents: Family and community environments. *Families in Society, 74*(7), 422–431.

Freire, P. (1970). *Pedagogy of the oppressed* (M.B. Ramos, Trans.). New York: The Seabury Press. (Original work published 1968.)

Freire, P. (1994). *Pedagogy of hope: Reliving Pedagogy of the oppressed* (R.R. Barr, Trans.). New York: Continuum.

Freitas, A.L., & Downey, G. (1998). Resilience: A dynamic perspective. *International Journal of Behavioral Development, 22*(2), 263–85.

Freud, S. (1999). The social construction of normality. *Families in Society: The Journal of Contemporary Human Services, 80*(4), 333–339.

Frey, L., Adelman, M.B., & Query, J.L. Jr. (1996). Communication practices in the social construction of health in an AIDS residence. *Journal of Health Psychology, 1*(3), 383–396.

Furman, W., & Gavin, L.A. (1989). Peers' influence on adjustment and development. In T.J. Berndt & G.W. Ladd (Eds.), *Peer relationships in child development* (pp. 319–340). New York: Wiley.

Garbarino, J. (2001). Making sense of senseless youth violence. In J.M. Richman & M.W. Fraser (Eds.), *The context of youth violence: Resilience, risk, and protection* (pp. 13–41). Westport, CT: Praeger.

Gairdner, W.D. (1992). *The war against the family.* Toronto: Stoddart.

Garmezy, N. (1976). *Vulnerable and invulnerable children: Theory, research, and intervention.* Journal Supplement Abstract Service, APA.

Garmezy, N. (1983). Stressors of childhood. In N. Garmezy & M. Rutter (Eds.), *Stress, coping, and development in children* (pp. 43–84). New York: McGraw-Hill.

Garmezy, N. (1985). Stress-resistant children: The search for protective factors. In J.E. Stevenson (Ed.), *Recent Research in Developmental Psychopathology* (pp. 213–233). New York: Pergamon.

Garmezy, N. (1987). Stress, competence, and development: Continuities in the study of schizophrenic adults, children vulnerable to psychopathology, and the search for stress-resistant children. *American Journal of Orthopsychiatry, 57*(2), 159–74.

Garmezy, N. (1991). Resilience in children's adaption to negative life events and stressed environments. *Pedicatric Annals, 20*(9), 462–466.

Garmezy, N. (1993). Children in poverty: Resilience despite risk. *Psychiatry, 56*(1), 127–136.

Garmezy, N., Masten, A.S., & Tellegen, A. (1984). The study of stress and competence in children: A building block for developmental psychopathology. *Child Development, 55*(1), 97–111.

Garwick, A.W., Kohrman, C.H., Titus, J.C., Wolman, C., & Blum. R.W. (1999). Variations in families' explanations of childhood chronic conditions: A cross-cultural perspective. In H.I. McCubbin, E.A. Thompson, A.I. Thompson & J.A. Futrell (Eds.), *The dynamics of resilient families* (pp. 165–202). Thousand Oaks, CA: Sage.

Gerard, J.M., & Buehler, C. (1999). Multiple risk factors in the family environment and youth problem behaviors. *Journal of Marriage and Family Therapy, 61*(5), 343–361.

Gergen, K.J. (1991). *The saturated self: Dilemmas of identity in contemporary life.* New York: Basic Books.

Gergen, K.J. (1994). *Realities and relationships: Soundings in social construction.* Cambridge, MA: Harvard University Press.

Gergen, K.J. (1996). Beyond life narratives in the therapeutic encounter. In J.E. Birren, G.M. Kenyon, J. Ruth, J.J.F. Schroots, & T. Svensson (Eds.), *Aging and biography: Explorations in adult development* (pp. 205–223). New York: Springer.

Gergen, K.J. (2001). Psychological science in a postmodern context. *American Psychologist, 56*(10), 803–13.

Gergen, K.J., Hoffman, L., & Anderson, H. (1996). Is diagnosis a disaster? A constructionist trialogue. In F.W. Kaslow (Ed.), *Handbook of relational diagnosis and dysfunctional family patterns* (pp. 102–118). New York: Wiley.

Gergen, M.M., & Gergen, K.J. (2000). Qualitative inquiry: Tensions and transformations. In N.K. Denzin & Y.S. Lincoln (Eds.), *Handbook of qualitative research*, 2nd ed. (pp. 1025–1046). Thousand Oaks, CA: Sage.

Germain, C.B., & Gitterman, A. (1996). *The life model of social work practice,* 2nd ed. New York: Columbia University Press.

Gilgun, J.F. (1996a). Human development and adversity in ecological perspective, Part 1: A conceptual framework. *Families in Society, 77*(7), 395–402.

Gilgun, J.F. (1996b). Human development and adversity in ecological perspective, Part 2: Three patterns. *Families in Society, 77*(8), 459–476.

Gilgun, J.F. (1999). Mapping resilience as process among adults with childhood adversities. In H.I. McCubbin & E.A. Thompson (Eds.), *The dynamics of resilient families* (pp. 41–70). Thousand Oaks, CA: Sage.

Gilligan, C. (1982). *In a different voice: Psychological theory and women's development.* Cambridge, MA: Harvard University Press.

Glantz, M.D., & Johnson, J.L. (1999). *Resilience and development: Positive life adaptations.* New York: Kluwer Academic / Plenum Publishers.

Glantz, M.D., & Sloboda, Z. (1999). Analysis and reconceptualization of resilience. In M.D. Glantz & J.L. Johnson (Eds.), *Resilience and development:*

Positive life adaptations (pp. 109–128). New York: Kluwer Academic / Plenum.

Glaser, B.G., & Strauss, A.L. (1967). *The discovery of grounded theory: Strategies for qualitative research.* New York: Aldine de Gruyter.

Goffman, E. (1961). *Asylums: Essays on the social situation of mental patients and other inmates.* Chicago: Aldine.

Goleman, D. (1994). *Emotional intelligence.* New York: Bantam.

Gooden, M.P. (1997). *When juvenile delinquency enhances the self-concept: The role of race and academic performance.* Unpublished doctoral dissertation, Ohio State University.

Gordon, C. (1994). Introduction. In J.D. Fabian (Ed.), *Michel Foucault: Power* (pp. xi–xli). New York: New Press.

Gordon, E.W., & Song, L.D. (1994). Variations in the experience of resilience. In M.C. Wang, & E.W. Gordon (Eds.), *Educational resilience in inner-city America: Challenges and prospects* (pp. 27–43). Hillsdale, NJ: Lawrence Earlbaum Associates.

Gordon, R.M. (2001). Criminal business organizations, street gangs and 'wanna be' groups: A Vancouver perspective. In T. Fleming, P. O'Reilly, & B. Clark (Eds.), *Youth injustice: Canadian perspectives,* 2nd ed. (pp. 101–24). Toronto: Canadian Scholars' Press. (Reprinted from *Canadian Journal of Criminology,* Jan. 2000, pp. 39–60)

Gorman, Jane (1993). Postmodernism and the conduct of inquiry in social work. *Affilia, 8*(3), 247–264.

Gorman-Smith, D., Tolan, P.H., Loeber, R., & Henry, D.B. (1998). Relation of family problems to patterns of delinquent involvement among urban youth. *Journal of Abnormal Child Psychology, 26*(5), 319–333.

Gottfredson, G.D. (1987). Peer group interventions to reduce the risk of delinquent behaviour: A selective review and a new evaluation. *Criminology, 25*(3), 671–714.

Graber, J.A., Brooks-Gunn, J., & Galen, B.R. (1998). Betwixt and between: Sexuality in the context of adolescent transitions. In R. Jessor (Ed.), *New perspectives in adolescent risk behaviour.* New York: Cambridge University Press.

Graham, J.R., & Barter, K. (1999). Collaboration: A social work practice model. *Families in Society, 80*(1), pp. 6–13.

Gray, J. (2000, 3 June). Teenage breakdown? *Globe and Mail,* A12.

Gregson, D. (1994). Normally very abnormal: A perspective on youth at risk. *Journal of Child and Youth Care, 9*(2), 31–41.

Guba, E.G., & Lincoln, Y.S. (1989). *Fourth generation evaluation.* Newbury Park, CA: Sage.

Guerra, N.G. (1998). Serious and violent juvenile offenders: Gaps in knowledge and research priorities. In R. Loeber, & D.P. Farrington (Eds.), *Serious
and violent juvenile offenders: Risk factors and successful interventions* (pp. 389–
404). Thousand Oaks, CA: Sage.

Hagan, J. (1991). Destiny and drift: Subcultural preferences, status attain-
ments, and the risks and rewards of youth. *American Sociological Review*,
56(5), 567–582.

Hagan, J. (1998). Life course capitalization and adolescent behavioral development. In R. Jessor (Ed.), *New Perspectives in Adolescent Risk Behaviour*
(pp. 499–517). New York: Cambridge University Press.

Hagan, J. & McCarthy, B. (1997). *Mean streets: Youth crime and homelessness.*
New York: Cambridge University Press.

Hallenbeck, M. (1998). A victory for the village. *Reclaiming Children and Youth*,
7(3), 182–6.

Hancock, Karen. (1999, May). London's sex trade industry: The politics of the
'problem.' Paper presented at the 16th Annual Qualitative Analysis
Conference, Fredericton.

Handel, G. (1992). The qualitative tradition in family research. In J.G. Gilgun,
K. Daly & G. Handel (Eds.), *Qualitative methods in family research* (pp. 12–
21). Newbury Park, CA: Sage.

Hardy, M.S. (2002). Behavior-oriented approaches to reducing youth gun
violence. *Future of Children, 12*(2), 101–17.

Hauser, S.T. (1999). Understanding resilient outcomes: Adolescent lives
across time and generations. *Journal of Research on Adolescence, 9*(1), 1–24.

Hawkins, J.D., Herrenkohl, T., Farrington, D.P., Brewer, D., Catalano, R.F., &
Harachi, T.W. (1998). A review of predictors of youth violence. In R.
Loeber, & D.P. Farmington (Eds.), *Serious and violent juvenile offenders: Risk
factors and successful interventions* (pp. 106–46). Thousand Oaks, CA: Sage.

Hawley, D.R., (2000). Clinical implications of family resilience. *American
Journal of Family Therapy, 28*(2), 101–116.

Hawley, D.R., & DeHann, L. (1996). Toward a definition of family resilience:
Integrating life-span and family perspectives. *Family Process, 35*(3), 283–298.

Health and Welfare Canada. (1988). *Mental health for Canadians: Striking a
balance.* Ottawa: Supply and Services Canada.

Henry, B., Caspi, A., Moffitt, T.E., Harrington, H., & Silva, P. (1999). Staying
in school protects boys with poor self-regulation in childhood from later
crime: A longitudinal study. *International Journal of Behavioral Development,
23*(4), 1049–1073.

Herrenkohl, T.I., Huang, B., Kosterman, R., Hawkins, J.D., Catalano, R.F., &
Smith, B.H. (2001). A comparison of social development processes leading

to violent behavior in late adolescent initiators of violence. *Journal of Research in Crime and Delinquency, 38*(1), 45–63.

Herrenkohl, T.I., Maguin, E., Hill, K.G., Hawkins, J.D., Abbott, R.D., & Catalano, R.F. (2000). Developmental risk factors for youth violence. *Journal of Adolescent Health, 26*(3), 176–86.

Hewson, D. (1991). From laboratory to therapy room: Prediction questions for reconstructing the 'new-old' story. *Dulwich Centre Newsletter* (3), 5–12.

Higgins, G.O. (1994). *Resilient adults overcoming a cruel past.* San Francisco: Jossey-Bass.

Hollin, C.R., Epps, K.J., & Kendrick, D.J. (1995). *Managing behavioural treatment: Policy and practice with delinquent adolescents.* London: Routledge.

Hollingshead, A.B., & Redlich, F.C. (1958). *Social class and mental illness: A community study.* New York: Wiley.

Hornby, S. (1993). *Collaborative care: Interprofessional, interagency and interpersonal.* Oxford: Blackwell Scientific.

Hoskins, R., Donovan, C., Merhi, S., Pascual-Salcedo, M. Cockcroft, A., & Anderson, N. (2000, Feb.). *Dialogue with Youth about Risk and Resilience.* Holyrood, NF: Health and Community Services Eastern Region.

Howe, D. (1987). *An introduction to social work theory: Making sense in practice.* Aldershot, England: Ashgate.

Howe, David. (1994). Modernity, postmodernism and social work. *British Journal of Social Work, 24*(5), 513–532.

Hoyt, M.F. (Ed.). (1996a). *Constructive therapies 2.* New York: Guilford.

Hoyt, M.F. (1996b). Postmodernism, the relational self, constructive therapies, and beyond: A conversation with Kenneth Gergen. In M.F. Hoyt (Ed.), *Constructive therapies 2* (pp. 347–68). New York: Guilford.

Huizinga, D., & Jakob-Chen, C. (1998). The contemporaneous co-occurrence of serious and violent juvenile offending and other problem behaviours. In R. Loeber & D.P. Farrington (Eds.), *Serious and violent juvenile offenders: Risk factors and successful interventions* (pp. 47–67). Thousand Oaks, CA: Sage.

Hurrelmann, K., & Engel, U. (1992). Delinquency as a symptom of adolescents' orientation toward status and success. *Journal of Youth and Adolescence, 21*(1), 119–138.

Hutchison, R.L., Tess, D.E., Gleckman, A.D., & Spence, W.C. (1992). Psychosocial characteristics of institutionalized adolescents: Resilient or at risk? *Adolescence, 27*(Summer), 339–356.

Irving, A., & Moffatt, K. (2002). Intoxicated midnight and carnival classrooms: The professor as poet. *Radical Pedagogy* [On-line], *4* (1). Available: HTTP: radical pedagogy.icaap.org Directory: content/issue4_1 File: 05_irving-moffatt.html

Irving, A., & Young, T. (2002). Paradigm for pluralism: Mikhail Bakhtin and social work practice. *Social Work, 47*(1), 19–29.

Jackson, S., & Martin, P. (1998). Surviving the care system: Education and resilience. *Journal of Adolescence, 21*(5), 569–583.

Jaffe, P.G., & Baker, L.L. (1999). Why changing the YOA does not impact youth crime: Developing effective prevention programs for children and adolescents. *Canadian Psychology, 40*(1), 22–29.

Jaffe, S.R., Moffit, T.E., Caspi, A., Fombonne, E., Poulton, R., & Martin, J. (2002). Differences in early childhood risk factors for juvenile-onset and adult-onset depression. *Archives of General Psychiatry, 59*(3), 215–222.

Jahoda, M. (1958). *Current concepts of positive mental health*. New York: Basic Books.

Jenkins, A. (1993, Sept.). Invitations to responsibility. Paper given at Workshop presented by the Faculty of Social Work, Wilfrid Laurier University, Waterloo, Ontario.

Jew, C.L., & Green, K.E. (1998). Effects of risk factors on adolescents' resiliency and coping. *Psychological Reports, 82*(2), 675–678.

Johnson, H.W. (1993). Rural crime, delinquency, substance abuse, and corrections. In L.H. Ginsberg (Ed.), *Social work in rural communities*, 2nd ed. pp. 203–217. Alexandria, VA: Counsel on Social Work Education.

Kaplan, H.B. (1999). Toward an understanding of resilience: A critical review of definitions and models. In M.D. Glantz & J.L. Johnson (Eds.), *Resilience and development: Positive life adaptations* (pp. 17–84). New York: Kluwer Academic/Plenum.

Kaslow, F.W. (Ed.) (1996). *Handbook of relational diagnosis*. New York: Wiley.

Katz, R. (1984). Empowerment and synergy: Expanding the community's healing resources. In J. Rappaport, C. Swift, & R. Hess (Eds.), *Studies in empowerment: Steps toward understanding and action* (pp. 201–26). New York: Haworth Press.

Kavanagh, A.M., & Broom, D.H. (1998). Embodied risk: My body, myself? *Social Science Medicine, 46*(3), 437–444.

Kaysen, S. (1994). *Girl interrupted*. New York: Vintage.

Kelly, K.D., & Totten, M. (2002). *When children kill: A social-psychological study of youth homicide*. Peterborough, ON: Broadview Press.

Kelley, P. (1995). *Developing healthy stepfamilies: Twenty families tell their stories*. Binghamton: Harrington Park Press.

Kerman, B., Wildfire, J., & Barth, R.P. (2002). Outcomes for young adults who experienced foster care. *Children and Youth Services Review, 24*(5), 319–344.

Kieffer, C.H. (1981). *The emergence of empowerment: The development of participatory competence among individuals in citizen organizations*, vols. 1 & 2. Unpublished doctoral dissertation, University of Michigan.

King, A.J.C., Boyce, W.F., & King, M.A. (1999). *Trends in the health of Canadian youth.* Ottawa: Health Canada. www.hc-sc.gc.ca/hppb/childhood-youth/spsc.html

Kirby, L.D., & Fraser, M.W. (1997). Risk and resilience in childhood. In M. Fraser (Ed.), *Risk and resilience in childhood: An ecological perspective* (pp. 10–33). Washington, DC: NASW Press.

Kirk, J., & Miller, M.L. (1986). *Reliability and validity in qualitative research.* Newbury Park, CA: Sage.

Klevens, J., & Roca, J. (1999). Nonviolent youth in a violent society: Resilience and vulnerability in the country of Colombia. *Violence and Victims, 14*(3), 311–22.

Kramer, M. (1992). Barriers to the primary prevention of mental, neurological, and psychosocial disorders of children: A global perspective. In G.W. Albee, L.A. Bond, & T.V. Cook Monsey (Eds.), *Improving children's lives: Global perspectives on prevention* (pp. 3–36). Newbury Park, CA: Sage.

Kuchuk, S. (1993). Understanding and modifying identification in an adolescent boys' therapy group. *Journal of Child and Adolescent Group Therapy, 3*(4), 189–201.

Kuehl, B.P. (1995). The solution-oriented genogram: A collaborative approach. *Journal of Marital and Family Therapy, 21*(3), 239–50.

Kumpfer, K.L., & Hopkins, R. (1993). Prevention: Current research and trends. *Recent Advances in Addictive Disorders, 16*(1), 11–20.

Kurtz, Z., Thornes, R., & Bailey, S. (1998). Children in the criminal justice and secure care systems: How their mental health needs are met. *Journal of Adolescence, 21,* 543–553.

Kvale, S. (1996). *Interviews: An introduction to qualitative research interviewing.* Thousand Oaks, CA: Sage.

Labonte, R. (1993). *Health promotion and empowerment: Practice frameworks.* Toronto: Centre for Health Promotion and ParticipACTION.

Ladner, J.A. (1971). *Tomorrow's tomorrow: The black woman.* Garden City, NY: Anchor Books.

Laing, R.D. (1967). *The politics of experience.* New York: Pantheon Books.

Laird, J. (1994). 'Thick description' revisited: Family therapist as anthropologist-constructivist. In E. Sherman & W.J. Reid (Eds.), *Qualitative research in social work* (pp. 175–189). New York: Columbia University Press.

Latimer, J., Dowden, C., & Muise, D. (2001) *The effectiveness of restorative justice practices: A meta-analysis.* Canada: Department of Justice.

Laub, J.H., & Sampson, R.J. (1993). Turning points in the life course: Why change matters to the study of crime. *Criminology, 31*(3), 301–325.

Lempers, J.D., Clark-Lempers, D., & Simons, R.L. (1989). Economic hardship, parenting, and distress in adolescence. *Child Development, 60*(1), 25–39.

Leonard, P. (1997). *Postmodern welfare: Reconstructing an emancipatory project.* Thousand Oaks, CA: Sage.

Lerner, M. (1986). *Surplus powerlessness.* Oakland, CA: Institute for Labor and Mental Health.

Lesko, N. (2001). *Act your age: A cultural construction of adolescence.* New York: Routledge Falmer.

Lewin, K. (1947). Frontiers in group dynamics. *Human Relations, 1*(1), 5–41.

Lewin, K. (1951). Defining the 'field at a given time.' In D. Cartwright (Ed.), *Field theory in social science* (pp. 43–59). New York: Harper.

Lightfoot, C. (1992). Constructing self and peer culture: A narrative perspective on adolescent risk taking. In L.T. Winegar & J. Valsiner (Eds.), *Children's development within social context* Vol. 2, pp. 229–245. Hillsdale, NJ: Lawrence Erlbaum Associates.

Lincoln, Y.S., & Guba, E.G. (1985). *Naturalistic inquiry.* Newbury Park, CA: Sage.

Linney, J.A., & Seidman, E. (1989). The future of schooling. *American Psychologist, 44*(2), 336–340.

Loeber, R., Drinkwater, M., Yin, Y., Anderson, S.J., Schmidt, L.C., & Crawford, A. (2000). Stability of family interactions from ages 6 to 18. *Journal of Abnormal Child Psychology, 28*(4), 353–369.

Loeber, R., & Farrington, D.P. (2000). Young children who commit crime: Epidemiology, developmental origins, risk factors, early interventions, and policy implications. *Development and psychopathology, 12*(4), 737–762.

Loeber, R., Farrington, D.P, Stouthamer-Loeber, M., & Van Kammen, W.B. (1998). Multiple risk factors for multi-problem boys: Co-occurrence of delinquency, substance use, attention deficit, conduct problems, physical aggression, covert behavior, depressed mood, and shy/withdrawn behavior. In R. Jessor (Ed.), *New Perspectives in Adolescent Risk Behaviour* (pp. 90–149). New York: Cambridge University Press.

Loeber, R., Green, S.M., Lahey, B.B., Frick, P.J., & McBurnett, K. (2000). Findings on disruptive behavior disorders from the first decade of the developmental trends study. *Clinical Child and Family Psychology Review, 3*(1), 37–60.

Loeber, R., Green, S.M., Lahey, B.B., & Kalb, L. (2000). Physical fighting in childhood as a risk factor for later mental health problems. *Journal of the American Academy of Child and Adolescent Psychiatry, 39*(4), 421–428.

Loeber, R., & Hay, D.F. (1994). Developmental approaches to aggression and conduct problems. In M. Rutter & D.F. Hay (Eds.), *Development through life: A handbook for clinicians*(pp. 488–515). Oxford: Blackwell Scientific.

Lonczak, H.S., Abbott, R.D., Hawkins, J.D., Kosterman, R., & Catalano, R.F. (2002). Effects of the Seattle social development project on sexual behavior, pregnancy, birth, and sexually transmitted disease outcomes by age 21 years. *Archives of Pediatric Adolescent Medicine, 156*(May), 438–447.

Lord, J., & Farlow, D.M. (1990). A study of personal empowerment: Implications for health promotion. *Health Promotion* (Fall), 2–8.

Lowenthal, B. (1999). Effects of maltreatment and ways to promote children's resiliency. *Childhood Education* (Summer), 204–209.

Luthar, S.S., Cicchetti, D., & Becker, B. (2000). The construct of resilience: A critical evaluation and guidelines for future work. *Child Development, 71*(3), 543–562.

Luthar, S.S., & Zigler, E. (1991). Vulnerability and competence: A review of research on resilience in childhood. *American Journal of Orthopsychiatry, 61*(1), 6–22.

MacFadyen, A.J. (1992, Oct.). *Environmental risk for children: Identification and assessment of risk variables.* Paper presented at the 2nd International Conference on the Child, Montreal.

Madden-Derdich, D.A., Leonard, S.A., & Gunnel, G.A. (2002). Parents' and children's perceptions of family processes in inner-city families with delinquent youths: A qualitative investigation. *Journal of Marital and Family Therapy, 28*(3), 355–370.

Madigan, S. (1996). The politics of identity: Considering community discourse in the externalizing of internalized problem conversations. *Journal of Systemic Therapies, 15*(1), 47–61.

Madigan, S. (1997). Re-considering memory: Re-remembering lost identities back toward re-membered selves. In C. Smith & D. Nylund (Eds.), *Narratives therapies with children and adolescents* (pp. 338–355). New York: Guilford.

Madsen, W.C. (1999). *Collaborative therapy with multi-stressed families: From old problems to new futures.* New York: Guilford.

Magnus, K.B., Cowen, E.L., Wyman, P.A., Fagen, D.B., & Work, W.C. (1999). Correlates of resilient outcomes among highly stressed African-American and white urban children. *Journal of Community Psychology, 27*(4), 473–488.

Maki, A. (2000, 4 Mar.). Serving as surrogate. *Globe and Mail* (Toronto), S1 & S5.

Margolin, L. (1997). *Under the cover of kindness: The invention of social work.* London: University Press of Virginia.

Martineau, S. (1999). *Rewriting resilience: A critical discourse analysis of childhood resilience and the politics of teaching resilience to 'kids at risk.'* Unpublished doctoral dissertation, University of British Columbia, Vancouver, BC.

Massey, S., Cameron, A., Ouellette, S., & Fine, M. (1998). Qualitative approaches to the study of thriving: What can be learned? *Journal of Social Issues, 54*(2), 337–355.

Masten, A.S. (2001). Ordinary magic: Resilience processes in development. *American Psychologist, 56*(3), 227–238.

Masten, A.S., P. Morison, D. Pellegrini, & A.Tellegen. (1990). Competence under stress: Risk and protective factors. In J.E. Rolf & A.S. Masten (Eds.), *Risk and protective factors in the development of psychopathology* (pp. 236–256). New York: Cambridge University Press.

Mastronardi, L. (1990). The Inuit community workers' experience of youth protection work. In L. Davies & E. Shragge (Eds.), *Bureaucracy and community: Essays on the politics of social work practice* (pp. 103–135). Montreal: Black Rose.

Matsueda, R.L., & Heimer, K. (1997). A symbolic interactionist theory of role-transitions, role-commitments, and delinquency. In T.P. Thornberry (Ed.), *Developmental theories of crime and delinquency* (pp. 163–213). New Brunswick: Transaction Publishers.

Matza, D. (1964). *Delinquency and drift.* New York: Wiley.

McAdams, D.P. (1993). *The stories we live by.* New York: William Morrow.

McCourt, F. (1996). *Angela's ashes.* New York: Simon & Schuster.

McCown, W.G., & Johnson, J. (1993). *Therapy with treatment resistant families.* Binghamton, NY: Haworth.

McCubbin, H.I., Fleming, W.M., Thompson, A.I., Neitman, P., Elver, K.M., & Savas, S.A. (1998). Resiliency and coping in 'at risk' African-American youth and their families. In H.I. McCubbin, E.A. Thompson, A.I. Thompson, & J.A. Futrell (Eds.), *Resiliency in African-American families* (pp. 287–328). Thousand Oaks, CA: Sage.

McCubbin, H.I., Thompson, E.A., Thompson, A.I., & Futrell, J.A. (1998). *Resiliency in African-American families.* Thousand Oaks, CA: Sage.

McKnight, J.L. (1991, Oct.). Beyond community services. Paper presented at Wilfrid Laurier University, Waterloo, Ontario.

McKnight, J. (1995). *The careless society.* New York: Basic Books.

McNamee, S., & Gergen, K.J. (Eds.). (1992). *Therapy as social construction.* Thousand Oaks, CA: Sage.

Mead, G.H. (1934). *Mind, self, and society.* Chicago: University of Chicago Press.

Mercy, J., & Hammond, R. (2001). Learning to do violence prevention well. *American Journal of Preventative Medicine, 20*(1S), 1–2.

Michell, L., & West P. (1996). Peer pressure to smoke: The meaning depends on the method. *Health Education Research, 11*(1), 39–49.

Micucci, J.A. (1998). The process of therapy: Principles and pitfalls. In J.A. Micucci (ed.), *The adolescent in family therapy: Breaking the cycle of conflict and control* (pp. 16–53). New York: Guilford.

Miech, R.A., Caspi, A., Moffitt, T.E., Wright, B.R.E., & Silva, P.A. (1999). Low socioeconomic status and mental disorders: A longitudinal study of selection and causation during young adulthood. *American Journal of Sociology, 104*(4), 1096–1131.

Miles, S. (2000). *Youth lifestyles in a changing world.* Buckingham: Open University Press.

Miller, A. (1991). *Banished knowledge* (L. Vennewitz, Trans.). New York: Anchor Books.

Miller, D. (1999). Racial socialization and racial identity: Can they promote resiliency for African American adolescents? *Adolescence, 34*(135), 493–501.

Miller, J.B. (1991). The development of women's sense of self. In J.V. Jordan, A.G. Kaplan, J.B. Miller, I.P. Stiver, & J.L. Surrey (Eds.), *Women's growth in connection* (pp. 11–26). New York: Guilford.

Mitchell, K.J., & Finkelhor, D. (2001). Risk of crime victimization among youth exposed to domestic violence. *Journal of Interpersonal Violence, 16*(9), 944–64.

Moffitt, T.E. (1993). Adolescence-limited and life-course-persistent antisocial behavior: A developmental taxonomy. *Psychological Review, 100*(4), 674–701.

Moffitt, T. E. (1997). Adolescents-limited and life-course-persistent offending: A complementary pair of developmental theories. In T.P. Thornberry (Ed.), Developmental Theories of Crime and Delinquency (pp. 11–54). New Brunswick, NJ: Transaction Publishers.

Moffitt, T.E., Caspi, A., Rutter, M., & Silva, P.A. (2001). *Sex differences in antisocial behaviour.* Cambridge: Cambridge University Press.

Monk, G., Winslade, J., Crocket, K., & Epston, D. (Eds.). (1997). *Narrative therapy in practice: The archeology of hope.* San Francisco: Jossey-Bass.

Monti, D.J. (1994). *Wannabe gangs in suburbs and schools.* Oxford: Blackwell.

Morgan, D.L. (1998). Practical strategies for combining qualitative and quantitative methods: Applications to health research. *Qualitative Health Research* [On-line], *8*(3), 362–376. Available: http://proquest.umi.com/

Mrazek, P.J., & Mrazek, D.A. (1987). Resilience in child maltreatment victims: A conceptual exploration. *Child Abuse and Neglect, 11*(3), 357–66.

Mullaly, B. (1997). *Structural social work: Ideology, theory, and practice,* 2nd ed. Toronto: Oxford University Press.

Murphy, L.B., & Moriarty, A.E. (1976). *Vulnerability, coping, and growth from infancy to adolescence.* New Haven: Yale University Press.

Myers, J.K., & Bean, L.L. (1968). *A decade later: A follow-up of social class and mental illness.* New York: Wiley.

Nadler, A. (2002). Inter-group helping relations as power relations: Maintaining or challenging social dominance between groups through helping. *Journal of Social Issues, 58*(3), 487–502.

Naess, A. (1989). *Ecology, community and lifestyle: Outline of an ecosophy* (D. Rothenberg, Trans.). Cambridge: Cambridge University Press.

Nagin, D., & Tremblay, R.E. (1999). Trajectories of boys' physical aggression, opposition, and hyperactivity on the path to physically violent and nonviolent juvenile delinquency. *Child Development, 70*(5), 1181–1196.

Neill, A.S. (1960). *Summerhill: A radical approach to child rearing.* New York: Hart.

Nettles, S.M., & Pleck, J.H. (1994). Risk, resilience and development: The multiple ecologies of black adolescents in the United States. In R.J. Haggerty, L.O. Sherrod, N. Garmezy, & M. Rutter (Eds.), *Stress, risk, and resilience in children and adolescents: Processes, mechanisms and interventions* (pp. 147–81). New York: Cambridge University Press.

Newcomb, M.D., Abbott, R.D., Catalano, R.F., Hawkins, J.D., Battin-Pearson, S., & Hill, K. (2002). Mediational and deviance theories of late high school failure: Process role of structural strains, academic competence, and general versus specific problem behaviors. *Journal of Counseling Psychology, 49*(2), 172–186.

Newman, D.L., Caspi, A., Moffitt, T.E., & Silva, P.A. (1997). Antecedents of adult interpersonal functioning: Effects of individual differences in age 3 temperament. *Developmental Psychology, 33*(2), 206–217.

Newman, F., & Holzman, L. (1997). *The End of Knowing: A New Developmental Way of Learning.* London: Routledge.

Newman, P.R., & Newman, B.M. (1976). Early adolescence and its conflict: Group identity versus alienation. *Adolescence, 11*(42), 261–274.

Nietzsche, F. (1968). *Twilight of the idols and the anti-Christ* (R.J. Hollingdale, Trans.). Harmondsworth: Penguin. (Original work published 1889.)

Noller, P. (2002). Twenty-five years of relationship research: A methodological journey. Paper presented at the 11th International Conference on Personal Relationships, International Society for the Study of Personal Relationships, Dalhousie University, Halifax.

Novac, S., Serge, L., Eberle, M., & Brown, J. (2002, Mar.). *On her own: Young women and homelessness* (pp. vii–ix). Ottawa: Status of Women Canada.

Nowicki, S. Jr., & Strickland, B.R. (1973). A locus of control scale for children. *Journal of Consulting and Clinical Psychology, 40*(1), 148–54.

Nylund, D., & Ceske, K. (1997). Voices of political resistance: Young women's co-research on anti-depression. In C. Smith & D. Nylund (Eds.), *Narrative therapies with children and adolescents* (pp. 356–381). New York: Guilford.

Nylund, D., & Corsiglia, V. (1996). From deficits to special abilities: Working narratively with children labeled 'ADHD.' In M.F. Hoyt (Ed.), *Constructive therapies: Vol. 2* (pp. 163–83). New York: Guilford.

Offer, D., & Sabshin, M. (1974). *Normality: Theoretical and clinical concepts of mental health* (Rev. ed.). New York: Basic Books.

Offer, D., & Sabshin, M. (Eds.). (1991). *The diversity of normal behavior.* New York: Basic Books.

Ogbu, J.U. (1981). Origins of human competence: A cultural-ecological perspective. *Child Development, 52*(2), 413–429.

Oglesby-Pitts, M.A. (2000). *Stories on resilience from childhood voices of adult African American males.* Unpublished doctoral dissertation, Peabody College of Vanderbilt University, Nashville.

Okamoto, S.K. (1999). Interagency collaboration with high-risk gang youth. *Child and Adolescent Social Work Journal, 18*(1), 5–19.

O'Leary, V.E. (1998). Strength in the face of adversity: Individual and social thriving. *Journal of Social Issues, 54*(2), 425–446.

O'Reilly, P., & Fleming T. (2001). Squeegee wars: The state versus street youth. In T. Fleming, P. O'Reilly, & B. Clark (Eds.), *Youth injustice: Canadian perspectives,* 2nd ed., pp. 185–204. Toronto: Canadian Scholars' Press.

Osherson, S. (1992). *Wrestling with love: How men struggle with intimacy with women, children, parents and each other.* New York: Fawcett Columbine.

O'sullivan, L.F., & Hearn, K. (2002). Beginner's lust: Adolescent girls venture into romance. Paper presented at the 11th International Conference on Personal Relationships, International Society for the Study of Personal Relationships, Dalhousie University, Halifax.

Padgett, D.K. (1998). *Qualitative methods in social work research: Challenges and rewards.* Thousand Oaks, CA: Sage.

Patton, M.Q. (1990). *Qualitative evaluation and research methods.* (2nd ed.). Newbury Park, CA: Sage.

Pavis, S., Cunningham-Burley, S., & Amos, A. (1998). Health related behavioural change in context: Young people in transition. *Social Science Medicine, 47*(10), 1407–1418.

Pearl, R., Bryan, T., & Herzog. A. (1990). Resisting or acquiescing to peer pressure to engage in misconduct: Adolescents' expectations of probable consequences. *Journal of Youth and Adolescence, 19*(1), 43–55.

Pease, B. (2002). Rethinking empowerment: A postmodern reappraisal for emancipatory practice. *British Journal of Social Work, 32*(2), 135–147.

Pease, B., & Fook, J. (1999). Postmodern critical theory and emancipatory social work practice. In B. Pease & J. Fook (Eds.), *Transforming social work practice: Postmodern critical perspectives* (pp. 1–22). New York: Routledge.

Penner, L.A. (2002). Dispositional and organizational influences on sustained volunteerism: An interactionist perspective. *Journal of Social Issues, 58*(3), 447–468.

Peterson, C., Maier, S.F., & Seligman, M.E.P. (1993). *Learned helplessness: A theory for the age of personal control.* New York: Oxford University Press.

Peterson, C., & Stunkard A.J. (1992). Cognates of personal control: Locus of control, self-efficacy, and explanatory style. *Applied and Preventive Psychology, 1*(2), 111–117.

Pettit, G.S., Laird, R.D., Dodge, K.A., Bates, J.E., & Criss, M.M. (2001). Antecedents and behavior-problem outcomes of parental monitoring and psychological control in early adolescence. *Child Development, 72*(2), 583–598.

Pilling, D. (1990). *Escape from disadvantage.* New York: Falmer Press.

Pipher, M. (1994). *Reviving Ophelia: Saving the selves of adolescent girls.* New York: Ballantine.

Pollard, J.A., Hawkins, J.D., & Arthur, M.W. (1999). Risk and protection: Are both necessary to understand diverse behavioral outcomes in adolescence? *Social Work Research, 23*(3), 145–158.

Pombeni, M.L., Kirchler, E., & Palmonari, A. (1990). Identification with peers as a strategy to muddle through the troubles of the adolescent years. *Journal of Adolescence, 13*(4), 351–369.

Prilleltensky, I., & Nelson, G. (2000). Promoting child and family wellness: Priorities for psychological and social interventions. *Journal of Community & Applied Social Psychology, 10*(2), 85–105.

Quinton, D., Rutter, M., & Gulliver, L. (1990). Continuities in psychiatric disorders from childhood to adulthood in the children of psychiatric patients. In L.N. Robins & M. Rutter (Eds.), *Straight and devious pathways from childhood to adulthood* (pp. 259–278). New York: Cambridge University Press.

Rak, C.F., & Patterson, L.E. (1996). Promoting resilience in at-risk children. *Journal of Counseling and Development, 46*(4), 368–373.

Ramon, S. (Ed.). (1991). *Beyond community care: Normalisation and integration work.* London: Macmillan.

Ramon, S., & Tallis, D. (1997). Seamless services and re-building identity. *Breakthrough, 1*(4), 35–44.

Rankin, C., & Aguayo, A. (2002). Perceptions of risky sexual behaviour: Personal and social benefits and costs of one-night stands. Paper presented at the 11th International Conference on Personal Relationships, International Society for the Study of Personal Relationships, Dalhousie University, Halifax.

Recklitis, C.J., & Noam, G.G. (1999). Clinical and developmental perspectives on adolescent coping. *Child Psychiatry and Human Development, 30*(2), 87–101.

Reich, J.W., & Zautra, A.J. (1988). Direct and stress-moderating effects of positive life experiences. In L.H. Cohen (Ed.), *Life events and psychological functioning: Theoretical and methodological issues* (pp. 149–80). Newbury Park, CA: Sage.

Reynolds, B.C. (1934). *Between client and community: A study of responsibility in social case work.* New York: Oriole.

Rich, J. (1998). *The nurture assumption.* New York: Simon & Schuster.

Richman, J.M., & Fraser, M.W. (2001). *The context of youth violence: Resilience, risk, and protection.* Westport, CT: Praeger.

Richters, J., & Weintraub, S. (1990). Beyond diathesis: Toward an understanding of high-risk environments. In J. Rolf, A.S. Masten, D. Cicchetti, K.H. Nuechterlein, & S. Weintraub (Eds.), *Risk and protective factors in the development of psychopathology* (pp. 67–96). Cambridge, MA: Cambridge University Press.

Rigsby, L.C. (1994). The Americanization of resilience: Deconstructing research practice. In M.C. Wang & E.W. Gordon (Eds.), *Educational Resilience in Inner-City America: Challenges and Prospects* (pp. 85–94). Hillsdale, NJ: Lawrence Earlbaum Associates.

Ristock, J.L., & Pennell, J. (1996). *Community research as empowerment: Feminist links, postmodern interruptions.* Toronto: Oxford University Press.

Roberts, B.W., Caspi, A., & Moffitt, T.E. (2001). The kids are alright: Growth and stability in personality development from adolescence to adulthood. *Journal of Personality and Social Psychology, 81*(4), 670–683.

Robertson, B.J. (1999). Leisure and family: Perspectives of male adolescents who engage in delinquent activity as leisure. *Journal of Leisure Research, 31*(4), 335–358.

Robinson, R.A. (1994). Private pain and public behaviors: Sexual abuse and delinquent girls. In C.K. Riessman (Ed.), *Qualitative studies in social work research* (pp. 73–94). Thousand Oaks, CA: Sage.

Rodwell, M.K. (1998). *Social work constructivist research.* New York: Garland.

Rosen, H., & Kuehlwein, K.T. (Eds.). (1996). *Constructing realities: Meaning-making perspectives for psychotherapists.* San Francisco: Jossey-Bass.

Rotter, J.B. (1966). Generalized expectancies for internal versus external control of reinforcement. *Psychological Monographs, 80*(1), 1–28.

Rounds, K.A. (1997). Preventing sexually transmitted infections among adolescents. In M. Fraser (Ed.), *Risk and resilience in childhood: An ecological perspective* (pp. 171–194). Washington, DC: NASW Press.

Ruth, J., & Kenyon, G. (1996). Biography in adult development and aging. In
J.E. Birren, G.M. Kenyon, J.Ruth, J.J.F. Schroots, & T. Svensson (Eds.), *Aging
and biography: Explorations in adult development* (pp. 1–20). New York:
Springer.

Rutter, M. (1983). Stress, coping, and development: Some issues and some
questions. In N. Garmezy & M. Rutter (Eds.), *Stress, coping, and development
in children* (pp. 1–42). New York: McGraw-Hill.

Rutter, M. (1985). Family and school influences on behaviourial development.
Child Psychology and Psychiatry, 26(3), 349–368.

Rutter, M. (1987). Psychosocial resilience and protective mechanisms.
American Journal of Orthopsychiatry, 57(3), 316–331.

Rutter, M. (2001). Psychosocial adversity: Risk, resilience and recovery. In
J.M. Richman & M.W. Fraser (Eds.), *The context of youth violence: Resilience,
risk, and protection* (pp. 13–41). Westport, CT: Praeger.

Rutter, M., Giller, H., & Hagell, A. (1998). *Antisocial Behavior by Young People.*
New York: Cambridge University Press.

Rutter, M., Quinton, D., & Hill, J. (1990). Adult outcome of institution-reared
children: Males and females compared. In L.N. Robins & M. Rutter (Eds.),
Straight and devious pathways from childhood to adulthood (pp. 135–57).
Cambridge, MA: Cambridge University Press.

Rutter, M., Maughan, B., Mortimore, P., & Ouston, J. (1979). *Fifteen thousand
hours: Secondary schools and their effects on children.* Cambridge, MA:
Harvard University Press.

Ryan, W. (1976). *Blaming the victim* (Rev. ed.). New York: Vintage Books.
Original work published 1971.)

Ryglewicz, H., & Pepper, B. (1996). *Lives at risk: Understanding and treating
young people with dual disorders.* New York: Free Press.

Saari, C. (1996). Relationship factors in the creation of Identity: A psychody-
namic perspective. In H. Rosen & K.T. Kuehlwein (Eds.), *Constructing
realities: Meaning-making perspectives for psychotherapists* (pp. 141–66). San
Francisco: Jossey-Bass.

Sampson, R.J., & Laub, J.H. (1997). A life-course theory of cumulative
disadvantage and stability of delinquency. In T.P. Thornberry (Ed.),
Developmental theories of crime and delinquency (pp. 133–61). New Brunswick,
NJ: Transaction Publishers.

Sands, R.G., & Nuccio, K. (1992). Postmodern feminist theory and social
work. *Social Work, 37*(6), 489–494.

Santor, D.A., Messervey, D., & Kusumakar, V. (2000). Measuring peer
pressure, popularity, and conformity in adolescent boys and girls: Predicting school performance, sexual attitudes, and substance abuse. *Journal of
Youth and Adolescence, 29*(2), 163–182.

Schatzman, L., & Strauss, A.L. (1973). *Field research.* Englewood Cliffs, NJ: Prentice-Hall.

Scheman, N. (1980): Anger and the politics of naming. In S. McConnell-Ginet, S. Barker, & R.N. Furmon (Eds.), *Women and language in literature and society* (pp. 174–187). New York: Praeger.

Scheman, N. (1983). Individualism and the objects of psychology. In S. Harding & M.B. Hintikka (Eds.), *Discovering reality* (pp. 225–244). New York: Reidel.

Schissel, B., & Fedec, K. (2001). The selling of innocence: The gestalt of danger in the lives of youth prostitutes. In R.C. Smandych (Ed.), *Youth crime: Varieties, theories, and prevention* (pp. 182–99). Toronto: Harcourt. (Reprinted from *Canadian Journal of Criminology,* Jan. 1999, pp. 33–56.)

Schmid, J. (2000). Family group conferencing: Giving families a voice in child protection. *Canada's Children, 7*(3), 18–20.

Scott, Dorothy. (1989). Meaning construction and social work practice. *Social Service Review,* (Mar.), 39–51.

Seale, C. (1999). *The quality of qualitative research.* London: Sage.

Sedgwick, P. (1982). *Psycho politics.* London: Pluto Press.

Seidel, J.V., Kjolseth, R., & Seymour, E. (1988). *The ethnograph* (Version 3.0). Corvallis, OR: Qualis Research Associates.

Seifer, R., & Sameroff, A.J. (1987). Multiple determinants of risk and invulnerability. In J. Anthony & B. Cohler (Eds.), *The invulnerable child* (pp. 51–69). New York: Guilford.

Selman, R.L., & Schultz, L.H. (1989). Children's strategies for interpersonal negotiation with peers. In T.J. Berndt & G.W. Ladd (Eds.), *Peer relationships in child development* (pp. 371–406). New York: Wiley.

Sharma, N., & Sharma, B. (1999). Children in difficult circumstances: Familial correlates of advantage while at risk. In T.S. Saraswathi (Ed.), *Culture, socialization and human development: Theory, research and applications in India* (pp. 398–418). Thousand Oaks, CA: Sage.

Sheehan, M. (1997). Adolescent violence: Strategies, outcomes and dilemmas in working with young people and their families. *Australia and New Zealand Journal of Family Therapy, 18*(2), 80–91.

Shelton, K. (Ed.). (1990). *Empowering business resources.* Glenview, IL: Scott, Foresman.

Sieppert, J.D., Hudson, J., & Unrau, Y. (2000). Family group conferencing in child welfare: Lessons from a demonstration project. *Families in Society: The Journal of Contemporary Human Services, 81*(4), 382–391.

Silberberg, S. (2001). Searching for family resilience. *Family Matters,* (22 Sept.).

Silbereisen, R.K., & von Eye, A. (1999). *Growing Up in Times of Social Change.* New York: Walter de Gruyter.

Silbereisen, R.K., & Walper, S. (1988). A person-process-context approach. In M. Rutter (Ed.), *Studies of psychosocial risk: The power of longitudinal data* (pp. 96–113). New York: Cambridge University Press.

Silva-Wayne, S. (1995). Contributions to resilience in children and youth: What successful child welfare graduates say. In J. Hudson & B. Galaway (Eds.), *Child welfare in Canada: Research and policy implications* (pp. 308–323). Toronto: Thompson.

Silverman, D. (2000). *Doing qualitative research: A practical handbook*. Thousand Oaks, CA: Sage.

Simmons, C.H., & Parsons, R.J. (1983). Developing internality and perceived competence: The empowerment of adolescent girls. *Adolescence, 18(72)*, 917–922.

Simmons, R. (2002). *Odd girl out: The hidden culture of aggression in girls*. New York: Harcourt.

Simon, T.R., Dent, C.W., & Sussman, S. (1997). Vulnerability to victimization, concurrent problem behaviors, and peer influence as predictors of in-school weapon carrying among high school students. *Violence and Victims, 12(3)*, 277–289.

Smaje, C. (1996). The ethnic patterning of health: New directions for theory and research. *Sociology of Health and Illness, 18(2)*, 139–171.

Smale, G.G. (1995). Integrating community and individual practice: A new paradigm for practice. In P. Adams & K. Nelson (Eds.), *Reinventing human services: Community- and family-centered practice* (pp. 59–80). New York: Aldine de Gruyter.

Smale, G.G., Tuson, G., Cooper, M., Wardle, M., & Crosbie, D. (1988). *Community social work: A paradigm for change*. London: National Institute for Social Work.

Smith, C. (1997). Introduction: Comparing traditional therapies with narrative approaches. In C. Smith & D. Nylund (Eds.), *Narrative therapies with children and adolescents* (pp. 1–52). New York: Guilford.

Smith, C., & Nylund, D. (1997). *Narrative therapies with children and adolescents*. New York: Guilford.

Sommers, C.H. (2000). *The war against the boys: How misguided feminism is harming our young men*. New York: Simon & Schuster.

Sparks, J.A. (2002). Taking a stand: An adolescent girl's resistance to medication. *Journal of Marital & Family Therapy, 28(1)*, 27–38.

Spira, MK., Grossman, S.F., & Wolff-Bensdorf, J. (2002). Voice and identity in a bicultural/bilingual environment. *Child and Adolescent Social Work Journal, 19(2)*, 115–138.

Stanton-Salazar, R.D., & Spina, S.U. (2000). The network orientations of highly resilient urban minority youth: A network-analytic account of minority socialization and its educational implications. *Urban Review, 32*(3), 227–261.

Statistics Canada. (1999, 21 Dec.). Youth Violent Crime. *The Daily* [On-line] Available http://www.statcan.ca. Directory: Daily/English/991221 File: d991221c.htm

Statistics Canada. (2002, Apr.). *Social Trends*. Available http:// www.statcan.ca

Stebbins, R.A. (1996). *Tolerable differences: Living with deviance* (2nd ed.). Toronto: McGraw-Hill Ryerson.

Steiner, A. (2001, Feb.). Out early. *Utne Reader*, pp. 16–17.

Steinhauer, P.D. (1996). Methods for developing resiliency for disadvantaged populations. In *Developing Resiliency for Disadvantaged Populations* [On-line] Available HTTP: www.sparrowlake.org Directory: docs File: resil.htm

Stern, S.B., & Smith, C.A. (1999). Reciprocal relationships between antisocial behavior and parenting: Implications for delinquency intervention. *Families in Society: The Journal of Contemporary Human Services, 72*(2), 169–181.

Stoppard, J.M. (2000). *Understanding depression: Feminist social constructionist approaches*. London: Routledge.

Stormshak, E.A., & Webster-Stratton, C. (1999). The qualitative interactions of children with conduct problems and their peers: Differential correlates with self-report measures, home behavior, and school behavior problems. *Journal of Applied Developmental Psychology, 20*(2), 295–317.

Stouthamer-Loeber, M., Loeber, R., Wei, E., Farrington, D.P., & Wikstrom, P.H. (2002). Risk and promotive effects in the explanation of persistent serious delinquency in boys. *Journal of Consulting and Clinical Psychology, 70*(1), 111–123.

Strauss, A., & Corbin, J. (1990). *Basics of qualitative research: Grounded theory procedures and techniques*. Newbury Park, CA: Sage.

Strickland, C.J. (1999). The importance of qualitative research in addressing cultural relevance: Experiences from research with pacific northwest Indian women. *Health Care for Women International, 20*(5), 517–525.

Surrey, J.L. (1991a). Relationship and empowerment. In J.V. Jordan, A.G. Kaplan, J.B. Miller, I.P. Stiver, & J.L. Surrey (Eds.), *Women's growth in connection* (pp. 162–180). New York: Guilford.

Surrey, J.L. (1991b). The 'self-in relation': A theory of women's development. In J.V. Jordan, A.G. Kaplan, J.B. Miller, I.P. Stiver, & J.L. Surrey (Eds.), *Women's growth in connection* (pp. 51–66). New York: Guilford.

Swadener, B.B. (1995). Children and families 'at promise': Deconstructing the discourse of risk. In B.B. Swadener, & S. Loveck, (ed.) *Children and families 'at promise'* (pp. 17–49). Albany: State of New York Press.

Tarter, R.E., & Vanyukov, M. (1999). Re-visiting the validity of the construct of resilience. In M.D. Glantz & J.L. Johnson (Eds.), *Resilience and development: Positive life adaptations* (pp. 85–100). New York: Kluwer Academic / Plenum.

Taylor, J.M., Gilligan, C., & Sullivan, A.M. (1995). *Between voice and silence: Women and girls, race and relationship*. Cambridge, MA: Harvard University Press.

Teram, E. (1999). A case against making the control of clients a negotiable contingency for interdisciplinary teams. *Human Relations, 52*(2), 263–278.

Thoits, P.A. (1995). Identity-relevant events and psychological symptoms: A cautionary tale. *Journal of health and social behavior, 36*(1), 72–82.

Thornberry, T.P. (1998). Membership in youth gangs and involvement in serious and violent offending. In R. Loeber & D.P. Farrington (Eds.), *Serious and Violent Juvenile Offenders: Risk Factors and Successful Interventions* (pp. 147–166). Thousand Oaks, CA: Sage.

Tidwell, R., & Garrett, S.C. (1994). Youth at risk: In search of a definition. *Journal of Counseling and Development, 72*(2), 444–446.

Tolan, P.H., & Gorman-Smith, D. (1998). Development of serious and violent offending careers. In R. Loeber & D.P. Farrington (Eds.), *Serious and violent juvenile offenders: Risk factors and successful interventions* (pp. 68–85). Thousand Oaks, CA: Sage.

Tomm, K. (1992, Sept.). Client empowerment through interventive interviewing. *Family therapy training program*. Workshop conducted by the Whitby Psychiatric Hospital, Whitby, Ontario.

Totten, M. (2000). *Guys, gangs and girlfriend abuse*. Peterborough, ON: Broadview.

Trieschman, A.E., Brendtro, L.K., & Whittaker, J.K. (1969). *The other 23 hours*. Chicago: Aldine.

Turner, S.G. (2001). Resilience and social work practice: Three case studies. *Families in Society: The Journal of Contemporary Human Services, 82*(5), 441–448.

Tyler, F.B., Tyler, S.L., Tommasello, A., & Connolly, M.R. (1992). Huckleberry Finn and street youth everywhere: An approach to primary prevention. In G.W. Albee, L.A. Bond, & T.V. Cook Monsey (Eds.), *Improving children's lives: Global perspectives on prevention* (pp. 200–212). Newbury Park, CA: Sage.

Tyyskä, V. (2001). *Long and Winding Road: Adolescents and Youth in Canada Today*. Toronto: Canadian Scholars' Press.

Ungar, M. (1995). *A naturalistic study of the relationship between the process of empowerment and mental health during adolescence.* Unpublished doctoral dissertation, Wilfrid Laurier University, Waterloo, Ontario.

Ungar, M. (2000). The myth of peer pressure: Adolescents and their search for health-enhancing identities. *Adolescence, 35*(137), 167–180.

Ungar, M. (2001a). Constructing narratives of resilience with high-risk youth. *Journal of Systemic Therapies, 20*(2), 58–73.

Ungar, M. (2001b). The social construction of resilience among problem youth in out-of-home placement: A study of health-enhancing deviance. *Child and Youth Care Forum, 30*(3), 137–154.

Ungar, M. (2002). *Playing at being Bad: The resilience of troubled teens.* Lawrencetown, NS: Pottersfield Press.

Ungar, M., Manuel, S., Mealey, S., & Thomas, G. (2000, May). *A study of community guides: Lessons for professionals for a community building practice.* Paper presented at Symposium 2000, Perspectives in Child Protection: Developments in Knowledge, Determinants of Optimal Health, Dilemmas in Practice, St John's.

Ungar, M., & Teram, E. (2000). Drifting towards mental health: High-risk adolescents and the process of empowerment. *Youth and Society 32*(2), 228–252.

Ungar, M., Teram, E. & Picketts, J. (2001). Young offenders and their communities: Reframing the institution as an extension of the community. *Canadian Journal of Community Mental Health, 20*(2), 29–42.

Updegraff, K.A., Madden-Derdich, D.A., Estrada, A.U., Sales, L.J., & Leonard, S. (2002). Young adolescents' experiences with parents and friends: Exploring the connection. *Family Relations, 51*(1), 72–80.

Van Den Berg, J., & Grealish, M. (1996). Individualized services and supports through the Wraparound process: Philosophy and procedures. *Journal of Child and Family Studies, 5*(1), 7–21.

Van Den Bergh, N. (Ed.). (1995). *Feminist practice in the 21st century.* Washington, DC: NASW Press.

Van Hoorn, J.L., Komlósi, A., Suchar, E., & Samelson, D.A. (2000). *Adolescent development and rapid social change: Perspectives from Eastern Europe.* New York: State University of New York Press.

Vanier Institute of the Family (2000). *Profiling Canada's families II.* Ottawa: Author.

Velleman, R., & Orford, J. (1999). How has our understanding advanced? Summary and integration. In R. Velleman & J. Orford (Eds.), *Risk and Resilience: Adults who were the children of problem drinkers* (pp. 215–52). Amsterdam: Harwood.

Veit, C.T., & Ware, J.E. Jr. (1983). The structure of psychological distress and well-being in general populations. *Journal of Consulting and Clinical Psychology, 51*(5), 730–742.

Wallerstein, N. (1992). Powerlessness, empowerment, and health: Implications for health promotion programs. *American Journal of Health Promotion*, 6(3), 197–205.

Walsh, F. (1998). *Strengthening family resilience.* New York: Guilford.

Walsh, F. (Ed.). (1982). *Normal family processes.* New York: Guilford.

Wang, M.C., Hartel, G.D., & Walberg, H.J. (1994). Educational resilience in inner cities. In M.C. Wang, & E.W. Gordon (Eds.), *Educational resilience in inner-city America: Challenges and prospects* (pp. 45–72). Hillsdale, NJ: Lawrence Earlbaum Associates.

Watzlawick, P., Weakland, J.H., & Fisch, R. (1974). *Change: Principles of problem formation and problem resolution.* New York: W.W. Norton.

Webster-Stratton, C. (1998). Preventing conduct problems in Head Start children: Strengthening parenting competencies. *Journal of Consulting and Clinical Psychology, 66*(5), 715–730.

Webster-Stratton, C. (2001). Preventing conduct problems, promoting social competence: A parent and teacher training partnership in Head Start. *Journal of Clinical Child Psychology, 30*(3), 283–302.

Webster-Stratton, C. & Hammond, M. (1998). Conduct problems and the level of social competence in Head Start children: Prevalence, pervasiveness, and associated risk factors. *Clinical Child and Family Psychology Review, 1*(2), 101–124.

Webster-Stratton, C., & Hammond, M. (1999). Marital conflict management skills, parenting style, and early-onset conduct problems: Process and pathways. *Journal of Child Psychology and Psychiatry, 40*(6), 917–927.

Webster-Stratton, C., Reid, M.J., & Hammond, M. (2001). Preventing conduct problems, promoting social competence: A parent and teacher training partnership in head start. *Journal of Clinical Child Psychology, 30*(3), 283–302.

Weedon, C. (1997). *Feminist practice and poststructuralist theory* (2nd ed.). Cambridge, MA: Blackwell.

Weihenmayer, E. (2001). *Touch the top of the world: A blind man's journey to climb farther than the eye can see.* New York: Dutton.

Weingarten, K. (1998). Sidelined no more: Promoting mothers of adolescents as a resource for their growth and development. In C.G. Coll, J.L. Surrey, & K. Weingarten (Eds), *Mothering against the odds: Diverse voices of contemporary mothers* (pp. 15–36). NewYork: Guilford.

Weis, L., & Fine, M. (Eds.). (1993). *Beyond silenced voices: Class, race, and gender in United States schools.* New York: State University of New York Press.

Wente, M. (2000, 28 Oct.). Eminem and Britney: Who scares you more? *Globe and Mail* (Toronto), A17.

Werner, E.E., & Smith, R.S. (1982). *Vulnerable but invincible: A longitudinal study of resilient children and youth.* New York: McGraw–Hill.

Werner, E.E., & Smith, R.S. (1992). *Overcoming the odds: High risk children from birth to adulthood.* Ithaca, NY: Cornell University Press.

Wheatley, M. (2000, Dec.). A new connected generation. *Utne Reader,* 80–81.

White, M. (1988). The externalizing of the problem and the re-authoring of lives and relationships. *Dulwich Centre Newsletter* (Summer), 5–28.

White, M. (1995). *Re-authoring lives: Interviews and essays.* Adelaide, South Australia: Dulwich Centre.

White, M. (1997). *Narratives of therapists' lives.* Adelaide, South Australia: Dulwich Centre.

White, M., & Epston, D. (1990). *Narrative means to therapeutic ends.* New York: W.W. Norton.

White, R.W. (1959). Motivation reconsidered: The concept of competence. *Psychological Review, 66*(5), 297–333.

Whyte, W.F. (1955). *Street corner society.* Chicago: University of Chicago Press.

Williamson, H. (1997). Status zero youth and the 'underclass': Some considerations. In R. Macdonald (Ed.), *Youth, the 'underclass' and social exclusion* (pp. 70–82). New York: Routledge.

Williamson, I.R. (2000). Internalized homophobia and health issues affecting lesbians and gay men. *Health Education, 15*(1), 97–107.

Windle, M. (1999). Critical conceptual and measurement issues in the study of resilience. In M.D. Glantz & J.L. Johnson (Eds.), *Resilience and development: Positive life adaptations* (pp. 161–178). New York: Kluwer Academic/Plenum.

Wolf, E.S. (1988). *Treating the self: Elements of clinical self psychology.* New York: Guilford.

Wolin, S., & Wolin, S. (1995). Resilience among youth growing up in substance abusing families. *Substance Abuse, 42*(2), 415–429.

Wolkow, K.E., & Ferguson, H.B. (2001). Community factors in the development of resiliency: Considerations and future directions. *Community Mental Health Journal, 37*(6), 489–498.

Yellin, E.M., Quinn, M.M., & Hoffman, C.C. (1998). Heavy mettle: Stories of transition for delinquent youth. *Reaching Today's Youth* (Summer), 4–8.

Ziervogel, C.F., Ahmed, N., Fisher, A.J., & Robertson, B.A. (1997). Alcohol misuse in South African male adolescents: A qualitative investigation. *International Quarterly of Community Health Education, 17*(1), 25–41.

Ziff, M.A., Conrad, P., & Lachman, M.E. (1995). The relative effects of perceived personal control and responsibility on health and health-related behaviors in young and middle-aged adults. *Health Education Quarterly, 22*(1), 127–42.

Zimmerman, M.A. (1990). Toward a theory of learned hopefulness: A structural model analysis of participation and empowerment. *Journal of Research in Personality, 24*(1), 71–86.

Zimmerman, M.A., Ramirez-Valles, J., & Maton, K.I. (1999). Resilience among urban African American male adolescents: A study of the protective effects of sociopolitical control on their mental health. [On-line] *American Journal of Community Psychology, 27*(6), 733–751. Available at http://proquest.umi.com

Zimmerman, M.A., & Rappaport, J. (1988). Citizen participation, perceived control, and psychological empowerment. *American Journal of Community Psychology, 16*(5), 725–750.

Zimmerman, M.A., & Zahniser, J.H. (1991). Refinements of sphere-specific measures of perceived control: Development of a sociopolitical control scale. *Journal of Community Psychology, 19*(2), 189–204.

Index

178, 191; and control, 177, 179–83, 186, 232–3; foster care, 172–4, 186; and identity construction, 174–95; institutionalized, 174–7, 183, 214; prisons, 176, 180, 188, 192

Peers: as health enhancing, 156–9; and identity, 90–2, 117–18; relations, 64–5, 67
Peer pressure, myth of, 290–6
Postmodernism: Michel Foucault, viii, 13; influence of, 25–6; and language, 86–7; relativism, 83–4; research, 7; and resilience, ix; therapy (*see* Narrative therapy); youth, 88
Power: in care, 179, 185, 232; Michel Foucault, 13, 129–30, 137, 169; Paulo Friere, 13; group identity, 89–90; identity, 134, 136–8; in treatment, 198, 200, 204–5, 224; mental health, 130–3; Friedrich Nietzsche, 129; over mental health resources, 150–2; relations, 211, 224, 229–31; research, 7, 10, 24; self-definition, 15, 109, 141–2, 172; social relations, 13
Powerlessness: definition, 81; in care, 174; surplus, 136
Problems: as social constructions, 28, 64; as solutions, 85, 229
Problem saturated: description, 122; identities, 6, 135, 172
Protective factors, 18–19, 54–5, 48–52, 94, 102

Relational self, 200
Research: biases of, 53, 69; method, 11; methodological shortcomings,

18, 68, 70–3, 175; naturalistic, 310; postmodern approach, 7, 10, 24
Research sample, 305–8, 310–11, 313–14; credibility, 315; confirmability, 316; dependability, 316; transferability, 315; trustworthiness, 314
Resilience: case study, Trish, 206–9; and construction of identity, 206; in care, 186; definition of, 70; in families, 58–60; narratives of, 204–6; pathways to, ix, 6, 56–8; and power, ii, viii; research findings, 17–21, 24, 56–60; social context, 21–3
Resistance, 100–4, 147, 174; case study, Cathy, 90–2
Risk factors, 19, 39, 40–2
Role models, 258, 260, 262

Schizophrenia, 94–5
Sex, sexuality, 90, 119–20, 208; behaviour, 218, 225, 294; expression, 264; social construction of orientation as a problem, 108–9; teenage mothers 223, 235
Social construction: of adolescence, 93, 107–9; definition, 25; of deviance, 64, 96–7; of diagnosis, 122; of health, 6, 69, 85–7; of identities, 15, 81, 91, 111; of knowledge, 28; of mental health, 175; as a problem, 108–9; of problems, 28–9, 64, 215; of resilience, ix, 10, 66, 95, 108, 112; of social expectation, 13; treatment, 193–4, 201, 215, 217; of truth, 84
Social narrative 201, 213
Social policy, treatment 176, 185, 186, 198